CHANGING CONTOURS OF WORK

Third Edition

To our hardworking students.

SAGE was founded in 1965 by Sara Miller McCune to support the dissemination of usable knowledge by publishing innovative and high-quality research and teaching content. Today, we publish over 900 journals, including those of more than 400 learned societies, more than 800 new books per year, and a growing range of library products including archives, data, case studies, reports, and video. SAGE remains majority-owned by our founder, and after Sara's lifetime will become owned by a charitable trust that secures our continued independence.

Los Angeles | London | New Delhi | Singapore | Washington DC

CHANGING CONTOURS OF WORK
Jobs and Opportunities in the New Economy

Third Edition

Stephen Sweet
Ithaca College

Peter Meiksins
Cleveland State University

Los Angeles | London | New Delhi
Singapore | Washington DC

Los Angeles | London | New Delhi
Singapore | Washington DC

FOR INFORMATION:

SAGE Publications, Inc.

2455 Teller Road

Thousand Oaks, California 91320

E-mail: order@sagepub.com

SAGE Publications Ltd.

1 Oliver's Yard

55 City Road

London, EC1Y 1SP

United Kingdom

SAGE Publications India Pvt. Ltd.

B 1/I 1 Mohan Cooperative Industrial Area

Mathura Road, New Delhi 110 044

India

SAGE Publications Asia-Pacific Pte. Ltd.

3 Church Street

#10–04 Samsung Hub

Singapore 049483

Acquisitions Editor: Jeff Lasser

Editorial Assistant: Alexandra Croell

Production Editor: Bennie Clark Allen

Copy Editor: Mark Bast

Typesetter: Hurix Systems Pvt. Ltd.

Proofreader: Rae-Ann Goodwin

Indexer: Maria Sosnowski

Cover Designer: Michael Dubowe

Marketing Manager: Johanna Swenson

eLearning Editor: Gabrielle Piccininni

Printed in the United States of America

Library of Congress Cataloging-in-Publication Data

Sweet, Stephen A., author.

Changing contours of work : jobs and opportunities in the new economy / Stephen Sweet, Peter Meiksins. — Third edition.

pages cm

Includes bibliographical references and index.

ISBN 978-1-4833-5825-3 (pbk. : alk. paper)

1. Technological innovations—Economic aspects—United States. 2. Labor market—United States. 3. High technology industries—United States. 4. Hours of labor—United States. 5. Industrial relations—United States. 6. United States—Economic conditions—21st century. 7. Globalization. I. Meiksins, Peter, 1953- author. II. Title.

HC110.T4S93 2016

331.0973—dc23   2015030397

This book is printed on acid-free paper.

Certified Sourcing
www.sfiprogram.org
SFI-00453

17 18 19 10 9 8 7 6 5 4 3 2

Contents

List of Exhibits

About the Authors

Stephen Sweet is an associate professor of sociology at Ithaca College and editor of the journal *Teaching Sociology*. His studies of work and its impact on and off the job have appeared in a variety of publications, including *Work and Occupations; Sex Roles; Research in the Sociology of Work; Family Relations; New Directions in Life Course Research; Journal of Vocational Behavior; Journal of Marriage and the Family; Generations;* and *Community, Work, & Family.* His books, *The Work-Family Interface* (2014), *Data Analysis With SPSS: A First Course in Applied Statistics* (2012), and *College and Society: An Introduction to the Sociological Imagination* (2001), have been extensively adopted in sociology courses. He has edited and coedited publications including the *Work and Family Handbook: Interdisciplinary Perspectives, Methods, and Approaches* (2006), *The Work and Family Encyclopedia* (2008–2011), and special issues of the journals *Teaching Sociology* and *Community, Work & Family.* His current research focuses on the factors that lead people to embrace work as part of their identity and the ways that organizations integrate flexible work practices. In his job at home, he provides support to (and receives support from) his wife Jai (a college administrator) and children Arjun and Nisha.

Peter Meiksins is professor of sociology and vice provost for academic programs at Cleveland State University. He has published widely on the sociology of work, particularly the sociology of technical work and of the professions, in journals such as *Work and Occupations; Sociological Quarterly; Work, Employment & Society; Theory and Society; Technology and Culture;* and *Labor Studies Journal.* He has coedited several books on work and labor and is the coauthor of two books, *Engineering Labour: Technical Workers in Comparative Perspective* and *Putting Work in its Place: A Quiet Revolution.* His current research focuses on engineers, the environment and the state, and gender and engineering. He has a daughter in university and he does all the cooking at home (he likes to cook; his wife doesn't); his wife barbecues and fixes the car.

Preface to the Third Edition

This book is an effort to make sense of work opportunity—as it was in the twentieth century and as it is today—and how it influences lives on and off the job. When we began writing the first edition of this book, we thought this would be a straightforward endeavor. First, we intended to discuss the "old economy" and the types of opportunities present when most of the labor force was employed in jobs critical to mass production industrial work. Then we were going to write about the emerging "new economy" and the ways new technologies, new organizations, new jobs, a new workforce, and globalization are transforming work. Our unique contribution would be to show the ways that current policies and practices, designed to correspond with needs in the old economy, fail to address the present-day concerns.

When we wrote the first edition, we spent well over a year blocking out chapters, going back into the research literature, writing chapter drafts, restructuring our arguments, and rewriting. With all of these efforts, we faced a recurring problem, namely, that our observations about the old economy kept intruding into what we wanted to say about the new economy, and vice versa. Our work in that first year would have been far easier if we had recognized then what was to become a central theme of this book: *the old economy has not been replaced by a new economy; the old economy is operating within the new economy.*

Once we understood the overlap of the old and new economies, we realized that our thesis would have to be modified, as would the structure of our project. The story of the old and new economies is one of *common social forces* that shape the development of work opportunity. Many features of the old economy, although sometimes in new forms, are central to the dynamics of the new. Our conclusion is that concerns facing workers today result from *structural lags* that have forestalled the implementation of effective responses to changes in the ways work is performed and from *enduring failures* to address the problems of inequality that developed in the old economy.

In the years that followed the publication of the first edition, the global economy tanked and the housing bubble burst. Job insecurity expanded, homes were lost, and working families experienced compounded strains. But not everything that happened was bad. There were some important expansions in workers' rights, such as increased opportunity to file discrimination suits and expanded opportunities for working women to breastfeed their children. There is now greater access to health care as well. But perhaps the biggest story, in respect to work and opportunity, concerns the reckless decisions made to serve the interests of those at the very top of the opportunity ladder and the consequences those decisions had on almost everyone else. Even with the ongoing economic recovery, large numbers of working families have been left behind, struggle to make ends meet, and live in precarious conditions. While the observations we presented in the previous editions remain largely the same, new and updated statistics presented in this edition show that opportunity divides have continued to expand, rather than contract. It is abundantly clear that the new economy, even in the context of an economic recovery, is not working for everyone.

In the chapters that follow, our goals are to identify the contours of work and how they have changed over time, considering both short-term changes that may have occurred over the course of the preceding decades, as well as the longer-term development of modern ways of organizing work. Our analysis relies primarily on the research of sociologists but also on that of labor historians and economists. Our goal is not to offer comprehensive histories of work, or to detail the experiences of all groups in the workforce, but to document the processes that shape work opportunity and how opportunities have been divided in the United States along class, gender, and racial lines. To do this, we adopted a comparative perspective, placing our analysis of opportunity and policy in the United States alongside the somewhat different realities of work in Western Europe and elsewhere. We also compare the experience of workers laboring today with those laboring in the mid-twentieth century and earlier, and we explore the American workplace in the larger context of an integrated global economy and emerging global networks of trade.

Chapter 1, "Mapping the Contours of Work," offers an introduction to the sociology of work and the unique contributions sociological analysis brings to the understanding of the changing economy. Our concern in this chapter is not so much to detail the nature of work in the new economy, or how changes in work have happened, but rather to indicate what needs to be examined if one is to understand work, society, and social change today. To do this, we outline observations sociologists have made about the ways culture, social structure, and agency shape the opportunity to work and the careers of workers. We introduce this chapter by describing the challenges faced by six workers laboring in the new economy. These individuals illuminate the *diversity* of workers' experiences and how the transition to a new economy is affecting career prospects and introducing distinct strains into family lives.

Chapter 2, "New Products, New Ways of Working, and the New Economy," considers the changing patterns of what is produced and how production occurs. In this chapter we consider the implications of concerns such as deindustrialization, the rise of service sector employment, and changing organizational designs and technologies. The primary question we consider here is the extent to which the new economy differs from the old economy in respect to what is created and the labor processes and practices involved in production. This chapter is designed primarily to illuminate why we have concluded that the old economy operates within a new economy.

Chapter 3, "Economic Inequality, Social Mobility, and the New Economy," examines the economic returns received from work and how work opportunity gives shape to the class structure of society. The analysis reveals sobering signs that economic transformations are contributing to a divided economy, one that sustains a two-tiered division between good jobs and bad jobs and one that is funneling substantial shares of the returns of work to a privileged elite. We also consider how the movement of "good jobs" from the United States affects the life chances of workers in emerging economies, as well as more peripheral areas of the global economy.

Chapter 4, "Whose Jobs Are Secure?" and Chapter 5, "A Fair Day's Work? The Intensity and Scheduling of Jobs in the New Economy," consider how security and time commitments to work have changed. We first show the ways work designs in the new economy are contributing to widening job insecurity. Our interest here is not just to detail the extent of risk present today but also to show how social policies implemented in the old economy set workers up to bear the burden of risk, often at the expense of their families and careers. Chapter 5 extends this history of the present by examining trends in the time spent working and the intensity of work. Here, we discuss the question of why American workers are working more than they did in the past, more than workers in almost every other society, and in many instances more than they want to. We also consider the implications of work in a 24/7 economy and the impact nonstandard schedules have on family lives.

Chapter 6, "Gender Chasms in the New Economy," examines the issue of gender inequalities at work. We revisit the fundamental question of what constitutes work and why women's contributions to society are commonly defined as something other than "real work" or not worthy of compensation commensurate to that received by men. We also consider the extent to which gender inequalities are disappearing in the new economy and detail why many inequalities persist. We conclude this chapter by examining the approach to handling care work in the United States, how it departs from the approaches used in Western Europe and its impact on both the quality of care and women's life chances.

Chapter 7, "Race, Ethnicity, and Work: Legacies of the Past, Problems in the Present," examines the proposition that race might be of declining significance in the new economy. We show that racial inequalities persist but that there are important differences in the ways various minority groups have responded to, and are being treated in, the new economy. We also detail the dominant reasons why racial and ethnic inequalities exist today. Because race continues to be a major policy concern, we consider two of the most pressing debates: the controversies about affirmative action programs and the impact of immigration on opportunity structures.

Chapter 8, "Reshaping the Contours of the New Economy," outlines what needs to change if work is to become a positive experience for all and how opportunities might be distributed more equitably in the new economy. Basing our recommendations on what has been done in other developed societies, we try to offer realistic goals that, if fulfilled, would enhance opportunity and life quality. We also acknowledge that the dehumanizing, unjust aspects of work in the new economy are unlikely to change by themselves and that positive steps must be taken to promote improvements. A variety of agents—including individuals, interest groups, unions, corporations, and government entities—will all need to play a role in reshaping work. In the end, we suggest that government intervention will be the key to bringing the expectations of employers in line with what should be expected of workers. Its level of engagement will hinge on the ability of individuals, activist groups, and unions to exert sufficient pressures.

Our hope is that this book will help readers to understand the origins of current problems confronting working people in the new economy. Beyond this, we hope this book will contribute to a much-needed dialogue about the strategies for liberating workers from poverty, from drudgery, from discrimination, from stress, and from exploitation.

Acknowledgments

This book is the result of the contributions of numerous people, from those who cut the trees, milled them into paper, drove the paper to our offices, designed our computers, filled our libraries with books (or at least electronic links to books!), fed us and our children, and heated our offices, to those who printed and delivered the book to your hands. Our intellectual efforts stand on the shoulders of the giants in the field, individuals who introduced the ideas we tried to advance and to whom our thoughts are indebted. We also relied on the efforts of the numerous researchers and officials who collected and organized the data we use to outline changes in work and opportunity. Here, we can only express our appreciation to those with whom we formed close interpersonal ties.

Our colleagues and mentors—including Cynthia Duncan, Phyllis Moen, Marcie Pitt-Catsouphes, and Peter Whalley—offered valuable guidance by directing our attention to the issues that need to be addressed and what to look for. Reviewers Judith Barker, Elizabeth Callaghan, William Canak, Carol Caronna, Marc Dixon, Linda Geller-Schwartz, Heidi Gottfried, Judith Hennessy, Martin Hughes, Arne Kalleberg, Charles Koeber, Kevin Leicht, Joya Misra, Cynthia Negrey, Vincent Roscigno, Gay Seidman, and Patrick Withen provided the sharp criticism that the book needed in its formation. Marissa Cardwell, Hillary Gozigian, and Stacy Sauppe offered insightful students'-eye views of the manuscript and helped us bring the manuscript together. Students in our graduate and undergraduate classes at Ithaca College and Cleveland State University, many of whom also are experienced workers in the new economy, raised questions that stimulated our thinking for this book. We also thank the incredibly supportive team at SAGE, including our editor, Jeff Lasser.

The Alfred P. Sloan Foundation provided support for the study of job insecurities (B2001–50, Stephen Sweet and Phyllis Moen, coprincipal investigators). In addition to Kathleen Christensen at the Sloan Foundation, we extend thanks to Yasamin Diciccio-Miller, Akshay Gupta, and the staff of the Cornell Careers Institute for their contributions to the Couples Managing Change Study.

Finally, we express gratitude to our spouses, Jai and Joyce, who gave us much-appreciated time to devote to this project, who listened to our struggles, and who offered their perspectives and guidance throughout.

Chapter One

Mapping the Contours of Work

Perhaps more than any other quality, the ability to plan, organize, and collectively engage in work sets human beings apart from other species. Work occupies most of our waking hours; it is a crucial part of identities and influences life chances. At the same time, work creates problems in lives and, at its worst, can become a sentence of grinding toil in jobs that offer few rewards. Our understanding that work can liberate but also enslave—and seeing both possibilities exemplified in the modern economy—inspired us to write this book. We wanted to take stock of work today—to consider the types of work opportunities available, chart how jobs emerge and disappear, and gauge the impact of workplace practices on and off the job. Beyond this, we wanted to reflect on how work could be organized so that it *makes sense*—so that it provides the resources people need and brings meaning to lives.

This chapter begins this discussion by considering the "contours of work." These contours can be thought of as the terrain on which work opportunities are distributed and traversed. The metaphor of contours is useful because, like geographic topographies, work opportunities have been etched into the landscape by long-term historical forces. Some of these forces resulted in profound changes, wherein old ways of working were abandoned and new methods introduced. This type of radical transformation occurred in the Industrial Revolution of the early nineteenth century, and some argue that computer and communication technologies are having a similar effect today. Other forces, however, shape opportunity landscapes in more gradual, ongoing, and cumulative processes. Social divisions created on the basis of gender, with its constantly evolving meanings and practices, are one such force. So are race and social class divisions.

To consider the impact of social forces on work, we introduce here a shorthand distinction that we use throughout this book: the division between the old and new economies. This dichotomy helps us identify the very real changes that occurred in work in the latter part of the twentieth century, including the introduction of computer technologies, the expansion of a global economy, shifts in the composition of the workforce, new organizational and managerial paradigms, and other transformations that we consider in the chapters to come. The **old economy** represents the various ways of assigning and structuring work that developed in the wake of the Industrial Revolution through the mid-twentieth century. This economy operated with systems oriented to mass production, gendered divisions of labor, unionized labor, and a variety of other enduring workplace practices. It was also an economy in which the United States was a central and dominating economic force. The concept of a **new economy** is used to examine the question of whether the nature of work has changed and, if it has, the extent to which these changes are affecting lives on and off the job. Our primary frame of reference throughout this book is work as it occurs in the United States but also as it is connected to the distribution of opportunities in the global economy.

Though we use the term *new economy*, we have come to conclude that many of the present-day contours reflect the way work evolved in the old economy.[1] Those arguing that there has been a "second industrial revolution" often ignore this. There are new jobs, new workers, and new work designs, and these are changing some of the ways work is performed, by whom, and the returns received. But many of the features introduced by the old economy remain. These "old" features are not simply vestiges destined to eventually die out; they are thriving and may be permanent features of the new economy that will continue to develop during the twenty-first century. Sometimes these old and new features are combined, for example, when low-skill factory work jobs are moved from the developed world to the emerging economies. The jobs may not have changed fundamentally, but the people who are performing them have. In Chapter 2, we consider the issue of production in the old and new economies in greater detail and assess the extent to which work in the new economy has changed and the extent to which it has remained the same.

Our discussion in this chapter is directed to identifying the dominant social forces that shape work opportunity. We organize this discussion by considering three interlocking concerns:

- **Culture**: meaning systems that attach individuals to work, harness their commitments, and direct their efforts.
- **Structure**: opportunities, as well as constraints, that shape what types of jobs can be pursued, by whom, and the returns received.

- **Agency**: personal effort and discretion, whether as individuals or in groups, to direct actions and decisions.

To open this discussion, we consider the lives of six workers laboring in the new economy and the rewards, strains, and constraints work produces in their lives. As you read these examples of what work is like in the new economy, reflect on the ways current opportunity structures allocate resources needed and think about how work provides meaning but also disrupts lives. The challenge we explore throughout this book is the means to bring culture, structure, and human initiative into harmony, so that work expands opportunity rather than constrains it. In other words, the goal is to reduce the incompatibilities between how jobs are arranged and what workers can bring to—and receive from—their work.

Scenes From the New Economy

The experiences of Meg, Tammy, Emily, Rain, Kavita, and Mike reveal how work lives on and off the job are being shaped by the contours of the new economy. All of these cases illustrate that the effects of historical change (in this case the transition to a new economy) can vary depending on its timing with respect to an individual's biography, as well as to his or her gender, class, and race (Elder 1999; Moen 2001a). The stories also reveal how careers unfold when new opportunities are introduced and old opportunities are dismantled.

Exhibit 1.1   Meg: A Successful Trader Strives to Manage a Demanding Career With a Child Who Has Special Needs

---

Meg started her career as a trader in the male-dominated world of the New York Stock Exchange. Although family connections and good fortune helped her gain entry to Wall Street, her early successes came from hard work, tough-mindedness, and interpersonal savvy. It also helped that she entered the world of Wall Street just as the stock market was to catapult to record high levels in the 1990s. By the age of twenty-five, Meg was promoted to head trader and received a remarkable salary. She also met her husband at the stock exchange.

To support her husband's transition into a law career, Meg followed him to Philadelphia. In Philadelphia Meg landed a position in a firm that was soon to manage one of the largest investment funds in the country, another remarkable leap in an already successful career. Along the way, Meg had two children and

(Continued)

(Continued)

benefitted from flexible work arrangements, moving intermittently between part-time and full-time work as the children matured. However, when her third child was born with serious medical needs, Meg decided to take a career break to provide more intense care and supervision, and her employer agreed. However, when Meg tried to return to her job in a part-time capacity, her firm gave her a choice: return full-time or resign. She chose to resign.

Note: Based on *Opting Out? Why Women Really Quit Careers and Head Home* (pp. 28–30) by Pamela Stone, 2007, Los Angeles: University of California Press.

Exhibit 1.2   Tammy: A Midcareer Manufacturing Worker Attempts to Salvage a Career and a Community

Tammy was born into a disadvantaged family in 1966 in Youngstown, Ohio. Early on, she was raised by her grandmother, who worked as a maid and companion to an elderly widow, but, at least for part of her childhood, she also lived with her mother, who was trying to recover from drug abuse. The city she grew up in entered a steep decline when she was a child; the steel mills began to close and the neighborhoods deteriorated as the people who lost their jobs left to find work elsewhere.

When she was fifteen, Tammy got pregnant; she broke up with the father and raised the baby on her own. She was determined not to drop out of school or be like many of the other girls around her, so she finished high school on time and later earned an associate's degree. She worked for a while in a supermarket and hoped for a manager's job, but nothing materialized. After a stint on welfare, she was able to find a job working in one of the region's few remaining industrial establishments, the Packard Electric Plant in nearby Warren, Ohio, making electrical components for GM cars. She worked there for two decades (earning as much as $25 an hour), as the plant slowly shrank around her and the union that represented workers grew steadily weaker.

In the early 2000s, a series of corporate and legal maneuvers resulted in the plant becoming part of GM's Delphi Automotive Systems, which was then spun off as a separate company. Delphi eventually filed for bankruptcy in 2005 in an attempt to get out of its union contract and wind the company down. Like many workers who had lived through the company's gradual shrinkage, Tammy did not fully foresee Delphi's decision to close or sell most of its units and eliminate two-thirds of its workforce. Some workers at Tammy's plant would be kept on—but with dramatic cuts to their wages and benefits and likely eventual job loss. The alternative was to accept a lump-sum buyout but also lose most of their pensions. Tammy accepted the buyout, determined to do something else with her life.

Tammy invested some of the money she received from the buyout with a relative who was speculating in real estate. At first, she received good returns on her investment but later lost most of her money when the real estate bubble of the late 2000s collapsed. She had to beg her relative to return a small portion of her investment so that she could keep her small house. She went back to school to earn a bachelor's degree and was approached by a professional organizer who was looking to hire community organizers to help combat the effects of Youngstown's decline. Tammy was passionate about her city and determined to do something, so she got the job. Since then, she has worked on several surveys of her city, which made her even more aware of the decline brought about by deindustrialization. Even as the fracking boom began to create jobs in the region, Tammy could see that most of the people like her in Youngstown were not finding jobs and were being passed by. By comparison, she considered herself lucky.

Note: Based on *The Unwinding: An Inner History of the New America* by George Packer, 2013, New York: Farrar, Strauss and Giroux.

Exhibit 1.3   Emily: A Contract Worker Navigates Insecure Employment

Emily is in her late forties and markets herself as a freelance editor/proofreader. While at one time she was a "regular employee," the job that she previously held vanished when her employer relocated. Her path to becoming a contract worker was not an intended career path. It was a means of rescuing a career that was dislodged.

Emily currently works as an editor with two different employers, a large law firm and small publishing company. She is not considered to be a career employee at either of these companies, does not have a private office, and shares a cramped workspace with another employee. She is not included in many of the office social functions, and her level of involvement with other regular employees is quite restricted. Nonetheless, her job as a freelancer provides her considerably more flexibility than her coworkers, and this is something that she values. And, because she is skilled at her work, her compensation is comparable to what the regular employees make.

Because the terms of Emily's employment rest on her employers' interest in hiring her for subsequent work, she keeps watch for opportunities. She believes that her type of job, based on short-term agreements between employees and their employers, is the wave of the future. While she feels secure in knowing how to do her work, she has a constant sense of insecurity in that she does not know what the future holds for her.

Note: Based on *Freelancing Expertise: Contract Professionals in the New Economy* (pp. 2–3) by Debra Osnowitz, 2010, Ithaca, New York: ILR Press.

Exhibit 1.4   Rain: A Chinese Immigrant Finds Work in the American Food Service Industry

---

Rain is twenty-nine years old and has been in the United States for five years. Born and raised in a village in rural China, Rain says that he came to the United States to escape religious persecution (but it is possible that this story is for the sake of his visa application). His journey to the United States was expedited by a "snakehead," whom Rain paid the equivalent of $70,000 to arrange transport and needed documents. Rain was initially flown from China to Mexico. Like immigrants from South America, he was escorted to the U.S. border and told to "run." Later he was picked up by an associate of the snakehead, who transported him from Houston to New York.

Within Chinatown in New York, Rain was connected to a network of opportunities to work in Chinese restaurants located throughout the United States. In fact, family run Chinese restaurants outnumber McDonald's restaurants in small towns. Moving from town to town, Rain learned to cook Chinese food to suit the American tongue, with its heavier emphasis on sweetness. It was in the United States that he tasted his first egg roll. Currently, Rain lives in a house owned by the restaurant owner, along with five of his coworkers, all of whom are Chinese immigrants.

Rain's treatment in each restaurant depends very much on the ownership, but a constant is an expectation to put in long hours and labor quickly. He commonly works six-day weeks, and his twelve-hour days begin with chopping vegetables and end with cleaning the kitchen. On the whole, he is thankful for the long hours, because that means more money for him and more money to send home. If an owner is too demanding, Rain's solution is to return to New York, find another restaurant in another small town, and begin again.

He is working hard to pay off his debt and is sending money home, but he has no immediate plans to return to China because his income in the United States is far greater than he could earn in his hometown or in any of the new factories in the urban centers. However, he does feel isolated and lonely. His biggest worry is securing U.S. citizenship.

Note: Based on "The Kitchen Network: America's Underground Chinese Restaurant Workers" by Lauren Hilgers, 2014, *The New Yorker,* October 13, 2014.

Exhibit 1.5   Kavita: A Young Indian Woman Navigates Night Work and Call Center Employment

---

Kavita is a twenty-two-year-old woman who works in a call center in Bangalore, India. Owing to the time difference that separates Bangalore from the United States, Kavita works a night shift so that her schedule fits American workday rhythms. She has learned to suppress her Indian accent, has familiarized herself with American vernacular, and takes pride in her work. Her job is very demanding, as she has to understand the scripts that guide interactions, quickly understand client needs, and sometimes diffuse hostile encounters from frustrated customers. As soon as one client hangs up the phone, another call is funneled into Kavita's headset and she begins anew.

The night shift that Kavita works carries with it perils. One concern is the very real physical danger that confronts women in Indian society when darkness falls. Even simple necessities, such as going to the restroom outside of the home, carry with them such risks that women try their best to avert physical need. Another concern is the stigma associated with night work, which is traditionally associated with prostitution and other morally suspect behaviors.

Call center work compares favorably to other industries in India, but it is demanding and competition for jobs is fierce. Any position might have as many as five hundred applicants. Kavita sought work at the call center because she wanted the freedoms that her income provides. Many of her coworkers labor because of more desperate financial needs. With her $300/month income she has been able to rent a small apartment and recently hired a maid.

Kavita sees call center work as a stepping-stone in her life but is not inclined to think about the next steps yet. She does heed (to a great extent) her parents' warning that her conduct needs to reflect favorably on family and to be mindful of how women should act if they are to find a good spouse. Living in modern India, Kavita can potentially form a relationship that might develop into a "love marriage" but is pressured by her parents to have an arranged marriage. By virtue of working in the global economy, Kavita and her coworkers are challenging many conventional ways of defining women's place in Indian society.

Note: Based on *Working the Night Shift: Women in India's Call Center Industry* by Rena Patel, 2010, Stanford, CA: Stanford University Press.

Exhibit 1.6   Mike: A Disadvantaged Youth Enters a Life of Crime

Mike lives on 6th Street in Philadelphia. Aside from its concentrated poverty and predominantly black racial composition, there are two things to note about Mike's neighborhood: few good jobs are to be found there and police surveillance is pervasive. Because of limited employment options, crime and the illegal work that operates in an underground economy are common. The hyperpolicing that attempts to control Mike and his friends operates with scant tolerance for illegal behavior, focusing on sorting the "dirty" residents from the "clean." Those who are dirty—like Mike, who engages in the drug

(Continued)

(Continued)

trade—face likely imprisonment. Not everyone on 6th Street is dirty. Compared to some other residents, Mike was not as entirely disadvantaged. His mother worked multiple jobs and kept a clean house.

Mike was first arrested at age thirteen for carrying marijuana, but unlike the lenient treatment that he might have received if the same infraction occurred in a middle-class community, he was convicted, given a record, and placed on probation. By the time Mike reached age twenty-two, he had two children with his girlfriend and was selling crack cocaine for extra money to supplement the limited income he earned in a part-time job at a pharmaceutical warehouse. Mike lost his job at the warehouse because he missed too much work while trying to also attend to the needs of his family, including the extra care demanded by his youngest daughter who was born with health problems. When he failed to find a replacement job, he turned to selling drugs as a primary source of income. The rest of his life has unfolded as a story of a life on the run, with incarceration and the prospect of jail time removing him further and further from the hope of ever attaining secure legitimate employment.

Note: Based on *On the Run: Fugitive Life in an American City* (pp. 14–19) by Alice Goffman, 2014, Chicago: University of Chicago Press.

The six vignettes, all based on real people performing real work, give a sense of the diversity, opportunity, and constraint that exist in the new economy. For Meg and Kavita, economic changes have opened new opportunities, but they coexist with enduring sets of expectations about what mothers and daughters should provide to their spouses, parents, and children. These cultural orientations seem more appropriate to another era and lag behind what these workers ideally want for themselves and, in many instances, what they can provide for others. For Tammy, the moving platform of history has introduced new career tensions because the types of jobs she performed during her entire career have become more difficult to find. And as she tried to find security by investing in the new economy, her meager savings vanished. Emily is one of a new breed of contract workers, and she is figuring out how to create security in a context where employers are increasingly inclined to hire workers for short-term task assignments. Rain exemplifies the type of worker who is commonly cast as a social problem—the illegal immigrant. On closer examination, his commitment to work is probably not displacing any American workers, and his commitment to work conforms to core American ideals of personal responsibility and effort. In contrast, native-born Mike is not integrated into an opportunity structure that lends itself to upward advancement. While he has made mistakes, even if he had not, the odds have been stacked against him from the start. All of these workers challenge archetypal images of the typical worker, someone who holds a secure 9-to-5 job. Taken together, these six individuals help establish the foundation of an important argument presented in this book: that in the new economy there is no "typical" worker.

The careers of these workers are influenced by demands and social ties off the job. All these workers are making career decisions in the context of their linkages to others. In some circumstances, children hold sway, whereas in other cases, it is the needs of spouses, aging parents, or both (Neal and Hammer 2006; Sweet and Moen 2006). These life stage circumstances play an important role in shaping worker behavior, expectations, and needs. How people respond to these circumstances is heavily influenced by cultural scripts (e.g., assumptions about what parents should provide for their children) and the availability of resources (which varies from person to person and group to group). And beyond family ties, the contexts of neighborhoods and communities influence one's ability to find work, the resources to prepare for work, and the security to engage in work (Bookman 2004; Sampson, Morenoff, and Gannon-Rowley 2002; Swisher, Sweet, and Moen 2004; Voydanoff 2007). In a word, a good characterization of workers' lives on and off the job is *complex*. Work today introduces various strains and tensions, and strains and tensions experienced off the job affect the capacity to work.

Culture and Work

One of the core questions guiding the sociology of work concerns how much work should be performed and the extent of work that should be expected of individuals throughout their life course. Most classic theories of work embrace cultural perspectives that view labor, in and of itself, as a noble endeavor. Karl Marx (1964 [1844]), for example, argued that work is what distinguishes humans from other species, and he highlighted how it enables people to transform their environments to suit human interests. Sigmund Freud (1961 [1929]) argued that work is a socially accepted means by which humans can direct their sublimated sexual energies. As such, he saw work as a means of achieving satisfaction when fulfillment in other parts of life is lacking or prohibited. Émile Durkheim (1964 [1895]) offered a different thesis, that work and the complex division of labor in society offered a means to create social cohesion. All these perspectives have in common the assumption that work has the potential to cement social bonds and advance the development of civilization. If this new economy is to live to its full potential, these perspectives suggest that the more work that people are able to perform, the more liberated their lives will be. This proposition should not be accepted too quickly.

Is it a cultural universal that work should be praised and that commitment to work is an indicator of social health? Anthropological and historical studies suggest otherwise. In many cultures, work is defined as the means for day-to-day survival. Subsistence economies operate on the basis of cultural assumptions that work is primarily a means to an end, so that once individuals have enough food and shelter, labor is expected to cease. Such an orientation to work in today's American culture would indicate a moral weakness and be perceived as a threat to social order. But from the point of view of many other cultures, our embrace of work could be considered pathological. If one can obtain enough to eat and gain sufficient shelter by working a few hours a day, so be it. Why should a hunter set out in search of game if the supply of food is adequate (Brody 2002; Sahlins 1972)?[2] And even within geographic regions such as modern-day Western Europe, expectations regarding the age at which individuals are expected to embark on careers, or to retire, vary remarkably. These varied life course scripts result in some cultures expecting ten years (or more) of additional attachment to the labor force than others, with policies that match these expectations (Sweet 2009). When viewed through this lens, Mike's loose attachment to work becomes more understandable and seems a lot less pathological. And note that Meg's decision to exit from the labor force at midlife (to care for her children) carries with it no stigma.

One important cultural question concerns why work plays such a central role in some societies but not in others. Part of the answer, according to Max Weber (1998 [1905]), is that the societies in the forefront of the Industrial Revolution had been swayed by changing religious doctrines. These religious beliefs, particularly those that underpinned the Protestant Reformation, created anxieties about one's fate in the afterlife. In response, Western European and American culture advanced the value of the work ethic, a belief that work is not something people simply do—it is a God-given purpose. Devoting oneself to work and doing a good job were considered to be ways of demonstrating that a life of virtue reflects grace. And as members of these societies embraced the idea that work is "a calling," they applied themselves to their jobs with greater vigor, creating wealth and affirming to themselves and others that God was looking favorably on their actions.

Although many now question Weber's thesis that the Protestant Reformation was responsible for the emergence of capitalism, the centrality of the work ethic to the development of Western society is widely accepted. So deeply is it ingrained in contemporary American culture that nearly three-quarters of Americans report that they would continue to work, even if they had enough money to live as comfortably as they would like for the rest of their lives.[3] Americans work to affirm to themselves and others that they are virtuous, moral individuals and deserving of respect (Shih 2004). Conversely, those who choose not to work, or workers like Mike who are unsuccessful in securing a job, are looked down upon and stigmatized. In American society, to be without work is to be socially suspect and unworthy of trust (Katz 1996; Liebow 1967).

The work ethic defines labor as a virtue, but it also has pathological dimensions. The cultural embrace of work may be akin to the flame that attracts the moth. It is telling that many who can afford to work less, and who have the opportunities to do so, choose not to (Hochschild 1997). Psychologists call these individuals "workaholics"(Machlowitz 1980), but as we discuss later in this book, many of those driven to work long hours do so because they are driven by organizational cultures that bestow rewards on those who live, breathe, and eat their jobs. The suspicion cast on those who do not hold jobs has created pressures to force work on those who get little benefit from it. Consider that welfare reform legislation, passed in the mid-1990s, requires even very poor mothers of young children to work in order to receive welfare assistance. This requirement defines mothering as "not work" (a concept we return to later) and ignores the reality that when these women do work, usually it is in low-wage dead-end jobs.

Why would people work above and beyond economic need? Thorstein Veblen (1994 [1899]) in *The Theory of the Leisure Class* observed that attitudes to work are bound up with materialistic values held in American culture. Markers of status include luxury autos, large homes, and expensive clothing. All of these commodities are conspicuously consumed, put on display to be seen and admired, and set standards for others to follow. By the mid-twentieth century, the drive to purchase social status permeated American society, compelling workers to labor hard "to keep up with the Joneses" and their neighbors' latest purchases (Riesman, Glazer, and Reuel 2001 [1961]). Contemporary American workers engage in the same status game that emerged in the late nineteenth century, but with new commodities (e.g., iPads, BMWs, and flat-screen TVs). Their competition now expands beyond their neighborhoods, as they are saturated with media images of success and have developed numerous ways to accumulate debt (home equity loans, student loans, and credit cards).[4] The result, some have argued, is "affluenza," the compulsion to purchase and spend beyond one's means (de Graaf, Wann, and Naylor 2001). For some members of the new economy, work has become the means to manage spiraling debts incurred while striving to keep up with others who are spending beyond their means as well (Schor 1998).

Because culture also shapes the attitudes workers and employers have toward each other, it is a social force that can create (but also dismantle) opportunity divides. One means by which culture contributes to social inequality is through the construction of social divisions and group boundaries. Racial and gendered divisions, for example, are based on assumptions that different social groups possess different capabilities. Whether these differences were originally real is immaterial; as the early twentieth-century American sociologist W. I. Thomas noted, what people believe is real often becomes real in its consequences (Thomas and Thomas 1928). In turn, these beliefs contribute to the formation of self-fulfilling prophecies. As we discuss later in this book, cultural assumptions about gender and race shape social networks, influence access to resources, and funnel people into different lines of work.

Beyond setting up boundaries, culture extends into job management practices and the design of technologies. Consider, for example, the enduring legacy of scientific management, one of the bedrock managerial approaches of the old economy. Frederick Winslow Taylor introduced this managerial philosophy (also known as Taylorism) at the beginning of the twentieth century to increase the productivity of workers laboring in factories. He advocated the benefits of redesigning work to wrest control from workers and place it in the hands of management. His *Principles of Scientific Management* (1964 [1911]) argued for the separation of "thought" from "execution" to establish clear divisions between managers (whose job was to think and design) and workers (whose job was to carry out managers' instructions). He used time and motion studies to decompose production jobs into the simplest component tasks in order to increase worker speed and accuracy. And managers' jobs were redefined to absorb worker skills into the machines and organization and to keep the flow of knowledge going in one direction—from the shop floor into managers' hands. The result was the creation of legions of deskilled jobs, the dissolution of many craft skills, and a decline in the individual worker's ability to control the conditions and rewards of work (Braverman 1974; Noble 1979; Pietrykowski 1999). It also fostered distrust and hostility between workers and their bosses (Montgomery 1979).

Why did Taylor advocate this way of organizing work, given its obvious negative consequences for the quality of work life and its negative effects on labor-management relations? In part, it was a response to something real— the fact that workers often did not work as hard as they could. His experiences had taught him that they did not show up to work consistently, took long breaks, and worked at a more leisurely pace than owners desired. These behaviors reflected workers' cultural values and their definition of what constituted a reasonable amount of labor. Likewise, Taylor's interpretation of this behavior was culture-bound. He interpreted workers' behavior not as a rational, class-based resistance to employers but as an irrational unwillingness to work to one's full potential. Taylor, like many Americans of his time, was embracing a cultural denial that class divisions within the workplace existed. His solutions also reflected the culture in which he was living. He advocated a reorganization of the workplace based on scientific methods, something that resonated tremendously in a society where science had come to be seen as the solution to many human problems. And he depicted the worker as essentially unintelligent and easily manipulated; Taylor was fond of using an example involving a worker named Schmidt (whom he described as "oxlike"), whom he persuaded to adopt his new system through a combination of simpleminded arguments and limited incentives. This, too, was typical of the dominant American culture at that time; many Americans believed that members of the lower classes, immigrants, and others at the

Exhibit 1.7   The Film *Modern Times* Offered a Poignant Illustration of the Alienating Nature of Work in Factory Jobs in the Old Economy

Source: Copyright © by Getty Images. Reprinted with permission.

bottom of society were inferior in various ways (including intelligence) to the more successful members of society. Taylor's ideas also reflected an abiding cultural belief in the correctness of capitalism, particularly the proposition that it is natural that some should be owners and others laborers, that the efforts of those at the top were more important and valuable, and that an extremely unequal distribution of the fruits of labor was not just defensible but actually desirable (Callahan 1962; Nelson 1980).

The legacy of managerial philosophies—in this case, scientific management—highlights how culture and social structure intersect. Managerial perspectives that embraced the proposition that workers are indolent and should not be trusted are directly responsible for the creation of many of the alienating, low-wage "McJobs" present in America today. These philosophies initiated the development and application of assembly lines, promoted the acceptance of the idea that some people should be paid to think and others to labor, and fostered divisions between "white-collar" and "blue-collar" jobs. This cultural orientation to work can explain the types of jobs that Tammy held at General Motors, as well as the rationale of dismantling those jobs and moving them elsewhere in the global economy.

These examples of how culture shaped workplaces in the past suggest interesting questions about culture's role in carving out the contours of the new economy. Have cultural attitudes about the role of work changed, and if so, have workplaces changed along with them? How long are people working, and why do they work so much? Have Americans begun to abandon long-standing (Taylorist) cultural assumptions about the proper way to organize work, or do we continue to construct workplaces on the assumption that workers are lazy, ignorant, and not to be trusted? To what extent do perceived divisions between the members of society continue to deprive some people of access to opportunity? We address these concerns in the chapters that follow.

Structure and Work

In contrast to culture and the way it creates meaning systems that orient people to work, social structure maintains enduring patterns of social organization that determine what kinds of jobs are available, who gets which jobs, how earnings are distributed, how organizational rules are structured, and how laws are formulated. Social structure does not exist independently of culture. Often, social structure reflects cultural attitudes, because people tend to create institutions that are consistent with their beliefs. And structure can also be in conflict with aspects of culture, creating tensions and contradictions with which individuals and societies must grapple. For example, consider how the structural reality of unemployment creates particularly difficult problems in a society such as the United States, where work is valued or structured as a mandatory part of citizenship. Americans are forced to make difficult choices between their cultural ideals and their social structural context: should the unemployed be made to work, or should they be helped because there are no jobs? If the latter, who deserves help, what kind, and for how long?

Throughout this book, we discuss various aspects of social structure, the access to different types of work, the division of labor, the social organization of workplaces, and legal and political arrangements that influence the design of jobs and the terms of employment. Here, we simply illustrate how social structure affects individuals' experience of work by considering how a few aspects of social structure—social class, job markets, and labor force demographics—may be affecting opportunities and workplace practices in the new economy.

Class Structures

One of the great contributions of Karl Marx (1964 [1844]) was his analysis of class structures and how they shaped workplace practices and opportunity structures. In his classic analysis of the industrial capitalist economy, he argued that employers' profits depend on the effort put forth by employees, which created incentives to limit wages and to push workers to labor as hard as possible. He also observed that the efforts of workers created far greater wealth for employers than it did for employees. Considering these class relations, Marx argued that the tendency for work under capitalism would be toward the creation of a polarized class structure, comprising a disenfranchised working class (the proletariat) and an affluent owner class (the bourgeoisie).

It is hard not to look at dead-end low-wage jobs in the new economy without some appreciation for Marx's core insight. Tammy (the former manufacturing worker) and Mike (the disadvantaged young adult) are what Marx might have expected to see in an advanced capitalist economy. However, the contemporary class structure of the United States is more complex than the bifurcated and polarized structure Marx envisioned, as evidenced by Meg (the trader) and Emily (the contract worker). And the experience of upward movement among the disadvantaged, as evidenced by Rain (the Chinese restaurant worker) and Kavita (the call center worker), adds even more challenges to simplistic Marxist structural models. Although laborers and capitalists exist, large portions of the workforce seem to fit into neither category. Numerous professional and managerial workers have substantial education, some (or even considerable) workplace authority, and higher salaries than the typical frontline worker. Yet it is difficult to describe them as captains of industry or members of the dominant class, given that they are not in charge and work for someone else (who has the ability to fire them). Sociologists have argued long and hard about how to describe these intermediate class positions. One sociologist described such workers as occupying contradictory class locations, combining elements of the classes above and below them (Wright 1985).

How best to map the precise shape of the class structure of capitalist societies is a matter for dispute, but what is not disputed is that class matters. For example, class affects people's access to work opportunities, although the precise way in which it does so has changed over time. Before the Industrial Revolution, most children inherited their line of work from their parents through a process known as ascription. Farmers' children tended to become farmers themselves, and craft workers would often learn their trade from their fathers. Women's roles were largely ascribed as well. One's occupation was to a great extent one of the things inherited from one's parents; the cross-generational effects of class were obvious and straightforward. With industrialization, however, the range of jobs expanded profoundly, many new occupations were introduced, and other occupations became less common or actually disappeared. As a result of these changing opportunity structures, fewer children could follow in their parents' footsteps or inherit occupations from the previous generation. By the late nineteenth century, geographic mobility and social mobility became more common, as children ventured farther from their home communities to find work (Thernstrom 1980). Class still mattered, however, because it affected one's access to resources such as education, skills, and connections that determined access to work in an economy where jobs no longer were inherited.

The existence of class also affects the structure of workplaces. Marx felt that the antagonism between labor and capital inevitably produced antagonism at work and led to the development of hierarchical, top-down managerial structures designed to control workers and ensure that the interests of employers predominated. Although the polarized workplaces envisaged by Marx may not be the dominant organizational form, managerial efforts to control labor reflect a strong desire to respond to class antagonisms. They reflect the reality that the workplace is a zone of contested terrain, one in which class conflicts take place, with each side using the weapons at its disposal—including layoffs, speedups, technology, strikes, and even sabotage (Edwards 1979; Montgomery 1979).

Throughout this book, we argue that social class remains one of the most powerful forces shaping employment opportunities and access to resources in the new economy. We examine how a changing economy has altered the reality of class and the extent to which changes in class structure have led to a fundamental restructuring of workplaces away from the familiar patterns of industrial America. We also examine how gender and race matter and how they interact with class to shape complex, contemporary structures of opportunity and workplaces. We focus on social class most directly in Chapter 3, but throughout we emphasize that other social markers (such as gender, race, or age) intersect with class in important ways.

Job Markets and Job Demands

Mike's (the disadvantaged youth) and Tammy's (the manufacturing worker) problems involve not simply finding work but also finding work that pays a reasonable income and work that they have been prepared to perform. Meg (the trader), on the other hand, possesses highly marketable skills and can command a handsome salary. For her, the problem is securing a job that matches her personal resources. For Emily (the contract worker), the problem is locating new opportunities that enable her to navigate from one job to the next. Rain (the restaurant worker) understood that few opportunities existed in his rural village in China that would allow him to provide for his family, which in turn led him to migrate to where he believed job opportunities existed. All of these workers have concerns that are structural in nature and involve the way opportunities are configured. All have to adapt themselves to the existing range of jobs and the prevailing ways in which jobs are organized. Their personal problems reflect the fact that workers— especially those laboring in times of economic change—face challenges in locating and adapting themselves to opportunities. For many workers, and those left involuntarily out of the labor force, the most recent economic recession has significantly compounded these problems. Tammy's job loss and failed venture into real estate speculation amply illustrate this concern.

The Industrial Revolution of the early nineteenth century was clearly a watershed, one that profoundly reshaped the types of jobs available to workers. The most obvious consequence of industrialization was that far fewer people were employed in agriculture and many more were employed in factory work. However, the changes were not limited to the shift from agriculture to industry. Traditional occupations outside of agriculture were also transformed, as new technologies and new ways of organizing work pushed older approaches aside. For example, the mechanization of weaving during the Industrial Revolution completely removed this work from the home and introduced new skills that fit factory labor. Similar stories can be told about many other traditional occupations, including hat making, shoe production, tanning, and tin smithing (Thompson 1963).

Is the range of employment opportunities available to American workers changing again? It certainly seems that way. Some jobs that used to be plentiful in America (such as the office typing pool) have virtually disappeared, and the skills needed to obtain jobs are changing as well. In the old economy, for example, it was common for children to follow their parents into the mill or factory and receive good wages for performing jobs that required little education. Today, few young people aspire to hold the type of factory job that Tammy used to occupy, largely because many of these jobs have disappeared. As steel mills and factories closed in the 1970s and 1980s, the impact reverberated throughout industry-dependent "rust belt" communities, forcing their residents to rethink long-standing beliefs about jobs, futures, and how one makes a living (Bartlett and Steele 1992; Bluestone and Harrison 1982; Buss and Redburn 1987).

One way of considering the changing opportunity landscape is to consider the process of creative destruction, a phrase introduced by economist Joseph Schumpeter (1989) to describe the tendency for old methods of production to be replaced by newer, more efficient approaches. In some cases, new technologies make old needs obsolete, as when the automobile extinguished the need for buggy whips. In other instances, technological innovation can replace workers with machines, as was the case with cigarette rollers (Bell 1973). New methods of organizing work can also be used to reduce production costs, for instance, by moving jobs to locales where labor costs are lower (Cowie 2001). And in the case of computers, technologies have not only replaced workers but also introduced entirely new markets and jobs.

The drive to create ever more efficient and profitable enterprises is influencing the distribution of work opportunities around the world, as we observed by introducing Kavita and her job in a call center. Production now occurs on a global scale, and the forces that disperse work to far-flung locations such as Indonesia (where athletic shoes are assembled) and Bangladesh (clothing) shape the life chances of workers both at home and abroad. Understanding the reasons why work is being dispersed, and the impact on workers' lives at home and abroad, is essential to revealing the trajectory of work and opportunity in the new economy. Throughout the twentieth century, the United States held a dominant position in the global economy. But in the new economy, lower-skilled production jobs previously held by Americans such as Tammy are increasingly being exported to countries such as China and India. While it is important to consider the impact on

American workers, we suggest that this is too narrow a focus, as analysis of the functioning of a global economy should not be restricted to the interests of any particular nation and its workers.

Changing employment opportunities also have redefined skill needs, reshaped job demands, and introduced new rewards. They also impose new burdens on workers' lives. Consider the large number of jobs available in various kinds of interactive service work that emerged in the latter part of the twentieth century. These jobs require a different type of work than that performed in the factory, in that the employees typically do not manufacture anything. Workers such as teachers, therapists, or servers provide a service for someone else with whom they are in direct contact. Sociologists have noted that this kind of work places different demands on the worker (Mills 2002 [1951]; Paules 1991). He or she must learn interaction skills— how to make others feel comfortable, how to produce the desired kind of social setting, how to deal with various kinds of difficult social situations— *because the interaction is a significant part of the product being sold.* Research on airline flight attendants performed in the 1980s offers a compelling illustration of how interactive service work is performed. At that time, flight attendants were trained to make customers feel safe in the rigid and sometimes frightening environment of an airplane. To do this, they were coached on techniques to change their internal emotional states to generate the display of warmth required by their employers. As a consequence, however, these types of workers were especially prone to experiencing emotional numbness or burnout (Hochschild 1983). However, today, much less emotional labor is expected from flight attendants, indicating that the definition of how service work is to be performed is open to social negotiation.

New jobs demand new sets of skills, and new technologies and organizational systems also are transforming many familiar jobs. An administrative assistant's job, for example, is quite different from the secretarial jobs that it replaced. In part this is because computer programs have eliminated aspects of the old job (repetitive typing) and created new ones (basic graphic design, data analysis, electronic communication). Bank tellers once were simply clerical workers who processed clients' financial transactions. Now, computerized information systems provide tellers with information about clients' financial positions and prompt tellers to sell various products to the client, all while a close electronic eye monitors what the worker is doing (Smith 1990). Even traditional manual labor is affected. For example, production workers who used to rely on their senses of touch and smell as guides now operate sophisticated computerized systems that make some of their old ways of working obsolete (Vallas and Beck 1996).

Finally, job opportunities may be less rigidly tied to space and time than they were in the old economy. Today, many workers have opportunities to telecommute and work from home offices. The economy operates 24/7, introducing the prospects of working alternate shifts and reconfiguring work around family lives. This may open opportunities to liberate workers from the traditional 9-to-5 grind and introduce new flexible schedules that more harmoniously mesh work with life—a work arrangement that the investment trader Meg's employer ultimately concluded was not viable. However, it may also allow work to intrude on lives in ways not possible in the old economy, perhaps forcing workers to be on call during "leisure" time in response to a round-the-clock economy. Understanding the impact of these new structural configurations is essential to charting the contours of work in the new economy.

Demography and the New Labor Force

Social structure can influence what jobs are available, but it can also affect who is available to perform that work. A full appreciation of the challenges and opportunities present in the new economy requires consideration of demography and how the composition of a society affects the placement of workers into jobs and the distribution of opportunities to prepare for and obtain work (Farnesworth-Riche 2006). The paid labor force is substantially different today as compared to the mid-twentieth century or earlier. It contains a far higher percentage of women workers, and the racial and ethnic makeup is also different. We devote two chapters of this book specifically to the intersecting concerns of gender (Chapter 6) and race and ethnicity (Chapter 7); here we introduce the importance of demographic forces by considering how age structures affect the availability of jobs, the availability of workers, the need to work, and the returns received from work.

The U.S. labor force, along with those of many other developed societies, is becoming older. Americans today can expect to live twelve years longer than could those alive in 1940 and twenty-six years longer than those who were alive in 1900.[5] Workers are living longer, and they are healthier when they reach ages that used to be considered "old." This presents new opportunities and new challenges to American workers and their employers. Consider, for example, retirement. Should workers continue to stop working at sixty-five? Why? If people are living longer and staying healthy longer, perhaps work careers should be lengthened. However, older workers generally do not want jobs that demand heavy schedules (Moen 2007). More common are desires to enter into second or third careers and to pursue work situations that focus less on earning money (although for many that remains

Exhibit 1.8 Age Distributions and Predicted Distribution in the United States: 1940–2060

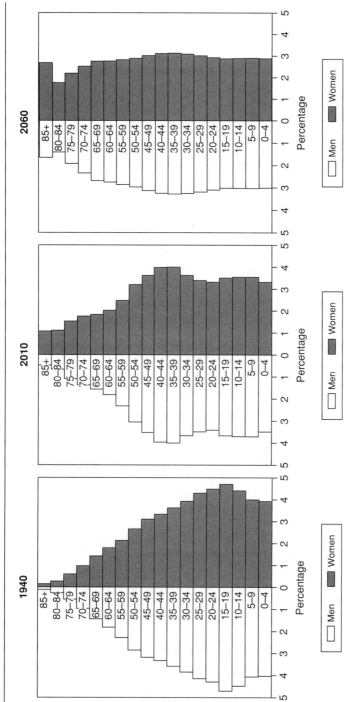

Source: U.S. Census Bureau.

21

important) and more on satisfying creative desires or making a difference in the lives of others. Unfortunately, most employers do not offer "bridge jobs" that accommodate the possibility of the types of scaled-back employment that fit the skills and interests of these workers (Hutchens and Grace-Martin 2006; Sweet et al. 2014).

The changing age structure of the workforce presents challenges to society as a whole, not just to employers. Exhibit 1.8 shows how the age structure of the United States has changed from 1940 to 2010 and how it is expected to change by 2060. Note that in 1940 the age structure of the United States resembled a pyramid, with most of the population in the younger age groups, with a steady attrition as one approached old age. Only a relatively small group lived beyond age seventy. In contrast, in 2010 the age pyramid looks more like a skyscraper, albeit with a bulge in the middle. This bulge is the baby boom generation, a birth cohort that is steadily aging its way into retirement years. A key structural question concerns how an aging society will provide economic support for the growing numbers of older people. Will they be required to work? Or will society continue to provide postemployment pensions for them? And, if the latter, how will that expense be financed? One can observe that this will be an especially big concern by the time the United States reaches 2060, because at that point 22% of the population will be over age sixty-five (triple the rate that existed in 1940). But, in comparison to many other countries, the United States actually is in a relatively favorable position in respect to aging. For example, Japan's National Institute of Population and Social Security Research (2012) estimates that by 2060, 40% of that country's population will be over age sixty-five. Again, note that while this demographic composition constitutes a structural concern, its origins are linked to both culture and agency. For example, Japan is far less accepting of immigrants than the United States; immigrants tend to be young, so Japan's approach to immigration exacerbates the consequences of native-born families having fewer children.

The aging of societies creates a pressure point because of the dependency of those outside of the labor force (the young and the old) on those in the labor force. Consider that the Social Security system, the most important source of retirement income for many Americans, is funded through taxes on currently employed workers. Those taxes become part of the general pool of Social Security revenue, which provides pensions to those who have retired. Some policy makers are concerned that if the pool of retired workers becomes larger and the pool of employed workers becomes smaller, the revenues available to fund the system will be squeezed (Weller and Wolff 2005). There is much controversy about whether this should be called a "crisis," but there is general agreement that ways need to be found to ensure that adequate revenues will be available for the growing population of retired workers.

Demographic factors such as age, gender, and race affect virtually all aspects of the economy and workplace. Demographics play a role at the organizational level, as the experiences of ethnic minorities and women are commonly shaped by their scarcity at the top levels of organizational hierarchies. They are critically important at the community level, as neighborhoods that lack job opportunities hinder the socialization of children into the types of workers needed in the new economy. The neighborhood that Mike grew up in exerted a powerful influence on his career decisions. We return to the critical issues of aging, gender, race, education, and immigration throughout this book.

Agency and Careers

Our last observation in this chapter, and a theme that runs throughout our analysis in this book, is that agency matters. All of the workers we considered made choices. Mike had a child at a young age and dropped out of high school, Meg elected to have three children and to pursue a high-powered career, Tammy took the initiative to return to school, Emily keeps her eyes and ears open for new work, Rain chose to move from his village to the United States, and Kavita applied to work in a call center even against her family's wishes. These observations highlight the ways in which people direct their life courses and how access to different resources and constraints shapes how lives are constructed over time (Elder 1998; Moen 2001b; Sweet and Moen 2006). The life course perspective is essential to understanding the contours of the new economy because it focuses on careers—the patterns of entry, exit, and movement between jobs. People do not just have careers, they forge them.

Sociologists are often accused of arguing that people are simply "pawns" or "cultural dopes" of the larger social structural and cultural contexts in which their lives are lived. The depiction of individuals as victims of external forces ignores the capacity of individuals to direct their own lives and those of others (Emirbayer and Mische 1998; Garfinkel 1967). However, the effective application of agency depends on resources. People with unlimited resources at their disposal are in a far better position to design their own lives than are those who have few resources. An important consideration is whether the new economy advances agentic capacity or undermines it. On the one hand, the new economy may be creating a context that is expanding the control individuals have to direct their life courses, in essence making lives less scripted than in the old economy (MacMillan 2005). Many old structural barriers have been removed (such as segregation laws) and so have the cultural barriers that funneled women and ethnic minorities into restricted ranges of occupations. Before the enactment of civil rights legislation and the women's movement, the prospects that women and racial/ethnic minorities like Barack Obama, Sheryl Sandberg, Hillary Clinton, or Sonya Sotomayor could move into positions of power were slim to nil. At the same time, each can rightfully claim that their successes should be attributed to agency, as their achievements would not have happened without the combination of incredible talent and incredible hard work. Today, one can quickly generate a sizable list of minority group members and women who have moved into professions in which they once had been entirely absent. And some have gone so far as to argue that personal effort can trump disadvantages imposed by concerns such as race and gender. However, as we discuss in detail throughout this book, ample evidence indicates that women and minorities are at distinct disadvantages in securing many types of jobs (Grusky and Charles 2004; Reskin, McBrier, and Kmec 1999). And beyond disadvantages created by social divisions, evidence indicates that more and more workers are in precarious jobs, undermining their control and the capacity to engage in planful action (Kalleberg 2013). The extent to which the new economy is fundamentally altering the possibilities for people to shape their own biographies is one of the central questions posed in this book.

Numerous ethnographic studies reveal that workers are not simply passive recipients of culture and structure; they use personal initiative to influence how their jobs are performed and the returns they receive from work (Darrah 2006; Richardson 2006; Roy 1955; Tulin 1984). To illustrate agency at work, consider Michael Burawoy's (1979) observations of production workers in the machining industry. These workers' jobs were regulated by quotas, wherein they had to make a specified number of parts to earn their base pay. But when they surpassed those quotas, they could "make out" and earn additional money. Quotas constituted a social structure, operating with explicit rules that were rigged by management to increase productivity. However, Burawoy observed that the machinists invented a variety of tricks to game this system. For example, they kept quiet about the easy jobs in which quotas were underestimated and complained incessantly about the impossibility of meeting quotas on virtually all other jobs. They bribed supervisors to get the easiest jobs and curried favor with coworkers to provide the stock needed to get their jobs rolling. When given an easy quota, workers overproduced and then hid their "kitties" that they turned in for extra compensation at later dates. In sum, these machinists showed that when workers are confronted by cultural and structural arrangements, they also engage in strategic action to influence how these arrangements affect their lives. Underpinning much of the research on agency is the question of equity and how it is socially negotiated. One wonders, if the economy has changed significantly, have the strategies workers use to assert their will changed as well?

Finally, it should be added that agency also operates at a collective level. Workers make efforts to carve out work lives for themselves, but they also collaborate to reshape the contours of work and create more satisfactory work opportunities for others. An obvious example is that workers band together in organizations such as unions or professional associations that use the strength of numbers to press for needed changes. Union publicity materials that describe unions as the "people who brought you the week-end" remind us that collective action obtained the taken-for-granted days off workers now enjoy. Similarly, the professional associations formed by doctors, lawyers, and others help protect those workers from competition, define what are acceptable (and unacceptable) professional practices, and generally shape the conditions under which those types of jobs are performed. Throughout this book, and particularly in the concluding chapter, we examine how collective action has shaped workplaces in the past and how it might do so in the future. Is the new economy making certain forms of collective action by workers obsolete? Is it creating openings and needs for new kinds of collective action? What are the key issues around which workers band together to effect change? Ultimately, if the workings of the new economy are to be improved, it will require the application of agency.

Conclusion

In this first chapter, we focused on the ways that sociological perspectives reshape the consideration of work. Our goal was simply to highlight the observation that a new economy does exist and that it can be evidenced by examining changes in culture, structure, and application of agency. Although work is commonly considered a means to obtain a paycheck, we argue that it is much more than that. The design of work corresponds with cultural templates that guide workers to their jobs and script social roles. Workers live within social structures that allocate opportunities and construct barriers that block access to meaningful employment. And within these contexts, workers have responded both individually and collectively to manage their responsibilities and reshape society.

The stresses experienced by workers like Meg, Tammy, Emily, Rain, Kavita, and Mike are probably familiar to readers of this book. Because of the instability of jobs, changing opportunity structures, the challenges of meshing work with family, and the challenges of finding good work, many workers find themselves struggling in the new economy. One of the great contributions of sociology is its capacity to reframe these types of personal problems as being public issues (Mills 1959). In the chapters that follow, we consider the extent to which work opportunities are changing as well as the impact these changes have on lives on and off the job. Our focus, throughout, is to identify stress points, opportunity gaps, the ways in which workers adapt to these strains, and what can be done to close the chasms that separate workers from fulfilling jobs and reasonable conditions of employment.

Notes

1. Of course, these are not the only phrases used. Others use the term *Fordism* to describe the old economy, and depending on the political slant of the analysis, *post-Fordism* and *flexible specialization* are used to describe the new economy, as are *knowledge economy, global economy,* and *postindustrial economy.*

2. It is worth emphasizing that describing hunting and gathering societies as "poor" is misleading. Though they lack the variety of possessions contemporary Americans enjoy, their members often live healthy and fulfilling lives.

3. Authors' analysis of the General Social Surveys. Retrieved from the General Social Survey website: www3.norc.org/GSS+Website.

4. Approximately one-third of American families rent their homes, one-quarter live at or near the poverty level, and nearly one-half will experience divorce. These facts are seldom represented in television's portrayals of the "typical" American family.

5. American men now live, on average, to be seventy-six years old, and American women have a life expectancy of eighty-one years.

Chapter Two

New Products, New Ways of Working, and the New Economy

One of the most popular themes in discussions of work is the idea that recent changes in work constitute the equivalent of a second industrial revolution. Consider, for example, the impact computers have had on the ways jobs are performed and designed. Computers enable workers to correspond at great distances, telecommute from home, and access a wide array of information. These "smart machines" have absorbed many workers' jobs and replaced human hands with robotic pincers that move with exacting precision. Computers also have spawned new markets for software and hardware, creating new jobs requiring new skills. Their reach spans the world, enabling near-instantaneous transmission of information, as well as the coordination of complex trade relationships that link companies with one another in global webs. It is hard not to conclude that computers have sparked revolutionary changes—not only in what is being produced and how jobs are designed but also in the geographic distribution of work. What impact do these types of changes have on current and future generations of workers?

The use of the concept of a "new economy" (or alternate terms such as *global economy*) is widely accepted as a shorthand way of saying that work today is remarkably different than it was in the recent past. But in this chapter, we open this assumption to debate. If there is a new economy, what are its distinguishing characteristics? We argue that jobs *have* changed in profound ways. There are new technologies, organizational designs, industries, and markets. The economy has become increasingly international. These changes have introduced the need to develop new skills to fit changing opportunity structures. But what is equally true is that many aspects of the "old economy," including the design of jobs to require limited skill, have either survived or been reproduced in new forms. After all, for every successful computer programmer who works at a company like Microsoft, one can find three poorly paid workers laboring on hamburger assembly lines at companies like McDonald's.[1] Understanding the new, the old, and the old in the new is the key to understanding the diverse needs and experiences of today's workforce.

In this chapter we consider some of the major changes said to characterize work in the new economy, including the decline of mass production and manufacturing work, new skill requirements, the emergence of new cultures of control, the gradual decline of organized labor, the rise of flexible work arrangements, and globalization. In each case, we argue that there have been significant changes but also that there are persistent features that reflect the perpetuation of the old economy within the new.

A Postindustrial Society?

One of the earliest forecasts of an emergent new economy came from sociologist Daniel Bell (1973), who argued in the early 1970s that America was entering a "postindustrial" era, in which the manufacturing-centered economy of the past was being replaced by an economy directed toward the provision of services. Bell was among the first to note something that subsequently became obvious to most Americans, particularly those located in the so-called rust belt of the industrial Midwest—employment opportunities had shifted away from manufacturing to other sectors of the economy.

Exhibit 2.1 shows that in 1940 the number of employees working in the manufacturing sector in America was more than double that in any other sector of the economy, accounting for over one-third of all employment. Until 1989, the manufacturing sector remained the dominant employer. But as the population of the United States grew during the latter part of the twentieth century, manufacturing employment did not. Today, instead of employing one in three workers, as it did in the mid-twentieth century, manufacturing enterprises employ only fewer than one in ten workers.

There are various explanations for this trend. Some argue that nearly all low-skill, low-wage manufacturing work is being funneled to developing economies, while the advanced economy of the United States focuses on knowledge work and services (Bell 1973; Fröbel, Heinrichs, and Kreye 1982). However, it is also possible to argue that this simply reflects something "old"—the continued effort of employers to find the least expensive ways to produce goods (Cowie 2001). From this point of view, manufacturing remains central to the economy; however, it now takes place on a global scale, rather than on a national one. Yet another interpretation emphasizes that the United States is unusual—the decline of manufacturing employment is more pronounced here than elsewhere. Rather than reflecting a long-term, general trend away from manufacturing, the U.S. pattern may reflect a choice by American employers to seek low-wage sites for manufacturing rather than invest more heavily in improving techniques at home (Appelbaum and Batt 1992). It may also reflect domestic economic policy choices favoring a strong U.S. dollar and the U.S. government's tolerance of policies in countries such as China, which keep their currencies artificially low. Such policies hurt U.S. manufacturing exports and make imported goods cheaper, resulting in stagnant or declining manufacturing employment in the United States (Scott 2015). All of these processes have played a role in shaping opportunity in the new economy.

Exhibit 2.1   Trends in Employment in Twelve Major Sectors: United States, 1940–2014

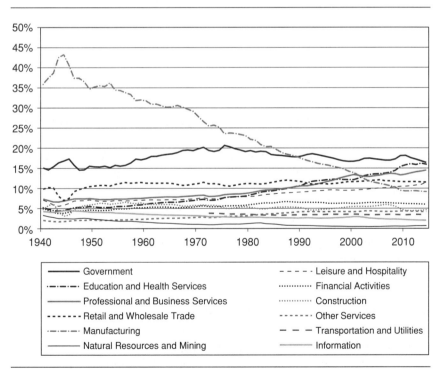

Source: Bureau of Labor Statistics.

The number of manufacturing jobs has declined in the United States and other economically advanced countries, but should we conclude that we are truly postindustrial? In the new economy, manufacturing enterprises continue to employ more than 12 million American workers. This may actually be an underestimate, as many industrial employers make increasing use of temporary workers, many of whom are not counted as industrial workers in government statistics. Although manufacturing employs a smaller percentage of Americans than it once did, it remains a major force in the economy and creates demand for the products and services generated in other parts of the economy (Hatton 2011; Scott 2015). It is not at all clear that manufacturing employment is in an inevitable long-term decline to the point where it will disappear entirely. Rather, it remains an important but less dominant part of what is now a more diversified economy.

Finally, it should be recognized that the practices of the old industrial economy have been woven into the design of many jobs central to the new economy. The fact that manufacturing opportunities have stagnated in the United States does not mean that the *ways of working* that developed in the old economy are on a path to disappearing as a result. The degree to which the old industrial economy has or has not been replaced can be examined by considering the extent to which mass production is disappearing.

The End of Mass Production?

It is generally agreed that economic activity in the old economy centered on the production of manufactured goods (e.g., automobiles, steel, chemicals, appliances) in large quantities for mass markets. The Ford Model T is the classic example of what the American manufacturing economy produced— an affordable and highly standardized car, mass-produced by American workers in a central factory location (Chandler 1990). Coordinating hundreds (and sometimes thousands) of workers at a single location meant that employers such as Henry Ford had to develop bureaucratic management systems, complete with rigid job definitions, rules of conduct, and productivity expectations (Edwards 1979).

The dominant managerial approach of the time was to follow the practices of scientific management, which encouraged the replacement of skilled workers with cheaper, more dispensable low-skill workers, while removing discretion from the shop floor and placing it in the hands of management (Braverman 1974). Finding ways to enhance productivity through job simplification, replacing people with technology, and improving managerial control over what was happening in the workplace were all central to this approach. The assembly line epitomized this philosophy, a combination of technology and organization that harnessed workers to labor at repetitive, simple tasks. To appreciate how this affected the performance of work, consider the difference between making automobiles using highly skilled workers (as many of the first automobiles were made) and the assembly line methods pioneered by Henry Ford. Instead of relying on a skilled (and hard to replace) craft worker who controlled how the work was done, the assembly line created jobs that required very little training, involved relatively simple repetitive operations, and dictated to the worker how the job should be performed. Perhaps most importantly, the worker lost control over the pace of work, as the assembly line pushed work forward at a speed primarily determined by management. The result was the creation of legions of deskilled jobs, the dissolution of many craft skills, and a decline in the worker's ability to control the conditions and rewards of work (Braverman 1974; Pietrykowski 1999).

This approach was enormously successful and formed the basis for the growth of the giant American manufacturing enterprises (e.g., Ford, General Motors, U.S. Steel) that dominated the American economic landscape and symbolized American economic power worldwide. This approach also fostered distrust and hostility between workers and their bosses, who developed an "us versus them" mentality, in which each side saw the other as having interests fundamentally opposed to its own. Thus, as managers tried various tricks to speed up work, those laboring on the front lines developed alternate approaches to try to restrict production (Burawoy 1979; Edwards 1979; Montgomery 1979; Tulin 1984).

If manufacturing is in decline, is mass production? To address this question, consider work as it is performed in different "megasectors"—broad groupings of different types of economic activity. Each of these sectors makes a distinct contribution to the economy—in extracting resources, in processing resources, in delivering goods, and in providing services.[2] The trends for employment in these sectors are represented in Exhibit 2.2, which shows the growing importance of service sector work, as well as the proportions of the labor force employed in other industries that seem (on the surface) to have helped society progress beyond mass production. However, consideration of many of the jobs within each of these sectors highlights how the typical strategies for organizing work in the manufacturing-based economy have been exported to other sectors and shape how work is performed outside manufacturing.

For most of human existence, most workers engaged in the extraction of raw materials—working in the areas of farming, fishing, forestry, or mining. But by the early twentieth century, these workers composed only a relatively small segment of the workforce. Those few who remain on farms today perform work that bears little resemblance to the pastoral ideals of the family farm. Rather, most farming occurs as part of agribusiness, in which the methods of mass production have been applied to the raising of livestock, poultry, and produce (Schlosser 2005). The extension of mass production into farm work has required some farmers to learn to use advanced technologies to manage production. However, it also has contributed to the creation of a divided opportunity structure that limits prospects for workers (such as migrant farm laborers) to grow and advance. Mining remains an intensely physical activity. Underground mining uses single-purpose machinery (such as "continuous miners") to grind the earth and place ore on conveyors. These technologies operate as assembly lines that run in reverse. Other forms of mining, such as strip mining (or even mountaintop removal, in which whole mountains are demolished and the ore removed in the process), rely on heavy equipment and systematic processing of materials and operate on a scale that could only be characterized as "mass" production. All newer mining technologies require the application of greater skills than the older manual operations, but they also substitute massive equipment and sophisticated technology for human labor. This is one enduring persistent feature of the old economy, the drive to improve productivity by replacing labor through the use of complex technologies and managerial innovations. It also operates on the basis of massive scale implementation, indicating that mass production is not on a decline.

Exhibit 2.2   Trends in Employment in Megasectors: United States, 1940–2014

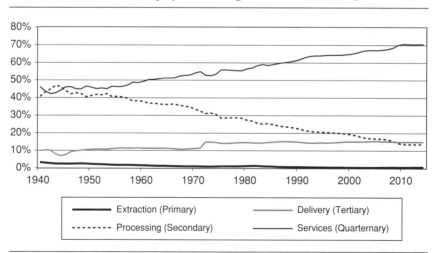

Source: Bureau of Labor Statistics.

The processing megasector focuses on the refinement of raw materials into finished goods, the intent of manufacturing and construction enterprises. As Exhibit 2.2 shows, processing work has declined significantly in the United States, which seems to support the "end of mass production" thesis. Yet, if we look at work within these sectors, mass production techniques have not been eliminated. It is true that there have been significant changes in this sector. For example, the traditional giant steel mill of the past has given way to smaller, more flexible "mini-mills" that produce smaller runs of more specialized steel products. But contemporary factories are still mass-producing consumer goods. And in certain parts of this sector, most notably the building trades, modern practices have made production more reliant on the use of standardized materials. Many homes are "prefabricated" in construction factories and simply assembled on site. Even the construction of "custom" homes (the largest of which are pejoratively termed "McMansions") depends heavily on cookie-cutter approaches to design and assembly. In short, flexible and custom production processes have taken hold in some areas, but they are being introduced in concert with a continued reliance on elements of mass production, not simply replacing them (Pietrykowski 1999).

The delivery megasector (which includes transportation, wholesale trade, retail trade, and utilities) is one of the most visible and important elements of the new economy, as just-in-time production methods rely on sophisti-cated systems to ensure that parts and materials arrive just when they are needed and as consumers increasingly demand immediate delivery of products they purchase online. Although associated in most people's minds with the new economy, this megasector, too, relies heavily on mass produc-tion techniques. For example, United Parcel Service (UPS) and Walmart (the world's largest private employer) use vast conveyor belt systems to sort and funnel parcels for delivery. Their successes are not built on unique products or customized services; rather, they are based on the application of mass production distribution techniques built with high technology and advanced accounting systems. And then there is Amazon, whose "fulfillment centers" now employ huge numbers of workers across the globe ensuring that online orders reach their destinations promptly and accurately. Amazon's employ-ment practices have been the subject of increasing journalistic scrutiny in the past few years, scrutiny that has revealed a twenty-first-century workplace that has married modern computer technology to very familiar, twentieth-century ways of organizing work. Here's how one observer described it:

> Amazon's shop-floor processes are an extreme variant of Taylorism that Frederick Winslow Taylor himself, a near century after his death, would have no trouble recognizing. With this twenty-first-century Taylorism, management

experts, *scientific managers*, take the basic workplace tasks at Amazon, such as the movement, shelving, and packaging of goods, and break down these tasks into their subtasks, usually measured in seconds; then rely on time and motion studies to find the fastest way to perform each subtask; and then reassemble the subtasks and make this "one best way" the process that employees must follow. (Head 2014)

Jobs like these are not skilled or challenging tasks that lead to career advancement; they are the type of routine work that one pursues as a means to earn a paycheck.

Finally, within the services megasector, which includes a wide array of enterprises—including leisure services, restaurants, hotels, real estate, financial, and public administration—mass production methods also can be found, often in highly developed, innovative forms. This sector includes some enterprises that do not rely on mass production—there are many relatively small enterprises in this part of the economy, such as bed and breakfast establishments. Businesses such as high-end restaurants rely on workers' skills to produce a "unique" product for the consumer. However, this sector also contains many highly standardized operations that use the techniques of mass production to good effect. Each McDonald's, for instance, is little more than a small factory, composed of deskilled jobs designed to execute production of a limited array of standardized goods. Every aspect of the process, including the dispensing of condiments, the design of the stores, and the way in which customers are greeted, has been standardized so that the experience of eating (or working) in a McDonald's is essentially the same wherever it is located. Even housecleaning teams are organized to work according to Taylorized methods, and the goals remain the same—to extract the maximum effort from each individual and minimize their chances of relaxing on the job (Ehrenreich 2001; Ritzer 2011).

In sum, there is a tendency to assume that the declining importance of manufacturing in the U.S. economy means that mass production is on the wane. It is not. Indeed, what has happened is that mass production techniques have been widely integrated into other sectors of the economy, including the rapidly growing service sector. Many of the key elements of traditional mass production, including the use of technology to pace work, careful design of routine work tasks, careful matching of workers to work tasks, and the use of insecurity and performance pressures to motivate workers, now characterize types of work that, in the past, were rarely organized in this way. It can be argued, in fact, that the ideas pioneered by Frederick Taylor and Henry Ford have become *more*, not less, influential in the contemporary "postindustrial" economy (Crowley 2010).

To be sure, new technologies and production methods have required an expansion in certain worker skills and transformed the ways in which work is performed. However, those same machines and methods also have replaced many workers, both in manufacturing and elsewhere, and the persistence and spread of mass production methods cannot be ignored. As discussed next, the reality is that the new economy relies on both high-skill and low-skill work, and it uses both mass production techniques and new flexibly specialized systems to produce goods and services.

New Skills?

The fact that the new economy is characterized by a new mix of industries and jobs has led some to conclude that it requires a new set of skills from the workforce. According to this argument, the traditional low-skill work characteristic of the industrial economy is being automated out of existence, while the new economy demands a workforce with "soft skills" needed for successful social interaction in service sector jobs. It also demands a more highly educated workforce, as the emergent "knowledge economy" relies heavily on highly trained workers with substantial quantities of technical and intellectual skills. Some argue that, as these new skills have supplanted manual skills, the trend toward work simplification also has been altered—even reversed. This is because the predictable, carefully designed, strictly managed, routine jobs typical of mass production might be difficult to transfer to activities that require face-to-face interaction or sophisticated knowledge and problem-solving skills. Thus, the new workforce will have to be more highly educated and able to work independently, outside the strict controls imposed on routine manufacturing work. Let us examine some of these "new" skills to determine whether the claims being made about them can be supported.

Interactive Service Work

Interactive service work involves direct personal encounters between employees and customers. This requires the workers who perform these jobs to interact effectively with clients and more often than not, to manage encounters that leave clients satisfied not only with the services rendered but also with the experience of being served. While an increasing proportion of jobs require "people skills," it should be obvious that interactive skills are not specific to the new economy, nor were they completely absent from the old economy. Even within the grind of production work, employees deftly used personal skills to manage work tasks and relations with coworkers and bosses (Burawoy 1979). It is true that some industrial jobs required few interaction skills, but there were other jobs (such as those involved in selling manufactured goods, managing manufacturing workers, doing the office work required by manufacturing enterprises, and so on) that clearly did. What this illustrates is that there is a range of jobs *within* industrial sectors. Not everyone employed in the manufacturing industry is a manufacturing worker, nor is everyone employed in a service industry performing interactive service work. Beyond this observation, it also bears noting that what constitutes service work varies widely. For example, the bedside manner that a doctor or nurse presents to patients is a critically important component of the work he or she performs. In contrast, the depth of the interactive experience between a fast-food worker and a customer is comparatively shallow, as are the expectations for emotional gratification.

One clear conclusion of a growing body of literature is that skills such as the ability to communicate effectively with others, to present oneself appropriately and effectively, and to function effectively in a range of social situations are essential components of contemporary jobs and are valued highly by employers. For some workers, these skills have been cultivated through years of informal socialization, such as that received from parents, so that they already know how to "fit in" with the types of people to be served. However, individuals from disadvantaged backgrounds often have developed very different types of interaction styles that lead to a poorer fit between their cultural tool kits and jobs. A young worker who grew up in an inner-city neighborhood may have a very difficult time "reading" the signals given off by the responses of a more privileged client and may also feel uncomfortable in the encounter. And the client may not necessarily treat the young worker in the same way as someone perceived as being more similar in habits and disposition. These types of interpersonal dynamics present new challenges in fitting workers into the new opportunity structures, as the work is not only about mastering technical skills but also social skills.

In theory, at least, it would seem that interactive skills would be resistant to routinization and simplification. However, as in the old economy, employers have attempted just that, and with considerable degrees of success. Perhaps the most familiar example of routinized interaction can be seen in the fast-food industry. As Robin Leidner documented in her pioneering study of interactive service work, McDonald's has worked out very specific guidelines not just for the production of the food their stores sell to customers but also for structuring the interaction between workers and customers. Frontline service workers in the stores are given very specific scripts to follow and are instructed (and their performance is monitored) regarding what to say and how to say it. Nor is the management of interaction confined to employees, as McDonald's has succeeded in finding ways to encourage customers to behave in predictable ways; for example, by physically arranging the store to encourage customers to behave in prescribed ways (line up here, pick up your food there, don't linger too long, dispose of your trash on the way out), as well as limiting or scripting menu choices ("I will have value meal number seven"). As has frequently been noted, the experience of patronizing a McDonald's restaurant is more or less the same, no matter where it is located, as a result of this careful routinization (Leidner 1993). Call center work is another type of interactive service work that has been successfully routinized and elaborately managed. Employees must follow carefully developed scripts, and calls are monitored for "quality assurance." Employees of call centers located abroad undergo accent modification programs so that their English will not be too foreign to callers; they are also asked to become familiar with aspects of Western culture (such as sports) so that they can interact more effectively with callers (Belanger and Edwards 2013).

Like routinization in manufacturing, interaction constraints can be experienced as oppressive and intrusive by both workers and customers. Much of the early research on scripted interaction speculated about the possibility that following scripts, and interacting with others according to externally imposed routines, rather than one's *own* reaction to the situation, can breed feelings of inauthenticity and psychological distress (e.g., Wharton 1999). But efforts to make interaction more routine and predictable can actually help employees do their jobs, with the result that they sometimes embrace the protocols and actively collaborate with employers in imposing routines. Hochschild's (1983) classic study of flight attendants, for example, describes the various routines and scripts airline employees are trained to use during commercial flights. She points out that some of the reason for this training is to promote the corporate brand and to ensure that employees project the company's desired image. However, it is also the case that some of the routines help flight attendants perform difficult tasks: creating a reassuring environment that calms potentially panicky passengers, coping with angry customers when in flight (when there are limited options for discipline), and so on. Far from resisting or resenting routines, flight attendants adopt them willingly and make use of them voluntarily. More recent research on nurses finds that burnout is common, in part, because of the emotional turmoil the work involves. In this context, scripts and routines that help nurses manage interactions with patients might actually help to reduce emotional fatigue (Erickson and Grove 2007).

For better or worse, like work in the old economy, interactive service work is subject to the pressure of routinization. Once work is routinized, there exists the potential to replace people with machines. Can this be done within the service sector? Clearly this is possible. Consider, for example, that inserting a credit card into the pump at a self-serve gas station is now the preferred means of payment, an act that completely eliminates the need to interact with the service station attendant. And it is possible to apply technologies to more sophisticated types of service encounters. However, there also appear to be limits. For example, one study of an attempt to implement an automated help desk found that computers have the capacity to respond to commonly experienced problems or needs of clients. However, what did prove to be an obstacle was that callers could not be controlled in the same ways that they are at a McDonald's restaurant. For example, callers to help desks typically did not know how to describe their problem in ways that the help desk computer could understand. Lacking technical sophistication themselves, callers often provided vague, incomplete, or even inaccurate descriptions of the problem they were experiencing, with the result that the computer was unable to ask many follow-up questions and lacked the capacity to respond appropriately (Head 2003). Similarly, employers have found it difficult or impossible to reduce their reliance on the care work provided by nurses, whose interaction with patients, as well as the various physical tasks they perform, remain essential to effective health care (Clawson and Gerstel 2014). So, while employers continue to attempt to apply old-economy techniques to the organization of work tasks, some of the complex services needed in the new economy may prove unsuited to those approaches.

High-Tech Work

The new economy is also frequently described as requiring a more educated workforce. According to this view the "knowledge economy" or the "information economy" depends on a large and growing supply of highly educated, technically sophisticated employees, rather than the low-skill workers needed by mass production industry. An important element of this high-skill workforce is the so-called **STEM** (science, technology, engineering, mathematics) workforce; policy makers argue that economic growth increasingly depends on an adequate supply of workers trained in these areas, individuals who can design and maintain new technologies.

STEM jobs have, in fact, grown significantly. These trends need to be interpreted carefully, however, because opportunities for work in some STEM occupations have not been expanding. While there are many more jobs for workers with computer science training, for example, the same cannot be said for physicists, chemists, or even certain kinds of engineers, where demand has grown more slowly, or not at all. Nor has the expansion of STEM employment been steady; on the contrary, since World War II it has been marked by a boom-bust cycle, as periods of high demand are followed by an overproduction of graduates, layoffs, and falling demand (e.g., what happened after the Vietnam War or the more recent dot.com bust of the early twenty-first century). In some instances, exaggerated predictions of actual or looming shortages of qualified STEM workers can be linked to advocates with political agendas at stake (Salzman, Kuehn, and Lowell 2013; Teitelbaum 2014). So, while the growth of STEM employment is real and likely to continue, it will likely remain a relatively small, if increasingly important, part of the contemporary economy.

As the STEM workforce has grown, so have hopes that the new economy will create large numbers of well-paying, secure, challenging jobs. The success of enterprises such as Apple, Microsoft, and, more recently, Facebook and other social media fuel enthusiastic visions of high-tech workers deeply engaged with creative work, making pioneering breakthroughs, and transforming knowledge into lucrative business opportunities. The demand for engineers, research scientists, and computer professionals, and the reality of success stories, indicate that these hopes are not irrational. However, there is reason not to jump to the conclusion that the low-skill mass production economy has been fully replaced by an economy dominated by autonomous, creative STEM workers.

First, it should be remembered that not *all* jobs in high-technology, science-based sectors are well-paid, high-skill jobs. The computer industry employs many professionals but also needs relatively unskilled workers to assemble, package, and transport its products. Similarly, while health care requires doctors, researchers, and other skilled professionals, no hospital can function without a significant number of orderlies, maintenance workers, aides, technicians, and clerks. Nor are the trends for the *professional* STEM workforce uniformly positive. For example, STEM salary growth has not outpaced salary growth in other occupations, suggesting that the demand for STEM professionals is not as great as had been anticipated (Hira 2010; Teitelbaum 2014).

In addition, the independent, creative, entrepreneurial STEM career exemplified by Steve Jobs of Apple and Mark Zuckerberg of Facebook is not the reality experienced by many employees in this sector. While earlier predictions (e.g., Kraft 1984) that high-technology work would be simplified and routinized in much the same way as manufacturing have proven exaggerated, STEM professionals work in jobs affected by a number of dynamics reminiscent of the old economy. For example, STEM employers in industries such as information technology (IT) can reduce the upward pressure on salaries produced by the shortage of well-trained workers by importing qualified employees from overseas. Much like manufacturing employers in the past, who encouraged and even sponsored immigration to keep labor costs down, contemporary IT employers look to countries such as India for sources of affordable labor. There is a growing controversy over the H1-B visa program that facilitates the import of technical professionals from overseas, as some claim that employers use this not because there is a shortage, but as a source of less expensive labor (Salzman, Kuehn, and Lowell 2013; Teitelbaum 2014). Moreover, the new economy offers novel opportunities to take advantage of the availability of lower-cost labor overseas. Many analysts have noted how the electronics revolution has made it possible to digitize steps in the work process and locate them offshore, retaining only portions of the work to be performed in the United States (Aspray 2010; Blinder 2006). Interestingly, the import of technical professionals and the outsourcing of jobs may be directly linked; among the largest users of the H1-B visa program are Indian technology companies, who sponsor technical professionals coming to the United States to work for a time, then return them to India where they become key components of the growing Indian high-technology workforce (Teitelbaum 2014).

The actual work performed by STEM professionals generally requires considerable skill and expertise. However, it is not uniformly creative or autonomous in the way suggested by the more euphoric visions of the contemporary, high-technology workplace. Not all computer programming work, for example, is fully creative. Some computer professionals are engaged in the design of new systems and products and apply genuine creative autonomy as they enjoy the freedom to play with new ideas and concepts in their work. However, much computer programming (while it can be technically demanding) also can be relatively routine, formulaic work. For example, composing the well-understood computer code that forms the core of even new programs, or checking and debugging programs, can be (and often is) performed by lower-paid and sometimes less-qualified employees. This type of work is most likely to be outsourced to countries such as India (Aspray 2010; Parthasarathy 2004).

Finally, even the more creative kinds of programming work are often managed in ways familiar to the old economy. Rather than being given a free hand to design and create whatever and however they please, computer professionals typically have to design programs on schedules set for them by managers or external customers (in the case of suppliers and subcontractors to larger firms). They also often are required to incorporate user suggestions into their designs, and their compliance with these and other expectations is closely monitored (Barrett 2004). The jobs of software developers are a long way from being the routinized work of mass production workers—they enjoy much more autonomy and have more creative decision-making ability than does anyone working on an assembly line. At the same time, as in the old economy, employers tend to seek ways to limit the cost of labor and attempt to manage and control it. In sum, there has been a growth in high-skill work in the new economy and some of this work is performed in new ways with new intents. Nevertheless, high-skill work has not replaced low-skill work, and even high-skilled workers have been subject to controls established in the old economy.

New Cultures of Control?

Some observers of the new economy have argued that changes in technology, organization, and markets are transforming jobs, including manufacturing jobs, into more highly skilled jobs in small, high-tech, "flexibly specialized" enterprises (Piore and Sabel 1984). The workforce envisioned for this new kind of workplace will be highly educated, multitalented, and required to exercise creativity and decision making on the job. In this vision of the new economy, managers are cautioned against "micromanaging" and are advised to form workers into teams with their own team leaders. Even low-level employees are hired as "associates," implying that their input will be valued. Others are not convinced. They point to the experiences of low-level service sector workers and agree with the critical philosopher Slavoj Zizek, who once quipped, "The employee of the month shows that one can be a winner and a loser at the same time." And, though acknowledging that new methods of organizing work are more common, these skeptics suggest that the reorganization of work is not just about introducing new markets or technologies but also about developing sophisticated new methods to control workers and undermine their power in the workplace (Curry 1993; Parker 1985; Parker and Slaughter 1988). Still others question whether even well-meaning managers attempting to create more creative, flexible work arrangements have the freedom, in the context of stockholder, financial, and other pressures, to create the workplaces they would like (Stuart et al. 2013; Thompson 2003). Thus, we must also ask, are new technologies and organizational designs increasing worker autonomy, creativity, and control?

Some of the most carefully conducted studies of this question have been performed by Steven Vallas, who has examined the introduction of computer technology and worker teams in the pulp and paper industry. His findings are important because they both support and refute core predictions regarding what happens to workers in organizations that use new technologies and managerial strategies. First, consider teamwork. Some analysts see worker teams as an ideological trick, a way of getting workers to believe that they have control when they do not. Vallas found that, rather than hoodwinking workers, work teams shared grievances, developed a heightened distrust of management, and developed class solidarities. And, by virtue of being a team, they expressed complaints to management with less fear of personal reprisal (Vallas 2003a). However, Vallas also found that the expectation for shared decision-making responsibilities between workers and managers has been exaggerated. In fact, the introduction of computer-regulating systems in the paper industry tended to increase the distinction between those who had the authority to make decisions and those who did not. Older workers interpreted the new technology as an affront to the craft skills they had developed through years of experience on the job, and they expressed dismay at the new reliance on meters and printouts that provided information they already possessed (Vallas and Beck 1996).

One of the important insights from Vallas's studies is that the new economy seems to be marked less by fundamental shifts in the amount of control workers have and more by modifications to systems of accountability. In the old economy, the assumption was that workers should have no control and that jobs and machines should be rigidly designed and managed from above. In the new economy, where commitments to Total Quality Management foster a drive to work with exacting perfection, and where the responsibility for creating this outcome is placed on the shoulders of worker teams, a new dynamic of collective pressure is introduced. Workers now have increased responsibility for production but not control over many of the decisions that shape it. These findings correspond with a number of other analyses that show that workplaces in the new economy do not operate on trust and cooperation and that workers and managers remain skeptical of each other's intentions and motivations (Appelbaum and Batt 1992; Osterman 2001; Rinehart, Huxley, and Robertson 1997; Smith 1990).

Another supposedly new dynamic is the re-creation of craft communities, which some believe are reshaping the ways work is understood and performed. For example, the success of Silicon Valley enterprises has been attributed to their operating in a regional community of similar companies that specialize in computer work (Pietrykowski 1999). In some ways, these regional centers operate in a manner similar to the craft communities of bygone eras and position workers to exert control through the development of a collective culture of standards and expectations. The work of skilled programmers in this environment is truly a team effort and requires considerable coordination of tasks that require varying levels of skill and control. In this environment, workers are often paid quite handsomely for their efforts. On the surface, it looks like a model example of optimistic predictions about what work can become.

Questions have been raised, however, about how real these "craft communities" actually are. The high-technology industry may have its share of start-ups and small, "nimble" companies, but it also is increasingly dominated by corporate giants: Apple, Hewlett-Packard, IBM, Microsoft, Google, Intel, and Cisco all were among the sixty largest companies in the United States in 2014. As we discuss further later in this book, some elements of life in the Silicon Valley and other high-tech strongholds appear more enslaving than liberating. For example, high-technology workers experience both external and internal pressures to labor twelve- to fourteen-hour days and sacrifice their lives for their jobs (a reality satirized in Dave Eggers's novel, *The Circle*). The project teams that form and reform within high-tech companies are subject to intense performance pressures and tight deadlines; the resulting managerial demands and coworker pressure both push workers to put in long hours. The reality that one's job may last only as long as the current project, and the hope that a show of commitment will lead one to be invited to join the next project, add to the external pressure (O'Riain 2007). But some of the pressure to work long hours is internal, as many high-tech workers embrace a sense of commitment to a culture in which the willingness to work long hours is taken for granted and normal (Harris and Junglas 2013; Shih 2004). It is paradoxical that a work environment that offers control also tightens the chains of work, resulting in workers laboring far longer hours than those preferred by most individuals.

A final aspect of change to the cultures of control in the new economy concerns the application of **flexible work arrangements**. In the old economy, workers were commonly expected to be physically present at their workstations and to structure their time commitments in accordance with rigid daytime/full-time schedules. But as the labor force shifted to include increasing proportions of women, and as new technologies and organizational designs developed, many argued that jobs need to become more flexible. In stark contrast to the practices and philosophies central to the old economy, the thesis underpinning the implementation of flexible work arrangements is that the rigid schedules and physical copresence among workers are not necessarily the best ways to design jobs.

Before discussing the extent of flexibility present in jobs in the new economy, it is important to note that flexibility is not always intended to help ease the balancing of work and family or to maximize the liberating potential of technology. Thus, we must ask, "flexibility for whom?" (Pollert 1988). For example, the fast-food worker who is sent home early because business is slack, or who is told to stay late because of an unexpected rush, has a flexible work arrangement that operates primarily for the employer's interests. Sometimes organizational flexibility is used to legitimate dismissal of workers or justify the dismantling of work sites. The temporary work industry has very effectively used the idea and rhetoric of flexibility to persuade employers, and even employees, that insecure temporary jobs benefit both employers and employees alike (Hatton 2011; Smith and Neuwirth 2008). These are not the types of flexible work arrangements we are concerned with here, although, as we discuss later in this book (especially in Chapter 4), this dark side of flexibility is a potentially growing phenomenon in the new economy.

The brighter side of flexibility is how it can be used to reconfigure job designs to suit the needs of workers. For example, sometimes workers seek flexible work arrangements to help them take care of a child or an aging parent. These types of needs might be satisfied by telecommuting, by reducing the number of hours worked, by scheduling work differently, or possibly by allowing a sabbatical from the job. Additionally, these arrangements may fit changing cultural preferences. For example, older workers commonly wish to remain integrated in the labor force but work fewer hours or work part of the year (Moen 2007). It is now clear that when they are applied with the employee's interests in mind, flexible work arrangements tend to help workers harmonize their lives with their jobs, as well as mitigate negative personal and family outcomes that result from work-family conflict (Kelly et al. 2008).

There are essentially three overarching types of flexible work arrangements. **Move work arrangements** include programs and practices that enable schedule variability, changes in starting and quitting times on a time-to-time basis, compression of workweeks, and opportunities to work at home, off-site, or at different worksites. Note that for these arrangements the amount of work remains the same, but the place or time at which the work is to be performed varies. In contrast, **reduce work arrangements** include programs and practices that enable workers to scale back work hours, to job share, to phase into retirement with reduced hours, or to work part of the year for a reduced amount of time. These options offer the prospect of temporarily limiting the amount of work to be performed. A third set of options can be considered **pause work arrangements**. These include programs and practices that enable workers to take temporary career breaks, sabbaticals, or paid or unpaid time for education or training to improve job skills. If employment opportunities are shifting in the new economy, we would anticipate that many of these move, reduce, and pause work opportunities would be available to workers. Are they?

Consider findings from one study of American companies, presented in Exhibit 2.3 (Sweet et al. 2014). Over half of the employers (54%) provided no flexible work arrangements to most or all employees. It is also evident that the availability of flexible work arrangements varies widely across sectors. Organizations in the manufacturing sector are the least likely to enable employees to move, reduce, or pause work, with 75% of organizations not offering any of these options to the majority of their workforce. In contrast, employers in the professional, scientific, and technical services sectors and in the accommodation and food services sectors are much more likely to offer

Exhibit 2.3   Percentage of Companies Offering Flexible Work Options to Most or All of Their Employees: United States, 2009

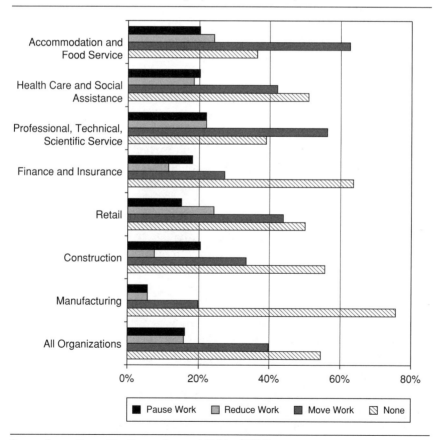

Source: Sweet, Besen, Pitt-Catsouphes, and Golden (2014).

access to flexible work arrangements (most commonly the option to move work in accordance with schedule flexibility). Among employers that offer flexible work arrangements, the most common approach is to enable workers to alter where or when they did their work (39%). Few employers provided most of their workers with the option to reduce work (15.8%) or pause work (16.1%).

The availability of flexible work arrangements also varies by the type of job being performed and by the type of worker performing that job. Ironically, the workers who often need flexibility the most—especially women—are the least likely to receive these options (Golden 2001; Swanberg, Pitt-Catsouphes, and Drescher-Burke 2005). Office administrative assistants, for example, are usually expected to work standard 9-to-5 shifts and to be at their desks during the workday, every day, even if work is slack. The managers for whom they work, however, may have numerous options to make "I-deals" that might configure their schedules to meet their personal needs, to work at home, or to negotiate reduced work if they wish (Rousseau 2005). The unevenness in the allocation of these types of opportunities is a critical concern in reconciling work and family for workers in all segments of the economy.

In sum, the existing evidence shows that some types of flexibility are more prevalent than others, but the option to reduce work or to take a break from work is not commonly provided to workers. Why is the availability of flexible arrangements so limited? Some evidence suggests that these practices help bolster workplace performance, facilitate retention, enhance the job, and may even contribute to a company's reputation (Arthur and Cook 2004; Richman et al. 2008). And if this is the case for all employers, then the limited implementation may simply reflect a structural or cultural lag that likely will be reconciled eventually. However, at present there is conflicting evidence about the extent to which different types of flexible work arrangements consistently result in positive "returns on investments" (Kelly et al. 2008). In the end, employers are the ones who decide whether to extend flexibility to employees, and they look for evidence that the benefits of doing so (increased productivity, decreased turnover) outweigh the costs. In the contemporary economy, in which managers find themselves under pressure to reduce labor costs, the case for truly flexible work arrangements must be based on evidence that it enhances the bottom line (Hatton 2011; Thompson 2003). In the absence of clear evidence of this result, it should be expected that the availability of flexibility will remain limited and uneven across industry sectors and occupations.

The technologies and organizations of the new economy are argued to expand control, and sometimes they do. However, evidence indicates that they have yet to live up to potentials identified and in some instances undermine control. Add to the equation that some jobs in the new economy continue to operate like jobs in the old economy, and the promise of a return to craft control appears even more distant.

The End of Organized Labor?

Another possible indicator of an emerging new economy is shifting balances of power between collectivities of workers and their employers. As Exhibit 2.4 shows, the rise of the old economy was accompanied by a dramatic increase in union membership in the United States. At the middle of the twentieth century, roughly one in three American workers belonged to a union. In the latter part of the century, however, membership plummeted, and, despite a short-lived increase in union membership in 2007 and 2008, by 2013, only 11% of workers belonged to unions. Overall, the decline of unionization in the private sector has been particularly sharp; less than 7% of private-sector workers belonged to unions in 2013. The one exception to the general pattern of decline has been in the public sector. According to the Bureau of Labor Statistics, government sector unions remain vigorous and have even grown, representing more than 35% of government employees in 2013. But, as we discuss next, even in this sector the union movement is being challenged.

One reason for falling union membership is that a declining proportion of the workforce is employed in manufacturing, the sector in which unionization has traditionally been strongest. In addition, as American manufacturing employment has contracted, employers have become

Exhibit 2.4   Percentage of American Workers Who Were Union Members: United States, 1930–2013

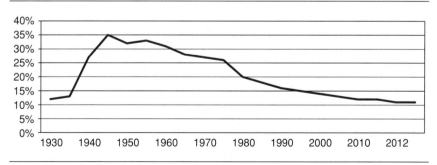

Source: Bureau of Labor Statistics.

increasingly willing to close facilities or to relocate both within the United States and abroad, so that unionization in the manufacturing sector has declined. In some cases, employers have moved away from areas where unions are strong to those where they are not; consider the shift of automobile manufacturing away from the union stronghold of Detroit to non-union states in the South. In other cases, efforts to unionize have been stymied by threats to close shop and by actual relocation. Free trade agreements such as NAFTA have made it easier for companies to move across borders, largely because those agreements often do not contain strong protections for labor organizations (Luce 2014). The development of complex supply chains, with major producers being supplied by a network of smaller companies scattered across the globe, has also contributed to union decline. Not only are the supplier companies small and mobile (making them hard to organize), they are also less economically secure, which in turn discourages collective bargaining (Luce 2014). Still, nonmanufacturing workers do join unions in many other countries (including Canada). And the decline of unionization in the United States has occurred not just in sectors exposed to capital mobility but also in sectors such as transportation and construction that cannot relocate. So, the real reason for declining unionization may be the failure of American unions to organize workers in the growth sectors of the new economy (Milkman 2006).

American unions have been criticized for their lack of emphasis on organizing new groups in the post–World War II era, but even when they try, unions often meet with failure. One hindrance they face is that laws in the United States have made it comparatively difficult. Although American workers won the right to organize with the New Deal–era Wagner Act (which also established the basic legal framework for collective bargaining in the United States), numerous restrictions have since been placed on unions and union organizing activities. The Taft-Hartley Act of 1947 was particularly important in this regard. This piece of legislation, strongly backed by an antilabor, postwar U.S. Congress, prohibited some of the most effective strategies that had been used to expand the reach and power of unions, most notably the closed shop (in which all workers at a particular place of employment are required to be union members), the sympathy strike (in which workers in one industry strike in support of workers in another), and the secondary boycott (in which unions attempt to persuade others not to do business with a particular firm whose workers are on strike). Even more importantly, Taft-Hartley made organizing new groups of workers much more difficult by authorizing states to pass "right-to-work" laws (which prohibit unions from making paying dues or fees a condition of employment), by strengthening employers' ability publicly to speak out against and resist unionization drives, by permitting strikebreakers to vote in union certification elections, and by making the process of union certification far less flexible than it had been.[3] In general, postwar U.S. labor policy has not favored new union formation, and the National Labor Relations Board, which regulates collective bargaining, has become more conservative in its rulings over time (Gould 2007). Moreover, employers have become increasingly hostile to unions and have successfully used a variety of tactics to discourage organization. In some cases, this involves the use of the "carrot"; that is, making union membership less attractive by providing, voluntarily, some or all of the good labor conditions that unions gain for their members (Milkman 2006). In others, it involves the "stick"; that is, aggressive efforts to block unionization through methods such as firing organizers and the use of experts to develop strategies of keeping unions out (Bronfenbrenner 2009; Head 2004).

Government workers in the United States have not had to contend with strong antiunion efforts by their employer. Though some states limit public-sector unions in various ways (e.g., New York State's "Taylor Law," which prohibits strikes by public employees), government workers in general have encountered fewer obstacles to unionization than their private-sector counterparts, which probably accounts for much higher rates of unionization in the public sector. However, in the aftermath of the financial crisis of 2009, a number of state governments, including states with strong union traditions such as Ohio and Wisconsin, took aggressive action to curtail public-sector unions. Arguing that salaries and benefits paid to current and retired government workers were crippling state budgets, and complaining that union job protections limited flexibility and prevented institutions such as public schools from rewarding merit, governors such as Scott Walker of Wisconsin and John Kasich of Ohio led movements to impose legislative restrictions on public-sector unions. Only Walker was successful, but the challenge to public-sector unions is real. Calls for similar limits on public unions have been heard in some European countries. Survey data indicate significant support for public-sector unionization rights, and efforts to overturn anti–public sector union legislation are under way. This indicates that the path to limiting the power of collective bargaining in the public sector may be politically risky. However, if state governments succeed in limiting public-sector unionization, that almost certainly will negatively affect the terms of employment for public-sector work (Greenhouse 2011a).

Some analysts have suggested that the new economy has the potential to change relationships between employers and employees for the better and that these new employer-employee relationships reduce the need for the checks that unions place on employers' inclinations toward exploitation.

For example, new management philosophies and new forms of work organization ostensibly promote collaboration and harmony between employers and their workers. Even if this is not evidenced in reality, the belief that this is the case can have significant power. Work in smaller enterprises involves direct face-to-face relationships between workers and their employers, which discourages a "them and us" mentality, and as greater shares of workers are laboring in smaller enterprises, this might be having an influence. In this culture of cooperation, traditional unions may not seem attractive to workers, who may see them as threatening the company's interests and their jobs (Heckscher 1988). It has also been pointed out that workers are less likely to devote their entire careers to single employers, instead building portfolios and moving from employer to employer. In this context, unions representing particular workplaces appear to become less relevant (Cappelli 1997). Still, portfolio careers are more typical of professionals, who generally move voluntarily, than of less-educated workers, who move because they have to (Kim 2013). A worker who is a victim of job insecurity is likely to view a union job more positively than someone who is building a career by "job hopping."

The decline of unionization has occurred simultaneously with declining wages and job security (Western and Rosenfeld 2011). Thus, it may not be that changing management practices are making unions unnecessary; rather, it may be that unions have lost much of their ability to negotiate for workers' interests or to persuade workers that they are better off with unions than without them. Some evidence suggests that unions have lost much of their teeth. For example, American unions' ability to use the strike to put pressure on employers to raise wages or improve work conditions has largely evaporated. Consider that, according to the Bureau of Labor Statistics, in 1970, 2,468,000 workers participated in 381 mass walkouts. In contrast, in 2013, there were only fifteen large-scale work stoppages, and these only involved 55,000 workers.

The downward trend in union membership has been witnessed in most industrialized countries outside the United States, but the extent of these declines has been variable. Scandinavian countries have retained remarkably high union membership. Countries such as Australia, Germany, and the United Kingdom have significantly higher union membership rates than does the United States. Neighboring Canada has unionization rates more than double those of the United States (see Exhibit 2.5). Outside the Organisation for Economic Co-operation and Development (OECD), in the developing world, unionization rates have been growing (Luce 2014). The United States stands out in the international arena because of the combination of dramatic declines in membership and its exceptionally low current levels of unionization. The fact that unions remain important in other advanced economies, and that service workers who are typically unorganized here belong to unions there, is strong evidence that unions can still matter. Early in the twenty-first century, a major national survey found that the majority of *unorganized* American workers would vote for a union if one were available to them (Freeman 2007). And, while support for unions waxes and wanes somewhat, the majority of Americans still view unions favorably and see them as beneficial to workers (DeSilver 2014). Unions may not be a vestige of the old economy, but whether they will thrive in the new economy depends on whether they develop effective strategies for attracting new members and organizing new sectors of the workforce. It also depends on

Exhibit 2.5   Trade Union Members as Percentage of All Employees: International Comparisons

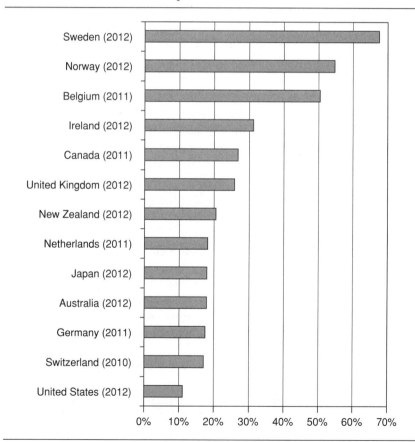

Source: Organization for Economic Co-operation and Development.

the resources made available to union organizers and the constraints placed on their actions.

A New Global Economy?

A final and much-discussed aspect of the new economy concerns globalization. Has the emergence of a global economy fundamentally changed the economy and the situation of workers worldwide? In some respects, the global economy is not really new. The histories of virtually all modern societies, from the sixteenth century onward, can be traced to international economic ties (Wallerstein 1979, 1983). For example, colonial America participated in international trade of slave labor, sugar, rum, tobacco, cod, and textiles (Kurlansky 1998). Had it not been for these exchanges, the present-day demographic makeup of the United States would be profoundly different, as would its culture. Likewise, the export of slaves to the United States had an enduring impact on the development of African societies. Trade with Asia is not new, and the European "discovery" of America was the result of attempts to find better trade routes. Indeed, international trade has long been in existence and has gone through numerous cycles of growth and decline (Chase-Dunn, Kawano, and Brewer 2000).

Nevertheless, one must still acknowledge that the extent of global economic activity is unprecedented and that the penetration of global capitalism to all corners of the world is both more complete and more complex than ever before. The new global economy can be described as a vast international network capable of rapidly developing and diffusing resources, technology, and information across the world. Among the key characteristics of the new global economy are the following:

- The immense volume of trade and consumption between societies;
- The rapid transmission of information between societies;
- Powerful and transportable technologies implemented throughout the world;
- Intense "dis-integrated" production, spread over national boundaries; and
- Flexible arrangements that enable employers to shift production and consumption from one society to another.

It should be added that the new global economy also is characterized by new types of legal and political arrangements designed to promote globalization. In the past, global economic activity was supported politically in various ways. Nineteenth-century colonial occupation created economic opportunities for employers in the dominant country (e.g., British enterprises benefitted greatly from British colonial activity in places such as India).

Even after the colonial empires dissolved, enterprises in the developed world often continued to derive considerable benefit from activities in the former colonies, aided by political, military, and diplomatic support from their home governments. On the other hand, international economic activity, especially among industrialized countries, was often limited in various ways by tariffs and other legal arrangements designed to protect domestic economies. It is this last situation that has begun to show signs of change in the new economy. Accompanied by economic theories that trumpet the benefits of free trade and the free movement of goods, services, and investment, many countries have joined in a variety of free trade agreements and even currency unions that remove many of the barriers to international economic activity. Notable examples include the North American Free Trade Agreement, designed to enhance free trade among the United States, Canada, and Mexico, and the European Union, which has created a large free trade zone among many of the countries of Europe and includes a common currency shared by at least some of its members. These arrangements make it much easier for goods and services to move across borders and for companies based in one country to establish facilities (or move them) to a range of others. One result has been that cultural and technological changes in developed and developing countries are accelerating at unprecedented rates. The speed of change, the extent of diffusion, and the flexibility of webs of connection set the current organization of work apart from the systems that preceded it (Castells 2000; Mattsson 2003; Milberg 2004). As one observer has remarked, the world is now, probably for the first time, approaching "universal capitalism" (Wood 2003).

Companies are integrating themselves into the global economy for a variety of reasons. An obvious reason is that companies try to move closer to emerging markets for their products; as countries such as China, India, and Brazil grow and industrialize, their residents emerge as new markets for products made by foreign companies, who often set up facilities nearby to be able to manufacture products for local consumption. Labor cost savings also are a major motivator; some companies locate in low-wage countries not to sell their products there but in order to reduce the cost of manufacturing goods to be sold in the United States and other developed economies. This is why some companies who had invested in production facilities in China, where labor costs have begun to rise, are now considering moving manufacturing operations to countries such as Vietnam and Indonesia.

Some critics argue that manufacturers, particularly those in highly polluting industries, are drawn to developing countries with lax environmental rules and enforcement. For this reason, many economists argue for more strict environmental standards as a means to control job flows. However, not everyone agrees, as counterevidence suggests that companies seek stable regulations, not necessarily loose ones, in making decisions about where to invest (Jones 2005; Rivera and Oh 2013). The tax structures of nation-state systems also encourage the movement of jobs. Companies that operate in multiple countries have the opportunity to concentrate their tax obligations in the country with the lowest tax rates. In some cases, they may even deliberately "move" outside the United States, while continuing to have operations in the United States, in search of tax havens. Major U.S. companies now have headquarters in places such as Bermuda, the Cayman Islands, and Luxemburg for this reason. In recent years, public attention has been drawn to the increasingly common practice of "inversion," in which U.S.-based companies merge with foreign companies and move their base abroad. The result is that large companies, such as medical equipment maker Medtronic and even Burger King, move at least a portion of their corporate operations overseas, in the process making huge tax savings by "locating" in a lower-tax country (Davis 2014). Companies also internationalize operations to secure government contracts and extend the global reach of their product lines.

The emergence of a global economy has had significant effects on workers in the United States and other industrialized countries, partly because the "national" character of companies has weakened and become ambiguous. American companies such as Ford have long had overseas operations in Europe. However, the scale of those overseas operations is something quite new. General Motors (like nearly all the major employers in the new economy) is a multinational corporation that operates both within and beyond the political realms of nation-states. Today, General Motors employs more workers outside the United States than it does within,[4] and it manufactures and sells cars around the world, with most of its sales *outside* the United States (Gregory 2012). Companies such as General Motors have been reconfigured to expedite shifts in production from place to place, as workers in Michigan have discovered. When companies move or open new facilities abroad, they bring more than jobs—they also sometimes spread culture and methods of organizing work. A good example of this can be seen in the case of Japanese companies, which have built facilities in both the industrialized and developing worlds. These plants became vectors through which Japanese production methods diffused to places such as Marysville, Ohio; northern Mexico; or Spain (Elger and Smith 1994). However, in other cases, foreign companies adopt local practices. A *Los Angeles Times* editorial argued that European companies, when they establish facilities in the United States, actually adopt American-style practices (such as "union-free" workplaces) that differ radically from the same companies' practices in their home countries (Meyerson 2011).

The emergence of a global economy has undoubtedly brought with it much that is new. Workers in the United States are much more likely to encounter technologies and managerial practices that originated elsewhere, and workers in developing countries have been drawn into more direct relationships with global webs of production. Still, arguing that all this is *entirely* new seems an exaggeration. Employers have relocated in the past, and even the earliest industrial firms in America "borrowed" practices from the pioneering British. It seems more accurate to say that globalization has accelerated and intensified existing dynamics at work. At the same time, the socioeconomic differences between the developed and developing world have not been erased by these changes (an observation that we document in the next chapter). Nor have national differences in workplace practices been eliminated by globalization (Smith and Meiksins 1995). As with the various other changes we have reviewed, there is much of the old within the new global workplace.

Conclusion

Does the existence of new products and new ways of working verify the existence of a new economy? The answer is both yes and no. The U.S. economy has shifted away from a primary reliance on its manufacturing base, and the expanding service sector is creating new job demands, as well as opportunities. So the economy is new in respect to the diversity of goods and services produced. But in many of the new jobs and industries, old ways of working and managing work are applied, indicating the persistence of the old economy. While some of the new jobs require different skill sets, substantial portions of the labor force work in low-skill jobs that require few skills, again indicating that not everything has changed. While organizations have redefined manager-worker relationships and are relinquishing more control to workers, some of these changes appear to be window dressing and in other circumstances have not led to a true enhancement of job quality. While the new economy offers prospects for flexible work, availability is limited and uneven. And while the global economy has shifted work opportunities, some of these changes are not so much new as they are extensions of tendencies that have been present for centuries.

We argued throughout this chapter that, while there is a new economy, it has been laid on top of and has not replaced the old economy. We also argue that the same forces that underpinned the development of the old economy continue to shape many of the contours of the new economy. The new economy offers great opportunities to liberate work, through new applications of technology, through new organizational designs, and by harnessing the contributions of a diverse workforce. But it also contains many elements of the old economy that block these opportunities and perpetuate and reproduce old ways of working. Both optimistic predictions that we are entering a new world of work and pessimistic comments about "old wine in new bottles" miss the complexity of contemporary work. Our analysis indicates that there will be both change and continuity in the emerging new economy and that there will be both positive gains for some workers and (if left unchecked) continued hardships for others.

Notes

1. The Bureau of Labor Statistics reports that in 2013, 3,696,180 people were employed in computer and mathematical occupations in the United States and 11,914,590 in food preparation and serving-related occupations.

2. Economists use the terms *primary, secondary, tertiary,* and *quaternary sectors*. However, because they also use the phrases *primary* and *secondary labor markets* to describe divided opportunity structures, we use the terms *extraction, processing, delivery,* and *service provision* in accordance with the divisions identified by Kenessey (1987).

3. The United States employs a cumbersome, two-step process for union certification in which workers must first sign cards indicating their interest in forming a union, then, at a later date, vote. Under the Taft-Hartley Act, all of this must take place under the watchful bureaucratic eye of the National Labor Relations Board. At the time of this writing, a proposal to substitute a one-step union certification process had stalled, despite initial support from the Obama administration.

4. GM's 2011 annual report indicated that the company employed 207,000 people worldwide, 74,500 of those in the United States.

Chapter Three

Economic Inequality, Social Mobility, and the New Economy

O ne would hope that the transition to the new economy is helping more families afford a better quality of life. One would also hope that it is increasing the opportunity to obtain quality jobs, the kind of work that offers prospects for growth and advancement. Better yet, one would hope that these improvements would be evident not only in the United States but also elsewhere in the global economy. And, finally, one would hope for equity, such that no one segment of the population reaps an inordinate share of the benefits or bears most of the risks and burdens. To what extent has the transition to the new economy enhanced the likelihood that these hopes will be fulfilled?

Social scientists have long argued that changes in work opportunity are intimately related to patterns of inequality, but in anticipating where societies are headed, theories often make very different predictions. Consider, for example, the debate about the effects on inequality that occurred in the early stages of industrialization. Karl Marx (Marx and Engels 1972 [1848]) argued that industrialization brought with it high levels of inequality and class antagonisms and that the ruling class (the bourgeoisie) obtained its wealth by appropriating it from the labor performed by the working classes (the proletariat). In predicting the future of the old economy, Marx believed that an oppositional class structure, the driving motor of capitalism, would polarize the structure of society into two classes, a small affluent class and a large exploited and disadvantaged class. In contrast, Frederick Winslow Taylor (1964 [1911]) countered the premise of antagonistic class interests by arguing that industrial capitalism would benefit all. In defending scientific management and the practice of dismantling the work of skilled craftsmen into repetitive unskilled jobs, Taylor argued that even if workers labored in low-skill jobs, they would be better off economically, as their companies would be more productive and create more wealth to distribute to everyone. Today, we are positioned much like Marx and Taylor were in the early stages of industrialization, as they tried to figure out the impact that a new economic order would have on the future of work and opportunity.

How is the emergence of the new economy reshaping patterns of inequality and opportunity? Is the decline of manufacturing and the rise of services liberating workers from economic hardship and spreading greater affluence to all? Or are these changes imposing new limits on opportunities and hardening already existing lines that separate the classes? Is the growth of industry in the developing world producing rising standards of living and more opportunities, or is it primarily benefitting a small elite and leaving existing class inequalities intact? In this chapter, we examine these questions, exploring how the changing contours of work affect structures of opportunity and the conditions under which the world's people live.

Are Economic Divides Narrowing or Widening in the United States?

Economic success is commonly gauged by a single measure, such as per capita income or median household income. While useful, these broad summary measures fail to capture the diversity of life chances, as it is possible for a society to have a very high *average* income but also for many individuals to be excluded from opportunity. For this reason, throughout this chapter we disaggregate economic data so that subgroups in the society are compared relative to one another, as well as over time. Our first concern is to identify the scale of social inequality as it currently exists in the United States and to gauge how that compares to the inequalities evident in the old economy. Our measures of the new economy rely on the most recent indicators available, and we mark 1970 as a high-water benchmark point from which to evaluate the opportunities present in the old economy. As discussed in the previous chapter, this year approximates the point at which the mass production industrial economy in the United States started to shift toward a more diverse postindustrial economy. With that shift, union membership declined, organizational practices were reconfigured, new flexible technologies were introduced, and the globalization of production took hold.

This benchmarking year also presents the old economy in perhaps its most favorable moment, as job security and wages were high for many workers, wage growth was nearing its plateau, and unemployment was low. Many of those features changed in the decades that followed, especially for blue-collar industrial workers in the northern rust belt, as factories closed during a period of deindustrialization in the 1970s and 1980s (Bluestone and Harrison 1982). Today, some of these communities have successfully made the transition to an employment base rooted in the new economy (e.g., Pittsburgh, Pennsylvania) while others suffer from stagnation or ongoing decline (e.g., Youngstown, Ohio, or Flint, Michigan).

In some ways, the situation present in 1970 affirmed the perspectives of both Taylor and Marx. In support of Taylor, the movement toward mass production work (even that which was deskilled) resulted in substantial wages and security for those employed in the manufacturing sector. In fact, income inequality declined during the early to mid-twentieth century in both the United States and in Europe. However, the declines in inequality were not because capitalism was working as Taylor believed it should but rather because of the impact that two world wars and the Great Depression had on class divides (Piketty 2014). The followers of Marx can rightly claim that the economic returns that manufacturing workers received were not inevitable outcomes of productivity. They were as much a consequence of organized labor acting in its own class interests. And while manufacturing workers had high wages and security, many others (especially women and minorities in the lower classes) were funneled into jobs that offered far fewer opportunities. The question we consider here is whether the shift to the new economy resulted in a fundamental shake-up of the amount of class inequality present in American society and if so, which groups have benefitted most.

Exhibit 3.1 offers a graphic illustration of the changes in incomes in the United States, examining the earnings received by five equal-sized portions of households (termed *quintiles*). To make comparisons over time possible, all of the dollar figures have been adjusted to their purchasing value in 2012. In 2012, the poorest fifth of households in the United States subsisted on incomes ranging from $0 to $20,599 (represented by the darkest-shaded band at the bottom of the graph), the next fifth had incomes that ranged from $20,600 to $39,764, and so on. One-fifth of households in 2012 had incomes higher than $104,097 (the top white-shaded portion of the graph). Because the range of incomes for these top-earning households extends into the millions of dollars (for people like Bill Gates), we capped the graph at a maximum income of $200,000 but added a line representing the threshold that separates the top 5% of households from everyone else ($191,056 in 2012).

Exhibit 3.1   Incomes Received by Each Fifth of Households: 1970–2012 (Prior Years Converted to 2012 Dollar Values)

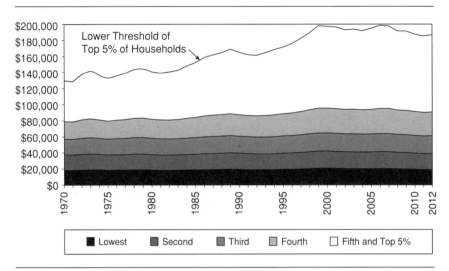

Source: U.S. Census Bureau.

To gauge the impact that the transition to the new economy has had on the relative earnings of different strata, consider the relative positioning of each fifth of the population in 2012, as well as how the maximum income threshold for each quintile changed in comparison to 1970. Exhibit 3.1 reveals that the threshold separating the poorest fifth of households from the rest of society increased by only $1,137, from $19,462 in 1970 to $20,599 in 2012. That means that roughly one in five households was living below or near the poverty level in 2012 and that this proportion has remained largely unchanged since 1970. The second quintile of households had maximum incomes of $39,764 in 2012. Again, we observe only a modest change in their overall economic condition, as the threshold that separates them from the next quintile only moved upward by $2,482 from 1970 to 2012. This stratum of households, like their counterparts in 1970, remained situated in a position that offers few possibilities to accrue savings and puts homeownership largely out of reach. Households in the third quintile had a maximum income of $54,226 in 1970, and that threshold rose by $10,356 to reach $64,582 in 2012. For the top two-fifths of households, however, the evidence suggests substantial income growth. Households in the second highest quintile saw maximum incomes rise from $77,366 in 1970 to $104,096 in 2012. Clearly the greatest change in incomes is reflected in the top-earning households. For the richest one in twenty households, the lower threshold that separated their earnings from those received by everyone else rose from \$122,294 in 1970 to \$191,156 in 2012, a 56% growth rate.

One can present an optimistic case that the new economy is creating prosperity and argue that a rising tide raises all ships. However, a more careful reading of the data reveals that the really significant gains in income went to top earners. In contrast, the lowest two-fifths of all households continued to earn incomes similar to what households earned in the early 1970s, and any differences observed probably do not reflect any substantial improvements when translated into capacities to purchase a better quality of life. While there has been some modest income growth even for these strata of households, as well as for the third quintile, the conclusion that they are modestly better off is open to debate, given that the incomes achieved are sometimes the consequence of working harder either to maintain one's standard of living or to satisfy new needs critical to career and family success in the new economy. For example, common strategies for supplementing a worker's declining wages can include having a spouse enter the labor force and/or increasing work hours. According to Jerry Jacobs and Kathleen Gerson (2004), if one measures the total amount of labor performed by the typical American household, American families now work the equivalent of an additional month each year as compared to the amount of work done in 1970. And to keep the income stream intact (most commonly by replacing a single-earner household arrangement with a dual-earner arrangement) requires making additional investments, such as purchasing a second car or allocating money for child care (Warren and Tyagi 2003). The key point to understand here is that even if the lower three-fifths of households are making modestly more than they did in 1970, they are not substantially better off in terms of their economic situation. They may be earning a little bit more, but they are working much harder to do so, and usually because they need to.

Exhibit 3.2 provides another lens on trends in inequality, here with a focus on equity. These graphs indicate the proportion of total income that went to different groups of households in 1970 and 2012. Looking first at 1970, observe that the richest 5% of households took home nearly one-fifth (17%) of the total income earned that year. If we add that figure to the share of income received by the remaining members of the highest quintile of the population (27%), we find that the top fifth of households received 44% of all of the income earned in 1970. Compare the proportion of earnings received by these top-earning groups to that received in 2012, when the richest quintile took home half (51%) of the collective income earned. The rich have gotten substantially richer. In contrast, those in the bottom tiers of the class structure are receiving a smaller piece of the income "pie." The poorest

Exhibit 3.2   Share of Aggregate Income Received by Each Fifth and Top 5% of
Households: 1970 and 2012

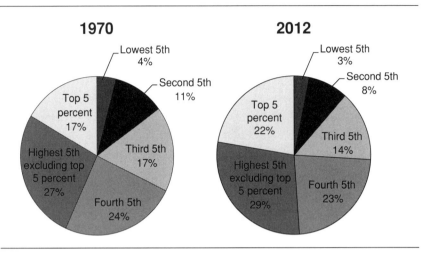

Source: U.S. Census Bureau.

fifth of households received only 3% of the total dollars earned in 2012, a smaller share than was received in 1970. Similar declining shares are observed for the second and third quintiles. Currently the income gap that separates the top tiers of American society from everyone else approximates the divide that existed in the early twentieth century. Unless fundamental changes occur to finance and tax laws, the investor class will continue to grow its wealth, and the divide will expand in the years to come (Piketty 2014).

Perhaps there is no better case than Walmart (now the world's largest private-sector employer) to illustrate the issue of compensation equity and what this means in the lives of individuals. Our friend Jodi worked at Walmart for three years and was considered to be an exemplary senior employee. Most commonly she worked the cash register or behind the returns counter. Jodi could request days off, but those requests were not always accommodated, and she earned the same amount whether she worked days, evenings, or on weekends. Her schedule changed week to week, as did her hours. Because she had solid evaluations, reflecting a positive attitude and diligence, her initial wage (which barely surpassed the minimum wage standard) increased by 40 to 60 cents per hour in each of her years of service. After three years of work for Walmart, she earned well beneath a living wage, estimated to be slightly above $11 an hour in the local community. While she wanted to work as many hours as possible, she was never scheduled to work full time because that would have required her employer to provide additional benefits. If she arrived late or failed to come in as scheduled, she lost the few privileges that she was awarded on the basis of her seniority with the company. Many of Jodi's coworkers had significant health concerns that could be directly traced to financial hardship (e.g., missing or decaying teeth) and commonly faced pressing concerns such as how to keep their cars on the road.

Contrast Jodi's meager income to that of Walmart's president and CEO, Michael T. Duke, whose total compensation was $5,643,677 in 2014 (according to AFL-CIO Executive Paywatch). If Jodi were to secure full-time work at Walmart (which she cannot), at her current wage rate she would have to work 247 years to earn what Michael earns in a single year. Conversely, in a single morning Michael earns far more than Jodi's annual income. Walmart is not exceptional in its differential treatment of employees at the high and low ends of its organizational structure. The AFL-CIO reports that in 1980 the average CEO made 42 times the pay of the average employee, but in 2014, the ratio had increased to 331 to 1. Nor is this just an American phenomenon. While the gap between CEO and worker pay is much higher in the United States than in other industrialized countries, the gap is still large elsewhere. Even in countries that prize social equality, the CEO-to-worker pay gap is substantial, such as Sweden's CEO-to-worker pay ratio of 89 to 1 in 2012 (AFL-CIO 2014). Calls for limits on CEO pay are commonly voiced, but, so far, there is no compelling evidence that real changes have resulted as a consequence of attention to this issue (Mischel, Bernstein, and Shierholz 2009). In fact, although widespread concern exists concerning CEO pay, in 2013 Swiss voters rejected an opportunity to limit CEO pay to a maximum of twelve times the pay of the company's lowest-paid worker (Ewing 2013). This shows that indignation does not necessarily lead to political will. The class divides that separate the incredibly affluent from the rest of society reflect the concentration of wealth and power that already existed in the old economy. However, the chasms that separate the "haves" from the "have nots" are widening, as the data consistently indicate that the richest segment of the population has received an increasingly large share of total earnings since 1970. While the "super-rich" existed in the old economy, the distance that separates this class from everyone continues to widen. Contributing factors include declines in labor unions, opportunities for wealth investment in global production, and much lower taxes on those earning very high incomes (Volscho and Kelly 2012). As we consider here, financial insecurity at the bottom and the diminished social commitment from those at the top are intricately intertwined and have consequences for everyone.

The terms of Jodi's employment place a burden on society as a whole, not just on Jodi. While her low wages make it possible for consumers (both the poor and the affluent) to purchase items at a lower cost than would otherwise be possible, the inability of low-wage workers to lead healthy lives results in higher medical costs for everyone, as these low-wage workers (and their children) are more likely to become ill as well as to seek medical attention only after it reaches critical conditions. To afford housing, they need heat and rent assistance. The fact that they cannot afford child care increases reliance on remedial services and correctional services. The costs of these (and other) services are increasingly carried by members of the middle classes, and less so by the super-rich or by corporations. As reported by the Tax Policy Center of the Urban Institute and the Brookings Institute (2014a), in 1970, the marginal income tax rate on the highest earners was 71%, but by 2013, this had been reduced to 39.6%.[1] While official income tax rates are structured so that the very affluent pay a larger share of taxes than the other income groups (owing to their larger incomes), the amount received is substantially less than that which could have been expected had their contributions remained at a level consistent with the standards applied in the old economy. And as Warren Buffett observed, because of various tax exemptions and because earnings from investments (capital gains) are taxed differently than earnings from wages, the investor class of the super-rich (who earn money off of their wealth) usually pay a *lower* share of their income to taxes than do members of the middle class (some readers will remember 2012 presidential candidate Mitt Romney reluctantly revealing an effective tax rate of 14%) (Nau 2013). In addition, corporations now contribute a smaller share as well, as their top tax rate declined from 49% in 1970 to 35% in 2013 (Tax Policy Center 2014b). Beyond that, corporations have become remarkably adept at skirting tax obligations. In 2010, for example, General Electric earned a profit of $14.2 billion, and nearly one-third of those profits came from work performed in the United States. Yet, not only did General Electric not pay any taxes, it actually claimed a tax benefit of $3.2 billion (Kocieniewski 2011). The problem, therefore, is two-fold. First, a choice is to be made between constraining the mechanisms that create a class of the super-rich or developing mechanisms that pull the disadvantaged up along with advantaged members of society. And, second, there is a need to develop equitable mechanisms that compel the super-rich and corporations to meet societal needs.

Reflect on one additional set of sobering statistics that reveal the lopsided outcome of the economic recovery. The recovery proved to be a great time to buy or own stock, reflected by the Dow Jones Industrial Average, which doubled from 8,000 in 2008 to 16,000 in 2013. But for those at the bottom (who can't afford to buy stock), the "recovery" has been a very different story. During this same period, the portion of children living below the poverty line in the United States increased from 18% to 22% (Annie E. Casey Foundation 2015). In simple dollars and cents, the transition to the new economy has benefitted those at the top of the class structure far more than those at the bottom. The extent to which the middle segments of the class structure have benefitted or lost in financial terms is debatable. However, it is clear that these households now have additional expenses that have resulted from new demands, and they also are working harder to earn what they have. It is also clear that members of the poorer classes of workers are no better off today in comparison to where they stood in the old economy, and many are worse off.

Are Career Pathways Opening or Closing?

The transition to the new economy has sustained the divides that separate the social classes, as well as expanded the chasm that separates the affluent from the rest of society. What is it about the new economy that has produced the higher levels of income inequality? Patterns of income inequality varied at different periods of the old economy—perhaps what we are seeing is just another one of those variations. Some of the changes in income inequality occurred because of factors such as government policy (e.g., not raising the minimum wage to keep up with the cost of living) and corporate policies (increased stockholder willingness to authorize huge compensation packages for CEOs) that are not directly related to the emergence of the new economy. However, there is good evidence that the characteristics of the new economy *are* responsible for a significant portion of the growth of inequality. Most important have been changes in the jobs that characterize the new economy and the skill demands associated with them. And with these changes, the prospects of personal movement from one social class to another have shifted as well.

As indicated in Chapter 2, one of the most important characteristics of the new economy is the shift away from manufacturing work toward service employment. In the old economy, the manufacturing sector was the essential source of well-paid jobs for those who lacked postsecondary education. However, the United States has lost a significant number of factory jobs in the past two decades, making them harder and harder to find, especially for younger workers (Scott 2015). Unionization was also an important characteristic of the manufacturing sector and helped win the good wages that some factory jobs provided. However, as manufacturing has declined, so has unionization (especially private-sector unionization); this decline has been identified as a major source of the growing polarization of wages (Western and Rosenfeld 2011).

As manufacturing declined, employment expanded in a wide range of service occupations and industries. Economists and sociologists who analyze the service-dominated new economy have concluded that recognizing this mix of occupations is the key to understanding changing patterns of income inequality and social mobility. Specifically, they argue that the service economy has tended to produce a more polarized workforce—highly paid jobs have not disappeared, but getting them now requires higher levels of education and significant levels of skill. As the service economy has expanded and matured, this polarizing tendency may actually be growing stronger. Middle-skill jobs in fields such as information processing, bookkeeping, and clerical work have proven to be good candidates for automation or offshoring and so have tended to disappear (Economist 2014). Growing sectors of the service economy, such as the provision of care, are particularly polarized, with the most highly skilled groups (e.g., nursing) able to organize professionally and demand good wages, while the rest of labor in poorly paid, devalued jobs (e.g. home health care aides) (Dwyer 2013). Good jobs for those lacking advanced education have become less common, and poorly educated workers now find only low-level jobs that offer little in the way of pay or opportunities to advance (Kalleberg 2013).

In short, the distribution of income is directly related to a polarized opportunity structure, with an expanding chasm that separates higher-paying jobs from lower-paying jobs and far fewer jobs available that fit somewhere in between (Autor, Katz, and Kearney 2006; Holzer et al. 2011; Moller and Rubin 2008; Mouw and Kalleberg 2010). This observation conforms to the perspective of **dual-labor market theory**, which divides opportunities into two different strata of jobs. The favored jobs are located in the **primary labor market**, which offers higher pay, predictable career paths, opportunities for skill development, and enhanced job security. These are the good jobs. In contrast, other workers are trapped in a **secondary labor market** composed of jobs that offer low pay, unstable opportunities, low security, and limited skill expansion (Piore 1977). Most of the low-skill jobs that workers hold today are nestled in the secondary labor market, offering neither significant material rewards nor stepping-stones to greater opportunity. Like Jodi's job at Walmart, these are dead-end positions that lack benefits, provide little security, and offer scant economic reward (Kalleberg, Reskin, and Hudson 2000). It is important to note that divided opportunity structures developed within the old economy and also that aspects of the division between the primary and secondary labor markets appear to be changing—not because bad jobs are becoming good jobs but rather through the extension of insecurity into some jobs in the primary labor market (making them more like secondary labor market jobs). As we discuss later in this book, some workers—even those in good jobs—are working longer hours, facing new forms of insecurity, and experiencing greater challenges in locating work than was the case a few decades ago. Nevertheless, the new economy is deeply divided and the availability of good jobs in the middle, particularly for those only requiring a limited education, is increasingly constrained (Perrucci and Wysong 2002).

In the old economy, a dominant career path was to expect income growth and security with advancing age (Cappelli 1997). While the prospects of obtaining a good job were unevenly distributed on the basis of race and gender, it was not unusual for workers with low levels of education to land, if not interesting jobs, ones that would (over time) eventually enable them to afford a middle-class standard of living. According to economist Frank Levy (1998), because the economy was expanding in the decades that followed World War II, the earnings potentials for all social classes expanded and the career experience for American men was akin to walking up an upwardly moving escalator. As we discussed, in the new economy, the escalator now seems to be moving along at a brisk pace for those at the top of the class structure; it might be moving at a slow pace for the upper middle class, but it is not moving at all for those in the middle and lower classes. The question we consider here is the likelihood of individuals being able to jump from one escalator to the next, to move from jobs that offer few prospects for advancement into jobs that do, or to walk up whatever escalator they are on (even if it is stalled or moving backward). We draw attention to two types of mobility, **intragenerational upward mobility** (the prospect of moving up a career ladder within one's lifetime) and **intergenerational upward mobility** (the prospect of landing jobs better than those held by one's parents).

Missing Rungs in the Ladder

It is clear that many workers in the new economy cannot "work their way up" in the manner that was evident in the old economy, and the entry point is increasingly important in determining the range of jobs that one might eventually be eligible to hold. For most workers, economic security in the new economy hinges on the attainment of a college or graduate degree. As a result, Americans are entering college programs and returning to school at unprecedented rates. Exhibit 3.3 shows that, in 1970, only one in two Americans earned high school degrees; in 2013 this figure had risen to nearly nine in ten. The proportion of adults who are college graduates has tripled

Exhibit 3.3   Educational Attainment of Adults, Age Twenty-Five Years and Older: United States, 1970–2013

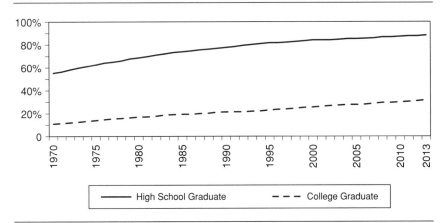

Source: U.S. Census Bureau.

during the same period, as younger Americans are increasingly likely to seek postsecondary education. According to the National Center for Education Statistics (2013), in 2012, 41% of young adults (age eighteen to twenty-four) were enrolled in college.

The dramatic increase in entry into college reflects personal responses to changing opportunity structures. And it is not only young adults who are investing in a college education in hopes of career success. Older Americans are returning to school in unprecedented numbers. More than one in three students (37%) enrolled in colleges and universities in 2008 was age twenty-five or older, and most of these students were women (Chronicle of Higher Education 2010). Among these nontraditional students, the most common reason for returning to school is to relaunch careers or adjust skills to keep up with today's job markets. While many older students find returning to school intellectually and socially invigorating, the combined burdens of student, worker, and parent roles place considerable strains on marriages and family lives (Hostetler, Sweet, and Moen 2007; Sweet and Moen 2007).

One wonders if a college education is worth it. After all, the time involved in pursuing an advanced degree requires deferring income and there is considerable expense involved in paying for tuition, room, and board. To answer the "is it worth it?" question, Exhibit 3.4 provides "synthetic work-life earnings"—what the average worker might earn over the course of his or her career, given the highest degree he or she ultimately earned. Of course actual earnings will vary from individual to individual; this is simply an estimate of the cumulative earnings obtained, given how people typically complete their degrees and attach themselves to the labor force. What is especially helpful is that the estimates also take into account other concerns, such as the likelihood that people with lower educational attainment are also more likely to be working in less stable jobs, which can introduce temporary income losses. Over the course of a career, people with a ninth- to twelfth-grade education earned on average $868,897. This equates to an average of $27,470 per year if they were full-time, year-round workers, but only $11,274 per year if they worked less than full time year-round. And one in three (35%) of those with this level of education did not work in any given year. Compare those earnings with workers who hold bachelor's degrees. Their expected lifetime earnings of $1,980,309 are more than one million dollars more than high school dropouts would earn over the course of a career and $844,999 more than high school graduates would earn. And careers of more-educated workers are much more stable, as only 12% of bachelor degree holders did not work in any given year. So the answer very clearly is yes, a college education is worth it.

Exhibit 3.4   Educational Attainment and Synthetic Work-Life Earnings Estimates for All Workers

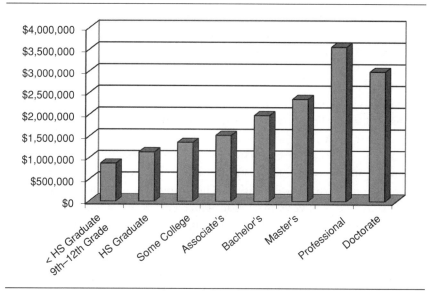

Source: Julian, Tiffany and Robert Kominski. 2011. *Education and Synthetic Work-Life Earnings Estimates ACS-14.* Washington, DC: U.S. Department of Commerce. U.S. Census Bureau. http://www.census.gov/hhes/socdemo/education/data/acs/index.html.

The evidence indicates that possession of a college degree is much more important now than it was in 1970, not only in respect to earnings potential but also having a job in which there is security and prospects for career growth. There is debate on the extent to which a college education actually makes workers more skilled or proficient, as part of what colleges may do is simply provide credentials that enable employers to sort prospective employees into piles of eligible and ineligible candidates (Arum and Roksa 2011). It may also be that the technical and creative skills often cited as the most valuable elements in a college education are less important to the acquisition of high wages than analytical and managerial skills (Liu and Grusky 2013). But even if this is the case, the certificate has tremendous value, and evidence suggests that attainment of a college degree has the greatest impact on the lives of those who are least likely to attend college (the disadvantaged) (Brand and Yu 2010).

Those who ignore the structural arrangements in the new economy argue that growing inequality is largely a result of choices—those who make the wise decision to attend college get good jobs, whereas those who do not fall behind (e.g., Herrnstein and Murray 1994). From this point of view, the types of jobs occupied by individuals with lower levels of education offer low pay because that is all that is justified by the limited human capital (skills) possessed by the occupants of these jobs. However, arguments such as these fail to appreciate structural circumstances; in particular, they ignore the fact that lower-educated workers may be able to secure good, well-paying jobs in conditions where their interests are protected by unions (Haley-Lock, Berman, and Timberlake 2013).

There are indications that a college degree is no longer the guarantee it once was. The pursuit of advanced degrees may reflect a growing reliance on credentials for entry-level jobs but does not necessarily reflect the need for greater skills in the performance of these jobs (Brooks 2005). In other words, what used to be a high school graduate's job (e.g., administrative assistant) is now a college graduate's job. As the number of college graduates has grown, more people find themselves underemployed, unable to find jobs commensurate with their education. The growing supply of college graduates has created a buyer's market in which wages are stagnant or even in decline (Perrucci and Wysong 2002). The result is that, although college graduates outearn those with less education, not all groups of college graduates experience income gains or land good jobs (Bernhardt et al. 2001). It should be pointed out that the American pattern is in some ways unusual. The pronounced emphasis on postsecondary education has not yet been replicated in Europe, although rates of university attendance are up and the demand for university graduates there is growing. What is common across all industrialized societies is the growth of economic inequality, indicating that the new class divides of the United States are not simply a matter of local peculiarities (F. Green 2006).

The changing relationship between the education system and work opportunity reveals the presence of serious structural lags. For example, the old economy mandated the support of public education through the high school level. High schools became the means to instill the fundamentals of reading, math, health, and social skills in future generations of workers and were primarily intended to ensure a supply of workers capable of filling the existing lower-skill jobs. However, the fact that many of the primary labor market jobs in the new economy demand skills that far surpass basic literacy may justify public support of education well beyond high school. Ironically, as the value of education has increased, public resources directed to under-privileged students have been cut, blocking the economically disadvantaged from the opportunity to attend college (Kahlenberg 2004).

But even if this support were to be provided, those resources alone would not be sufficient to eliminate the disparities that exist between those occupying good jobs and bad jobs. While obtaining credentials may help some individuals move into more desirable employment, the secondary labor market jobs will remain. Increasing proportions of these jobs are now (and will be) filled by the college educated. These observations highlight the challenges that lay ahead. In an economy where education is increasingly a necessary qualification for access to quality employment, there is a need to enhance opportunities to develop college-level skills. The growing cost of education is an increasingly burdensome challenge for families hoping to help their children get ahead, especially for those at the bottom of the socio-economic ladder. Since not all jobs are good jobs, there is a need to create career stepping-stones such that workers can progress from lower-skilled work into higher-skilled work. And, for those who can't make this progression, there is a need to enhance the quality of lower-skilled employment such that it is not synonymous with bad employment. In the end, increasing access to a college education can facilitate mobility, but it cannot resolve the underlying structural problems that funnel some workers into good jobs and others into bad jobs.

Entry Points: Securing the Good Job in Young Adulthood

Because it is more difficult to secure good jobs with a high school education, greater proportions of young adults are delaying entry into full-time work in favor of pursuing advanced degrees. And even when they do this, they often have a difficult time obtaining a good job. For those young adults who come from families with economic resources, the difficulties are buffered, as parents can provide a variety of supports to advance the development of skills, as well as to sustain their children as they work to secure employment. For those young adults coming from disadvantaged positions, the jump from school to work is more difficult.

Today's older workers are expected to provide more resources to their children far later in their lives than was the case for previous generations, a dynamic illustrated in Exhibit 3.5. These changes have resulted from shifts in the timing of work and family careers, a sustained redefinition of parent-child and child-parent responsibilities, and new opportunity structures that block the younger generation from independently achieving sustainable careers as they enter adulthood. Note that the intergenerational transfer of resources can vary in the following ways: the type of resource (direct transfer of finances or provision of care work), directionality (from parent to child or child to parent), volume (how many resources are being channeled), intensity (the amount of effort involved), duration (for how long the provision of resources continues), and timing (age and life course station). All of these means of providing support have shifted, and in the new economy parents are expected to provide more for their children, and for much longer, than was previously expected.

Exhibit 3.5   A Schematic of Intergenerational Resource Transfers

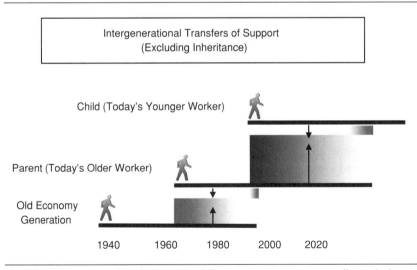

Note: In the figure, graphics indicate the following ways resources are allocated: duration (length), volume (height), intensity (shading), directionality (arrows), and timing (position).

Historians inform us that, until the early twentieth century in America (and even today in developing countries), children's roles were defined largely in terms of what they could contribute to the family economy. At very young ages, children worked side by side with their parents and commonly provided a greater share of the household income than did wives (Gratton and Moen 2004). Children also provided considerable support for parents as they reached old age. But over the course of the development of the old economy in the twentieth century, children's roles were redefined as dependents. Today, this dependent status is rigorously embraced by the culture, as Americans do not expect children or young adults to channel support up to their parents (who wish not to be a "burden"); rather, parents are supposed to funnel resources down to their children (who now have come to expect this as an entitlement). As children's roles shifted to dependency, so did the cultural expectations of the types of resources parents should provide. Today childhood is viewed as a distinct life stage that should be free from the grind of life. In this context, a parent's obligation is not only to provide care but also to give substantial supports that enable growth and exploration. While these expectations began to be established over a century ago, the quantity and quality of resources that are expected have escalated, as has the duration of provision in the new economy. As a consequence, it is not unusual for children in middle and upper classes to begin "resumé building" in their teenage years, pursuing extracurricular activities that can be marketed in college applications.

Adolescence has extended itself well into ages that were previously defined as part of adulthood, and now the culture is embracing the perspective that there is an in-between stage of "emerging adulthood" that extends beyond age eighteen and perhaps continues into the early thirties. These emerging adults expect freedom from parental authority but do not assume they must be self-sufficient. They commonly rely on support from parents and take advantage of options to return home if need be. The lives of these "emergent adults" are characterized by instability in financial circumstances and interpersonal ties (Arnett 2007). With this change, the resources provided by parents comprise a critical safety net for younger workers. Today it is common, for example, for parents to provide support for "boomerang children" who leave home but then come back (Goldscheider et al. 1999).

Studies vary in their estimations of the quantity of resources that parents provide to adult children, but all conclude that substantial proportions of children in their twenties remain reliant on parents for significant housing and financial support (Arnett 2004; Gitelson and McDermott 2006). Schoeni and Ross (2005), in an analysis of the Panel Study of Income Dynamics, found that during the transitional years (ages eighteen to thirty-four), parents contribute (on average) about $38,000 in material assistance to each child. But this support varies considerably by socioeconomic class. Children from families in the top income quartile received $70,965 during this transition period. Aside from helping children navigate the types of unstable careers that are common in young adulthood, parental resources are also the primary source of financial aid used to fund college educations. How do parents afford this? Commonly by borrowing money, using home equity loans, or forgoing investing in their personal retirement accounts (Cha, Weagly, and Reynolds 2005). While access to parental resources helps young adults prepare for work in the new economy, deprivation of these supports significantly limits opportunities and life choices (Aquilino 2005).

In sum, substantial investments from parents are a major factor in increasing the odds that a young adult may enter into the primary labor market. For children from disadvantaged families, these resources are limited, which weighs against their career prospects (Eccles and Zarrett 2006). For parents in the middle class, the provision of these resources is commonly accompanied by increasing the pressure to be more intensive parents, to earn more, and to take on personal debt, all for the sake of helping one's children secure their careers. Not only has the structure of opportunity become more polarized, with a growing gap developing between winners and losers, the chances of establishing a career increasingly depends on coming from families with parents who have good jobs.

Is the Global Economy Becoming More Flat or Bumpy?

A major part of the reason for declining opportunities in the United States can be attributed to the loss of high-paying manufacturing jobs, the type of work that was obtainable with a limited education in the old economy. The reasons for the decline of manufacturing are complex, as discussed in Chapter 2. However, at least some of the decline can be attributed to the movement of jobs overseas. But what has happened to inequalities related to the opportunity structures in emerging economies in the global economy? Perhaps the loss of manufacturing jobs in the United States has improved the quality of life elsewhere, and perhaps the divide that separates the "developed countries" from the "developing countries" is narrowing. In this section we consider that issue, as well as how the class structure and work opportunities within developing countries have been affected by the shift to the new global economy.

There is much disagreement about the ways the developing world is being affected by the new global economy. At one extreme in this debate are those who suggest that globalization is creating a global race to the bottom in which employers seek out those countries in which wages are lowest and worker protections are weakest, resulting in deteriorating work conditions and economic fortunes on a global scale (Cowie 2001; Lash and Urry 1987). On the other side of the debate are those who argue that globalization is expanding fortunes and creating opportunity, both at home and abroad (Friedman 2005). And it is important to note that the path globalization takes, and its effects on inequalities, is not inevitable. As in the past, the future will be shaped by regulations that determine what can be traded and the terms under which those trades are to occur (Piketty 2014).

No matter how one assesses its effects, it is clear that the global economy is transforming work in developing countries, influencing workers' opportunities and behaviors in the process. One such change can be observed in accelerated urbanization in developing nations. Exhibit 3.6 reveals that in 1950, for every one person residing in a city in developing nations, there were three other people living in the countryside. By 2050, the developing world will have nearly five times the population it did in 1950, and most of its people will be living in urban centers. By 2050, more than 70% of the world's population will live in cities, and even the poorest countries of sub-Saharan Africa will be primarily urban (Saunders 2010). In some respects, the causes of urbanization are similar to those that drove this process in the United States in the latter part of the nineteenth century. People are establishing communities that coincide with current opportunity structures. Urban centers are expanding because of push factors (the scarcity of jobs in rural areas) as well as pull factors (the perception that jobs will be available in the cities). In some cities, such as Lagos, Nigeria, the populations have expanded far more rapidly and in volumes so heavy that they far surpass their carrying capacities.

As they move to urban centers, people in developing countries are transformed as workers. In a process that parallels what happened in Europe and the United States in the eighteenth and nineteenth centuries, they are proletarianized. That is, they are transformed from peasants and other nonemployees into wage workers (Deyo 1989). But in the developing world in the new economy, the problems of urbanization and proletarianization are magnified by scarcities of resources, by outmoded (and sometimes nonexistent) infrastructures that operate amid contemporary technologies, and by overpopulation. Some migrants, such as Kavita (the Indian call center worker introduced in Chapter 1), successfully find work. But many cannot, resulting in the growth of huge concentrations of marginally employed people in places such as the favelas of Rio and Sao Paulo or the swollen urban centers of nonindustrial Africa.

Exhibit 3.6   World Population Projections (in Millions): 1950–2050

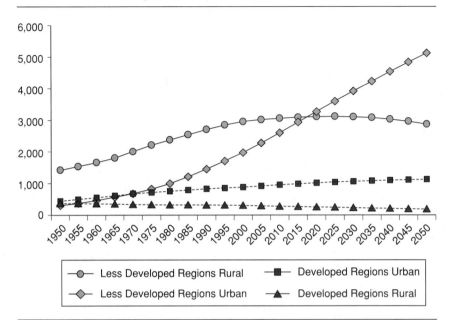

Source: United Nations, Department of Economic and Social Affairs, World Urbanization Prospects 2011 Revision.

Grappling with the social problems associated with urbanization—including employment, health, safety, sanitation, and housing needs—will be one of the greatest challenges for the new global economy (Cohen 2003; Economy 2005; Kim and Gottdiener 2004; Roberts 2005; York, Rosa, and Dietz 2003). Employment prospects in the urban centers of the developing world are often grim. There simply are not enough conventional jobs available to absorb the enormous mass of city dwellers. One result has been the growth of the "informal economy" in the developing world. This refers to a variety of both legal and illegal activities, including begging, drug dealing, making and selling food, various kinds of domestic work, jitney and pedicab driving, and many other jobs that are unregulated and unprotected. Disagreement about the consequences of this type of work is intense. Some see it as positive and as opening opportunities for urban dwellers to engage in entrepreneurship that can be translated to the formal economy. These small entrepreneurial activities are seen as the basis for the gradual acquisition of wealth and, eventually, providing a springboard to middle-class status (Saunders 2010). Awarding microloans to individuals, as practiced by Nobel

Peace Prize recipient Muhammad Yunus's Grameen Bank, reflects this way of thinking about cultivating work opportunity in developing societies. Others respond that the informal economy actually competes with and eliminates more desirable employment opportunities. In this manner, it is "stealth" formal economy work—as when home workers produce goods that directly or indirectly make possible the low-cost production of goods that eventually are sold in retail outlets such as Walmart and Costco (Davis 2006).

The movement of population within the developing world and the limited employment opportunities for migrants add to the pressure to move across national borders (Mattingly 1999; Sassen and Smith 1992). But even though jobs are highly mobile in the new economy, significant barriers discourage workers from moving across borders. The proportion of the world's population living outside its country of birth has only risen from 2% to 3% in the past thirty years, and the extent of migration slowed in the aftermath of the 2008 economic downturn (Glyn 2005; Tilly 2011). According to the U.S. Census, in 2012, 13% of the population of the United States was foreign born. For some, such as Rain (the Chinese restaurant worker introduced in Chapter 1), migration is a route to economic prosperity, as the experience of many immigrants in the United States demonstrates. However, dangers exist as well. Once immigrants are removed from their local residences and social networks—and especially if they migrate illegally—they labor with fewer protections. This problem is dramatically illustrated in the lives of migrants from Indonesia who serve as domestic workers in the Middle East. These young women are socially isolated, labor for meager compensation, and receive little protection from government agents in their home or host countries. In the worst cases, they are treated more like slaves than employees (Rudnyckyj 2004).

Decentralized production and internationalization have fostered the development of what is now a hallmark of twenty-first-century work—**global supply chains**. In the new economy, workers seldom create commodities, start to finish, at a central location within a nation-state. More often, production is network driven, divided up between companies spread across the world (Schrank 2004). Some of the most recognized names in the new economy—including Liz Claiborne, the Gap, and Nike—do not directly employ any production workers. Instead, these companies develop designs and marketing strategies and then contract work with independent manufacturers operating abroad (Gereffi 1994; Tracy 1999). In this system, Nike employees can be well paid and live in good, stable communities, but the workers who produce Nike shoes often are not. The operations of these supply chains expand wealth in a progressive fashion, a dynamic illustrated in

Exhibit 3.7. Relative to the profits obtained at the final stages of production and distribution, workers laboring upstream (concentrated in the developing world) produce and accumulate smaller shares of wealth (Bair and Gereffi 2003). This dynamic helps to explain the paradox that the global economy is simultaneously expanding wealth in both the developed and developing worlds, as well as expanding and extending preexisting economic disparities across the globe. It can be added that global supply chains are highly sensitive to costs; they seek out regions where labor costs and the other costs of production are low. However, if as a result of increased economic activity, costs in those regions begin to rise, supply chains can quickly seek out alternative regions where production costs remain low, creating a global, downward pressure on production workers' wages (Economist 2014).

If global supply chains operate in the manner presented in Exhibit 3.7, we would expect that in the wake of the transition to the new economy, the divide that separates the rich countries from the poorer countries would remain intact and perhaps even expand. According to a study by Milanovic (2005), a lead economist at the World Bank, this has in fact happened. Of the countries that were identified as being either in the third world (poor) or fourth world (very poor) in 1960 and 1978, nearly all remained in the same economic position in 2000, and for those that changed position, the most common direction was *downward*. And among the countries identified as being "contenders" in 1978 (who might possibly transition to the status of being a rich country—countries like Costa Rica, Mexico, and South Africa), most remained in the same position or slipped downward. From 1978 to 2000, the downward mobility rate (i.e., slipping from contender status to third-world status) of all countries was 29%, and the upward mobility rate (i.e., moving from third-world status to contender status) was only 3%. In fact, only two countries in the past forty years moved out of the fourth world—Botswana and Egypt.

Exhibit 3.7   How Value Accumulates in a Global Supply Chain

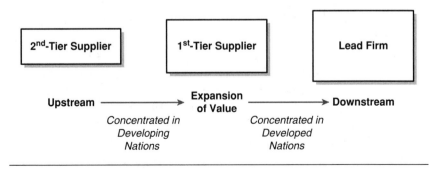

A few illustrations will help clarify how multinational organizational structures and global supply chains affect international inequalities and opportunities for individuals. As points of comparison, we focus on two countries, China with its remarkable economic expansion that coincides with globalization and Ghana with its continued positioning as a marginal economy, as compared to the United States. Suppose we wanted to see if the typical Chinese or Ghanaian worker is gaining ground on the typical American worker in the new economy. How do we determine this? One method is to compare wage rates such as the per capita share of the gross national income. This is the sum of all incomes received in a country, divided by the country's population. Analysis of per capita incomes would reveal that this has increased in all three countries in the past two decades, with China showing the highest growth rate. It is safe to conclude that aggregate incomes have expanded in all three countries. This is the story of a rising tide raising all ships. But it is also important to note that this does not mean that expanded societal wealth within each country was equitably distributed.

If we used the per capita share of the income to gauge if countries are catching up to one another, analysis would be clouded by the fact that costs of goods and services are remarkably different in China and Ghana in comparison to the United States. In other words, one dollar buys more in China and Ghana than it does in the United States, so each dollar increase means more in China and Ghana than it does in the United States. In order to solve this concern, we adjust the per capita gross national income to reflect purchasing power parity (PPP), which takes into account costs of housing, food, and so on. Once these adjustments are made, comparisons can be made using a standard currency that represents how earnings translate into ability to consume within the societies under study. In this case PPP earnings are reflected in the currency of the United States as its purchasing power is adjusted to each country's economy.[2] The differences between these three countries are shown in Exhibit 3.8.

In 2013, in the United States, the per capita PPP was $53,960, in China it was $11,850, and in Ghana it was $3,880. In other words, for every one dollar a Ghanaian had to purchase needed items, an American had $14. For every dollar available to a Chinese citizen, the American had nearly $5. Will the average Chinese or Ghanaian worker "catch up" to the average U.S. worker? Exhibit 3.8 does not offer compelling evidence to support the expectation that Chinese workers are on a path to catch up to American workers, as the gap that separates the two countries did not narrow. In contrast, Ghanaian workers are even worse off relative to the workers in the United States, as the gap that separates these two countries has expanded over time. Time will tell how far the gaps continue to narrow between China

Exhibit 3.8   Per Capita Purchasing Power from 1990 to 2013: Comparison of the United States, China, and Ghana

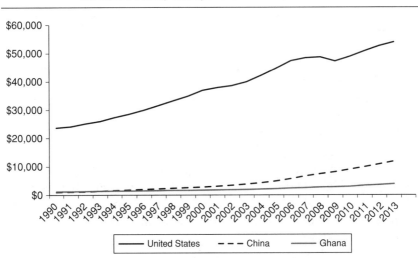

Source: World Bank as Reported in Google Public Data Explorer http://www.google.com/publicdata/explore?ds=d5bncppjof8f9_.
Note: Reported in current dollars (not adjusted for inflation).

and the United States, but these types of data give a clear indication that the Chinese have a long way to go, and those in weaker economies (like Ghana) further still. This discussion highlights the fact that income inequalities can expand even as incomes grow. And we add one other major caveat—there is no "average" worker. In all three of these countries many workers labor in positions very far below the mean wage, and comparison of conditions under which low-wage work occurs across countries reveals the differences to be even more profound. As a case in point, consider that history's deadliest garment factory disaster occurred in 2013 in Bangladesh, killing more than 1,100 workers (Greenhouse 2014).

As further illustration, consider Ohio Art's famous Etch A Sketch, which used to be manufactured by workers in Bryant, Ohio, who earned a livable wage before their jobs were outsourced to the Kin Ki Corporation. This toy, along with most other toys available to American consumers, is now manufactured in China by low-wage workers who are expected to work twelve hours a day, seven days a week. These workers receive no overtime pay (even though it is required by Chinese law), have no "weekends," and are docked wages whenever they miss work (Kahn 2003). Overall standards of living in China have risen in recent years, reflecting the fact that at least some Chinese workers benefit from the new economy. However, many Chinese workers are not allowed to migrate permanently from the countryside to better-paid factory jobs (Peng 2011). They thus become migrant workers, temporarily housed in "dormitories," and eventually are forced (often unwillingly) to return to their villages after a few years of labor (Ngai 2005). Many migrant workers in China are victimized by employers who fail to pay them their wages and/or maintain unsafe workplaces, all with the protection of corrupt local officials. And, as China has moved from a state-dominated to a more market capitalist orientation, workers in the older, state-run enterprises complain that their jobs have disappeared and that the economic benefits on which they once counted have disappeared (Lee 2007). Levels of inequality within China have grown, indicating both winners and losers in the process (Glyn 2005).

Economic development in places like China and India has had particularly profound effects on the situation of women such as Kavita (the call center worker introduced in Chapter 1). In many traditional cultures, women live in rigid patriarchal cultures where women's roles are highly circumscribed. Industrialization creates the potential for change because many of the workers who enter the new factories are women. This experience could advance gender equality, alter women's roles, and give women a degree of economic independence. The reality turns out to be more complex. On the one hand, as women become more independent, traditional forms of patriarchal domination by fathers and husbands have weakened. On the other hand, women in factories and call centers remain embedded in patriarchal kinship and community networks that restrict what they are allowed to do, and they encounter highly patriarchal work organizations in which women are the workers and men (often from their hometowns or part of their kinship network) are the supervisors (Lee 1998; Ngai 2005; Tiano 1994).

The economic gains that China and India experienced with their entry into the global economy also have come at a considerable environmental cost. As the land, water, and air quality in the United States became cleaner in the latter part of the twentieth century (global warming effects excepted), the trend is reversed in China. Chinese rivers are now dangerously polluted, and five of China's seven major waterways are deemed unsuitable for human contact. In only six of China's twenty-seven largest cities do residents have access to clean drinking water, and the wells of those living in rural environments have been fouled by industrial contaminants. The air is so polluted that factories had to be shut down to allow the 2008 Beijing Olympic Games to be held, and airplane pilots frequently cannot see skylines when approaching Chinese cities (Economy 2005). The impact of industrialization goes beyond pollution. For example, in its effort to harness waterpower for the industrial economy, the Chinese government developed numerous river dam projects that displaced millions of Chinese from their ancestral homes (Hessler 2003). Chinese and Indian economic development thus illustrates the complex effects of globalization—economic growth and rising living standards, combined with growing inequality, pollution, and community disruption. Workers in the emergent economies have reason to be both optimistic and concerned about their future.

More than low-skill manufacturing work is being directed to the developing world. As global communication becomes more sophisticated, and as trade with Asia becomes more liberalized, it is quite possible that many of the jobs in the IT sector will be offshored as well (O'Riain 2007). India, for example, has experienced a remarkable growth in high-tech work during the past thirty years. Its successes can be attributed to a number of cultural factors, including strong work ethics and a large literate population fluent in English. The policies of the Indian government also have played an important role by directing resources to public schools, as well as to the training of engineers and medical specialists in state-supported universities. The International Institute of Information Technology (IIIT) in Hyderabad graduates 65,000 engineers and programmers a year (Bradsher 2002). As Thomas Friedman (2005) points out in *The World Is Flat*, these workers are highly skilled and are eager to perform jobs that had been concentrated in the United States.

Jobs that use information and computer technologies in the developing economies do not necessarily require workers to have technological sophistication. For example, one of the major opportunities in India is call center work. Call centers gravitated to India in the mid-1990s. The global movement of call center work reflects a broad trend to disperse service work throughout the global economy. For example, in the 1970s, companies such as IBM outsourced consumer questions to call centers in Ireland and Scotland, as well as to lower-paying rural locales in the United States (Head 2003). By employing Indians, companies shave as much as 80% off the costs of performing this same work in America and Europe (Batt et al. 2005). Call center employees tend to be young and well educated. Their work involves processing an unending stream of calls to and from Western consumers. The shifts are long (eight to ten hours per day, six days a week), and the pay is low by American standards but high in comparison to what women typically earn in India. And because of international time differences, most call center employees work at night. Though the jobs are clean, the work is repetitive, standardized, and intense, involving rapid transitions between conversations that last only a few minutes. The job requires the skills to bridge cultural divides and the skills to navigate the protocols of response to customer queries, tasks that can take a month or longer to master. However, these skills are not transportable to other jobs beyond the call centers and do not offer strong prospects for upward career mobility. Also note that the work hours in India are aligned to the needs of Western callers, and the need to adjust to the Western languages and culture also reflect the subordinate status of these call center workers (Batt et al. 2005; Taylor and Bain 2005a, b). As a consequence, women workers like Kavita face hazards associated with nighttime work in that society, including sexual assault and stigmatization as being morally suspect (Patel 2010).

Other high-tech jobs in India require far greater technological sophistication. An estimated half million skilled workers labor in the Indian software industry, making it the second largest pool of software engineers in the world (Khadria 2001; Mir, Mathew, and Mir 2000). The work of computer programmers is demanding, and in India they typically work ten-hour days (and often longer). On the surface, the daily tasks of computer programmers are similar in both India and in the United States. However, the purpose of their work is often different. Indians are commonly expected to write component pieces or debug systems within larger programs designed abroad. They are less often engaged in the creative work that results in the development of a Google or YouTube. As a result, India is unlikely to emerge as a new knowledge creation center but rather is more likely to remain an upstream link in knowledge creation, which will continue to be centered in America and other highly developed societies (Parthasarathy 2004).

The structure of high-tech work has challenged traditional Indian customs and introduced Western cultural values. For example, traditional Indian norms largely prohibited young men and women from engaging in casual interaction, dating, and having romances in advance of arranged marriages. Call centers, with their comparatively high pay, mixed-gender workforce, and night work, are promoting sexual experimentation and increasing the number of "love marriages" among a young generation of workers. The long hours of work in the computer industries are creating the same types of stresses and overburdened schedules that American workers experience. In India, many of the strains of long schedules are buffered by the work of stay-at-home wives, as well as by grandparents who are willing and available to watch young children (McElhinney 2005; Patni 1999; Poster and Prasad 2005). But one wonders if the current generation of Indian professional women will challenge these intergenerational roles as their children have children.

Though the growth in the number of Indian programmers and engineers is remarkable, the popular image of high-tech India is somewhat misleading. In comparison with the United States, Indian high-tech workers compose an extremely small proportion of the overall workforce (there is approximately one skilled software engineer for every 2,200 Indians). Moreover, although some work in India is strongly linked to the work being performed in the Silicon Valley, the quality of life in India is still a far cry from the postindustrial experience of California (Chakravartty 2001; Patni 1999). Most Indian workers continue to engage in traditional agrarian work in rural villages or in menial jobs in urban centers; the bulk of the Indian workforce continues to subsist on extremely low incomes. Day-to-day business involves contending with power outages and political corruption. In India, like China, there exists a significant, and perhaps growing, divide between the opportunity structures and rewards characteristic of rural agrarian work, urban industrial work, and employment in the emerging high-tech sector.

So is the new economy flattening the divides that separate rich countries from poor countries or leveling the class divides that exist in developing nations? Evidence is considerable that some poorer countries are economically better off now than they were a few decades ago but that environmental risks have been transferred to these societies as well. While standards of living may be improving in some respects, and deteriorating in others, we find scant support for the proposition that poorer countries are "catching up" to the economically powerful countries. The reason for the continued "bumpiness" has much to do with the types of jobs distributed in the developing economies and how those differ from the types of jobs present in the advanced economies. The exception to this observation, however, can be found by considering the life chances and experiences of relatively privileged members in developing economies, whose experiences can be quite comparable to those of the more privileged members of developed economies.

Conclusion

In this chapter, we considered whether the new economy is fundamentally reshaping the distribution of economic returns received from work and if the doors that grant access to opportunity are opening or closing. Although some have argued that the new economy is fostering a new era of opportunity at home and abroad, we caution against embracing this assumption without strong reservations. The new economy is creating affluence, but all too often it is in a manner that reshapes and reinforces opportunity chasms that separate those who have from those who do not. This is reflected in the changing income structures in the United States, as well as in the persistence of global inequalities. In American society, work in the new economy is shaped by two key divides. One divide separates those at the top from the rest of society. The truly affluent enjoy a radically better quality of life than does the rest of the society, and their level of economic commitment to the collectivity is weakening. The second divide separates those in the middle from those at the bottom, whose prospects for career advancement are largely blocked by the design and allocation of opportunity. In respect to the divides that exist in the global economy, the transformations that shape the opportunities at home are reshaping opportunities abroad. Those fortunate enough to occupy good jobs in developing societies can enjoy a quality of life remarkably similar to that of the fragile middle in America. But once one considers the types of jobs being performed, the conditions under which this work is performed, the proportions of workers who are involved in "good" versus "bad" jobs, and the environmental conditions in which this work occurs, the perception of a flat world disappears. And though the successes of China and India receive considerable attention, much of the developing world has been excluded from the prospects of benefitting from the global economy. This is especially true in Africa, where incomes and life expectancies remain desperately low.

Are workers better off today than they were a few decades ago? Advocates of either an optimistic or pessimistic perspective can gather numerous examples to support their beliefs. This is possible because economies have become far more diverse than they were in the old economy, not only in terms of what is expected of workers but also the returns that work offers. Which workers are we talking about, and in what types of jobs? Considering these dynamics reveals that multiple trajectories are at play in the new economy, trajectories influenced by social class but also by gender, race, and nationality. In the remaining chapters of this book, we focus on the issue of work diversities and divides, both of jobs and workers, as well as the tensions emerging in the new economy.

Notes

1. Marginal income tax rates vary according to income levels, but the same standards are applied to all individuals irrespective of their income levels. For example, the first $100,000 that a millionaire makes would be taxed at the same rate as that of another individual who only earned $100,000. It is only the earnings obtained beyond specified thresholds that are subjected to higher tax rates. This point is commonly lost in discussions of how taxes are applied to the incomes of the affluent. Capelli (2008) has argued that declining marginal tax rates for high earners fueled the growth in CEO pay packages, as it is possible for companies to offer incentives to lure CEOs from one organization to another at costs lower than would be possible were the higher rate in effect.

2. But even the PPP has problems, as the purchasing needs are not equal across countries (e.g., people in a country with a national health care entitlement do not need to purchase that service), and if an individual needs to purchase goods beyond the local level (e.g., fly from China and stay in the United States) the calculations are thrown off.

Chapter Four

Whose Jobs Are Secure?

In the latter part of 2008, the United States (and many other countries in the global economy) experienced the onset of what proved to be a prolonged recession. In the years that followed, the stock market plummeted, unemployment increased, the housing market collapsed, homes were foreclosed on, and bailouts were offered. As we write this book, Wall Street has not only recovered, it is thriving. The value of stocks continues to increase, and the kingpins of the financial sector are once again securing six- and seven-figure bonuses on top of their lucrative salaries. But the recovery looks very different when a focus moves from Wall Street to Main Street, as the average American worker earns less today compared to the average worker fifteen years ago. Many in Middle America lack jobs, and those who are employed fear losing them. Others have given up hope of finding jobs or are working in positions mismatched to their skills and needs. In this chapter, we suggest that it is a mistake to view this most recent economic downturn and insecurity as an isolated event and that refuge will be found when the "jobs recovery" hopefully happens. The evidence suggests a very different future is in store for most workers in the new economy, one in which attachment to jobs will remain far more tenuous and conditional than was the case in the old economy (Kalleberg 2013).

In this chapter, we focus on the issue of job insecurity and how the prospect or experience of job loss shapes workers' lives and experiences. To do this, we first consider how job and career threats were intertwined in the old economy and how the approaches to managing these perils in the United States differed from those adopted in many European countries. We then consider workers' exposure to risk in the new economy and gauge the extent to which job insecurity has grown and why. We show that the spread of job insecurity has occurred because of the decline of older, more secure types of jobs but also because of new strategies for organizing work and the changing composition of the labor force. The result is that more families are grappling with economic and emotional turmoil, and they do so in a society ill-equipped to meet their needs.

Risk and Work: Historical and Comparative Views

One critical question in the sociology of work concerns who bears the burden of risk. For instance, if production orders fall, is it the employer's responsibility to continue to provide paychecks to workers? If a new technology can be developed to replace workers, is it the employer's responsibility to find obsolete workers new jobs? If an applicant is willing to work for less than an existing employee, does that employee have any right to keep that job? And in an economy built on wage labor, should unemployed citizens receive support if no jobs are available? In the wake of the Industrial Revolution in both Europe and America, the answers to all of these questions would have been no. Employers were expected to provide jobs but at their discretion and according to terms and conditions of their own choosing, as well as with respect to what the labor market would bear. Government was not charged with the responsibility of providing assistance to those who lacked jobs or to those who could not work.

In the early phases of industrialization, workers labored without any of the protections present today. To secure work, they commonly had to bribe foremen for jobs, and they could expect discrimination on the basis of their ethnicity, age, and gender. If they refused to give their foremen kickbacks, or if they caused any trouble on the shop floor, they could expect to be vindictively dismissed. And if they were cast out onto the street, there were virtually no government-sponsored social supports to help them find work or survive extended joblessness (Engels 1936 [1845]; Jacoby 1985; Katz 1996; Thompson 1963; Trattner 1999). Even as the problems of an emerging industrial economy became increasingly apparent, U.S. politicians at the national level remained reluctant to involve themselves in workplace affairs or tackle the issue of unemployment (Lipset 1996; Skocpol 1992). In part, this inaction was the result of individualistic values deeply ingrained in American culture, beliefs that individuals are primarily responsible for their own fates and that government regulation impinges on personal liberty (Bellah et al. 1985). Political inaction also reflected the control early industrialists had over political processes and their ability to discourage legislation to regulate the terms under which work was performed. In sum, in the early phases of industrialization, risk in America was primarily shouldered by individual workers and their families.

In the United States, a dearth of government regulations and programs to protect workers created opportunities for entrepreneurs to offer risk management services in the form of **private insurance**. By the early twentieth century, workers could pay premiums to purchase health and long-term disability insurance (Jacoby 2001). During the twentieth century, these insurance policies (sometimes purchased by individuals, sometimes offered as a job benefit) remained one of the central means of managing the risks associated with job loss or the prospects of disability. Today, this private insurance approach to handling risk has come to haunt the American worker because insurance companies are powerful political forces that shape government-sponsored health and job-protection programs, introducing costs higher than would otherwise occur.

During the nineteenth and twentieth centuries, workers also developed collective ethnic and class-based strategies for mitigating the risks of personal hardship. Starting in the 1840s, a variety of fraternal organizations, such as the Masons and the Odd Fellows, emerged. These urban social clubs formed along ethnic lines and provided member families with small death benefits and, in some instances, health insurance. This **mutual assistance** approach to managing risk, whereby collective resources were pooled to provide support in times of hardship, was later adopted by the trade unions that formed in the second half of the nineteenth century. But unlike the ethnic affiliations of the early fraternities, trade unions distributed mutual assistance to members of occupational groups, thus providing skilled workers with resources that could help them survive unemployment and disability (Jacoby 2001).

As organized labor expanded its power and membership during the twentieth century, collective bargaining agreements provided unionized workers with some protection from the risk of job loss. Unions fought for limits on arbitrary dismissal, and victories included the implementation of seniority rights (so that veteran employees could not be laid off as easily) and grievance procedures (that discouraged vindictive attacks on individual workers) (Edwards 1979). Unions helped large portions of the workforce gain access to jobs that were well paid and stable. But union initiatives in the management of risk focused primarily on advancing their members' interests. Although some nonunion employers emulated unionized firms, many nonunionized workers (who were disproportionately women and minorities) were left lacking social supports and job protections (Jacoby 2001; Lichtenstein 2002).

A legacy of these approaches to managing risk in the United States is that access to job security and benefits is heavily dependent on what kind of job workers have and for whom they work. Their ability to "make ends meet" requires holding a job and, if that job is lost, finding a replacement job quickly. In contrast, the approach adopted in most European countries was to address the problem of risk by introducing **entitlements**—rights and resources available to all citizens independent of attachment to the labor force. These transfers from the government to individuals take a variety of forms, including assistance for unemployment, disability, sickness, old age, housing, family leave, and child care. Exhibit 4.1 reveals that 20% of the U.S. gross domestic product is directed to public social assistance, considerably less than the percentage budgeted in most Western European countries. As a result, workers in Europe have access to a greater quantity of resources that can be used if they lose jobs, and workers in America assume far greater amounts of individual risk in comparison with workers in Europe.

The social programs common in many Western European countries are costly, and for that reason some countries are struggling to generate the funds needed to support these collective resources. This problem of funding generous social programs is magnified by the aging of the workforce, which creates greater resource demands to service larger proportions of the population in retirement and increases burdens on those who remain in the labor force. It is an open question whether these pressures will cause Western Europe to become more like the United States or if the opposing pressures of individualized risk will compel the United States to become more like Western Europe. Likely both will happen to some degree, and the extent of change will be dependent on social pressures and the actions of interest groups.

American workers do have some protections (see this book's appendix for a regulatory time line). The U.S. government's first major advances in the management of risk came as a result of the large-scale job losses that occurred during the Great Depression. In 1935, the **Social Security Act** introduced supports for those who cannot work, including aid to the elderly, the disabled, and some children. The **Fair Labor Standards Act**, implemented in 1938, introduced many of today's most important workplace regulations, including short-term unemployment insurance and a national minimum wage. Legislative acts such as these provided vital assistance to American workers. But again, these protections are much less extensive than those enjoyed by workers in other industrialized countries.

The primary buffer against job loss for American workers is **unemployment insurance**, a program operated through federal and state government partnerships. The goal of unemployment insurance is to provide short-term assistance so that workers have the financial resources to seek suitable replacement jobs. Because the program is administered by individual states, eligibility and compensation vary within the nation. Most states provide partial wage replacement (most commonly 50% of wages—with a cap for high-income earners) for a maximum of twenty-six weeks. It is possible,

Exhibit 4.1   Government Public Expenditure as Percentage of GDP: International Comparisons, 2013

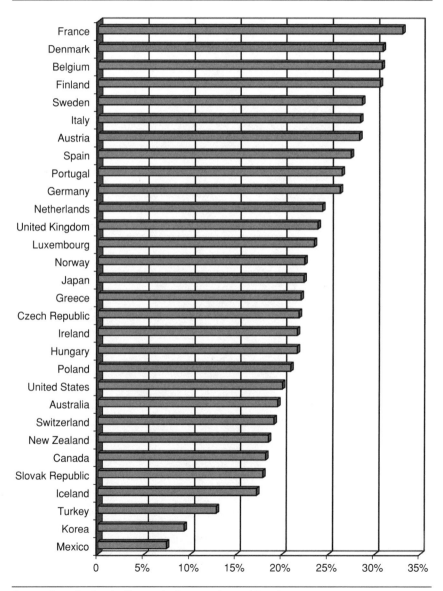

Source: Organization for Economic Co-operation and Development.

however, for unemployed workers to receive extended benefits in times of high unemployment. But even then, this is insufficient to cover the needs of substantial portions of displaced workers. According to the Bureau of Labor Statistics, in 2011, the average length of an episode of unemployment was twenty-one weeks, and 44% of the unemployed were out of work for more than twenty-seven weeks. Exhibit 4.2 shows that the support received by American workers is meager in comparison with what is available to workers in most other developed countries. As a point of contrast, Denmark provides displaced workers with 90% of their previous salary for up to two years.

Exhibit 4.2   Unemployment Entitlements: International Comparisons

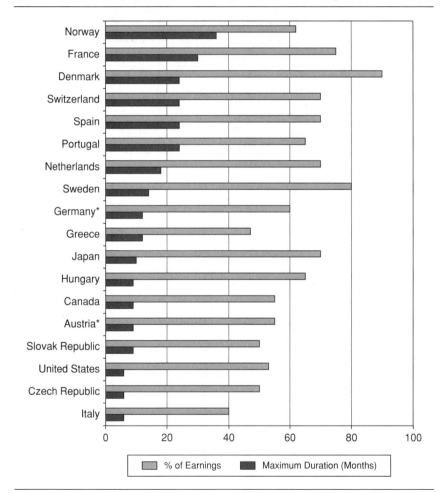

Source: Organization for Economic Co-operation and Development (2004).

Note: *Net earnings.

In the United States, only one in three unemployed workers receives unemployment insurance. This is attributable, in part, to restrictions on who is eligible. Unemployment insurance generally does not cover temporary workers, the self-employed, agricultural workers, part-time workers, those who were out of the labor force for extended periods, those who voluntarily left their jobs, or those who are trying to reenter the labor force after an extended absence. It also fails to protect parents (most commonly women) who take time off to raise families. As a result, unemployment insurance covers only 40% to 60% of those who lost jobs, 10% to 15% of those who left their jobs, 25% to 35% of those trying to reenter the labor force, and only 10% of those who are attempting a new entry into the labor force. Additionally, many workers do not apply for benefits because they lack an understanding of how to apply, assume that they will find replacement work soon, or feel a sense of stigma in using social assistance programs (O'Leary and Wandner 1997; Wandner and Stettner 2000).

In sum, job loss protections, developed during the twentieth century in America, are modest, short term, and restricted, leaving workers who lose their jobs with few resources on which to fall back. As we demonstrate in the next section, this approach is increasingly out of step with the needs of workers laboring in an economy where job loss is commonplace.

How Insecure Are Workers in the New Economy?

The advent of industrial capitalism brought with it the business cycle, with its characteristic boom and bust periods, exposing employees to the risk of job loss. However, as the old economy matured, the risk of unemployment came to be unevenly distributed. Many unionized workers successfully negotiated seniority systems that ensured that the longer one worked for an employer, the lower the likelihood of job loss. Managers and professionals were protected by reward systems designed to retain highly skilled employees and reward organizational loyalty (Cappelli 1997). Employers provided these protections not out of the goodness of their hearts but because they were persuaded that it was in their own competitive interest to retain hard-to-replace employees and to invest in their professional development. Those at the bottom, who worked in insecure secondary labor market jobs, experienced frequent bouts of unemployment and faced high risks of destitution. As the U.S. government strove to control the destabilizing effects of financial speculation and to stimulate the economy when it threatened to go into recession, these countercyclical economic policies limited those risks for all workers, somewhat—especially after the Great Depression of the 1930s. Today, however, evidence is ample that something has changed, as we have seen two major bursts of very high (10% or higher) unemployment in the past three decades, and it is becoming clear that even workers in "good jobs" are far less secure than in the past (Beck 2000; Kalleberg 2009; Rubin and Brody 2005; Sweet, Moen, and Meiksins 2007).

How insecure are today's workers? The answer depends on how insecurity is defined. One way of measuring insecurity is to examine the percentage of workers who are **unemployed,** that is, people who are actively looking for work but cannot find it. At any given point in 2014, over 11 million Americans—approximately one in fifteen working-age adults—were unemployed. The rates for men were somewhat higher than for women, and African American men were unemployed at twice the rate of white men. Unemployment rates have fluctuated considerably during the past forty years, from a low of 3.5% in 1969 to a high of 10.1% in 2010. These rates also vary monthly, within industries, and by geographic locale. For example, construction workers are commonly laid off during the winter months, but retail employment opportunities grow in advance of the holiday season.

Relying on unemployment statistics as the exclusive measure of job insecurity tells only part of the story. According to the standards used by the Bureau of Labor Statistics, to be classified as "unemployed," an individual would have to be not currently working *and* actively seeking a job. As a result, these statistics exclude **discouraged workers** (people who have given up trying to find work), those who are forced to accept jobs that are inappropriate to their qualifications and needs, and those laboring in jobs that offer no protection beyond short-term contracts (Cottle 2001; Kalleberg, Reskin, and Hudson 2000; Smith 2002). One illustration of the limitations of these figures can be observed by examining job creation data, also collected and reported by the Bureau of Labor Statistics. Notable is that when new jobs are created, the numbers of unemployed do not go down proportionately because better job prospects encourage more people to seek work (Thurow 1999). In other words, unemployment statistics fail to recognize many potential workers, people who could be working but are not.

It should be emphasized that unemployment statistics also do a poor job of revealing the number of people who lose their jobs involuntarily. As Jacob Hacker (2006) argues, rates of involuntary job loss have grown, and the increasing rate of these types of job losses expanded well in advance of the most recent economic recession. He concluded that many people who lose jobs find replacement jobs that are inferior to their previous positions, with lower pay and benefits, and are mismatched to their education and experience. As a result, these workers remain employed but still fear (and experience) employment insecurity (see also Kalleberg 2007). They are not, however, unemployed.

Most workers are let go one by one, in numbers too small to register as events worthy of a newspaper's lead story. But in the new economy, these trickles of job loss combine to form rivers of insecurity. Other workers are let go together with sizable numbers of other employees. Beginning in the mid-1990s, the Bureau of Labor Statistics began tracking **mass layoffs,** events in which establishments had fifty or more employees applying for unemployment insurance within a five-week period. Exhibit 4.3 shows that in 2012, during the "jobless recovery," at least 15,236 establishments had large-scale layoffs affecting more than 1.5 million workers overall. This was good news in comparison to the number of mass layoffs that occurred in 2009, but the number of workers affected remains high. The three most common reasons for mass layoffs were seasonal work ending, company restructuring, and permanent plant closure. Although reliable data on mass layoffs are not available for a long-term analysis, the number increased significantly in the early 1970s, particularly in the manufacturing sector, and has subsequently remained consistently high. Unfortunately the Bureau of Labor Statistics is no longer tracking mass layoff events, making it harder to document the extent of insecurity present today.

As the old industrial economy gave way to the new economy, decreased job security was especially noticeable among production workers in the manufacturing sector. Even unionized production workers in core industries could no longer count on the protections offered by collective bargaining agreements. Some of the most visible mass layoffs and plant closings occurred in industries (such as automobile assembly) and in states (such as Michigan and Ohio) that had traditionally been the heart of strong labor union organizations. In addition, the sharp decline in work stoppages in recent

Exhibit 4.3   Trends in Mass Layoffs in the United States: 1996–2012

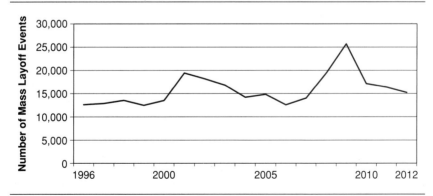

Source: Bureau of Labor Statistics.

years is strong evidence that workers are less well-equipped individually or collectively to fight for improved job security or to resist employers' efforts to gain "flexibility" and undercut seniority protections. Hourly workers in most industries, skilled or unskilled, unionized or not, can no longer count on the security provided by large employers and seniority rules.

The growth of job insecurity is, in part, the product of a more volatile, boom-or-bust economy, in which deregulation and efforts to shrink government's economic role have helped to fuel speculative bubbles and weaken countercyclical economic policies. However, this insecurity now also affects workers in high-skill, high-paying occupations. For example, the high-tech sector (which is often touted as one of the key elements of the emerging new economy) has been characterized by the same pattern of job loss and mass layoffs as traditional manufacturing. Even in advance of the recession that began in 2008, Intel eliminated 10,000 jobs in 2006 and Hewlett-Packard cut 15,000 in 2005. Some estimate that between 500,000 and 800,000 high-tech jobs moved offshore in the early twenty-first century (Schultz 2006). Although some employers continue to place an emphasis on retaining high-skill employees, many employers have responded to increased economic competition and unstable market conditions by weakening their commitment to reward structures designed to encourage employee loyalty. Thus, efforts to promote "flexibility" encourage looser commitments to all employees. The flexibility push is reinforced by stockholder pressures to engage in periodic bouts of downsizing and layoffs, by new forms of work organization that assign managerial tasks to worker groups, and by new organizational structures that make it harder to advance careers by moving up within a single organization. Managerial and professional employees once could count on generous benefits packages and stable, steadily growing incomes. Today, these workers have good reason to feel less confident that these arrangements will be available and that security will expand as their careers progress. Additionally, fiscal pressure has increased insecurity among the many professionals employed in the public sector (such as teachers), and some states such as Wisconsin have taken steps to limit the ability of public-sector employees to collectively bargain. Though some managerial and professional workers have done well in the new economy, it is also apparent that at least some of these once-secure workers cannot be as confident that they will retain their jobs and have to think seriously about the possibility of midcareer changes (Cappelli 1999; Jacoby 1999; Moen and Roehling 2005).

Hacker (2006) notes that American society has increasingly shifted "risk" onto the shoulders of employees. Instead of defined-benefit health care plans, for example, employees are encouraged to open health care savings plans (which means they risk not saving enough). Instead of traditional pensions, employees are offered stock ownership plans, investment opportunities, and other market-based opportunities that promise greater payouts but also involve the risk of loss. And those risks are real. This lesson was learned by Enron employees who lost nearly all their retirement savings when the company failed, because much of it was in the form of Enron stock contributed by Enron or purchased by the employees themselves. They were not alone; the 120,000 employees at United Airlines saw most of their retirement savings disappear when the company declared bankruptcy in 2004 (Marks 2004). Newspaper accounts of companies closing operations, underfunding their pensions (and petitioning the government for financial assistance), and engaging in legal maneuvering to get out of pension commitments to current and retired workers are now commonplace. By 2010, talk of modifying previously ironclad pension agreements with public-sector workers was becoming widespread (Cooper and Walsh 2011).

Income stability also has weakened in recent years. In the old economy there were people who suffered sudden, temporary drops in income (because of illness, job loss, business failure, and the like). But the numbers of people who suffer sudden losses in income have grown significantly. And although the risks of such income fluctuations are still greater among the less educated, the risks grew more rapidly for better-educated Americans in the 1990s (Hacker 2006). With budgets stretched to the breaking point, for many dual-earner couples, an unexpected event such as a job loss or illness can quickly plunge a family into bankruptcy (Warren and Tyagi 2003).

There is also a subjective dimension to job insecurity, the anxiety felt at the prospect that one's own job might disappear (Schmidt 2000). The General Social Survey, a widely used national opinion poll, indicates that feelings of job insecurity are widespread. In 2012, one in ten workers (11%) believed that it was very likely or somewhat likely that they would lose their job in the next year. Another survey, the Couples and Careers Study conducted from 1998 to 2000 by the Cornell Careers Institute, surveyed dual-earner middle-class workers in upstate New York. This study revealed that most higher-level workers were only about 80% to 85% confident that their jobs would exist for the next two years. Only one in four (27%) men and one in three (35%) women in this study were fully certain that they could keep their jobs (Sweet, Moen, and Meiksins 2007). Likewise, the 2012 General Social Survey indicates that only two in three workers (60%) had high confidence that it was "not likely" they would lose their jobs in the next year.

Finally, job insecurity is expanding because of the changing composition of the labor force, as well as the changing organization of work. In an economy dominated by dual-earner families, the loss of one spouse's job creates strong prospects that the other partner—even one with a secure job—may need to reconsider career options. Those partners can be put into the position of trailing spouses and be forced to rework their careers to match the direction charted by their partner. Alternatively, displaced workers could have spouses who hold jobs they are reluctant to relinquish. In this circumstance, displaced workers are anchored to communities, and their options can be limited. To fully understand the realities of job insecurity, therefore, requires thinking of families of jobholders as well as individual jobholders.

To highlight how this operates, let us reexamine the data from the Cornell study from the perspective of couples and link spouses' careers together as they actually are in the lives of most Americans. Recall that the typical professional worker is about 80% confident that his or her job will remain for another couple of years. Using this as a dividing line, we can consider those at or above the 80% mark as holding comparatively "secure" jobs and those below as being insecure. Remember that these workers are married to spouses who also hold jobs that may be secure or insecure. What are the prospects of both partners in a dual-earner family holding secure positions at the same time? Exhibit 4.4 reveals a sobering state of affairs in America—*secure working conditions are the exception*, rather than the rule, for dual-earner professional couples. Only 44% of American dual-earner households have both partners feeling fairly secure in their jobs; most families have one or both partners feeling insecure. If we raise the threshold to *full* confidence that jobs are completely safe, the numbers plummet even further, as only about one in ten (12%) dual-earner households has both partners feeling fully secure (Sweet, Moen, and Meiksins 2007).

Exhibit 4.4   Job Security Configurations of Dual-Earner Professional Couples (80% Confidence That Jobs Will Be There in Two Years)

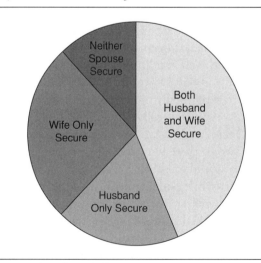

Source: Sweet, Moen, and Meiksins (2007).

Finally, we note that insecurity has been intentionally built into the design of some jobs with the purpose of maximizing the power and control of employers. This is the case in the Taylorized "McJobs" in the secondary labor market, where complaints concerning work conditions can be countered with "if you don't like the job, find another one—you are replaceable." Even worse conditions are found in the employment of day laborers, who must renegotiate the terms of employment on a daily or weekly basis. This and other kinds of marginal employment have become more common as employers have found ways to avoid regulations through subcontracting work to smaller companies that rely on this type of labor (Bernhardt et al. 2008). Many of these laborers are undocumented workers and have no recourse other than to accept whatever terms are offered. Other day laborers use their jobs to buy drugs, and these relationships feed into a vicious cycle of substance abuse and economic marginalization, while at the same time securing the employer's ability to obtain low-wage work on an "as needed" basis (Williams 2009).

The Costs of Job Loss and Insecurity

Losing a job has immediate and long-term consequences for household finances. Even among displaced professional workers, two in three receive no severance pay after being terminated. For those who do get severance packages, the compensation varies greatly. Most receive only a modest sum of money (two weeks' pay being the most common), providing little relief from the financial strains of finding new work (Sweet, Moen, and Meiksins 2007).

The economic impact of losing a job is not a new concern. What has changed in the new economy is the ability of families to weather these disruptions. In the old economy, the husband/breadwinner arrangement made it possible for wives to act as financial reserve units, as well as to hold jobs temporarily when their husbands lost work. Today, the incomes of both spouses are essential to meet family budgets. As a result, short periods of joblessness can devastate family finances in ways that were less common in the old economy (Moen and Roehling 2005; Warren and Tyagi 2003). And this experience is becoming increasingly common. Recent estimates indicate that the percentage of dual-earner families in which one spouse lost a job doubled from 2007 to 2010, with more than a million such couples being reduced to one earner in 2010 alone (Uchitelle 2011). In our own studies, when we asked displaced workers and their spouses what they wished they had done differently, the most common responses were to have saved more and to have put more energy into finding new work before losing their old jobs. But when families are putting in long, stressful hours of work already, this is often difficult to do. As one displaced engineer, a mother of an eight-year-old boy, told us, "When I think of myself at that time [before I lost the job] . . . I felt like I was doing just about all I could do."[1]

Another problem facing insecure workers is that even though jobs are unstable, they remain tightly tied to individuals' senses of identity and feelings of self-worth. As a result, losing a job can have a major impact on health and social-psychological well-being (Uchitelle 2006; Young 2012). Job losses also strain marriages, sometimes to the breaking point (Westman, Etzion, and Horovitz 2004). Consider, for example, how job loss affected Lisette, a displaced forty-eight-year-old clinical nurse, and her relationship with her husband:

> [My boss] just told me that she had some bad news. That, you know, that they had to make the budget cuts. And my position was one of the positions that was being eliminated. And, I mean, I just burst into tears. . . . And I was just so shocked. Everybody that worked with me was shocked. Just, um, it was just really unexpected and nobody had thought that, you know, it would happen to somebody like me, you know, who had done such a good job and had worked so hard and I was really well liked by everybody there.

Feeling "lost," and perhaps in a state of denial, Lisette had difficulty understanding the permanence of her employer's decision and returned to meet with her boss in the following week to negotiate a means to get her job back. In shame, she avoided telling her husband, Damon, about the job loss and for an entire week she pretended to go to work. Damon, in turn, interpreted this as a "personal rejection" and their mutual satisfaction with their marriage dropped precipitously.

It is not only those who lose jobs and their spouses who are negatively affected. Simply witnessing coworkers being displaced increases anxieties and stress in the workplace (Grunberg, Anderson-Connolly, and Greenberg 2000). However, studies show that this stress can be moderated if employers make visible the rationale for organizational restructuring, provide advance notification that job loss may occur, and give evidence that procedural justice has been used to determine who will (and who will not) lose jobs (Trefalt 2010). In other words, if workers know that jobs have to be lost, agree that job losses are necessary, and are given opportunities to plan, they are in a stronger position to adjust their lives accordingly. Unfortunately the resource of advanced knowledge is seldom provided to displaced workers.

Psychologists and sociologists have documented how planning and a sense of control facilitate social psychological adjustment to change (Bandura 1982; Emirbayer and Mische 1998). Toward this end, advance notification can be the key to helping workers adjust *in anticipation* of job loss. If workers know ahead of time that layoffs are being planned, they are in a position to seek additional training well before they find themselves without a job. In addition, advance notice can give workers and their representatives time to negotiate with employers either to limit the numbers of people affected or to arrange for assistance of various kinds for those employees who are displaced (Uchitelle 2006).

Outside of individually negotiated contracts and collective bargaining agreements secured by unions, in the United States the only "right to know" about job futures was established by the **Worker Adjustment and Retraining Notification (WARN) Act.** This law mandates that companies with more than one hundred workers provide sixty days of notice if they anticipate terminating or laying off fifty or more employees. Though of significant benefit to workers in large companies, this act leaves most workers unprotected—those employed in smaller companies, those who are not part of a mass layoff, those who have worked for the company for less than six months, and part-time workers. Unfortunately, most employers are reluctant to extend advance notification of impending job loss. Exhibit 4.5 shows that half of the displaced workers we interviewed said they received

Exhibit 4.5   Percentage of Displaced Professional Workers Who Received Notification That Their Jobs Would Be Eliminated

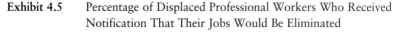

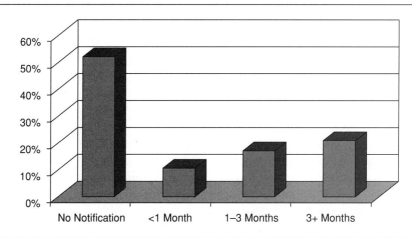

Source: Sweet, Moen, and Meiksins (2007).

no notification, formal or informal, that their job would be eliminated. Only a small minority, one in five workers, had three or more months to prepare for the loss of their jobs. And even when employers extended severance packages, the callous methods used to inform employees of layoffs remained a bitter pill. Our in-depth interviews with managers and skilled professionals revealed sobering accounts of what it is like to lose a job in the new economy. For example, Edwin, a forty-year-old engineer and father of three young children, told us of how he lost his job:

> How did I learn my job was gone? Um, just all at once. I had no idea I was going to be let go. I was actually saying goodbye to people that were being let go. And, you know, kind of comforting them and telling them it would be okay. And I was sitting at my desk later that afternoon and I just see my boss walk up to me and ask me if I had a minute. And I kind of saw it in his face. And I say right then, "You got to be kidding." He says, "Yup, sorry, bad news." So that was it. It was that cold.

This case is typical. Before being let go, Edwin and his wife had it all—two good jobs, a satisfying family life, and a happy marriage. Their success came after years of working together to locate two jobs, select their community, and reconfigure their work schedules to raise their children (Moen and Sweet 2003; Pixley 2008; Sweet, Swisher, and Moen 2005). In the course of an afternoon, their lives were turned upside down, forcing them to confront difficult, fundamental decisions: how to manage dwindled resources, whose job to favor in the next stage of Edwin's career, and how to cope with the prospect of losing their home and neighborhood ties.

Even when employees have some advance knowledge of impending layoffs, the consequences can be significant. This is particularly true when layoffs affect declining regions, single-employer communities, and older workers (Sweet 2007). In these situations, workers often have great difficulty finding new jobs because little else is available locally to employ them or because of discrimination or skill mismatches. Younger workers may be willing to move away, but older workers typically are more reluctant and are more likely to experience prolonged or even permanent unemployment. The result can be both economically and psychologically devastating, undermining a worker's sense of self as a breadwinner and causing workers, both young and old, to look at work more as a way to pay the bills and less as a source of personal satisfaction and community (Koeber 2002).

Women and racial minorities are especially vulnerable when organizations downsize, reflecting their comparatively tenuous attachments to careers. One would expect that establishing rules that guide impartial decision-making processes would buffer this dynamic, but this does not necessarily happen. If, for example, the rule is that employees with the longest job tenure or the highest rank have the greatest job protections, this tends to favor white men, as women and racial minorities tend to have held jobs for shorter durations. However, if decisions are based on individual evaluation of each employee's individual contributions to the organization and their performance review, gender and race play a far lesser role in the outcomes. Notably, when antidiscrimination protocols govern layoff decisions, the result is often substantial reductions in differential termination on the basis of gender or race. Thus, formal rules that guide selection of which individuals will be downsized can level tendencies for differential treatment, but the outcomes depend on how those rules operate (Kalev 2014).

Finally, we introduce a counterintuitive observation. Approximately one in four workers who lose jobs actually report that their lives (but not their finances) *improved* in the aftermath. Here it is important to consider who these workers are. The new economy operates on the basis of jobs that can introduce considerable stress in workers' lives and is less forgiving to those who chose to exit these jobs. So when workers' lives improve following an unexpected job loss, usually the job they exited had been taking a toll, but the workers had felt that they had no option other than to persevere in what were sometimes toxic environments (Sweet and Moen 2011). The layoff forced these workers out of a bad situation and made their lives better in a sense. But this experience must be considered in the context of the array of options available to workers, which sometimes offer a choice between a rock (a job that isn't rewarding) and a hard place (unemployment).

Responding to Insecurity: Old and New Careers

The old economy encouraged an orientation to work and careers that is largely discredited in the new economy. Yet some still cling to the career mystique that loyalty will be reciprocated and that finding the good job will result in finding the good life (Moen and Roehling 2005). Today, many are starting to question these assumptions. In the old system, for those in the primary labor market, a "good employee" was someone who had found a well-paid, stable job and who committed his or her career to the employer. Jumping from employer to employer tended to be seen either as opportunism or as a sign of a troubled work history. For those in the secondary labor market, unstable work histories reflected career patterns that were fostered by limited opportunity but also were used as evidence of individuals' unsuitability for jobs that required greater responsibilities. As a result, demonstrating a lasting commitment to employers or unions became essential for upward mobility, and an employee's loyalty became synonymous with her or his "character." To prosper as an "organization man" or a "union man" required embracing an employer's or union's interests as one's own and seeing oneself as part of an association of like-minded employees (Mills 2002 [1951]; Whyte 1956). Emily, the contract worker introduced in Chapter 1, no longer orients her career expectations in this fashion, nor do her employers consider her character to be suspect. In fact, it is her willingness to hold short-term contracts and complete the work diligently that make her an attractive employee.

For those in primary labor market jobs, employee loyalties in the old economy were commonly reciprocated by employers, who adopted an ethos of **corporate paternalism**—the belief that it is the employer's responsibility to provide for their employees, much as it is parents' responsibility to provide for their children. For instance, in the 1950s, IBM CEO Thomas Watson Jr. proudly stated, "There are many things I want this company to become, but no matter how big we become, I want this company to be known as the company that has the greatest respect for the individual." Consistent with Watson's words, IBM extended generous pay, lifetime employment, and jobs to widows (Kanter 1977). In the latter part of the twentieth century, the CEO's role as the benevolent employer was replaced by a new kind of corporate leader, exemplified by Sunbeam CEO Albert "Chainsaw Al" Dunlap and the legions of corporate raiders who made quick profits by dismantling otherwise profitable enterprises (Bartlett and Steele 1992).[2] Perhaps the most vivid portrayal of the new corporate ethos is offered in the Michael Moore film *Roger and Me*, which shows General Motors CEO Roger Smith dodging the question of why American jobs were being moved offshore. In contrast to Watson, Smith defined his responsibility as being primarily to the investors of General Motors.

Jobs are insecure in the new economy in part because of a growing acceptance, especially among managers and captains of industry, that jobs should be insecure. An earlier view of employees as assets to be retained has been replaced, not surprisingly encouraged by the temporary work industry, by the view that employees are costs to be minimized in order to maximize profits (Hatton 2011; Smith and Neuwirth 2008). As Brian O'Reilly stated in a widely cited article in *Fortune* magazine, the "new deal" for workers is this:

> There will never be job security. You will be employed by us as long as you add value to the organization, and you are continuously responsible for finding ways to add value. In return, you have the right to demand interesting and

important work, the freedom and resources to perform it well, pay that reflects your contribution, and the experience and training needed to be employable here or elsewhere. (O'Reilly 1994, 44)

O'Reilly was writing to the select workers (and their employers) who benefitted under the old system of rewarding seniority with job protections. He presented a case for the continual restructuring of work, fitting people to jobs (as opposed to the reverse), and the dismantling of jobs when work is completed. His view reflects the themes of "rightsizing" and "organizational flexibility" emphasized in numerous managerial publications of the past forty years. The accepted goals of modern business are to be "lean and mean" and to restructure continually—even as a number of critics argued that this often has negative effects on corporate profitability in both the short and the long term (Grunberg, Anderson-Connolly, and Greenberg 2000; Wagar 2001). Though the new social contract has been packaged as providing flexibility, from a worker's perspective it can often look much more like an effort to extend the power to displace employees at will (Pollert 1988).

The problem of job insecurity is pervasive in secondary labor markets, where workers enter jobs with virtually no protection against dismissal. For example, an application for work at a Burger King restaurant informs workers that they "can resign or be terminated . . . at any time without notice or requirement of cause." Though their job application form states that they have access to an arbitration program, there is virtually nothing to arbitrate if the signed agreement says that employers can fire workers at will (Wolkinson and Ormiston 2006).

Fast-food workers are not the only ones who experience this one-sided arrangement. Our interviews with displaced professional workers revealed many stories that show how little loyalty is extended from the top down. Even dedicated, long-service employees are displaced at will and often in ways that show little or no appreciation for employees' past contributions. The account offered by Duke (a thirty-six-year-old engineer at a major manufacturing company) was similar to those of many other workers who had lost their jobs:

> They had everybody in the organization go to a meeting. They handed out paper slips, some of the people went upstairs, some of the people went downstairs, and the people who went downstairs were informed that they were done as of that day, and the people who went upstairs were informed that they were going to be kept on for a couple months but their jobs would also be gone. . . . It was a real lousy way to do something like that.

As we made comparisons between workers, and looked at how employees were terminated, we found that Duke and his coworkers actually reported comparatively favorable treatment, in that they received two weeks' severance pay for each year they had been with the company, as well as temporary continuation of their health insurance and access to an outplacement company. In contrast, Tobias, a fifty-three-year-old information specialist, recounts a worse and sadly common experience. After working a series of twelve-hour days to complete an important contract, he was called into his supervisor's office, told that his job was terminated, and was escorted out of the building a few minutes later. Because of fear that he would sabotage work stored on his computer, he was not allowed to log back into the system or remove any personal communications or files on his machine. He was not alone. In the weeks that followed, twelve other employees at his company were treated in a similar manner. Tobias's story is particularly harsh, but he is among many others we interviewed who were "tapped on the shoulder" and escorted out of their buildings within a half hour of being notified that their jobs were gone.

To what extent is the new social contract reshaping workers' commitments to their jobs and employers? Workers, on average, have lesser tenure with their employers, meaning that they are less likely to stay with the same employer for the same amount of time compared to the old economy, and this is especially true among older white males (who were the biggest beneficiaries of tenure-based security systems) (Kalleberg 2013). Other workers (especially women and younger workers) were much more likely to have shorter tenure and less enduring relationships with employers even before the transition to the new economy. Some have argued that the new economy is corroding the character of American workers and undermining lasting commitments to fellow workers and employers. This portrait depicts modern workers as pursuing immediate self-interests but lacking a commitment to labor for a greater good. This perspective suggests that with the transition to the new economy, workers, like their employers, no longer see loyalty as a virtue (Sennett 1998). Although this may be true for some employees, our interviews with displaced workers did not indicate this to be as common as is often argued. Instead of being disloyal, we found that many of the problems experienced by displaced workers resulted from their perhaps being *too loyal* to their jobs. It is possible that they did not feel that sense of connection to their employers that workers felt in the old economy, but they were intensely committed to their work and labored long hours not only because they had to but because they saw it as their duty. For the most part, they continued to behave according to preexisting models of what a good employee should be and to give as much as they could to their employers and to their coworkers. As a result, the most common response we heard from workers (even those who had a sense that their jobs were unstable) was that learning of their job loss was like "being a deer in the headlights" or "being hit on the head." They were "stunned," "shocked," "distressed," and "incredulous in disbelief." Had these workers constructed their value systems and personal strategies to correspond with the new economy, they would not have reported that "employers do not take care of their people" and that they felt "unappreciated," "annoyed," "miffed," "frustrated," and "extremely angry." Workers adopting a new set of work values would be much more likely to anticipate job loss and be better prepared to cope with it both practically and psychologically. Most displaced workers do not orient their perspectives in such a manner.

Still, workers' orientations to jobs and careers seem to be changing. The Bureau of Labor Statistics reported that in 2014 the average length of time workers had been with their current employer was just 4.6 years. The average baby boom generation worker in the United States held eleven jobs between the ages of eighteen and forty-six (Bureau of Labor Statistics 2012). More importantly, far fewer workers expect, or plan, to stay with their current employers throughout their career, a sharp departure from the old ways of working. These data suggest that workers may be redefining career paths, as well as their strategies for navigating labor markets over the life course. Insecurity is also playing a role in reshaping identities. For example, in the old economy, members of the working class relied heavily on the transition to work to mark the biographical transition to adulthood. Today, because working-class jobs are sometimes unavailable and are usually unstable, young adults are not in a position to use employment in the same manner to signal that they have "made it" to adulthood. Instead, adolescence is now extended into a vague stage of "emerging adulthood," with twenty- to thirty-year-olds defining their status as adults on therapeutic grounds, such as overcoming adversities experienced in childhood (Silva 2012). Similarly, career disruptions undermine the capacities of older workers to create a cohesive retrospective account of life events. Rather than viewing their own life stories as a progression of successes that have accumulated over time, workers now commonly see their biographies as loosely connected and sometimes disjointed experiences (Gabriel, Gray, and Goregaokar 2013). So at both ends of careers, as well as in the middle, job insecurity not only undermines economic security, it also fragments the sense of self.

Some have argued that redesigned workplaces offer some segments of the workforce expanded prospects to develop skills and to be liberated with new horizons of opportunity. These skills may not ensure security in internal labor markets, as they might have in the old economy, but they are transportable to other places of employment. This optimistic view envisions a mobile workforce charting **boundaryless careers**, engaging in transient relationships between different employers and thereby expanding a variety of portable skills (Arthur and Rousseau 1996; Raider and Burt 1996). Most analysts who adopt the phrase "boundaryless career" use it to emphasize the ways that ranges of individual choices are expanded in the new economy. Such is the case for computer programmers in Silicon Valley. As these workers rotate through a variety of companies, they gain a variety of experiences and earn significant financial rewards, simultaneously enhancing innovation and expanding knowledge (Saxenian 1996). However, the cavalier use of the word *boundaryless* to describe careers needs to be questioned when considering the constraints on worker mobility. For some workers, especially young, educated, single workers, movement from job to job or community to community might be comparatively less constrained and can result in upward mobility. However, the boundaryless concept ignores the everyday constraints on workers that stem from their relations with others. Relocating, for most workers, entails considering how a career move may affect the career of a spouse, their children's well-being, and the ability to care for aging parents. Older or less-educated workers, in particular, find it difficult to move and are less able to acquire the new skills they might need to "job hop" successfully (Holzer et al. 2011). Rather than having unconstrained careers, workers in the new economy face increased constraints—in terms of social relations and economic demands.

The problem of career instability is also apparent in worker experiences in retraining programs. Many laid-off workers are encouraged to seek additional training, either by going back to school or by taking advantage of either publicly funded or employer-sponsored retraining programs. Workers are told that they should retool, acquire new skills, and adapt to changing patterns of opportunity. Unfortunately, worker retraining often produces cynicism and disappointment, rather than employment. It is hard to know what to retrain for, especially when there may be few jobs of any kind to be found. But beyond this, retraining programs and supports tend to emphasize short-term skill acquisition, rather than the broad education that would make employees truly "flexible"; and retraining often winds up training people for jobs that do not exist. Displaced workers are often reluctant (quite understandably under the circumstances) to abandon their long-standing ties to occupations and industry sectors (Uchitelle 2006).

Additionally, the focus on the upward mobility of unattached professionals pursuing boundaryless careers ignores the careers of workers who labor in less favorable arrangements. A large proportion of the workforce labors in **contingent jobs**, "as-needed" positions, filled by short-term agreements between workers and employers. These jobs include on-call work, temporary help, agency work, and contract work positions designed to be temporary and unstable. Because of their short-term employment arrangements, contingent workers are commonly treated differently from "regular workers." For example, temporary workers are sometimes given different-colored security badges, assumed by coworkers to be less competent, not offered employer-sponsored training, and excluded from office rituals such as birthday parties. Because of their perceived marginal status, coworkers are less inclined to express interest in these workers' lives outside of the workplace and often fail even to learn their names (simply referring to them as "the temp") (Henson 1996). A widely cited study found that contingent workers earn considerably less pay, have less access to health insurance, and are less likely to receive pension benefits than those who work in more conventional arrangements (Kalleberg, Reskin, and Hudson 2000). Temporary workers sometimes report liking aspects of their jobs, but as Vicki Smith (2002) forcefully demonstrates in her book *Crossing the Great Divide*, nearly all long for secure jobs, something harder to find in the new economy.

It is important to recognize that not all contingent workers are alike. While many contingent workers labor in marginal temporary jobs, others operate as **contract workers**; that is, they provide services to an organization but do not work for them directly as employees. Some companies may use contract arrangements to get around labor laws that protect employees or to avoid having to pay benefits to some of their workforce. However, there also is strong evidence that many contract workers, like Emily, enjoy a sense of freedom in not attaching themselves to long-term commitments to organizations. These contract workers can sometimes command high compensation in exchange for the temporary use of their expertise, and many feel a sense of liberation by removing themselves from the confining walls of any particular organization's bureaucracy. Still, these workers usually lack the conventional security offered by longer-term employment, so their careers hinge on continually seeking replacement work (Bidwell and Briscoe 2009; Kalleberg 2013; Osnowitz 2010).

Conclusion

In this chapter, we considered risk and job insecurity for American workers in historical and international comparative contexts. We showed that the element of risk is not new and that workers today are far better off than were workers in the early phases of industrialization. At the same time, many workers remain excluded from these protections in the new economy, and new problems have emerged, including an expanded spectrum of jobs that offer little security. Contemporary employees face different types of risk than were experienced by employees in the old economy, not only in their employment contracts but also in the ability of their families to weather career disruptions. And the demography of the American workforce has changed, not just jobs. Dual-earner families are in a unique position of double jeopardy because the loss of one partner's job can disrupt both partners' careers, while single-earner families (some of whom are single-parent families) also face mounting risks of job loss.

Unlike their European counterparts—who enjoy some protection from risk simply by virtue of citizenship—American workers have few resources to protect them from the consequences of job insecurity and loss. American workers need to hold jobs as well as locate jobs that offer protections in the form of "benefits." When these jobs are lost, they need to find replacement work quickly. The safety nets established during the twentieth century were built to shelter husband/breadwinner–wife/homemaker families through brief periods of joblessness. These risk management strategies are now woefully insufficient to protect most working families. Similarly, providing pensions and other benefits through employers has become more and more problematic, as workers are forced to move laterally from job to job and from employer to employer.

The new economy has fundamentally weakened the social contract between employers and employees. Employers once believed it was in their own interest to retain valuable employees, but economic instability, global competition, and stockholder pressure have encouraged them to move workers out of jobs at will. This new managerial ethos enables employers to serve the interests of stockholders through flexible labor management strategies but at great cost to American workers, who often are unsure if they can depend on employment beyond the short term. And because employers seldom provide employees with solid information about planned layoffs, workers typically lack the ability to gauge their future job prospects accurately. A more equitable arrangement would necessarily involve providing workers the opportunity to plan careers proactively in an economy of expanded risk and to make tactical career decisions based on solid information about their future employment prospects. Instead, most workers are obliged to be reactive and to redirect disrupted lives in response to decisions they had no part in making.

A return to traditional seniority-based systems of job security does not appear likely, nor would it be unambiguously a good thing. While those systems provided some workers with badly needed protection, they never covered more than a portion of the overall workforce. Moreover, questions can be also raised about the effects of these practices on labor markets and the quality of work. For example, tenure-based systems in the teaching profession have been criticized for placing younger teachers with fresh approaches (but less experience) at a decided disadvantage relative to older teachers. In an economy in which change occurs rapidly and teachers are called on to continuously retool and upgrade their knowledge and skills, employment practices that simply reward seniority are problematic. This does not mean that the elimination of employment security is a solution to motivating workers, however. What *is* needed are employment systems that reward and encourage creative, forward-looking workers that do not rely on high levels of insecurity as motivators.

In the United States, employers value workers who can be "all in," which can include taken-for-granted expectations that workers labor full-time and overtime as needed. When labor needs diminish, the solution is to lay off subsets of these "all-in" workers and to retain other employees who are expected to continue working long and hard. This is not the only potential path to managing the complex processes of matching labor supply to meet demand. Consider, for example, that in many Western European countries, employer freedom to retrench workers is constrained even when work becomes more scarce. In response, employers fit labor supply to demand by reducing work hours expected of individual workers, while retaining far larger numbers of employees. The work hour adjustment strategy puts a greater financial burden on employers than the displacement approach, but at the same time it reduces the financial strain experienced by families and the consequences of career disruptions (Applebaum 2011). As we identified at the beginning of this chapter, the big question is who is expected to bear the burden of managing risk and its consequences. Currently, far too many burdens of risk are placed on workers and their families, who also experience far too many of the negative consequences of employment insecurity.

One might expect that as families have become subjected to greater risk, the workings of the new economy would lead more Americans to agree that government intervention is needed to instill safety in a turbulent economy. This has not happened. In fact, as an aggregate, Americans are now less inclined to view government as a solution in comparison to attitudes held before the Great Recession. However, a more careful analysis reveals that Americans are becoming more divided on this issue, with Republicans having much stronger beliefs against government involvement and Democrats having modestly greater faith in government involvement. This indicates that there is not an agreed-upon understanding of how—or if—government should be involved in the risk issue and that there is a need to see this issue as intertwined within larger political debates (Brooks and

Manza 2013). The underlying question is whether Americans can be persuaded that government can be an effective tool for change, a consideration we return to in the conclusion of this book.

Job insecurity will likely remain a contour of work in the new economy. Given this situation, we believe that discussion needs to shift from a focus on *job security* to enhancing *career security* across the life course (Moen and Sweet 2004). This involves allocating resources that help workers transition from one job to the next and eliminating the structures that force workers to be either "all in" or "all out" of the labor force. This also requires a rebalancing of the employee-employer relationship with respect to access to information, so that employees are better positioned to understand the prospects of their jobs being eliminated and so that deterrents to high labor turnover are introduced. And in an economy where many workers either lack jobs or labor in jobs that poorly fit their talents, attention needs to be devoted to increasing work opportunity. As we discuss in the next chapter, this may involve thinking about ways of redistributing some work from those who have jobs to those who do not.

Notes

1. Quotes in this chapter are taken from the Couples Managing Change Study (Stephen Sweet and Phyllis Moen, coprincipal investigators), which included in-depth interviews with 125 dual-earner couples who either held insecure jobs or who had recently lost jobs. For details on methods, see Sweet, Moen, and Meiksins (2007).

2. This nickname was originally coined by workers protesting his labor management practices but was also one he embraced.

Chapter Five

A Fair Day's Work?

The Intensity and Scheduling of Jobs in the New Economy

The workers described at the beginning of this book face a number of challenges in managing the time and intensity of their work. Meg, the trader, experienced challenges straddling a demanding job and caregiving responsibilities, ultimately leading to a decision to exit her career. Tammy, the manufacturing worker, went from being "work rich" to being "work poor" as her job at Delphi vanished. Emily, the contract worker, has work contracts that ebb and flow depending on the jobs she is able to secure. Rain, the Chinese restaurant worker, labors consistently long hours. Kavita, the call center worker in India, works the night shift and faces social challenges as a result. And Mike, the inner-city young adult, has difficulty finding and maintaining stable employment. All of these workers face common problems: negotiating work arrangements that enable them to meet their family needs, keep their careers intact, and gain a fair day's wage for a fair day's labor. What is a reasonable workday for an employee in the new economy? And should employees be expected to perform, as Frederick Winslow Taylor (1964 [1911]) prescribed in his *Principles of Scientific Management*, the absolute maximum amount of labor possible? Or should their work occur at a more relaxed and (some would argue) humane pace?

This chapter focuses on the intensity and scheduling of work to understand the challenges that job expectations pose for workers and their families in the new economy. We consider the factors that cause some workers to labor longer than they want to, while (ironically) others work less than they want to, or even not at all. We consider why so many Americans feel over-worked, and we place job demands in historical and comparative perspective to highlight the ways in which American culture and policy contribute to both work poverty and overwork. Finally, we consider the impact new schedules have on working families and their strategies for reconciling job schedules with family demands.

Time, Intensity, and Work

One obvious way to measure how much work people are performing is simply to count how many hours they spend laboring. Interestingly, this way of thinking about work commitments is relatively recent and in many ways is a very poor standard to judge the actual amount of work that is performed. Only in the past two centuries have jobs become things people "clock into." By contrast, in preindustrial times, work centered on the home and constituted a stream of activities that varied according to the rhythms of the day and the season. Workers responded to (among other things) cows returning from the field, crops in need of sowing or harvest, and children in need of nursing (Osterud 1987). Labor historian E. P. Thompson (Thompson 1967) termed this *task-oriented labor*, a systemic approach that organized, measured, and compensated work on the basis of the completion of specific assignments. When work was organized according to task, schedules varied remarkably throughout the year and typically interspersed intense labor with prolonged periods of relaxation. And because work was performed in and around the home, people in preindustrial societies did not make a clear distinction between what was "work" and what was "life" because the two were inextricably intertwined.

Industrialization sparked a radical reorganization of work, shifting the criteria for compensation away from the completion of tasks toward the *length of time* engaged in tasks. This system of **time-oriented labor** led to the development of hourly wages and shift work, and it reoriented the rhythms of work and family lives around clocks and calendars (Hareven 1982; Marglin 1982). Although the hourly wage is now a taken-for-granted arrangement, in the early nineteenth century this alternate way of measuring and compensating work was not immediately embraced. Workers had to learn to arrange their schedules to match that of the factory and structure their family lives to perform shift work. As Thompson (1963) noted, the end of the Industrial Revolution can be marked by the moment workers stopped protesting over *how much* they were expected to produce and started protesting over *how long* they were expected to work—a change already in evidence by around 1830. The factory bells that echoed throughout New England in the nineteenth century are mostly silent, but twenty-first-century workers still watch the clock. Many taken-for-granted divisions of the day, week, and year—including vacations, the weekend, and the lunch hour—were all literally invented in the late nineteenth century and reflect the triumph of time-oriented systems of controlling work (Rybczynski 1991).

Arguably, a task orientation to work is a more natural means of organizing labor than a time orientation. Consider, for instance, that when college students are assigned to write a term paper, their most common question is "How long does it have to be?" Students never ask, "How much time will I be required to spend writing?" The first question is more natural because it concerns the product of one's efforts. The latter question is of greater concern for most workers in the labor force because their compensation is not determined directly by how productive they are but by how long they spend engaged in the activity. Today, even some skilled knowledge work is measured by the hour. For instance, lawyers seek to maximize their "billable" hours because this constitutes the measure by which they are commonly paid (Yakura 2001).

In the twenty-first century, most workers are accustomed to the logic of time-oriented labor and to the idea that compensation is linked to the number of hours they work. Surprisingly, the struggle over how long workers should work has not turned out the way many earlier observers expected. Although progress would suggest that work would have grown easier, more fulfilling, and more economically rewarding, the sixty-hour workweeks of the nineteenth century have not faded entirely away. As we discuss in the next section, many Americans find themselves laboring very long hours, often longer and harder than they want to, as well as more than their parents did.

Understanding time-oriented labor as a socially negotiated system of managing work presents interesting and important questions about what activities should be compensated in the new economy. Many of the problems workers confront today emerged from the ways the terms of labor came to be negotiated in the old economy. For example, one old question concerns when work begins and ends. When miners and mine owners in the late nineteenth century faced this question, miners ultimately were forced to agree to walk or crawl several miles to reach the coal face before they could clock in to their jobs; paid work commenced only after they had begun to dig.[1]

Exhibit 5.1   Use of Time as a Means to Organize Work Remains a Legacy of the Old Economy

Source: Copyright © by Paul Edmondson/CORBIS. Reprinted with permission.

Today, this seems unreasonable. However, consider this fact: the American Community Survey documented that the average worker in the United States spends fifty minutes a day (approximately two hundred hours in a year) commuting to and from his or her job, but few workers are compensated for this effort. Acknowledging this, however, would require developing mechanisms for rewarding labor in all its forms, including work in and around the home, and replacing the restricted definitions of work created in response to industrialization. The fact is that many jobs today require workers to labor before they enter and after they leave the workplace. Workers in many service jobs, for instance, commonly have to perform additional work tasks, such as cleaning their uniforms, on their own time. Some of this is legal, but in other cases, employers have been found guilty of not paying workers for set-up or clean-up work for which they were entitled to wages (a practice known as "wage theft") (Meixell and Eisenbrey 2014). The time and expense it takes to be educated and trained for skilled jobs in the new economy is rarely included in calculations of worker effort. As a result, many young workers enter their careers burdened with tens of thousands of dollars of debt accrued during their college educations. This is a burden that *they* carry, not their employers.

Even some workers whose hours are not unusually long, and whose hours of work have not increased over time, complain of feeling overworked. Research conducted in 2011 by the American Psychological Association found that more than a third of Americans reported that they were "stressed out" at work on a typical workday and that "too heavy a work load" and "long hours" were two of the top five sources of stress for American workers. Findings such as these indicate a collective belief that the pace, intensity, and the duration of work expected are unreasonable, a view that scholarly research supports. And more workers are increasingly feeling that their jobs require intense pressures to work fast, to work hard, and to work too much, and along with these trends, they feel less job satisfaction (Kalleberg 2013).

Low-skill restaurant jobs, like other forms of work designed in the old economy, were structured to pressure workers to "hustle" and "bull and jam." As many of these jobs remain in the new economy, new pressures have been introduced by new workplace practices and opportunity structures. For example, although smart technologies have eliminated some of the unpleasant, physically demanding tasks of the past, they also pressure workers to keep up with machines that work steadily and fast. Even workers whose jobs involve monitoring technology can experience high levels of stress because this type of work often involves a combination of repetitive tasks with the need to stay alert. To get a sense of these pressures, consider what it is like to be a baggage screener at a major airport; a job like this involves monotony (a seemingly endless stream of routine examinations of travelers' bags) but also requires the agent to be vigilant enough to notice the occasional dangerous item that passes through the screening mechanism.

In contrast to the collective pressure exerted in the old economy to restrict production and adhere to the "stint" that limits the amount of work everyone will perform, the new economy appears to operate with the opposite pressure to "keep up" with everyone else (Burawoy 1979; Shih 2004). One reason for this shift has been the introduction of managerial approaches modeled after those initially adopted in Japan. These systems create work teams structured so that each member of the group becomes a supervisor for everyone else, creating a collective peer pressure to work harder. This type of informal social control may be more powerful in extracting labor than the older top-down managerial systems that relied on supervisors "driving" workers, as workers who fail to keep up feel that they are letting everyone down, not just their supervisor.

Another aspect of contemporary work that leads to intensified effort is the need to do many things at once. Jobs in the new economy require workers to "wear many hats" and to have the capacity to "multitask." Time management and prioritization have become mantras of contemporary human resources departments, not just because workers have too little time but also because they have so many (different) things to do. In addition, workers who are expected to perform many tasks are less likely to find themselves with "downtime." Compounding the problem further is the blurring of work-family boundaries. For example, computers can open avenues for workers to labor while at home (e.g., respond to e-mails) and to connect with family while at work (Kreiner, Hollensbe, and Sheep 2009). At the same time, computers may make it more difficult to disengage from work roles. As anthropologist Charles Darrah (2006) observed, these time-strapped families do not "balance" work and family; their lives are endlessly busy.

Finally, contemporary workers are often pressured to labor with intensity because employers deliberately limit staffing levels to keep their companies "lean and mean." The result of these efforts to reengineer and downsize corporate workforces is a smaller number of workers carrying out more work. Resisting or protesting these pressures to intensify work is difficult or unlikely as they are often invisible. Consider, for example, that employers of certified nursing assistants deliberately employed fewer staff than were really needed, concealed that fact, and then pressured their employees to get the work done anyway (Clawson and Gerstel 2014). In the context of pervasive job insecurity, economic recession, and weakened union power, individual workers feel intense pressure to work hard, lest the axe fall on their necks next. A poignant example is offered by American air traffic controllers, whose union was shattered during Ronald Reagan's presidency and whose growing workload has been a subject of controversy ever since (Vaughan 2006). Whether these changes contributed to mishaps (such as controllers falling asleep on duty) is open to speculation.

These observations illuminate that the problem of overwork is not simply a concern of the number of hours spent on the job. Work in the new economy also is colonizing domains from which it was previously absent. Consider, for example, the extinction of the lunch hour, as well as the growing tendency to take work home on weekends, in the evenings, and along on vacations (or to forego vacations altogether). These behaviors were the exception in the 1950s; now they have become the norm. Workers find that entering careers requires earlier demonstration of significant accomplishments and larger preinvestments in training than was the case for the previous generation of workers. College faculty offer a useful case in point, as junior faculty are now expected to publish multiple articles while pursuing graduate degrees and then to jump higher bars for favorable tenure reviews than their colleagues who entered the profession in the 1970s. Nor is it only workers at the high end of the human capital spectrum who need to make precareer investments. A high school diploma used to be the requisite for a secretarial job, but those applying for administrative assistant positions today commonly compete with others who possess associate's and bachelor's degrees. And the drive to compete is extending downward through the life course, as evidenced by the intense pressure high school students experience to "stand out" among their peers. Even then, many of these students are finding that near-perfect performance provides no guarantee of access to the elite college programs that would have been a lock for high achievers of the previous generation (Rimer 2007).

Compared to the assessment of time spent working, measuring the extent to which work has intensified is a challenging endeavor. One approach is to consider the average hourly output of workers, which the Bureau of Labor Statistics reports have consistently advanced during the latter part of the twentieth century. Interpreting these types of data is complicated, however, because some of these increases can be attributed to technological and organizational advances. But even if this is the case, these innovations have not reduced the burden of work. If anything, they have increased the polarity between those who have steady work (and are intensifying their efforts) and those who do not (for whom not working is hardly "leisure"). Indeed, there is a deep irony in the fact that the technological and organizational transformations of work that increased productivity have not resulted in an expansion of leisure or an increase in wages.

How Much Should We Work? Comparative Frameworks

The question of how much work is the right amount of work focuses on five basic issues:

- How much work is necessary to meet needs?
- How much work do people actually want to perform?
- How have the standards for consumption and work commitment changed over time?
- How do these standards vary from one society to the next?
- What are the consequences of laboring greater or lesser amounts?

In considering the answers to these questions, it is immediately apparent that a universal work standard does not exist. What one person and her or his family might view as the right amount of work might be considered insufficient (or too much) for the next. Cultural values play a role in determining ideals, as do structural opportunities and the extent of needs that might exist. And as important, the amount of work an individual wants to perform changes as he or she progresses through the life course. Still, there are pretty clear indications that having too much work, or too little work, not only takes its toll on workers, their families also suffer as a result (Kleiner and Pavalko 2014). As we discuss shortly, calibrating the right amount of work is also a political question, as the need to labor is intrinsically tied to larger questions of how societies are designed to operate.

In the early days of industrialization, work hours were often quite long. In some cases, workers were required to put in twelve-hour days (or more) on a regular basis. Accurate historical statistics are hard to come by, but economic historians estimate that workweeks of sixty hours or more were typical in U.S. manufacturing in the latter part of the nineteenth century (Whaples 2010). Workers and their representatives responded to long workdays by pressing for reductions in work time. Many of the most famous confrontations in American labor history centered on the issue of the working day (including the famous Haymarket riot of 1886), and the effort to win a standard, eight-hour day became one of the most important rallying cries for American workers (J. Green 2006). Average work hours did decrease slowly in the early decades of the twentieth century, but it was not until the passage of the Fair Labor Standards Act in 1938 that the eight-hour day became the norm in the United States. Its passage underlined what had become a central assumption shared by many Americans—that as workers became more productive, it should be possible to reduce work hours without decreasing wages.

The hope that work hours would continue to decrease as productivity grew has not been realized. Americans continue to work close to forty hours per week, despite enormous productivity gains since the 1930s. Averages are informative, but equally important are statistics that document the diversity of work schedules within American society. According to the Bureau of Labor Statistics' Time Use Survey, during their workdays men spend on average eight hours and women spend seven hours laboring in their jobs, and the "average" worker labored thirty-eight hours per week. But as Exhibit 5.2 shows, fewer than one in two Americans worked the conventional full-time commitment of forty hours a week. One in five Americans worked fewer than thirty hours per week, and one in four worked more than full time. One startling fact is that nearly one in seven workers commits forty-nine or more hours a week to their jobs. This is the group considered by pop psychologists to be workaholic, people so addicted to their work that their jobs have become their primary focus in life, which in turn causes their personal lives to suffer (Machlowitz 1980). And it appears that professional and managerial workers, particularly men, often "choose" to work really long hours in the contemporary economy (Clawson and Gerstel 2014; Jacobs and Gerson 2004). However, many such workers also report that they would prefer to work fewer hours. Surveys show that a sizable proportion of the workforce (as many as one in five) would be willing to take a reduction in pay if it would enable them to work shorter hours (Golden 2005). When highly committed workers are asked why they work longer than their ideal, the most common reason they offer is that "my job requires it" (Moen and Sweet 2003). Ethnographic accounts of workers at the other extreme of the economic spectrum reveal that, for them, long hours often are not a choice or the result of an "addiction" to the pleasures of fulfilling work. People in poorly paid, working-class, and service jobs work long hours because it is the only way to make ends meet (Ehrenreich 2001). These statistics and qualitative information reveal that the study of work hours requires considering whether workers' jobs provide them with the hours of work they need, want, and/or are capable of performing.

The problem of overwork takes on a different and more significant meaning if we shift analysis from a focus on individual workers to household economies. Analysis of data from the Current Population Survey (CPS) reveals that men's average work hours have not changed much during the

Exhibit 5.2 Percentage of Workers According to Weekly Work Hours: United States, 2010

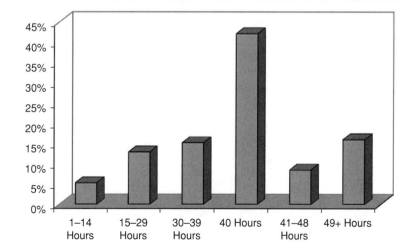

Source: U.S. Census Bureau.

past forty years. However, what has changed is the likelihood that there will be *two* paid workers in the family and that wives will be holding full-time jobs. Jacobs and Gerson (2004) reveal in *The Time Divide* that the single biggest explanation for the expansion of work hours is the increasing prevalence of dual-earner couples. As such, the most common work family arrangement is to have two workers performing three jobs (two at work and one at home). In 1975, the average wife worked only 704 hours (thirteen hours per week), but by 2009, these hours had nearly doubled.[2] The increase in women's paid employment was not associated with a decline in men's work hours, which also increased slightly during this period. As a result, in comparison with 1970, the "average" couple now puts nearly ten more hours into paid work each week. During this same period, there was little change in the total time spent on "home work," which in the 1980s (twenty-seven hours) remained approximately the same as in 1965 (twenty-four hours). As a result, considerable strains are created by dual-earner work arrangements, which often pit work commitments against family obligations, leaving workers—especially working mothers—stressed and exhausted (Hochschild 1989; Moen and Roehling 2005; Pitt-Catsouphes, Kossek, and Sweet 2006).

Another means of gauging American overwork is to examine how much time is spent working in other countries. Comparisons reveal that people in only a few countries labor as many hours as workers do in the United States. Exhibit 5.3 shows that Americans work, on average, fifty-three hours more per year than Japanese workers (roughly one and a half extra weeks), 119 hours more than British workers (roughly three extra weeks), 299 hours more than French workers (roughly seven extra weeks), and 408 hours more than workers in the Netherlands (roughly ten extra weeks). Although Mexico, Greece, and Poland all report higher average work hours than the United States, women in these countries are less likely to be in the labor force. They are also more likely to exit the labor force into retirement at younger ages (Sweet 2009). Thus, the United States is exceptional in the amount of time its population devotes to work.

In comparison with most other countries, the United States is unusual in its lack of policies to limit the extent to which employers can overwork their employees. Two in three countries in the world have established laws to regulate the maximum number of hours employees can be expected to work (most commonly from forty-eight to sixty hours per week). Employees in most countries have a right to rest breaks, which in some countries are taken collectively, thus enabling nearly the entire society to pause from work. In the United States, no such laws exist at the federal level. In fact, laws and corporate cultures in the United States reinforce the *employer's* right to demand that workers engage in overtime work, even when that work directly conflicts with family needs (Wolkinson and Ormiston 2006).

Exhibit 5.3   Average Annual Work Hours: International Comparisons, 2013

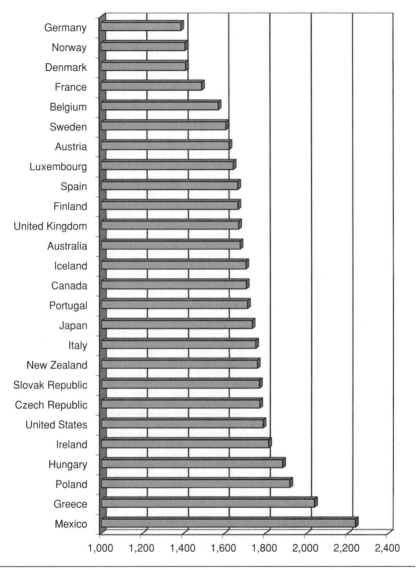

Source: Organization for Economic Co-operation and Development.

The United States has fewer public holidays than most other developed countries and has no law guaranteeing its workers a right to vacations (McCann 2005). Exhibit 5.4 reveals that most European nations mandate that employers give workers four to six weeks of paid vacation a year, with an additional one to two weeks of paid holiday leave. In contrast, the typical full-time worker in the United States, though not entitled by law, gets about two weeks of vacation per year. Unionized employees receive more vacation, but with declining numbers of employees covered by collective bargaining agreements, the ability to secure vacation time has eroded (Mischel, Bernstein, and Allegretto 2005). Additionally, American workers fail to use all of their vacation time, or take work with them on vacation, for fear that they will fall behind in their jobs or careers.

Of note, Americans and Europeans took similar amounts of vacation in the 1930s, 1940s, and early 1950s. The subsequent divergence occurred because of different approaches to implementing vacation policy. In the United States, vacation leave was introduced in the 1930s and 1940s by employers, who regarded it as a means of increasing productivity by increasing employee satisfaction and health. It also was included in collective bargaining agreements, which expanded the amount of vacation time available to union workers. By contrast, most European countries introduced vacation time as part of

Exhibit 5.4   Annual Paid Vacation Days and Paid Holidays: International Comparisons

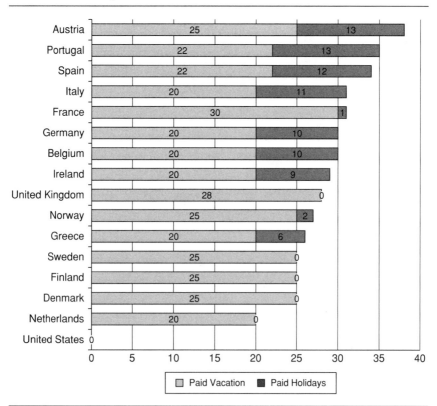

Source: Center for Economic Policy Research (2013).

government policy, along with a host of other entitlements such as universal health care and job protections. Because of this, vacations are available to all workers in these countries, not just workers who have jobs that offer benefits or those protected by union contracts. If similar mandatory vacation laws were enacted in the United States, American workers would be laboring closer to the number of hours worked by Europeans (Altonji and Oldham 2003).[3]

In sum, many workers in the United States are laboring long hours and families are working more than they did a few decades ago. They work more than workers in other developed nations and often more than they want to. It is also important to recognize, however, that many American workers lack jobs or would like to work more (or more steadily) than they currently do but have trouble finding enough work (Lambert 2009). Some part-time workers voluntarily work reduced schedules, but the number of involuntary part-time workers has been growing. According to the Bureau of Labor Statistics, in 2014, one in four (25%) part-time workers was working part time involuntarily, meaning that they could not find full-time work because of either slack work conditions or because a part-time job was all that they could find. These contrasting situations of overwork and underwork are a consequence of a divided economy, one in which there is a work-rich labor force that labors long hours and a work-poor labor force that lacks sufficient work opportunities and compensation. Arrangements that compel some workers to perform the jobs of two workers (a product of both the number of hours and the intensity of work) block the creation of opportunities that could lead to employment for all. The problems of overwork and underemployment, therefore, need to be viewed as two sides of the same coin (Rifkin 2004).

Finally, it is also important to remember that the reconfiguration of work demands is affecting developing societies as well. In factories in China, and in the maquiladoras that line the Mexican border with the United States, workers commonly labor twelve-hour days throughout the entire week. As factory work has expanded in these industrializing regions, rural migrants find themselves subject to the rigid, clock-driven rhythms of time-oriented labor. Although these labor practices make it possible for Americans to purchase inexpensive commodities for use in their scarce leisure time, they are a burden placed on other workers. It is hard not to conclude that the new economy, in both its domestic operations and global operations, is compelling workers to labor more, not less, and is expanding the chasms that separate workers from the opportunity to have a life off the job.

Why Are Americans Working So Much?

A variety of factors contribute to Americans working longer hours than workers in most other countries, but chief among these is economic need.

For those workers at the bottom of the opportunity divide, working long hours is a means of making ends meet. Consider the fact that the 2015 federal minimum wage rate was $7.25 per hour, a rate of pay that has been unchanged since 2009. The purchasing power of the current minimum wage is well below what it was at its peak in the late 1960s. A full-time minimum wage weekly paycheck of $290 is barely sufficient to provide for individual needs, let alone enable a worker to raise a family. So some workers work multiple jobs or willingly work beyond the forty-hour norm. It is also important to recognize that many minimum wage workers are employed as part-time workers but work for multiple employers, thus putting in full-time (or often greater than full-time) commitments with no prospects for overtime pay. Economic considerations also contribute to overwork among individuals who hold managerial and professional jobs. Such workers often have considerable control over their work schedules, for example, they can take an afternoon off or come in early or stay late without much difficulty. However, as one observer has noted, such workers often have achieved control over *when* they work but not over how long (Lopez 2006). For these workers, career considerations or the threat of job loss are typically the factors motivating them to work long hours. Workers in such jobs fear that resisting pressures to work long hours will be interpreted as a lack of commitment, hurt their chances for promotion, or mark them as expendable when cuts are to be made. Workers in comparatively good jobs also face conditions of wage stagnation and declining benefits. For example, thirty years ago, the types of jobs that many managers hold would have included defined pension plans, meaning that their retirement income was secured based on how long they worked for their employer. Today, workers in these same types of jobs have contribution plans, in which their own contributions to retirement accounts matter. These workers are laboring not only to meet the needs of their weekly budgets but also to secure a bankroll to secure well-being in retirement, saving money into accounts that their employers are less invested in maintaining (Kalleberg 2013).

Workers often lack control over their work schedules. When workers have this control, they sometimes use it to limit work hours. Such is the case for registered nurses, who are not easily replaced and who are in high demand (Clawson and Gerstel 2014). Few other occupations enjoy such a privileged labor market position, so workers who want to limit their hours are unable to do so. Indeed, the structure of employment and limited social supports in the United States provide workers with comparatively little leverage to control their work schedules, so when Americans want to work less, they have a lesser capacity to do so than workers in some other industrialized societies (Lyness et al. 2012).

American workplace cultures also play an important role in pressuring workers to labor long hours. One of the most important studies to reveal this dynamic is Arlie Hochschild's (1997) *The Time Bind*. This book examined the work and family lives of professionals employed at "Amerco," a company that offered numerous family friendly programs, including options for reduced hours and family leave. To her surprise, Hochschild observed that even when Amerco introduced family responsive policies, few workers used them. This raises an interesting question: if some American workers have access to leaves of absence or reduced hours, why do they not take greater advantage of existing opportunities to work less? The answer can be found in organizational cultures that encourage Americans to see long hours of work as evidence of personal competency and the stigma that is associated with use of flexible work options (Blair-Loy 2003; Munsch, Ridgeway, and Williams 2014; Shih 2004). Workers who occupy "good jobs" in the new economy labor with peers and supervisors who distribute badges of honor to those who can put in long hours and stigmatize those who do not. In companies like Amerco, workers who failed to put in long hours were viewed by their coworkers and supervisors as "nonplayers" who lack the qualities needed to move up the corporate ladder. The prospect of falling off the career track kept many working longer than they wanted, but others recognized that a choice to scale back could reduce their jobs to the least interesting and rewarding tasks (Barnett and Gareis 2000a).

The Time Bind also offered a radical new interpretation that inverted the "home is a haven in a heartless world" thesis, concluding that many workers in the new economy find their lives enhanced in the workplace, rather than in the family. One of the subjects in the study explained why she gladly puts in overtime:

> I walk in the door and the minute I turn the key in the lock my older daughter is there. Granted, she needs somebody to talk to about her day. . . . The baby is still up. She should have been in bed two hours ago and that upsets me. The dishes are piled high in the sink. My daughter comes right up to the door and complains about anything her stepfather said or did, and she wants to talk about her job. My husband is in the other room hollering to my daughter "Tracy, I don't ever get any time to talk to your mother, because you're always monopolizing her time before I even get a chance!" They all come at me at once. (Hochschild 1997, 37)

In contrast to the romantic ideals of family life, *The Time Bind* argued that time-strapped Amerco workers experienced home lives of whining children, nagging spouses, and an unending backlog of onerous household chores. By contrast, their jobs offered friendly coworkers, concrete rewards, and interesting tasks, leading workers to *prefer* to be in the office rather than in the home.

Hochschild's thesis that the rewards of work now surpass those derived from family has been criticized for overstating the degree to which American workers are *voluntarily* choosing work over home. Even some of her own interview subjects indicated that they worked long hours because they *had* to (Meiksins 1998). It is also important to remember that the type of worker studied at Amerco tended to be from the creative class, representing the values and perspectives of workers whose jobs offered numerous intrinsic and financial rewards (Florida 2002). The lives of these employees stand in stark contrast to the legions of workers, such as maids, fast-food workers, or retail clerks, who labor in backbreaking jobs or in hostile work environments. Even within its analysis of the creative class, the Amerco study failed to consider other professional workers who engage in creative work but who are exploited by new organizational structures. For example, colleges and universities employ increasing numbers of part-time adjunct faculty, who commonly work long hours, often at multiple jobs, for a fraction of the pay commanded by their full-time counterparts. Still, some lower-skilled occupations conform to the time-bind thesis. Such is the case of nursing assistants, who find work preferable to home life, contrasting their difficult lives as parents with limited resources to the fulfilling, long-term relationships they developed with the patients for whom they cared (Clawson and Gerstel 2014). Another study, this time of British employees in the construction industry, reminds us that many workers labor long hours not simply because they have to but also because they want to and truly enjoy working (Sturges 2013). It is fair to say that *The Time Bind* drew attention to two crucial aspects of contemporary American life: the difficulties of home life in families where both parents work and the fact that many workplaces offer real rewards to workers willing to put in long hours.

Long hours in the workplace offer opportunities to earn badges of honor for American workers, but this cultural orientation to work is less common in Europe. For example, Americans take pride in broadcasting their heavy schedules to coworkers to increase their status. In contrast, when German workers put in long hours, their colleagues view them as inefficient and wonder what is slowing them down. Thus, cultural differences may account for some of the disparities between American workers and European workers. But there are structural reasons as well. While Americans have been increasing their work hours, European nations have experimented with shorter workweeks. Most notably, during the 1990s, the French government passed legislation discouraging French companies from employing workers beyond thirty-five hours a week (Fagnani and Letablier 2004). This legislation reflected a desire to reduce the problem of overwork, to translate productivity gains into increased leisure, and to spread the available work around to all members of the society.

What are the consequences of legislating shorter work hours? Many European employers (and some European governments) fear that overall economic productivity and competitiveness is being harmed. Voices have been heard in many European countries (notably in Germany and France) calling for a relaxation of limits on the workweek and a move to a more American-style approach to employment, but this is not favored by organized labor or most workers. In 2008, arguing that French employment law was hobbling French business, the more conservative government headed by Nicholas Sarkozy passed changes significantly weakening the thirty-five-hour rule and allowing longer workweeks for many workers. Nevertheless, the thirty-five-hour week remains the reference point for French workers and remains very popular; French workers who labor beyond thirty-five hours are still entitled to extra pay beyond their normal hourly wage (Bennhold 2008). Elsewhere, counterarguments and proposals have been made, and there has been an effort to "standardize" work hours across Europe by establishing a forty-eight-hour ceiling for how many hours a worker can be required to work per week in European Union countries. This would force some countries, such as Great Britain (which thus far has opted out), to alter their current practices. The controversy continues, and, so far, European work hours appear to be continuing their gradual decline, indicating that the U.S.–Europe gap in work hours is unlikely to disappear (European Foundation for the Improvement of Living and Working Conditions 2011; Meiksins and Whalley 2004).

Another reason for overwork in the United States is that Americans face greater penalties than Europeans if they choose to reduce their work hours. For example, most working families in the United States secure medical care as a benefit from working a full-time job. In contrast, citizens of many European countries can cut back on work, or exit the labor force entirely, and still retain access to medical care (Meiksins and Whalley 2004). Similarly, most other developed nations have invested in extensive public transportation systems, infrastructures that afford residents the option not to purchase automobiles. In contrast, the minimal public transportation infrastructure in the United States builds in an expectation that Americans purchase cars and pay for their upkeep.[4] Consider, too, the impact of educational funding in the United States, where the system ties school quality to local property values. This system entrenches social inequalities and propels economic competition to purchase property in desired school districts (Kozol 2006).

Finally, overwork is structured into the American system of allocating jobs. To understand how this happened, we need to go back to the Great Depression, an era in American history remembered as the time when many citizens lacked jobs. Less commonly recognized is that during the Great Depression, those who did have jobs commonly worked very long hours. To resolve this dilemma, the Roosevelt administration introduced overtime provisions as part of the Fair Labor Standards Act (FLSA). This law introduced a financial penalty for overworking employees, requiring employers to pay time-and-a-half for each additional hour worked beyond forty hours per week. This legislation helped redistribute work opportunities from those laboring too many hours to those not working at all (Costa 2000). But because of the high costs of health insurance and other employer-sponsored benefits, it is now far less expensive to expect a smaller number of full-time employees to work overtime than to hire a larger number of workers to work forty-hour weeks or less. These expenses also increase incentives to create part-time or temporary jobs that are not eligible for benefits. When employers face pressures to increase production, they tend to do so by asking their current workforce to labor more or by hiring workers to whom they do not have to pay benefits.

The FLSA defined two classes of workers: hourly workers who are entitled to overtime pay and "exempt" salaried workers (most commonly employed in managerial or professional jobs) whose work hours are not regulated. These exempt employees are among the most time-strapped in the new economy, having experienced an incremental expansion in job expectations during the past century. As Jacobs and Gerson (2004) note in *The Time Divide*, the exemption of some workers from overtime rights has increased the incentives to overwork salaried employees and to push more workers into jobs designed to have fewer protections. One illustration of this process can be found in the ways job boundaries can be blurred in the new economy. Such is the case for "team leaders" on production crews—workers who are primarily engaged in production work but who also have some supervisory responsibilities. How should these employees be classified—as hourly workers with rights to overtime pay or as salaried workers who have no such rights? In 2004, the Bush administration passed legislation that excluded some hourly workers who performed supervisory work, as well as those achieving higher incomes, from overtime eligibility. The Economic Policy Institute estimated that this simple act of redefinition, which redrew the boundaries of exemption from the FLSA, resulted in 8 million fewer workers being entitled to overtime pay. It also created incentives for employers to shift hourly workers into salaried "management" positions that, in reality, have few managerial responsibilities. What changed were not the day-to-day tasks but rather, the right to extra compensation when laboring beyond the forty-hour threshold (Eisenbrey and Bernstein 2003).

In sum, why are Americans working so long and hard? Part of the answer rests in economic need—reasonable hours for those at the bottom do not provide a livable income, and reasonable hours for those in the fragile middle do not secure a stable career. Other answers can be found in an American culture that praises those who overwork, as well as policies that fail to discourage overworking employees. And some of the reason can be attributed to agency—some Americans genuinely want to put in long hours. It is also clear that there are significant penalties for not working according to schedules that are oftentimes imposed on workers with scant consideration of demands in workers' lives off the job. For low-wage workers, the problem is finding enough work. These workers understand that if they do not show up and work according to a schedule that has been posted with little advance notification, they may find themselves without work the following week (Lambert, Haley-Lock, and Henly 2012). Developing mechanisms that enable workers to exert control over their schedules is an element needed to make the new economy operate to its fullest potential.

Nonstandard Schedules: Jobs in a 24/7 Economy

The old Dolly Parton song "9 to 5"—the theme for the film of the same name—included the exasperated statement, "What a way to make a living." Though many working women (and men) still labor in the traditional forty-hour-a-week grind, they compose a far smaller proportion of the workforce. Workers in the new economy adhere to a diversity of schedules, including part time, split shifts, full time, and overtime. Fewer work by the hour and more are employed by the contract or in salaried positions that demand fifty to seventy hours of labor per week (or more). Workers labor during the day but also in the evening, at night, and on the weekend. Some clock in and out of their jobs, but other employees are placed "on call" and can be summoned to work at a moment's notice. While some workers still labor according to traditional schedules, more are demanding flexible arrangements. For still others, flexible schedules are designed by employers to meet their own needs.

The reorganization of work, allowing it to be performed around the clock, and just in time, is one of the contours of work in the new economy. Of course, working outside of "standard" hours is not an entirely new phenomenon. Even in the old economy, certain kinds of workers could expect to work nonstandard schedules. Industrial workers, in particular, typically worked "shifts," and those shifts might involve early morning starts or late ending times, or might even involve night shifts, especially when production was booming and a third shift was laid on. Similarly, safety workers such as police officers or firefighters often worked nights, and employees in the limited numbers of businesses that were open at night (e.g., restaurants and entertainment venues) worked unusual hours. Still, until recent decades most stores and businesses were closed in the evenings and on Sundays, and the 9-to-5 schedule was perceived as the norm for workers outside manufacturing (and day shifts were the norm even for industrial workers).

The new economy has made the idea of a "standard" workday or week problematic. The new economy operates with no week "ends." It continues twenty-four hours a day, seven days a week. In the United States, no Sabbath, blue Sunday, or holiday compels workers to take a break. Notice, for example, how some stores proudly announce that they are open "24 hours a day, 365 days a year." Increasingly, some workers find they are being told that they must work on national holidays, such as Thanksgiving, New Year's Day, or (ironically) Labor Day. As the demand for workers to fill jobs around the clock increases, so too do the challenges faced by working families. The elaborate family schedules (typically posted in kitchens) that reconcile conflicting obligations of working parents and children attest to the complexities of melding work and family schedules. Just as the Industrial Revolution forced the culture to adjust to new rhythms, the emergence of a 24/7 economy is creating profound changes in work and family lives, as well as in other institutional arrangements. This presents new opportunities for working in new ways but also new challenges in adjusting lives to nonstandard work schedules.

Exhibit 5.5 illustrates one means of capturing the extent to which nonstandard work schedules are common in the new economy. While it is true that the daytime schedule is the time when most workers are laboring, note that at 6:00 a.m., one in seven workers are at their jobs, and the same is true at 7:00 p.m. When the number of work hours and the timing at which work occurs are taken into account, fewer than one in two employees (40%) works a standard day shift approximating the notion of a 9-to-5 full-time job, and younger workers and women are among the most likely to work nonstandard shifts (Presser 2003a). Note also that nonstandard hours are common in the service sector, so that as the economy continues to shift to expand service jobs, work temporalities will continue to shift as well.

Part of the reason for the expansion of nonstandard scheduling is the emergence of new markets. For instance, evenings and weekends present lucrative opportunities for retailers to increase sales. The same is true for employers in the fast-food industry, which in the 1980s expanded business hours to enable the introduction of breakfast menus. The importance of offering shopping hours at nonstandard times has grown with the increasing

Exhibit 5.5   Percentage of Employed Persons Working on Their Main Job at Different Hours of the Day and Night: 2005–2009

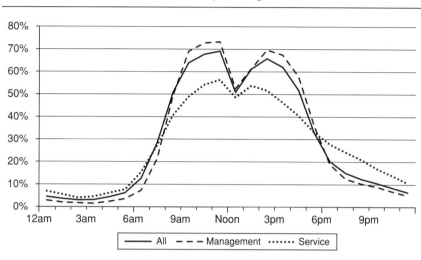

Source: Bureau of Labor Statistics, American Time Use Survey, 2005–2009.

prevalence of dual-earner couples. Few families can function if stores and other businesses are open only between 9 and 5, and many time-strapped families rely on restaurants and other commercial outlets for services they once performed themselves. Many of the jobs created by the expansion of work time beyond 9 to 5 are part-time jobs, as evidenced by the fact that part-time workers have been found to be most likely to work nonstandard shifts outside core daytime hours (Beers 2000).

New managerial practices and philosophies also increase pressure on manufacturers to extend work into the nights and weekends, thus contributing to the creation of nonstandard schedules. Flexible production methods discourage employers from keeping a large stock of component parts ready for assembly, instead favoring the just-in-time approach, in which parts are manufactured (and often received) close to the time at which they will be needed. But producing goods "just in time" requires the creation of demanding production schedules that may operate into the evenings and weekends. In the wake of expanded markets and reconfigured production methods, distribution companies such as UPS have expanded their operations, employing legions of workers to labor throughout the night processing packages, enabling a lobster caught in Nova Scotia to be transported live to a restaurant in Kansas (McPhee 2005).

Why do people work nonstandard shifts? One reason is linked to the desire for part-time work. For example, students who need to work before or after school or workers who are trying to work more than one job may find nonstandard shifts a useful expedient. But part of the answer also can be found in job markets and the types of opportunities available to workers. For those in the lower classes, for whom well-paid work is more difficult to find, the need to find any work can require bending one's schedule to fit the needs of employers. Survey data indicate that the most common reasons for working odd hours are that they are built into job definitions and that opportunities to work regular shifts are not available. Employers seek flexibility in scheduling and have long tried to find ways to link employment levels to fluctuations in the demand for staffing (having more workers at busy times, fewer when things are quiet). New technologies have made this easier. Scheduling software enables employers to develop a more precise picture of when staff are needed and to design shifts that match, rather than employing people for a standard eight-hour shift. This software can operate as a two-edged sword. On the one hand, it can enable workers to bid on shifts that they prefer and advance flexibility. On the other hand, it can expand the likelihood that schedules become less predictable and more variable (Bailyn, Collins, and Song 2007; Schneider 2015).

The next most common reason offered for working nonstandard shifts—and this is more often the case for women—is that nonstandard job schedules offer greater opportunity to manage personal or family needs, such as helping with child care or enabling workers to continue their education (Presser 2003a). It is not unusual for spouses to engage in a tag-team strategy of managing family—as one spouse returns from work to home, the other spouse leaves the home to go to work. This adaptive strategy of "off-shifting" can facilitate the capacity of parents to provide hands-on care to children (Pagnan, Lero, and MacDermid Wadsworth 2011). However, it comes at a cost, as spouses' lives are reduced to short intervals of contact based largely on task transference ("I did this, now you do that") and increase the absence of rituals such as the collectively experienced evening dinner (Ochs et al. 2006). An award-winning study revealed that recently married couples with young children who adopted alternating schedules were *six times more likely to get divorced* than were similar couples who worked regular schedules (Presser 2000).

Finally, it is important to note that some workers are "always on," meaning that their jobs require them to be available at a moment's notice. An obvious example of this might be physicians who set up practices in rural communities or those with specialization such as neonatal care. However, many self-employed workers also experience difficulties in "clocking out" and face challenges in disengaging from jobs. These workers view balance as something that might be unattainable (Hilbrecht and Lero 2014). So while many jobs offer the prospect of setting boundaries that can be constructed according to the clock, some types of employment are not so easily confined.

How Americans Deal With Overwork

Having a good job is often accompanied by the expectation that one will labor long hours, uninterrupted, year in and year out. Those who hold bad jobs, many of which are located in the expanding service sector, need to labor extremely long hours to afford even a scaled-down version of the American dream. Forgoing work comes at great costs, and many American workers face a stark choice: accept long hours as a way of life or choose to work shorter hours for considerably less compensation or fall off the career track. As a result, the most common response of workers is not to challenge employers or government leaders to change workplace policy and instead bend their lives to fit within existing structures (Moen and Roehling 2005).

Younger, childless workers are more apt to be willing to put in long hours, whereas those later in the life course, who have caretaking responsibilities, or whose health may be failing, experience greater difficulty adjusting their lives to fit the expectations of employers. Notable is that most young men and women do not plan to make radical changes in their work hours following the birth of a child. But after trying to "have it all," many find the demands of work and family too overwhelming to manage. Faced with mounting pressure, the most common response is to fall back on gender roles developed in the old economy (Becker and Moen 1999; Stone 2007).

Exhibit 5.6   Work Hour Arrangements of American Middle-Class Dual-Earner Couples

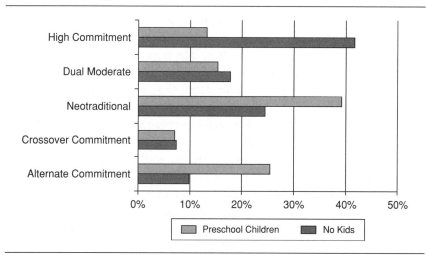

Source: Adapted from Moen and Sweet (2003).

One way of capturing this dynamic is by studying the different schedules dual-earner couples adopt before, and after, they have children. Exhibit 5.6 shows the work hour arrangements adopted by two groups of dual-earner couples, those who are younger nonparents (dual incomes, no children) and those who have a young child. Five work hour arrangements are identified:

- High-commitment couples (both spouses working long hours—more than forty-five hours a week)
- Dual moderate couples (both working full time—thirty-five to forty-five hours a week)
- Neotraditionalists (husband working long hours but the wife not)
- Crossover-commitment couples (wife working long hours but the husband not)
- Alternate-commitment couples (neither working long hours and one working reduced hours)

Notice that in the new economy, the high-commitment arrangement (with both partners working long hours) is the most commonly adopted schedule for young nonparents. In contrast, the most common strategy for couples who have preschool-age children is to adopt either a neotraditional arrangement (the wife scaling back her work commitments) or for both partners to work less than long hours. This arrangement remains largely the same until children mature and leave the household (Moen and Sweet 2003). Most Americans espouse (at least in words) fairly egalitarian attitudes regarding women's and men's opportunities, believing that all members of society should have the same options and equitable rewards. Exhibit 5.6 reveals gendered responses to time strains. When faced with a deficit of time available for care work, families tend to revert to the patterns laid out in the old economy, normative arrangements that push women into the home and men into the workplace. The result is the perpetuation of gendered opportunity structures, arrangements in which men have careers while sacrificing family time, and women sacrifice careers for the rewards of family. It's interesting that this tendency to respond to time deficits by retreating into traditional gender roles is most pronounced for salaried professional and managers. Census data reveal that men's overwork increases the likelihood that their female partners will drop out of the labor force, while the reverse is *not* true for women's overwork. However, when the data are examined more carefully, they reveal that the effect of gender is limited to professional women—this is a result *both* of their partners' earning power and of cultural attitudes to professional mothers (who are judged harshly for working long hours and excused, if they quit, for making a wise choice in managing work/family conflict) (Cha 2010).

The consequences of time strains are resonating in a variety of other ways that map onto life quality. Nearly half (43%) of all workers feel that they do not get enough sleep, and most workers do not feel highly successful at "balancing" work and family (Moen, Waismel-Manor, and Sweet 2003).[5] Faced with the choice of "making a career" or "making a family," Americans are now having fewer children, having children later in life, or sometimes even giving up on family altogether (Altucher and Williams 2003; Farnesworth-Riche 2006). Consider the startling fact that women now have their first child nearly four years later than they did half a century ago. More women are opting not to have children at all; according to Current Population Survey data, in 1975, only one in ten (10%) women aged forty to forty-four had never had a child, but by 2010, this figure had risen to nearly one in five women (19%). Families that do have children are increasingly obliged to make use of child care providers (e.g., professional caregivers, neighbors, relatives), even though they are often reluctant to do so. Job demands appear to be having a profound impact both on the shape of family lives and on the prospects of forming families in the first place.

Some workers are demanding changes, requesting that their employers reconfigure work arrangements to accommodate personal needs. Technological innovations and the rise of service work have made it possible for many jobs to be performed in settings outside the workplace (e.g., the home, in transit) and at a variety of times. These changes open the prospects for **flextime** and **flexplace** schedules that enable workers to labor at home, to negotiate the number of hours expected, to refashion the starting and ending times of work as well as break lengths, and to create opportunities to bank time. Advocates of flexible work arrangements point to the fact that flexibility does not necessarily involve reducing how many hours jobs are expected to take but does require expanding the amount of control workers have in setting schedules that match their needs off the job. They emphasize shifting a focus from the amount of time spent working to measures of actual productivity.

As discussed in Chapter 2, the extent to which flexible work arrangements are available to workers remains limited and uneven. Some workers, particularly those with scarce skills, have been able to arrange reduced work schedules without suffering the severe economic and career penalties usually linked to part-time work. Although flexibility offers new opportunities to bridge work and family more effectively, new work arrangements also can create new concerns for working families, especially in respect to establishing boundaries that enable one to disengage from work. Some workers have found that options to work into the evening or at home create new portals through which work can intrude into leisure time and domestic life (Kreiner,

Hollensbe, and Sheep 2009). However, this may not be the most common outcome, as other studies show that when workers have greater control in determining how and when their work will be performed, it reduces work-family conflict and enhances healthful behaviors such as exercising and sleep (Moen et al. 2011). What may matter most is creating job designs such that workers are able to position their jobs to match their own work-life style (Kossek and Lautsch 2012). These arrangements must be two-way streets, however, as employers expect to receive a fair return on their investment in individual workers. The reality is that few employers have actually crossed a crucial divide: from making limited sets of accommodations allocated on a case-by-case basis to integrating flexibility as a normal way of working (Kossek, Lewis, and Hammer 2010).

When jobs are rigid or demanding, families are forced to be flexible and to sacrifice. Some families adapt by doing without, such as by having fewer children, or by changing the ways in which affection is delivered, such as by purchasing readymade items rather than engaging in more time-consuming hands-on affection (Pugh 2009). Under the pressures of time strain, over-worked individuals also develop strategies of laying out blocks of time to compartmentalize work and family commitments or of shifting their lives around, for example, by rising before dawn (Moen et al. 2013). Many families also place an increased emphasis on efficiency, which can be achieved by purchasing prepackaged goods as well as by multitasking. However, growing evidence points to the deleterious consequences of hectic lives and their impact on emotions, stress, distress, and work-family conflict (Offer and Schneider 2011). In a word, the way many families respond to overwork is by suffering.

Conclusion

In the new economy, honor is commonly bestowed on those employees whose cars are the first ones in the parking lots and the last ones out. Those who cannot keep up with escalating job demands, or meet the higher requirements to get jobs in the first place, are forced to the margins into jobs that offer limited rewards and opportunities. For the growing number of salaried workers, there is no cap on the number of hours that employers can demand or limits on the expectations of what it takes to keep a job.

Even though organizational and technological innovations have opened up possibilities to liberate work (such as through the use of flexible arrange-ments), they are being implemented in a culture that still equates productivity with time spent at work and that fails to prevent overwork. As a result, requests for shorter hours, or failures to put in "face time," usually come with career penalties. As American culture has embraced overwork as a virtue, the new economy has unleashed new sets of pressures (largely unchecked) to labor longer hours with intensified effort. This in turn has helped to create work poverty, limiting the availability of jobs for others who want them. And the problem is not just too many hours, or too few hours, it is when those hours are to be committed. Growing evidence suggests that a key element to the solution is to be found in control—the extent that workers themselves are able to determine when and where work is to be performed. By escalating control, workers are better able to position jobs fit within the contours of their lives (Kelly et al. 2014). And it is important to note that workers do not only seek flexible work options to help them perform their family roles; they do so to enhance their job performance as well (Shockley and Allen 2012).

For workers at the bottom of the opportunity structures in the new economy, schedules and wages intertwine in problematic ways. Current minimum wage standards, for example, do not require employers to structure work schedules in a manner that enables employees to make a living; the standards require only that employers pay a (woefully insufficient) base hourly wage. Even the more ambitious efforts to ensure a living wage (estimated at roughly $11 an hour in most locales) assume that workers who receive this wage would have the ability to work full time. Little public discussion has been directed to the need to provide adequate compensation and supports to those who need to work less. Many workers—such as single parents—cannot maintain full-time schedules and perform their family responsibilities outside the workplace. Moreover, living wages are, in almost every instance, calculated on the basis of day-to-day needs, leaving long-term needs such as paying for college tuition or saving money for retirement unaddressed. Nor are the problems of the many Americans who lack sufficient, steady work being addressed adequately. Finally, while flexible work options show promise for helping workers who have too much work, for many low-income workers the problem is securing sufficient work. In those circumstances, flexible work arrangements can undermine their capacity to maintain predictable levels of work that match their needs (Lambert, Haley-Lock, and Henly 2012).

Resolving these issues requires tackling—head on—the institutionalized practices that push some workers to labor beyond their capacity and prevent others from contributing up to their capacity. It also requires countering cultural values that keep Americans from putting work in its place. In some respects, contemporary workers are facing as profound a transformation in the developing new economy as their counterparts did during the Industrial

Revolution. Rethinking the concept of a fair day's work—how much, how hard, and how long employees should be expected to work for their compensation—needs to be front and center in a national dialogue on ways to refashion the new economy.

Notes

1. Before becoming an academic, one of the authors of this book was a professional carpenter and worked for a company that required him to haul tools from the equipment shed and make them operational before he could "clock in" and wrap up equipment after he "clocked out." This added more than a half an hour of uncompensated labor to each day.

2. When the Current Population Survey calculates average work hours, it excludes those who are not in the labor force, which can create an impression of more time spent pursuing paid labor than actually occurs. The estimates reported in Exhibit 5.3 include working-age adults who are out of the labor force and who are categorized as working zero hours. This reduces the estimated number of hours worked but enables us to reveal the remarkable changes in the average working hours created by women's entry into the paid labor force.

3. Long vacations, however, can create their own problems. Such was the case when a heat wave enveloped Europe in 2003. Because the French customarily take holidays during the summer months, elderly citizens had scarce access to health services, resulting in high mortality.

4. One in three motor vehicles in the world is located in the United States, and the U.S. vehicle-to-person ratio is nearly double that of countries in Western Europe (Freund and Martin 2000).

5. Authors' analysis of the Ecology of Careers Study. Data represent a sample of middle-class, dual-earner couples.

Chapter Six

Gender Chasms in the New Economy

Today, the number of American women participating in the labor force approximately equals the number of men, and women's contribution to family finances is critical for household economic stability. Yet gender remains a significant force in shaping the contours of opportunity in the new economy. It affects aspirations, shapes access to jobs, influences the compensation received, sways relations with coworkers, affects opportunities for promotion, and complicates labor force attachment. When viewed from a global perspective, gender has a greater impact on life chances than any other characteristic attributed to individuals (Fuchs-Epstein 2007). While *sex* and *gender* are commonly treated as synonymous, it is important to recognize that in the world of work, gender is not something that is simply possessed, it is something people do to each other (West and Zimmerman 1987). Gender creates the expectation that women and men will be capable of different things, and conflating gender with biological sex makes it seem "natural" to divide labor along gender lines. Throughout this chapter we call this assumption into question. Furthermore, we suggest that as gender chasms in labor markets and at work subordinate women in terms of both power and resources, men lose out as well.

To illustrate these complex processes, in this chapter we consider why women and men gravitate to different types of occupations and how gender intersects with the capacity to perform work inside and outside of the home. We argue that the new economy has expanded and diversified employment opportunities for both women and men but also that enduring forces continue to segregate workers on the basis of gender and impose hurdles that block mobility. Some of the chasms that separate men and women in the workplace can be attributed to the choices people make concerning what careers to pursue and where to concentrate their energy. But these gaps also are established by differential treatment on the job and by the various ways workers are subject to discrimination. Some inequalities are the product of interpersonal dynamics, but others result from job designs, as well as the value placed on different types of work.

While equity is a major reason to consider gender inequality, we also ask readers to consider a related problem—how work in the paid labor force affects the capacity to provide care. In a society where most adults are expected to work outside the home, developing new means to support the young, the old, and the disabled has become a pressing policy concern. For example, recall in Chapter 1 the brief discussion of Meg (the trader), who had to make some difficult choices between her job and her family. Her experiences reflect those of the baby boom generation. On the one hand, Meg's story is one of liberation, because she successfully entered into a career that had been largely sex segregated in the old economy. On the other hand, Meg's family demands ultimately dislodged her career, in part because she had to make a choice to either be "all in" or not in at all. Throughout this chapter, we reflect on the need to support work performed both inside and outside of the home and identify how disconnects between the demands of the workplace and those of the home differentially impact women's careers and undermine families.

When Did Home Work Become Nonwork?

Our friend Erika is a stay-at-home mother who left her job to support her husband's career and raise their two young children. While Kevin is at work in his research lab at a prestigious university—a job that requires long hours and frequent travel—Erika manages the home front—tending to scraped knees, arranging play dates, and doing all the other things that keep their family integrated into their community. For his efforts, Kevin receives accolades, retirement benefits, and a handsome salary. Although she receives occasional pats on the back from her friends who speculate about "how difficult it must be to stay home with the kids all day," Erika's social status is decidedly lower than that of her husband. She receives far less social recognition for her efforts, no awards, and no pay. Her status as a nonworker is most tellingly revealed when she is asked about her intentions to "go back to work" after her children get older. Her numerous frustrations with mothering work (which are more serious than her culture admits) are felt alone and in private. As a result, Erika is beset with ambivalent feelings about her career choices. Though taking pride in her work as a mother, she misses the rewards of having a good job in the world of paid work. And her husband also loses out, not in the workplace but in having only brief windows of time to spend with his children.

Erika and Kevin have what is commonly considered to be a "traditional" household arrangement. In reality, when viewed in a historical perspective, this clear-cut separation of husbands' and wives' roles is anything but traditional. For most of human existence, almost all work centered in and around the home. In these **household economies**, there were gendered divisions of labor, with some tasks primarily assigned to women (cooking and child care being the most notable), but both genders contributed to the family economy. Shared responsibilities also were common. For example, in colonial America, when husbands became ill, wives served as "deputy husbands" and assumed responsibility for virtually all the activities previously performed by their spouses. Though women were not the political equals of men, they were considered workers and their efforts were considered absolutely essential to family survival (Boris and Lewis 2006; Boydston 1990; Ulrich 1982). Furthermore, the culture did not make a distinction between "going to work" and "going home," because work and family life were, to a great extent, one and the same. As a result, women who worked in and around the home were defined as being real workers, and their efforts were visible and socially recognized. A close approximation of agrarian work-family life worlds can still be witnessed on family farms, where the work of wives and husbands intertwines in proximate physical spaces (Cohen 1991).

Following the Industrial Revolution, and during the late nineteenth and early twentieth centuries, American culture reconfigured its orientation toward home work and embraced a breadwinner-homemaker arrangement. But this did not happen immediately with industrialization. In fact, when the early factories physically separated paid employment from work around the home, the first workers were often women and children. Men sometimes refused to participate in these new arrangements (Hareven and Langenbach 1978). However, within the two succeeding generations, men's and women's roles became sharply differentiated. The new system, supported by the **ideology of separate spheres**, cast men in the role of wage earners, which in turn encouraged them to evaluate self-worth in terms of career success and the ability to provide for their family's economic needs. Many women, however, were expected to stay in the home and tend to the needs of their spouses and children. Although this husband/breadwinner–wife/homemaker arrangement is commonly termed *traditional*, it is actually a modern arrangement unique to the new industrial order. Its influence had major effects on divisions of work in the home, women's access to jobs in the paid economy, and social policy. Women were cast as the weaker sex, were considered dependents rather than workers, and were thought of as being less capable of "real work" than men. A landmark Supreme Court decision (*Muller v. Oregon* 1908), for example, ruled that it was not only acceptable, but also desirable, for employers to limit the number of hours their female employees worked. These are the words of Justice David Brewer, who wrote the majority opinion:

> That woman's physical structure and the performance of maternal function place her at a disadvantage in the struggle for subsistence is obvious . . . and, as healthy mothers are essential to vigorous offspring, the physical well-being of a woman becomes the object of public interest and care in order to preserve the strength and rigor of the race. (Boris and Lewis 2006, 81)

Justice Brewer's comments reflected the dominant cultural attitudes of the early twentieth century that a woman's place is in the home. This ideology of separate spheres not only assigned home work to women and legitimated discrimination against them, it also redefined the economic value of women's efforts in the home. Rather than the home being a place of work (as it was in the eighteenth century and before), the home came to be viewed as a haven from work, the place where men recovered from the toils of the factory and the office (Lasch 1995). What was previously considered work was recast by an emergent **cult of domesticity** that asserted that household tasks were something other than labor, could be effortlessly performed, and offered so many intrinsic rewards that financial compensation was not necessary. In 1965, for every one hour working fathers spent on household tasks, working mothers performed eight. In 2010, men were performing more of the labor around the home, but working women still perform twice the labor that working men do around the home, and this ratio has not changed appreciably since 1985 (Bianchi et al. 2012). Doing domestic labor remains a significant component of cultural definitions of femininity. Women who earn more than their husbands do more domestic labor than comparable women whose husbands outearn them. One prospect is that even when women are primary earners, they still conform to traditional female roles and thus counteract the gender-altering consequences of being the primary earner in the household (Schneider 2011). Alternately, it might reflect an unwillingness on the part of their husbands to assume a larger share of these responsibilities. Either prospect highlights the impact of gender on the way work is divided in households.

Even today, some cultural and political leaders call for a renewal of policy to support the supposedly natural arrangement of the husband/breadwinner–wife/homemaker model (e.g., Santorum 2006). Their vision of a traditional family corresponds with how families were represented on television shows that aired in the mid-twentieth century, such as *Leave It to Beaver*, *Ozzie and Harriet*, and *Father Knows Best*. These archetypes were of young, healthy, self-sufficient, heterosexual couples that could prosper on the efforts of one breadwinner. Even if they do not directly say that society is better off when women concentrate their energies in the home, the assertion that life was somehow better or easier in the 1950s as compared to today has been strongly implied. But as Betty Friedan documented in her pathbreaking book *The Feminine Mystique* (1963), home work in the 1950s bore little resemblance to the image presented on television. For most stay-at-home mothers, home work entailed a grinding repetition of alienating tasks, social isolation, and subservience. Idealizing these families reflects inaccurate ahistorical assumptions about the merits of the gendered division of labor and the organization of household work and the fact that the husband/breadwinner–wife/homemaker arrangement was largely restricted to two-parent families who had opportunities to get good jobs. This arrangement was not an option for those working in low-paying jobs, which included many immigrants and members of racial minorities (Coontz 1997, 2000; Gerstel and Sarkisian 2006). Class biases are evident as well, as middle-class men typically earned incomes that enabled them to support an unpaid wife, but working-class and poor men did not. Furthermore, the notion that women should be "free" from work to tend to matters in the home was not applied to all families, as many African American women were clearly expected to work as servants in support of the new ideal household arrangements for a privileged white society (Nakano Glenn 2002). Early twentieth-century immigrant women were also far more likely than were their native-born counterparts to work outside the home. When they attempted to conform to the dominant view that women should be homemakers, they encountered financial hardship (because their husbands' incomes were often low). In response, many found ways to make significant economic contributions to the household *within* the home by taking in laundry, managing boarders, or by producing clothing and other necessities (Amott and Matthaei 1996).

In sum, the problems faced by Erika are a legacy of her culture's adaptation to industrialization but are also specific to her racial identity and class position in the new economy. For women in less desirable economic circumstances, the prospects of choosing to stay home and mold their lives to conform to the mythic "traditional" arrangements were (and are) not commonly available. Since the 1950s, expectations regarding middle-class white women's paid employment have changed significantly and the cult of domesticity has weakened. However, the assumption that women will have primary responsibility for the management of the home remains. Moreover, this work is still not recognized for the vital economic role it plays in preparing the next generation for work and enabling workers (like Kevin) to put in long, undistracted hours on the job (Crittenden 2001).

Women's Participation in the Paid Labor Force in America

While the husband/breadwinner–wife/homemaker arrangement was only available for a portion of the families in the United States in the old economy, it was a dominant model for organizing family lives. Women, especially married women with children, were far less likely to work than were men. And, although this arrangement presented very different opportunities, the clear-cut gendered division of labor created a means to maximize collective family resources for the middle class (Becker 1981). Today, this arrangement is less common: women are almost as likely to work outside of the home as men, and most married-couple households contain two working adults. Exhibit 6.1 shows the magnitude of this change. In 1940, only one in four women were in the paid labor force, but by 2013, nearly two in three were.

Exhibit 6.1   Men's and Women's Labor Force Participation Rates (Age Sixteen Years and Older): United States, 1940–2013

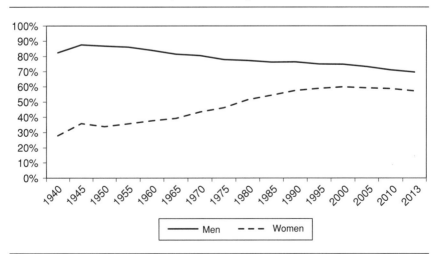

Source: Historical Statistics of the United States, Bureau of Labor Statistics.

Men's participation declined slightly, reflecting the aging of the population (there are now more retirees) as well as increases in the numbers of young people who delayed their entry into the labor force to complete school. Clearly a convergence is occurring with respect to the labor force participation of men and women.

Exhibit 6.2 shows that the normative arrangement of the old economy, in which the husbands went to work and the wives stayed home, is now the exception. In 2012, most opposite-sex married couples in the United States were dual earners, with both the husband and wife in the paid labor force. There are several reasons for the increase in women's labor force participation and the growing numbers of dual-earner couples. First is the changing perception of women's place in society and the remarkable transformation in gender role ideologies. Changes in the structure of the economy have been equally important. Stagnant male incomes made it increasingly difficult for the average husband to support a family on his wage alone (a situation long familiar to immigrant and minority families). Married women, whether they wanted to or not, found that they *had* to work if their families were to maintain their expected standard of living (Bernhardt et al. 2001; Warren and Tyagi 2003). Also, the remarkable growth of the service sector (a significant employer of female workers even in the old economy) created a demand for

Exhibit 6.2   Employment Configurations of Married Couples: United States, 2012

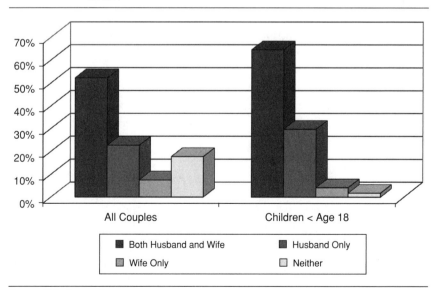

Source: U.S. Census Bureau.

an expanded female labor force in jobs that do not challenge conventional attitudes about gender. Exhibit 6.2 also shows that married couples with children (including those with young children) usually have two earners in the labor force, a remarkable reversal of the earlier preference for stay-at-home mothers. However, among married couples with only a single earner, it remains the case that wives are more likely than husbands to be the ones to drop out of the labor force; in that sense, children still affect the labor force attachment of wives more than husbands.

The rise of the dual-earner couple has forced families to confront issues less commonly present in the old economy, such as who will care for children while both partners are at work, whose career will take priority, and how to select and pay for day care. As we discuss later, old gender templates play a strong role in determining couples' responses to the stresses they experience in the new economy.

Gender Inequalities in Compensation

Men and women still face very different prospects of ever rising to the top of career ladders, falling off those ladders, or even making it beyond the lowest rungs. The data are sobering. On virtually every measure of earnings, women trail well behind men. According to the U.S. Census Bureau, in 2013, the average woman worker earned $13,165 less than the average male worker. Women are twice as likely to be poor and are much more likely to hold low-paying jobs that offer slim prospects for upward mobility (Gilbert 2003; Kalleberg, Reskin, and Hudson 2000). They are half as likely as men to make it into the ranks of top income earners and are far less likely to achieve the very highest of ranks in corporations. As an example, consider that in 2014, among Fortune 500 CEOs, for every woman there were twenty men (Catalyst 2014). Simply stated, while women are catching up to men with respect to labor force attachment, they have not caught up in respect to pay and position in the new economy. Recent trends indicate that the gaps are not narrowing as much as one might hope and some of the gender gaps remain as wide as ever.

Many complexities are involved in analyzing the extent of gender inequalities in earnings. For example, should one compare all women with all men or only those who are working in the paid labor force? Note that the latter analysis tends to underplay the extent of gender inequality because women who are not in a position to earn any income are excluded from the calculations. The fact that women are much more likely to be working in part-time jobs creates additional biases in wage disparity calculations that base analysis on full-time workers. But even when the comparisons of men and women workers are restricted to those who are working full-time, year-round jobs, women still tend to earn considerably less than their male counterparts.

First consider the good news. Exhibit 6.3 shows that the women-to-men earnings gap has been closing. As the top line in the graph shows, in 1960, for every one dollar a man (working a full-time job) earned, women earned about 61 cents. In 2012, full-time women workers were earning 77 cents for every dollar earned by full-time working men. Now consider the bad news. A sizable wage gap still exists between men and women full-time workers. Again, because we have restricted the analysis to full-time workers, note that this analysis underplays the differences that would be revealed if part-time workers were included in the equation. In addition, while women's wages have been rising, much of the reason for the reduction in the gap between men and women workers is stagnation in men's wages. In other words, while women seem to be making some progress in enhancing their incomes, men's real incomes are actually a bit lower than they were in the early 1970s. So the closing wage gap can be explained both by an enhancement of women's earnings and a leveling of men's earnings. Also, the most recent decade of data suggests the rate of convergence between men's and women's earnings is slowing, at least in comparison with the gains made from 1970 through 1995. The reasons for this slowing convergence are not altogether clear. One study suggests that it may be the result of contemporary women pursuing jobs that offer lower pay

Exhibit 6.3   Women's and Men's Earnings (in $1,000s) and Income Ratios for Full-Time Year-Round Workers: United States, 1960–2012 (Earnings Adjusted to 2012 Dollars)

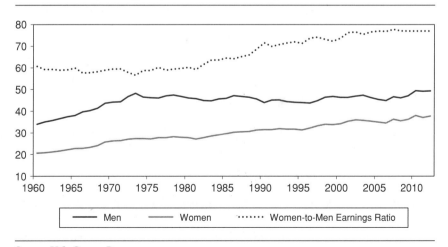

Source: U.S. Census Bureau.

(Blau and Kahn 2006). In other words, if women were gravitating to jobs that paid more, the gap would be closing further still. We return later to the question of why they are not. Additionally, the persistence of the gender-wage gap results not only from men's wages being higher than women's but also because men work longer hours now in comparison to women. So as more women enter into the labor force and into the types of jobs held by men, they are not working long enough to fully catch up (Youngjoo and Weeden 2014). Thus work hours, allocation of job opportunities, and compensation differentials on the basis of gender combine to create and sustain income disadvantages.

A number of mainstream media publications have considered an interesting trend: approximately one in five wives make more than their husbands, a remarkable change considering that in 1970 only one in twenty couples was in a comparable situation (Perpitone 2010). However, more careful study of this dynamic indicates that the change is not as dramatic as these figures suggest. According to research by Sarah Winslow-Bowe (2006), if one were to follow couples in which the wives outearn the husbands over time, within a few years the vast majority shift to the husband having a higher income. The reason for the wife's income advantage commonly occurs because the husband lost his job or is temporarily out of the labor force. It is actually quite rare to find couples in which the wife maintains an income that is consistently higher than her husband's over time. And if one were to identify couples in which wives have consistent income advantages, most of these couples are low earners. In dual-earner families in the bottom economic quintile, wives outearn their husbands 70% of the time, compared to only 34% for top quintile dual-earner families (Glynn 2012). While the wife might make a significantly higher percentage of the household earnings than the husband in these couples, the actual monetary difference in their incomes is quite small, given that both are earning low incomes.

In sum, wide gaps exist between men's and women's earnings. Some of the explanation can be found in the fact that household work is not compensated, which leaves many women without paychecks. The expectation that women will assume disproportionate household and child care responsibilities increases the odds that women will be funneled into part-time jobs, which also results in lower earnings. But even among full-time workers, women's pay lags well behind that of men. Why is this?

Socialization, Career Selection, and Career Paths

The large-scale entry of women into the paid labor force reshaped how men and women view their roles and capabilities and opened doors that were previously closed. As a result, the gender composition of entire fields has shifted. For example, women are now the majority of graduates in veterinary colleges, a profession that in the 1960s and before was exclusively male. And growing evidence suggests that men want to be more involved in intensive provision of care to their children (Harrington, Van Deusen, and Mazar 2012). Nevertheless, gender segregation remains a central part of the contours of work in the present-day American economy.

One reason for these imbalances is that gender templates encourage men and women to have different aspirations. From early childhood, individuals make choices about what kinds of activities to engage in, what skills to develop, and what interests to pursue. Along each step of the way, they develop skills that, in turn, become part of the tool kit they use to construct future encounters. Ultimately, these choices influence eventual occupational goals and destinations. However, *choice* might not be the most accurate term to use because decisions are made in the context of powerful social expectations about gender. Various **agents of socialization** (including parents, schools, and the media) instill beliefs that boys/men and girls/women are not equally suited to all tasks. The confluence of social pressures and transmission of taken-for-granted paths, over time, explains why men and women place different emphases on their identities as breadwinners, why they select different occupations, and their willingness to sacrifice their careers for the needs of their children, spouses, and aging parents. The result of socialization is that boys and girls (and men and women) are continuously molded to have interests and identities suited to different types of endeavors.

Americans are socialized to expect women to fill certain positions in society, and in that respect many jobs are "gendered." Not every culture views gendered lines of work in the same way. For example, in the United States most secondary school teachers are women (60%), but in India, two in three (69%) secondary school teachers are men (United Nations Statistics Division 2011). Similarly, three in four doctors in the United States are men, but in Russia nearly three in four doctors are women. Statistics such as these firmly establish that expectations about which jobs should be done by men or women are culturally determined (Harden 2001). Although women have made remarkable forays into many professions that were previously nearly exclusively male, Exhibit 6.4 shows that many occupations remain almost exclusively filled by women workers. Notably, nearly all preschool and kindergarten teachers are women, as are secretaries, dental hygienists, dental assistants, dietitians, typists, and child care workers. Conversely, women are nearly entirely absent in construction industry jobs such as those performed by plumbers, carpenters, and electricians.

Gender expectations interact with class and racial differences to produce a complex, varied pattern of gender segregation in American workplaces. For women at the bottom of the opportunity divide, a major problem is the existence of **occupational ghettos**, gendered jobs that typically offer few paths to upward mobility (Grusky and Charles 2004). As Exhibit 6.4 shows, most maids, day care workers, and secretaries are women. The fact that the income gap between white and black women is relatively small (far smaller than it is for white and black men) is linked to the fact that women of all races are funneled into lower-paying jobs such as these.

Socialization encourages workers to feel well-matched to gendered lines of work. For example, one study of secretaries found that most of these

Exhibit 6.4   Occupations With High Percentages of Women Workers: United States, 2013

Occupation	Number Employed (1,000s)	Percent Female	Women's Median Weekly Earnings
Preschool and kindergarten teachers	484	98%	$624
Childcare workers	410	95%	$418
Secretaries and administrative assistants	2,113	94%	$677
Receptionists and information clerks	828	92%	$527
Licensed practical and licensed vocational nurses	404	92%	$732
Billing and posting clerks	380	92%	$629
Registered nurses	2,023	90%	$1,086
Nursing, psychiatric, and home health aides	1,207	89%	$450
Bookkeeping, accounting, and auditing clerks	702	89%	$670
Teacher assistants	501	89%	$475
Maids and housekeeping cleaners	605	88%	$406
Office clerks, general	734	84%	$596
Personal care aides	539	84%	$445
Elementary and middle school teachers	2,138	81%	$937
Social workers	507	80%	$818
Cashiers	932	72%	$379
First-line supervisors of office and administrative support workers	828	70%	$748
Waiters and waitresses	558	70%	$400

Source: U.S. Department of Labor.

women (especially older women) enjoyed their jobs. Rather than perceiving gender ghettoization as a source of oppression, they had accepted what they were socialized to believe—that men and women are different from one another, that women are skilled at doing tasks that men are bad at performing (especially nurturing), and that they personally possessed these skills (Kennelly 2002, 2006).

Men with lower levels of education traditionally enjoyed advantages over women with comparable credentials in the old economy. These men were encouraged to seek, and generally found, jobs in manufacturing, construction, or automobile repair—work that offered opportunities for skill and income expansion and stronger prospects for economic security in both the short and long term. But less educated African American men were a notable exception because they often were excluded from jobs of this kind. In recent years, the perception has grown that the situation of boys from poor and working-class backgrounds has deteriorated and that girls now have the advantage. The decline of well-paid manufacturing jobs, and evidence that girls are outperforming boys in school, seem to indicate that boys who do not have high levels of education are aspiring to jobs that no longer exist. However, a careful look at the evidence indicates that race, rather than class, is interacting with (not replacing) gendered aspirations. Less-educated white men are not aspiring in large numbers to enter traditionally female fields but continue to find desirable, "masculine" work in areas such as construction or criminal justice. Poorly educated African American men continue to hope for traditionally male jobs that are unavailable to them and thus are falling behind (Kimmel 2006; Young 2003). Gender segregation at the bottom of the opportunity divide persists but takes different forms for members of different racial groups.

Gender socialization also plays a role for men and women holding comparatively good jobs in the new economy. One means of illustrating its power is to consider how young adults select college majors, a critical step in determining subsequent career options. Exhibit 6.5 reveals that even today, young men continue to gravitate toward traditionally male-dominated fields (e.g., computer science and engineering) and women tend to gravitate toward college majors associated with helping professions (psychology, education, health care). In part, this is the result of gender beliefs, one of which is that men tend to be better at math than women. Research into this issue reveals that differences in mathematical abilities are actually small or even nonexistent. And even when differences are identified, scant evidence exists to support any conclusion that these are based on biology (Ceci, Williams, and Barnett 2009). But these beliefs create self-fulfilling prophecies. Once the perception of capabilities is embraced by young men and women, even when those individuals have equivalent skills, it influences their aspirations to pursue mathematics-related professions. In other words, boys pursue math-related careers not because they actually have better skills than girls; they do so because they *believe* that they are better (Correll 2001, 2004). These beliefs, in turn, lead them to take additional courses and further develop their skills. While socialization may lead individuals to develop certain interests and skills, agency is enacted as young women and men self-select into career paths, expressing interests in college majors and particular types of entry-level jobs because these are viewed as compatible with self-conceptions (meaning "who I am") (Cech 2013a). But this is not the only factor in play in understanding gender contours within the new economy. As we discuss later, some women enter male-dominated fields (such as engineering and science), only to find themselves marginalized or that jobs prove to be incompatible with their family responsibilities (Ceci, Williams, and Barnett 2009; Committee on Maximizing the Potential of Women in Academic Science and Engineering 2006; Preston 2004).

Aside from its role in career selection, gender socialization influences how men and women respond to work and family strains. Among working-class

Exhibit 6.5   Gender Compositions of Bachelor's Degrees Conferred: United States, 2010–2011

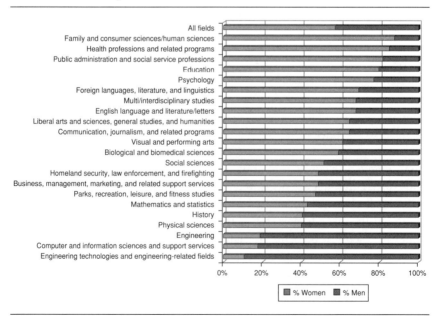

Source: Chronicle of Higher Education Almanac (2013 edition).

and poor families, women are more likely than men to arrange work schedules to allow involvement in their children's lives (Garey 1999). Among higher-income families, men seldom sacrifice their careers for family (Becker and Moen 1999). In fact, the opposite is the case, as men devote themselves more intensively to their work because they see this as a duty to their families. To compensate for their husbands' reluctance or unwillingness to relinquish career goals, women modify their work lives, scale back their work hours, and redirect their professional interests toward alternate careers (Moen and Sweet 2003). As a result, dual-earner families are transforming the twentieth-century separate spheres model into new **neotraditional arrangements,** wherein women retain primary responsibility for child care while keeping one foot in the labor market in lower-pressure (and typically lower-paying) jobs.

The strategic choice to scale back work hours comes with significant costs to professional women, not only in immediate compensation but also in long-term career prospects. Working women who are able to arrange shorter hours or flexible schedules with their employers are at risk of being placed on mommy tracks and assigned tasks that offer fewer rewards and less opportunity for growth compared with workers who remain on the fast track (Barnett and Gareis 2000b). And even when more attractive opportunities to scale back on work are present (which can be the case for professional workers such as lawyers and academics), there is a very real prospect that they may never get back on track once they step off (Meiksins and Whalley 2002; Moen and Roehling 2005). Particularly in occupations where time commitment is valued highly, mothers' efforts to limit their work hours are a major cause of the gender pay gap in contemporary America (Goldin 2014).

For dual-earner couples, neotraditional arrangements create marked disparities between wives' career opportunities and those afforded to their husbands. As one partner's job is put on hold, the other's continues to grow, which reverberates into subsequent life course decisions, such as whose job to favor, when and where to move, and who should assume responsibility for family care work. Exhibit 6.6 illustrates this dynamic. When dual-earner couples manage their relationships, they can choose to favor either one partner's career (leaving the other as a trailing spouse), to take turns, or to give priority to neither partner's career. Most husbands and wives start their careers on relatively equal footing, with neither partner's career being favored, but as their lives develop over time, wives' careers tend to be towed along and follow the direction charted by their husbands' job opportunities. Their options are constrained by investments in husbands' careers, which in turn limits their options to advance and grow, even after children have left the household (Pixley 2008; Sweet, Moen, and Meiksins 2007). It is important to recognize that when jobs demand long hours, they tend to create unequal spousal commitments to work inside and outside the home. These unequal commitments play out in a gendered way, such that when husbands work long hours, wives are significantly more likely to exit the labor force. It is rare for husbands to quit their jobs in order to adjust to their wife's job demands. As such, overwork tends to exacerbate gender inequalities (Cha 2010).

Catherine Hakim (2001) argued that the reason for this type of dynamic is that many women express a preference to center their identities in the home rather than in the workplace and that this may explain some (but not all) of the divergences in husbands' and wives' careers (Ceci and Williams 2010; Kan 2007). It is important to recognize, however, that for most women the decision to leave the labor force, or to scale back on career aspirations, is not a happy choice but one that is necessary when the combined demands of work and family outstrip time and energy resources (Stone 2007). When faced with these types of tensions, a common strategy is to give up either on career goals or family goals, so it is not that women prefer to drop out of the labor force but that this is the preference among very constrained options. Some women try to resolve these tensions by locating work situations that are more compatible with responsibilities held outside of the job. For example, some women use self-employment as a means to balance

Exhibit 6.6   Percentage of Husbands and Wives Reporting That Their Career Was Favored Over Their Spouse's Career (by Life Stage)

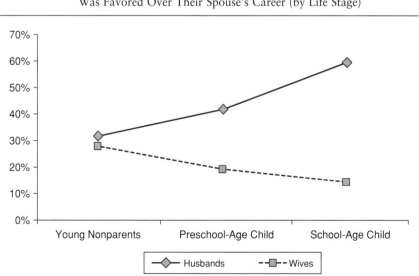

Source: Sweet and Moen (2006).

work and family commitments, and these types of jobs are commonly pursued after the birth of children. Such is the case for African American female entrepreneurs who establish beauty salons (Harvey 2005). In contrast, children have little effect on men's pursuit of self-employment, and men tend to use self-employment as a means to advance career objectives (Carr 1996). A more recent study revealed that a woman's social class may affect her reasons for self-employment. The study found that women in lower-level jobs pursue self-employment as a means of balancing work and family, but women pursuing higher-powered professional careers act like men, and when they do become self-employed, they do so primarily for career reasons (Budig 2006). Preferences may be changing, however. In interviews with young women about their career aspirations, Kathleen Gerson (2009) asked young women what they wanted out of life. Not surprisingly, most wanted a family (including children and a spouse), as well as a career. When she pressed them and asked, "Suppose you could only have two of these things . . . a husband/partner, a child, or a career, which two would you pick?" most of the young women chose to discard the husband! Social class plays a role when women are confronted by this choice. A recent study found that affluent women are more likely to marry because they are increasingly able to find partners willing to accommodate their careers; lower-income women have less access to such partners, so are decreasingly likely to marry, although they still work and have children (Carbone and Cahn 2014). And interviews with fathers who stay at home with their children report feeling the same types of rewards (and frustrations) that stay-at-home mothers experience (Harrington, Van Deusen, and Mazar 2012).

Exhibit 6.7 presents a graphic image of an important dynamic operating in the new economy. As revealed in the research by Phyllis Moen and colleagues, if we were to trace back to the old economy, we would find that women and men did, in fact, occupy separate worlds, and within those worlds, members of each gender had common interests and values (Moen and Spencer 2006). But the transition to the new economy has brought with it a far greater diversity of what women want and a greater diversity of what men want as well. Thus, over time, it could be said that there are "converging divergences" in interests, values, and goals. And if we were to add a life course dimension to this analysis, it becomes apparent that what any woman or man wants or needs is likely to change over time. For example, some workers might want to labor intensely when they are age twenty to thirty, to reduce work commitments in the midthirties, and ramp back up in their fifties. When they reach retirement age, some might still want to work, but in "not so big jobs" (Moen 2007). Focusing on the diversity of values and goals reveals that the career paths women and men follow are not necessarily paths of preference and that if opportunity structures were not as limited, likely far greater degrees of gender equality would be evident in the new economy.

In sum, socialization continues to shape men's and women's career pursuits, as well as their expectations about what they should do off the job. The tensions evident in the new economy tend to push workers to revert to the gender templates established in the old economy, with women assuming primary responsibility for the management of the domestic sphere and men adopting roles as breadwinners. But this adoption of old gendered strategies for managing work and home occurs in a new economic and cultural context in which most workers want and need to remain attached to the paid labor force. Liberating work in the new economy will require a serious response to the culturally based forces that create cookie-cutter jobs that push working families to adopt neotraditional arrangements—a practice that tends to cost both men and women the opportunity to work as equals inside and outside the home.

Interpersonal Discrimination in the Workplace

Socialization contributes to gender inequalities at work by influencing the supplies of workers seeking entry into different fields. But gender also plays a role in shaping the demand for workers with specific qualities. To illustrate how this happens, imagine interviewing a series of applicants for a demanding job, a position that will require long hours of work and some travel. Your

Exhibit 6.7   Converging Divergences in Women's and Men's Values and Preferences Over Time

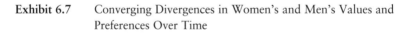

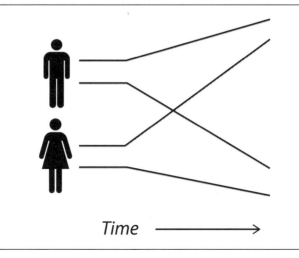

Time ⟶

choice comes down to two candidates, Jane and John, individuals who have identical qualifications and who performed equally well at all stages of the interview process. The only difference between the candidates is that Jane is visibly pregnant, but John (obviously) is not. Which person would you hire? We have posed this question to hundreds of students over the years, but only rarely has a student offered even mild support for hiring Jane. They have eloquently (and often emphatically) argued that her candidacy poses a number of concerns, including the inevitability that she will want to take time off from her job, that she will be unable to put in as long hours as John, and that she will be in no position to travel once her child is born. As uncomfortable as it may make them, they conclude that it would be their responsibility to hire the person most fit to meet the demands of the job—John.

All of these conclusions are based on **gender schemas**, culturally based models concerning the core differences that distinguish men from women and assumptions about men's and women's places in society (Cech 2013a). Notice how parental status becomes a master status for Jane in a way that it does not for John (who conceivably could have an infant waiting for him at home). There is a ready acceptance of the assumption that Jane would want to have reduced hours after she had her child and that the child would detract from her work. But it is also possible that she could have a partner who wants to stay home or has an excellent day care arrangement. What takes precedence in favoring John is the emphasis on crudely constructed visions of how women and men behave in different situations and the assumption that Jane and John would behave in a corresponding manner. This is a process termed **statistical discrimination**, wherein perceptions of group tendencies become the rationale for differential treatment of individuals. Statistical discrimination is problematic for a number of reasons, not least of which is the widespread use of **stereotypes**—often erroneous assumptions about social groups that obscure the range of behaviors and abilities present within any population.

In the new economy, evidence indicates that gender schemas may have less power than they did in the old economy, but this may be conditional on parental status. An important study by Shelley Correll (2007) found that when presented with comparable job candidates, evaluators perceived women as being largely as capable and committed as men. However, she also found that childless women were called back at twice the rate of mothers. Other studies show that motherhood is associated with lower earnings, especially for those occupying lower-income jobs (Budig and Hodges 2010). In contrast to the motherhood penalty, associated with perceived deficits in competence and commitment, marriage and fatherhood status actually offer men a premium, improving perceptions of worker competence, pay, and prospects for promotion (Bygren and Gähler 2012; Glauber 2008; Killewald 2013). So while the perceived competence of women has gained more solid footing, the perception of mothers as being good workers has not.

Women are sometimes subjected to **hostile sexism**, the belief that they are inferior to men at specific tasks (Masser and Abrams 2004). An example can be found in the comments made by former Harvard University president Lawrence Summers, who in 2005 expressed his opinion that one reason why female scientists are scarce at top research universities is because of innate differences between the sexes. When power holders accept these types of beliefs, the likelihood increases that they will operate on the assumption that women are likely to fail and to view their accomplishments with skepticism. The denial of the opportunity to succeed contributes to self-fulfilling

Exhibit 6.8   Instead of Hiring This Woman, Most College Students Would Hire an Equally Qualified Man. Would You?

Source: Copyright © by Getty Images. Reprinted with permission.

prophecies, as workplace stratification systems lopsidedly allocate opportunities to men and then reward their successes with even more opportunities to excel. One would expect that egalitarian and meritocratic values would hold sway among entrepreneurial teams, which operate under considerable pressure to succeed. While experience counts, even here men tend to rise into leadership positions, in part because gender is used as a quick and dirty means of sorting individuals into levels of perceived leadership potential. And perhaps even more telling is the observation that when husbands and wives are members of the same team, the husband is far more likely to assume a leadership position (Yang and Aldrich 2014).

Note that women also can be the objects of **benevolent sexism**, which operates on the assumption that they are better than men at other types of activities, such as planning social events, organizing files, or caring for children. This, in turn, prompts gatekeepers to open doors for their entry into jobs that have been traditionally defined as "women's work." The problem here is that women tend to be viewed as exceptionally qualified for work that is less rewarding than "men's work," an issue we return to shortly. Benevolent sexism also can lead employers or managers to "protect" female workers and lead them not to challenge them or involve them in difficult or dangerous tasks. The result is that women may not have as many opportunities as men to develop new skills and to demonstrate their capabilities on the job. One especially compelling illustration of this dynamic can be found in the U.S. military, which protects women soldiers from field combat and in so doing, shields them from the opportunity to demonstrate the valor and leadership needed for promotion to the top ranks. Sexist practices also map onto strategies of advancing collective interests of workers. One example of this can be seen in the use of a "brotherhood" ethos in groups such as Vendors for Justice. By using "brotherhood" rhetoric, the organizers of street vendors in New York City sought to unite workers who shared particular values, including the notion that men stand with one another to protect women. On one level, "brotherhood" created cohesion among a restricted group of men, but at the same time it alienated women and men who held more progressive values (Roychowdhury 2014).

Overt discrimination involves visible, conscious, and intentional decisions to bar entry into occupations. In the old economy women were excluded from most professional occupational fields and it was customary for them to be paid lower wages than men, even when they performed the same work. Not until the late 1960s and early 1970s did elite colleges such as Dartmouth and Princeton admit women into many of their professional programs. Similarly, overt discrimination excluded women from well-paid jobs in the skilled trades. Entry into apprenticeship programs was difficult or impossible for women; union membership was largely restricted to men, and women who did succeed in entering male-dominated trades were often met with a hostile reception that made it difficult for them to "learn the ropes." Today, there are far fewer instances of overt discrimination, largely because of the **Civil Rights Act of 1964**, which prohibited employment discrimination based on sex (as well as race, color, religion, or national origin), and the **Equal Pay Act of 1963**, which prohibited paying men and women different wages for equal work. These laws, and a series of successful lawsuits against employers, helped to change work policy and employment practices, which in turn has opened avenues for women to enter historically male-dominated professions and industries. Overt discrimination still occurs in the new economy, but at least in comparison with the 1950s and before, the problem is less severe and women now have legal recourse. Notably absent are federal labor laws prohibiting discrimination on the basis of sexual orientation, and limited numbers of states have legislation to this effect. This kind of legislation matters. One experiment, for example, revealed that when job seekers signaled a possibility that they were gay in application materials (for example, by listing that they were treasurer of a LGBT organization), they were only about half as likely to be contacted after submitting a job application. However, the same study revealed that the degree of discrimination was buffered in states that had prohibitions, providing compelling evidence that legislation makes very real differences in leveling playing fields (Tilcsik 2011).

When faced with overt discrimination, workers who know they are being treated in an unfair manner are ostensibly in a position to level complaints or to sue their employers. Such was the case for Ramona Scott, one of 115 women who testified in a class-action gender discrimination lawsuit against Walmart. Scott testified that, after being passed over for promotion, her manager told her, "Men are here to make a career and women aren't. . . . Retail [work] is for housewives who just need to earn extra money." Stephanie Odle, an assistant manager, joined the same class-action lawsuit against Walmart only after she learned by chance that her male coworker earned $10,000 more a year than she did (Head 2004). In the summer of 2011, the U.S. Supreme Court ruled that such large class-action suits were unacceptable. A major concern for the court was the question of how reasonable it is to make awards to most or all women who work for an employer, based on a limited number of identifiable instances of problems in employment practices. The decision is likely to make it much more difficult to use class-action suits in cases of suspected employment discrimination affecting large numbers of employees (Liptak 2011). An added barrier in establishing class interests is that employees often do not know when and how they have been discriminated against, in part because information on employee pay is usually kept closely guarded. As a result, many workers never learn the extent to which they have been treated unfairly. Even female scientists at MIT had little understanding of the extent to which they were disadvantaged in work assignments, promotions, and allocation of lab space until a group of them shared their experiences and saw patterns that otherwise were invisible (MIT 1999). Leveling complaints also can involve career costs because even when these complaints are legitimate, the victims can be perceived as troublemakers.

Even when they want to, employees face uphill battles in lodging complaints against their employers. One of the most notable cases in recent history is that of Lilly Ledbetter, a manager at Goodyear who repeatedly received lower raises than the men who worked with her. Over time, the accumulation of smaller pay increases led to her making tens of thousands of dollars less than men who were hired at the same time as she was and who were working in comparable positions. In a stunning decision, the U.S. Supreme Court ruled (by a narrow majority) that Ledbetter was *not* entitled to damages under Title VII of the Civil Rights Act of 1964 because she did not protest the compensation differences shortly after each of the pay-setting decisions was made. The fact that she lacked the information needed to do so, as well as the implications that seeking redress might have had on her career, were captured in the dissenting statement by Justice Ginsberg:

> The Court's insistence on immediate contest overlooks common characteristics of pay discrimination. Pay disparities often occur, as they did in Ledbetter's case, in small increments; cause to suspect that discrimination is at work develops only over time. Comparative pay information, moreover, is often hidden from the employee's view. Employers may keep under wraps the pay differentials maintained among supervisors, no less the reasons for those differentials. Small initial discrepancies may not be seen as meet for a federal case, particularly when the employee, trying to succeed in a nontraditional environment, is averse to making waves. (*Ledbetter v. Goodyear Tire & Rubber Co.* 2007)

To address this concern, the first act of legislation signed into law by President Obama was the Lilly Ledbetter Fair Pay Act, which changed how the statute of limitations for filing grievances against employers is defined. Rather than requiring that the grievance be filed within 180 days of the employer's decision in respect to *the determination* of pay levels, employees can now file a grievance within 180 days of *the receipt* of each paycheck in which discrimination is argued to be evident. While a significant step forward, the onus remains on employees to show that they have been discriminated against, and, as we discuss shortly, more often than not employees remain in a position that limits their ability to do so.

Another concern is that women and members of minority groups also can be subject to **covert discrimination,** wherein power holders structure opportunities in a biased manner but in ways that the employee may find difficult to detect or prove. A manager who is reluctant to employ or promote women, for instance, can try to increase the chances of failure by making the employee's life exceedingly difficult. An employee may find herself short-staffed, have her hours cut, or be assigned unfavorable tasks or scheduled for work at times incompatible with her needs off the job. Similarly, she may be set up for failure by being placed in situations for which she has not been properly trained or on jobs that have low odds for success. Covert discrimination is one of the most frequently cited contributors to the existence of a **glass ceiling**—an invisible barrier that prevents female white-collar workers from rising to the highest ranks.

It is also important to consider motivations when discrimination occurs. In the new economy, it is possible that discrimination is less often practiced deliberately *against* employees but rather *for* employees whom managers see as especially worthy of opportunity. Among managers, "fitting in" is of paramount importance, which influences their tendency to gravitate to, and create, gender and racially homogenous work teams. White men hold most positions of power, so they have the greatest leverage in reproducing gender and racially homogeneous managerial teams (Elliott and Smith 2004). The protégé, the junior employee who looks, acts, and identifies with the (white male) boss, has a decided advantage in this culture and may be rewarded by supervisors' designing new jobs fitted to his strengths. The women excluded from "old boys' clubs" sometimes suspect that they have been wrongly passed over, but proving the existence of discrimination in such a culturally mediated process can be challenging (if not impossible).

An additional problem confronting women (as well as racial and sexual minorities) can be the existence of a **hostile work environment,** a situational context so caustic that it undermines the ability to perform jobs. Although not formally barred from working in the company of men, women can find themselves in uncomfortable situations or subjected to unwanted sexual propositions. Fully one in three women in their midtwenties has experienced unwanted touching or invasions of their personal space on the job (Uggen and Blackstone 2004). Work in such contexts can send subtle and not-so-subtle messages to women that they either do not belong or that they are primarily valued on the basis of sexual interests; it also can undermine their productivity and advancement. Of note, similar reports of hostile work environments are offered by men who try to enter traditionally female-dominated professions such as clerical work or nursing (Henson and Rogers 2001). However, the uncomfortable gender environment men encounter in these situations also can produce **glass escalators** that lead them into higher-level, better-paid jobs. A classic study found that male kindergarten teachers encounter a difficult work environment (especially from hostile parents) in which questions are raised about their motives, their sexuality, and so forth. Far from harming their career prospects, this can actually encourage the transformation of these teachers into school principals, a more conventionally male role in which they acquire greater authority and higher pay (Williams 1991). More recent research confirms the continued existence of glass escalators for men in many female-dominated occupations (Smith 2012).

Some women are placed by their superiors in no-win situations, forced to choose whether to acquiesce to unwanted relationships or resist and experience near-inevitable, career-damaging repercussions. Male-dominated workplaces tend toward masculine cultural values and behavior, and in this world, sexual jokes and horseplay can be especially problematic if only a few women are represented. This also poses problems for sexual minorities, whose participation in sexual discussions or office romance is unwelcomed and received with hostility. It is commonly assumed that the victims of sexual harassment are the least powerful members in organizations, but this is not always the case. In fact, female supervisors experience more harassment than nonsupervisors. One likely contributing factor is that women are statistical minorities among supervisors, suggesting that the performance of work in male-dominated social contexts leaves women especially vulnerable to harassment (McLaughlin, Uggen, and Blackstone 2012).

Policing sexuality in the workplaces of the new economy is problematic for a number of reasons. One concern is that many consensual romantic encounters (and marriages) are formed as the result of working together, and it is not unusual for spouses to seek work within the same organization (Creamer and Associates 2001; Schiebinger, Henderson, and Gilmartin 2008; Sweet and Moen 2004). Additionally, work cultures (accepted by both male and female employees), such as those of restaurant waitstaff, are often accepting of sexually tinged coworker interplay, including pinching, joking, and even casual encounters (Williams, Giuffre, and Dellinger 1999). Other jobs, such as those of comedy writers and those in the publishing industry, require employees to develop materials that some may find objectionable, and this in turn may influence the gender composition of fields (see Exhibit 6.9). Attempting to constrain discussions or eliminate potentially offensive materials could ultimately undermine the prospect of actually doing this work (Dellinger and Williams 2002). In the service economy, selling sexual titillation (such as at a Hooters restaurant) is part and parcel of some jobs.

Exhibit 6.9   *Colbert Report* Writers Receive Their Emmys in 2013: Why Are
There So Few Women?

Source: Copyright © by Getty Images. Reprinted with permission.

How do most workers respond when they feel they are being discriminated against or find themselves in hostile work environments? Among those
in low-level jobs, such as employees in the fast-food industry or retail sector,
the most common response is to tolerate the situation and when that
fails, to try to find work elsewhere. But for women in higher-level positions,
harassment or inequitable treatment on the job can present a classic
catch-22. Even in situations where the worker can document unfair treatment, registering a complaint (which typically would require complaining to
someone in authority) tends to be taken as evidence of a failure to "fit in"
or "get along." Ultimately the boundaries of acceptable conduct in the new
economy will be played out in the courts, as well as in the ongoing negotiation of informally established workplace cultures.

Structural Dimensions of Gender Discrimination

Thus far, we considered the problem of gender discrimination largely by
focusing on how individuals respond to one another on an interpersonal

level. If gender inequality were simply a matter of interpersonal discrimination, solutions would involve changing attitudes through sensitivity training initiatives or by penalizing misconduct (such as leveling fines against those who act irresponsibly). However, even if these initiatives were successful, deeper structural forces that reinforce gender inequities in the new economy would remain. In this section, we focus on two institutionalized practices that limit women's ability to compete in the modern workplace: the ways women's work and men's work are valued and the ways job designs conflict with gender scripts.

The Devaluation of "Women's Work"

Consider the differences between two low-status occupations, one of which is primarily occupied by men, the other by women. The job descriptions in Exhibit 6.10 are quoted from the Bureau of Labor Statistics *Occupational Outlook Handbook*, a handy source of information about the nature of different jobs and the economic returns workers receive for their efforts.

Exhibit 6.10   Two Different Job Descriptions: Why Does One Job Pay Less Than the Other?

Hand Laborers and Material Movers
Hand laborers and material movers typically do the following: manually move material from one place to another; pack or wrap material by hand; keep a record of the material they move; use signals, when necessary, to assist machine operators who are moving larger pieces of material; and ensure a clean and orderly workplace. In warehouses and wholesale and retail operations, hand material movers work closely with material moving machine operators and material recording clerks. Automatic sensors and tags are increasingly being used to track items that allow hand material movers to work faster. Some workers are employed in manufacturing industries in which they load material onto conveyor belts or other machines. **Median pay in 2012: $11.04/hour; $22,970/year.**

Child Care Workers
Child care workers typically do the following: supervise and monitor the safety of children in their care; prepare meals and organize mealtimes and snacks for children; help children keep good hygiene; change the diapers of infants and toddlers; organize activities or implement a curriculum that allows

(Continued)

(Continued)

children to learn about the world and explore interests; develop schedules and routines to ensure that children have enough physical activity, rest, and playtime; watch for signs of emotional or developmental problems in children and bring the problems to the attention of parents; and keep records of children's progress, routines, and interest. Child care workers introduce babies and toddlers to basic concepts, such as manners, by reading to them and playing with them. For example, they teach young children how to share and take turns by playing games with other children. Child care workers often help preschool-age children prepare for kindergarten. Young children learn from playing, solving problems, questioning, and experimenting. Child care workers use play and other instructional techniques to help children's development. For example, they use storytelling and rhyming games to teach language and vocabulary. They may help improve children's social skills by having them work together to build something in a sandbox or teach math by having children count when building with blocks. They may involve the children in creative activities, such as art, dance, and music. Child care workers also often watch school-age children before and after school. They help these children with homework and take them to afterschool activities, such as sports practices and club meetings. During the summer, when children are out of school, child care workers may watch older children as well as younger ones for the entire day while the parents are at work. **Median pay in 2012: $9.38/ hour; $19,510/year.**

Source: Bureau of Labor Statistics, *Occupational Outlook Handbook,* 2010–2011 edition.

Why do hand laborers and material movers earn on average $1.66 per hour more than day care workers? One could suggest a variety of reasons, but none of them eliminates the fact that day care work is more challenging and requires greater skill. Even the argument that greater pay to compensate for the dirty nature of work crumbles when one remembers that providing care for young children involves more than a little dirt and quite a few unpleasant smells! Disparities such as these have led feminist scholars to consider the **comparable worth** of different types of jobs. Their research indicates that wage disparities are not simply the result of labor supply and demand; instead they are intrinsically tied to the valuation of the jobs that men and women are expected to perform. Of course, one should use caution in generalizing from a selective comparison of two specific occupations. To address this concern, Paula England and her colleagues developed a variety of statistical approaches to document how comparable worth affects women's earnings, considering not so much who is working but, rather, the jobs associated with men's and women's roles in society. England's statistical models show that if a man with the same level of education moved from an occupation entirely composed of men to an occupation entirely composed of women, his earnings would substantially decline. Jobs that require care work (which is culturally associated with women's responsibilities) pay 5% to 10% less than do jobs that do not, even if other relevant factors are considered (e.g., jobholders' education, years on the job, supervisory responsibilities). It is hard not to conclude that "women's work" is systematically undervalued in the paid economy (England, Budig, and Folbre 2002; Karlin, England, and Richardson 2002).

There are often marked disparities in the comparable worth of *tasks* within jobs as well. Most occupations require workers to perform a wide range of activities, all of which are central to organizational success. New employees need to be trained, notes need to be taken, interpersonal conflicts need to be resolved, and a variety of other personnel and technological concerns need to be addressed on a day-to-day basis. Men and women employed in the same type of job may be directed to perform different aspects of that work. For example, women professors tend to be assigned a disproportionate share of student advisees, which in turn frees their male colleagues to spend more time on more highly valued research activities. Although colleges and universities give lip service to the importance of advising students (and cannot succeed without this work), the time spent on this work can hurt, rather than enhance, an employee's performance review. In the end, the tasks that men tend to be assigned carry greater weight in decisions about promotions and pay increases (Fletcher 2001).

How Job Designs Discriminate

Discrimination is commonly understood in terms of unfair evaluation of people who perform the same type of task. However, it is also possible to discriminate on the basis of selecting what tasks to use as a basis for evaluating performance or to structure jobs in such a manner that it disadvantages particular groups of workers.

Consider police work and careers within policing. Nearly all police departments require patrol officer candidates to demonstrate physical aptitude for the job and rely on tests that commonly include measures of physical prowess. On the surface, tests of agility and strength appear to be gender-neutral because the same standards can be applied to all candidates. But when one looks at the effects, and how fitness exams tend systematically to screen out women applicants, structural biases in their construction and application are revealed. At one police department in Pennsylvania, for example, only about one in ten (12%) female applicants successfully passed the running test, compared with more than half (60%) of the men (Brooks 2001). On measures of strength, women also fare poorly. The average woman can only perform sit-ups and push-ups at about 75% the capacity of men, and the average grip strength for women is only 57% of that of men (Shephard and Bonneau 2002). These differences are real, but one must ask how often a police officer actually will need to perform push-ups or run long distances in the line of duty. One also wonders how much grip strength it actually takes to fire a pistol and why tests of strength, such as these, are on fitness exams. Nevertheless, these are the standards commonly used to screen applicants.

Part of a patrol officer's job requires physical work, and applicants should not be exempt from those responsibilities. However, it should be the case that the tests used to assess applicants are *relevant* to the job. Most day-to-day police work involves mundane rides in patrol cars, writing up reports, processing people, and handing out tickets. When force is needed, it is commonly performed as a team effort rather than being performed by lone officers. Technologies such as Tasers also make the successful management of physical altercations depend less on strength. Perhaps most devastating to the argument regarding the need for physical tests for police work is the observation that physical tests are used to determine who can *enter* into police jobs but not who can *keep* them.

Beyond these observations, consider how the existing selective testing techniques tend to ignore the skills that women are especially likely to possess. For example, only about half of all police departments include situational tests, wherein a simulated real-life encounter is constructed and recruits are judged on their ability to handle routine traffic stops or more dangerous encounters (Shephard and Bonneau 2002). In these simulation exams, the ability to read emotional states and intentions is the needed skill, a strength more commonly associated with feminine qualities than masculine attributes. Arguably, interpersonal tests are more important than physical tests because the ability to read a person's motivations and emotional state, and respond accordingly, could help officers avoid having to use physical force in the first place. Because these tests are not as widely used, the likelihood that candidates with poor interpersonal skills will make it through the screening process is increased, which favors the candidacy of underqualified male applicants. Also, note that the work of police supervisors or detectives almost never requires the use of force, but the career path to those positions is through patrol jobs, which in turn requires demonstration of physical prowess.

Structural forms of discrimination are built into the very design of work. Therein lays the problem, because most jobs and professional expectations have been designed with men in mind. For example, to become a pilot in the U.S. Air Force, one needs to be sixty-four to seventy-seven inches tall, a standard that is squarely in the midrange for American men but that screens half of all women from eligibility.[1] Here we observe something different from the police exams, in that height criteria are not arbitrary or irrationally selected. Pilots need to be able to reach the levers and buttons that surround them on all sides of their cockpit seats. In this case, the structural discrimination occurred in the design of the plane itself, which was tailored to fit a typical man, not a typical woman. And sometimes professional communities distinguish masculine/high-value jobs from feminine/low-value jobs, as is the case of engineers who divide themselves into "technical" and "social" subfields. Women are more likely to be directed into (and direct themselves into) the engineering subfields that require "soft" (people) skills but pay lower wages as well. As a point of comparison, consider that an engineer's limited ability to interact effectively with others can be viewed as a marker of being especially well suited to higher-paid work opportunities on technical matters (Cech 2013b). Similarly, within the medical profession women doctors tend to gravitate to "people oriented" specialties, such as family practice or pediatrics, whereas men gravitate to technical specialties such as surgery, radiology, or pathology (Ku 2011). Again, the latter subspecialties within the profession tend to offer greater financial rewards, but one must wonder if the job demands warrant the pay differentials. Both of these examples illustrate the ways professions need employees with diverse skills but divide, assign, and value work according to a gender regime.

Legal scholar Joan Williams (2000) identified a number of interesting cases such as these in her book *Unbending Gender*, which examined the templates used to construct job expectations. She concluded that the current structure of work itself can be discriminatory because it uses the image of the male worker as the metric for determining the characteristics of **the ideal worker.** Ideal workers, in today's economy, are people who can put in long hours, uninterrupted, throughout their careers. They are available when the company needs them, can work late when called on, can spend weekends in the office, and will not have any prolonged absences from the job. Their performance will not be hindered by sickness, aging parents, children, or pregnancy. These expectations are largely insensitive to the normal life courses of women and their roles off the job. In a word, ideal workers are men.

As another example, consider how inhospitable most workplaces are to breastfeeding—a normal part of women's lives but not men's. Exhibit 6.11 reveals the numerous health benefits of breastfeeding, for both children and nursing mothers. The American Academy of Pediatrics recommends that newborn children be exclusively fed breast milk for the first six months of life and then be provided with breast milk along with other food until at least twelve months of age. But fewer than one in four American women who work full time nurse their children to the six-month marker, a much smaller percentage compared with new mothers who are out of the labor force (Galtry 2000, 2002). And when working women do breastfeed their children to the six-month marker or longer, they suffer significant income losses in comparison to women who rely on formula or a shorter duration of breastfeeding combined with formula use (Rippeyoung and Noonan 2012).

The breastfeeding problem can be attributed to the fact that most working women cannot afford temporary leaves from their jobs and that newborn children are not welcomed in most workplaces. However, there exists an underused technological solution that can help women stay strongly attached to jobs. Breast pumps (which used to be bulky and somewhat noisy appliances) are now quiet and small enough to be carried like briefcases. These devices enable nursing mothers to express milk while away from their children and then store it for later use. Using these machines only requires privacy, access to a refrigerator, and the provision of brief breaks (twenty to thirty minutes a few times a day). These are modest resources to provide, but they remain unavailable to most workers. In 2010, the Fair Labor Standards Act was amended to require employers to provide reasonable break time and a private, nonbathroom place for nursing mothers to express breast milk during the workday, for one year after the child's birth. Time will tell if this legislation has a marked effect, and as with other similar types of legislation, compliance is not always assured. Nonetheless, this type of responsiveness to concerns central to the operation of the new economy provides hope, as it illustrates that expectations about workplace practices are shifting.

Exhibit 6.11   Health Benefits to Breastfeeding

Benefits to Children	Benefits to Mothers
Less urinary tract infection	Less breast cancer
Less respiratory infection	Less ovarian cancer
Less diarrhea	Less osteoporosis
Less allergic disease	Earlier weight loss
Less middle ear infection	Enhanced self-esteem
Less bacterial meningitis	Enhanced infant bonding
Less botulism	Enhanced feelings of success
Less bacteremia	
Less gastrointestinal infection	
Less atopic eczema	

Source: American Academy of Pediatrics (2005).

In sum, a focus on job designs and the standards used to evaluate employees reveals structural considerations that disadvantage women in the paid labor force. Creating change in this area requires rethinking taken-for-granted assumptions concerning the best means to attach people to jobs and how to design jobs and careers such that they do not create de facto disadvantages that are predictable. This requires new talent management strategies to generate interest in jobs, screen applicants, design work spaces, construct work schedules, and evaluate employee performance. The first step in this process is to rethink who is the "ideal worker" and thereby bring workplace policy and practice into line with what is reasonable to expect from today's diverse workforce.

Strategies to Bridge the Care Gaps: International Comparisons

The increased participation of women in the paid labor force has contributed to resource gaps in the provision of care for children and aging parents. This problem will escalate in coming decades as the aging baby boom generation continues to transition into retirement and then into old age. As this happens, ever-larger proportions of the workforce will find themselves sandwiched between the need to work, care for their parents, and care for their children (Neal and Hammer 2006; Sarkesian and Gerstel 2004). Here we consider two core policy considerations—provision of care alternatives and family leave options—and how those policies in the United States compare with those in other advanced societies.

America's approach to handling child care is a hodgepodge of stopgap approaches that create divergent experiences among different classes in the workforce. For workers at the top of the class structure, such as Erika, the stay-at-home mother discussed at the beginning of this chapter, high incomes afford not only the luxury to stay home but also the resources to employ others to cook, clean, and at times watch children. Professional women with demanding jobs can purchase care privately, although usually at considerable expense, and rely on a variety of prepackaged care items, such as prepared foods. These strategies work but eat into couples' incomes and stall careers. They are also not the preferred arrangements, as many parents feel deprived of the opportunity to engage fully in the provision of hands-on care of their children. For workers in jobs that pay low wages, the strains are far greater and solutions are even less satisfactory.[2] Many parents in working-class families deliberately work alternating shifts, so that someone is home at all times. This can work, but it has obvious negative effects on marriages and can create high levels of stress in people's lives (Presser 2003b). It is not unusual for children in low-income families to be left to care for themselves (Heymann 2000). Note also that a full understanding of the problem with the American system of care provision requires considering the ways that care needs are connected with class and racial relations. Today, America's child care system operates on the backs of poorly paid workers, who are almost exclusively women and disproportionately members of minority groups or recent immigrants. The affordable labor they provide makes it possible for professional women to devote time to their jobs, revealing that the ability of some women to integrate themselves into the new economy depends on the exploitation of other women (Mohanty 2003).

The uneven quality of child and elder care options in American society compares unfavorably with the situation in many countries in Western Europe, which have implemented national child care programs that fund publicly financed child care centers, which in turn promotes high use (Gornick and Meyers 2003; Pettit and Hook 2005). For example, because most child care workers in Sweden are well paid and have university degrees, virtually all working parents can go to their jobs assured that their children are receiving high-quality care (Morgan 2005). Some embrace the notion that children are best raised in the warm arms of their mothers and consider paid care providers to be comparatively "cold." This perception is not shared in Denmark, a country with universal child care supports. Danes believe that children served in quality state-sponsored centers receive "warm" care that helps them grow and mature, and it is not considered inferior to the care received in the home (Kremer 2006a).

Subsidizing care centers is one means of promoting family responsive policies. But this does not address the fundamental problem that most care work is uncompensated and performed by family members (Crittenden 2001). Here another social experiment is enlightening—the provision of direct payments to individuals to purchase care assistance. In the United States, professional home health care assistance, such as in-home nursing, is available only to those who have financial resources. Those lacking resources commonly go without care or rely on family members to provide this care (which in turn can interfere with their work). In Denmark, those need-ing home assistance are given a "Personal Budget" that they can use to purchase the assistance of their own choosing. Notable is that two in three of the people employed by those controlling their own Personal Budgets are the spouses, parents, or adult children of the person purchasing care. In essence, this system enables family members to compensate each other finan-cially for providing care work and legitimates their taking time out from the paid economy. However, this system is not without its own problems, because role conflicts can result when family members employ one another. It also has undermined the power of professional groups to define reasonable care standards (Kremer 2006b).

There have been some advances in the U.S. approach to work-family policy, but they are modest by international standards. One of these occurred in 1993 with the passage of the **Family and Medical Leave Act** (FMLA).[3] This legislation provides workers with the right to take twelve weeks of leave from their jobs to care for newborn and newly adopted children or to assist other family members in need. By recognizing workers' need to take "time-outs" to tend to family matters, the FMLA was a tremendously important step in helping address existing care deficits. But it has not helped all workers. Because the leave allowed is relatively short (twelve weeks), the amount of time that care work can be performed is very limited. Employees who have worked for their employers for less than one year, those who work part time (less than twenty-five hours per week), and those who work for smaller employers (with fewer than fifty workers) are not covered by the FMLA. This disadvantages low-income workers, who are much more likely to be employed in smaller enterprises, to have less stable job histories, and to work part time. Most importantly, because the leave is unpaid, it is useful only to those workers who can afford to take time away from their jobs. Ironically, the result is that those who most need to take time away from their jobs—those who cannot afford to pay for care services—are excluded from reaping the benefits of the FMLA. And when employers voluntarily offer the option for care leaves, they are more likely to be offered to men in upper-tier professions than to women in lower-tier occupations (Swanberg, Pitt-Catsouphes, and Drescher-Burke 2005).

The FMLA is family leave American style; it assumes that most families have a breadwinner who can remain in the labor force to provide for family economic needs. For those eligible at the lower end of the economic spectrum, family leave can be considered a right but not an option. Exhibit 6.12 shows that the American approach is vastly inferior to the leave policies adopted in nearly all other developed nations. For example, Norway and the United Kingdom offer new parents an entire year off after the birth of a child, and these workers receive 80% or more of their base pay during that time. As we discuss next, provisions in Sweden are even more generous. In most of the countries that have paid parental leave, it is not the employer who pays (as Americans commonly assume would be the case). Rather, the government provides stipends (supported through higher taxes) that replace the wages new parents would have earned from their jobs. Though most Western European countries have developed more supportive family responsive policies, important cultural variations also influenced the forms these

Exhibit 6.12   Statutory Family Leave Entitlements in Developed Countries

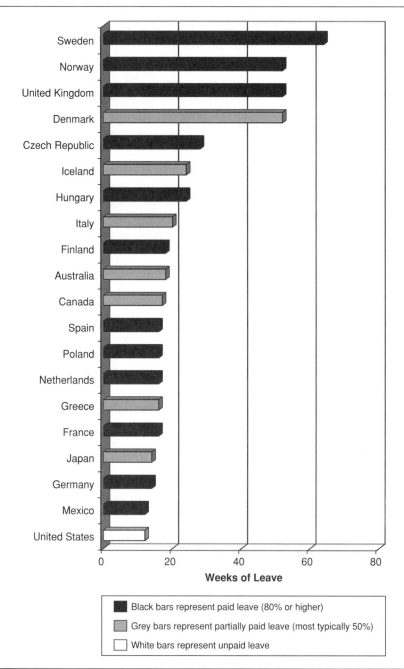

Source: United Nations Statistics and Indicators on Men and Women (2011).

policies take. Some societies seek to emancipate women from the home and to dismantle traditional gender roles (e.g., Finland), while others seek to facilitate the fulfillment of traditional gender roles with some integration of women into the paid labor force (e.g., the Netherlands and Germany) (Haas and Rostgaard 2011; Pfau-Effinger 2004).

Sweden offers an interesting case study of the possibilities for policy change, as well as cautionary findings on the impact family responsive legislation can have on men's and women's behavior inside and outside the workplace. Currently, families are entitled to a total of 480 days of family leave, most of which is compensated at 80% of the salary earned (with a cap on higher-earning households). In the early 1970s, the Swedish government formed a commission to study family needs. Its findings pushed the nation to enact and actively promote family leave with legislation that was initially designed to encourage both mothers and fathers to be involved in the nurturing of children. It soon became clear that men, on the whole, were reluctant to make use of parental leave benefits. In response, in 1995 the government initiated legislation and public relations campaigns to promote a "daddy month"—an incentive specifically directed to encourage men to take paid time out from their jobs to tend to their children. Of note, the impetus for this initiative to motivate men to take time out for work came first from women's groups, who saw rebalancing family divisions of labor as a critical condition for increasing gender equality. Later men became highly involved and helped win passage of the legislation (Bergman and Hobson 2002). Because the daddy month is defined such that one must either "use it or lose it," men were motivated to take time out from work. Having observed the impact on parental behavior, Sweden subsequently expanded fathers' leave to two months, which in turn has led to more men taking longer leaves from work. Other countries, such as Iceland, have tried even more aggressive schemes, such as expecting equal shares of leave to be taken by husbands and wives, and have seen even stronger effects on men's willingness to pursue parental leave. These case studies show that "gender blind" policies are not sufficient to reshape commitments in the home; what is necessary are incentives that draw men into committing time for care work and policies that minimize the penalties associated with temporarily leaving work (Haas and Rostgaard 2011).

Sweden's experiments with family responsive programs also helped reveal a paradox. While paid family leave facilitated women's participation in the labor force and helped them care for young children, it also *exacerbated* the level of gender occupational segregation and the earnings gap that separates men from women workers. The reason for this dynamic is that paid family leave is almost exclusively used by women (Morgan and Zippel 2003).

When employers know that men are unlikely to request time away from the job, but that women are more likely to make that request, clear incentives are created to discriminate against women workers, especially those who will be expected to assume positions of responsibility. As a result, countries with the most family friendly legislation (such as Sweden) have even higher levels of sex segregation than the United States does, and women are less likely to advance to the highest levels in the paid labor force (Mandel and Semyonov 2004, 2006). This paradoxical outcome—the more generous the family leave, the more severe the gender inequality—has intrigued researchers interested both in supporting gender equality and in resolving work-family tensions. What is clear is that the provision of family leave tends to expand gender inequalities for those in upper-tier professions, but inequalities are leveled among those further down the occupational scale. Thus there needs to be caution in assuming that any work-family policy affects all classifications of workers in the same way (Mandel 2011; Misra, Budig, and Boeckman 2011). It is also clear that the type of work-family policy being considered, and the quantity of resources provided, can make a marked difference in shaping women's attachment to the labor force and men's attachment to care work (Hegewisch and Gornick 2011). Therefore, even if some unanticipated consequences are identified, these do not indicate a need to discard family leave policies but rather to modify them—for example, by introducing use incentives for men.

At a time when many European countries have been expanding their supports for working families, the United States enacted regressive policies directed at those at the bottom of the class structure. Ironically, as the need to care for disadvantaged children increased, welfare reform undermined the prospects for poor single mothers to stay home with their children. The Personal Responsibility and Work Opportunity Reconciliation Act of 1996 reworked the previous major welfare program, called **Aid to Families with Dependent Children (AFDC)**, into the current program called **Temporary Assistance for Needy Families (TANF)**. The AFDC system provided monthly welfare checks to poor families as a substitute for attachment to the labor force. Political leaders came to believe that this approach was promoting a culture of dependency, one in which poor people accepted "welfare as a way of life" (Murray 1995). In its stead, TANF was designed to limit support to a lifetime maximum of five years (states are free to set the limit lower, and some have done so), as well as to create an expectation that recipients work while receiving assistance and continue to work after the assistance ends. In this way, TANF was designed to get the poor into the labor force. But it did so with inadequate provisions to enable poor families (disproportionately single mothers) to manage the care of their children (Hays 2003). Studies of these families on the fault line indicate that they are typically placed in jobs that pay at or near the minimum wage, that these jobs seldom have any prospects for upward mobility, that care responsibilities interfere with women's abilities to keep these jobs, and that the lack of child care resources forces families to place children in situations untenable by middle-class standards (Crouter and Booth 2004). So, whereas many societies in Europe have enabled women to take sabbaticals from their jobs, America introduced initiatives to require the participation of the poor in jobs that pay little and offer few opportunities for advancement. Time will tell what impact this has on the next generation, but it is reasonable to predict that forcing poor women to take low-wage jobs will do little to alter existing gendered wage disparities and will maintain or even exacerbate racial disparities as well.

Conclusion

In this chapter, we surveyed and mapped the contours of gender inequality in the workplace, as well as considered the reasons for their occurrence. We showed that even though women comprise nearly half of the American workforce, only a small fraction rise to the top and become corporate or government leaders. Instead, they are disproportionately funneled into lower-paying jobs and face greater prospects than men of having their careers dislodged midstream. We also showed that women perform substantial amounts of work that is economically unrecognized or undervalued. Although interpersonal discrimination remains an important consideration in the new economy, deeper structural problems exist that differentially affect women's and men's careers. To be successful in today's workforce requires molding oneself into jobs designed for men who had stay-at-home wives.

The chasms that separate men's and women's careers are created by a variety of forces that have the consequence of fostering disadvantages that accumulate over their life courses. Women are coached early on to have different aspirations than men, and men and women are encouraged to accept—as a given—that "women's work" is of lesser economic value. If this work is undervalued, men will not seek it, with the result that large numbers of women will remain trapped in low-paying occupational ghettos. There have been advances in encouraging girls to aspire to enter "men's" careers. But there is a crying need to teach boys (and men) the rewards that can be obtained in the performance of "women's work," both in the home and in the paid economy, and to alter existing practices that systematically undervalue care work.

Although not a panacea or without problems and concerns, America's adjustment to the new economy can benefit from considering the far bolder European social experiments that advance opportunities to care for children and other community members. Ultimately, the future structure of the new economy will reflect the decisions made to address the question of gender inequality, the level of commitment to dismantling the gendered divisions of labor both inside and outside the home, and the concern for providing care when most parents are in the paid labor force.

Notes

1. The average height of American men is 69.2 inches, for women, 63.8 inches.

2. Parents in the United States can take a pretax deduction for child care expenses, but this policy does little to help low-income families who commonly pay little in income taxes to begin with.

3. In California, legislation took effect in 2004 mandating that employees be eligible to receive as much as half pay for a period of six weeks to care for a sick or injured family member or following birth, adoption, or foster care placement. Unlike the FMLA, there is no restriction on organizational size or tenure with the employer. Time will tell if the country follows California's lead, one that was met by considerable opposition from business groups (Nowicki 2003).

Chapter Seven

Race, Ethnicity, and Work

*Legacies of the Past, Problems
in the Present*

Mike, the young African American man introduced in Chapter 1, has the odds stacked against him. But one wonders what factors caused his current situation, his tenuous hold on work in the new economy. Are his problems simply the result of his (and his parents') choices? Or are they the result of his lower-class social origins? No doubt both played a role. But, beyond that, the resources and opportunities available to Mike have been influenced by race as well. As we discuss in this chapter, while some of the racial barriers that existed in the old economy have been partially countered by legislation and changing public attitudes, the structuring of the new economy also has introduced new challenges that disadvantage racial and ethnic minorities, which is in turn leaving a generation of young, lower-class minority workers at the margins. And even among members of the middle class, race continues to influence how high one can rise.

In this chapter, we offer an overview of race, ethnicity, and work, looking both to the past for the origins of contemporary problems and to the future challenge of creating a fully racially integrated workforce. We first consider race and ethnicity from a historical perspective to provide a context for considering the ways in which racial and ethnic exclusion manifested itself in the old economy. Though patterns of exclusion have changed in some ways, they continue to influence the allocation of the resources needed to prepare for work, as well as access to jobs themselves. As a result, members of some racial and ethnic minorities are at a distinct disadvantage in today's workplace and labor market. These observations lead us to several critical policy issues concerning work, race, and ethnicity in the twenty-first century, including immigration control and affirmative action programs.

Histories of Race, Ethnicity, and Work

Concurrent with the transition to a new economy have been remarkable changes in ways that race and ethnic identities are understood and defined. Consider, for example, that in the old economy people were fitted into rather neat racial categories, whereas today multiracial and multiethnic identities are commonplace. It is also clear that the relative importance of different racial and ethnic affiliations has also shifted in public discourse, such as increased attention to Hispanic heritage and Muslim religious affiliations. While this seems new, shifting definitions of social groupings and understandings of those groupings occurred in the old economy as well. For example, Americans now refer to all persons of European descent as being "white," whereas early twentieth-century Americans would have categorized them into many different racial groups. Sociologists and others have increasingly come to define race as a social construct, in which physical differences between groups (such as skin color) are assumed by members of society to mean that those groups inherently differ in many other ways (e.g., ability, intelligence). The term *ethnicity* (or *ethnic groups*) is generally used to describe the cultural differences (e.g., language, diet, costume) between groups (for example, between Americans of Polish and Irish descent).[1] Our purpose in this section is not to provide a comprehensive overview of racial histories (a mighty task indeed!) but simply to illustrate how history maps onto the present and has shaped some of the contours shaping the distribution of opportunity along racial and ethnic lines.

African American Exceptionality

One question commonly posed is why African Americans, who have been in America nearly as long as white Americans (and much longer than many other ethnic groups) are economically so far behind. One explanation is that, unlike virtually all other immigrant groups, most people of African descent were brought forcibly to America, severed from family ties, and sold into bondage. In early America, African Americans were, in most instances, forbidden to hold property or to advance their positions. The dominant ethnic group, white Anglo-Saxon Protestants (WASPs), accrued wealth and later came to control the economic and political fortunes of the nineteenth century, but African Americans were left behind. Although American history marks the resolution of the Civil War as the formal end to slavery, it did remarkably little to change the day-to-day work experiences of African Americans in the South, where most newly freed African Americans remained propertyless, sharecropped the fields for their old masters, and accrued debt rather than wealth. As previously discussed in Chapter 3, as well as elaborated on in this chapter, the intergenerational transmission of wealth is an incredibly important ingredient for success in the new economy, placing African American children at profound disadvantages, then and now.

Although a significant number of African Americans worked outside of agriculture even under slavery, it was difficult for them to find work in industry in the post–Civil War South. Some did find employment, but even those with significant skills were typically relegated to work as unskilled laborers. Whites and most trade unions (especially unions of skilled workers) devoted considerable energy to keeping African American workers out. And the racial hostilities that permeated American culture were strategically exploited by employers in some parts of the country, using African Americans as strikebreakers or threatening to replace low-wage white workers with African Americans unless workers acquiesced to management's terms. African American women were much more likely than were their white counterparts to work in the post–Civil War period, but they were largely kept out of industrial employment. Most found work in various menial service occupations, such as washing clothes (Gerstel and Sarkisian 2006).

Around the time of World War I, large numbers of African Americans (along with rural whites from Appalachia) traveled from the South to the North to find work in the rapidly industrializing cities. Even though African American men succeeded in finding work in industry, most remained confined to unskilled jobs at the bottom of the employment ladder and were generally less likely to be employed than were new immigrants coming from Eastern and Western Europe. African American women had far less success entering industry than did African American men, so they continued to be concentrated in low-level service occupations. In the South, as well as in the North, a stable African American middle class emerged, but the black-white division was so strong that they formed separate castes within a supposedly free society, separated into distinct communities, and shared few social ties or common experiences with the white middle class (Myrdal 1995 [1954]).

In general, throughout the period of rapid industrialization, most African American workers, whether they were in the South or the North, were channeled into the least desirable forms of employment, were far more exposed to unemployment in bad economic times, and were prevented from acquiring the education or training that might gain them access to better-paying jobs. But there was some progress. Some unions, for example (particularly those that organized all categories of workers, not just skilled workers), crossed racial lines. And during World War II, because of labor shortages, some African American workers moved up, temporarily, into better jobs. However, once the war was over, many of these gains evaporated, leaving African Americans in much the same condition they had been in before (Honey 1999). Unfortunately, as union membership has declined, so has the influence of unions on limiting the extent of wage disparities that exist on the basis of race (Rosenfeld and Kleykamp 2012).

In the latter half of the twentieth century, many aspects of race in American society changed. Key pieces of civil rights legislation, such as the **Equal Pay Act of 1963** and the **Civil Rights Act of 1964**, established the legal standard barring employers from excluding anyone from employment on the basis of race or ethnicity. Civil rights legislation also put an end to legalized segregation in the South. Evidence also shows that overt hostility to African Americans was on the wane in the latter part of the twentieth century and that the United States has become a more racially tolerant society (Schuman et al. 1998). Does this mean that race no longer matters? Some, like the highly influential sociologist William Julius Wilson (1987), argued that race, as a master status, has declined in its significance. He observed that African Americans who had moved out of the central cities, who had entered college, and who had developed marketable skills stood reasonable chances of making it in the rapidly changing economy. If African Americans continued to be economically disadvantaged, he argued, it was not primarily the result of race but of *class*, that is, of the declining opportunities for well-paid employment for those with limited education and skills. Others disagreed, finding evidence that race still mattered. Even though legalized discrimination had been abolished, and overt forms of prejudice weakened, the United States is still not a color-blind society, and various forms of "subtle discrimination" continue to affect all aspects of social life, including workplaces.

The Immigrant Experience

African American workers faced particularly well-organized and harsh systems of oppression, but they were not alone in encountering obstacles to employment in the industrial United States. Americans frequently succumbed to "nativist" sentiments, and many immigrant groups found themselves excluded from certain kinds of employment ("Irish need not apply"), trapped in poorly paid ethnic economies (e.g., the Jews in the garment trades), exploited by unscrupulous employers, and suspected of radical or anti-American sentiments. In the factories of the late nineteenth century, jobs were distributed to ethnically homogenous work teams, and favoritism to one's own ethnic group was considered a normal way of distributing work (Jacoby 1991). Various stakeholders of the time produced a variety of documents demonstrating the dangers new immigrants posed to American society (Gusfield 1963; Thomas and Znaniecki 1958). As Exhibit 7.1 shows, these hostilities were compounded by concerns raised in the mid-nineteenth century about Asian immigrants. This cartoon not so subtly suggests that immigrants, and their foreign ways, had the potential to swallow up American values and liberties. Racial and ethnic diversity was then—and is now—viewed by some as a threat rather than as a strength.

In the early part of the twentieth century, immigrant groups, African Americans, and native-born white Americans competed for jobs within a split labor market, such that employers would gravitate to employing workers from specific ethnic groups as first or second preferences, depending on

Exhibit 7.1   An Editorial Showing Fear of Immigrants (Circa 1860)

THE GREAT FEAR OF THE PERIOD
THAT UNCLE SAM MAY BE SWALLOWED BY FOREIGNERS.

Source: Copyright © by Corbis. Reprinted with permission.

need and interests in potentially driving down wages by playing off interethnic hostilities (Restifo, Roscigno, and Qian 2013). During the twentieth century, some hostilities faded as immigrants gained citizenship and assimilated. For the most part (and unlike the African American experience) immigrant families who had initially seemed foreign and threatening were amalgamated into the new economy, improving their fortunes within the expanding U.S. economy. But suspicion of immigrants remained strong, as evidenced by the passage of highly restrictive legislation that established strict quotas on immigration from virtually all parts of the world (Alba and Nee 2003). Certain groups received particularly unfriendly treatment, as the following examples illustrate.

- Male Chinese workers were imported to the United States, largely to help build the transcontinental railroad, but they were not allowed to bring along their families or become citizens. Once the railroad was completed, Americans reacted to the arrival of immigrants from China and Japan by pressing for legislation to keep them out. These efforts were successful; Chinese immigration was stopped with the 1882 Chinese Exclusion Act and Japanese immigration with the Gentleman's Agreement of 1907 and the Immigration Act of 1924.

- Japanese immigrants to the United States (Issei) succeeded as farmers in western states and hoped that their children (Nisei) would gain acceptance into the American mainstream. However, despite doing well in school, few managed to find jobs outside the ethnic labor market before World War II. Isolated and disliked, Japanese Americans were easy targets for the internment policy of World War II (Takaki 2008).

- The Bracero program, established to respond to labor shortages during World War II, created work opportunities for immigrants from Mexico. As "guest workers," Mexicans were allowed to enter the United States temporarily to work and then return to Mexico, but the program did not permit long-term residency and restricted their employment to low-level jobs that American employers found difficult to fill (Alba and Nee 2003).

Changes in immigration law in the post–World War II period put an end to the exclusionary laws affecting Chinese and Japanese immigration and eliminated the immigration quotas, with their racial overtones that had shaped immigration policy since the 1920s. The Bracero program was also discontinued in the mid-1960s, eliminating the special category of guest worker, to which many Mexican migrants had been confined. Recent immigration law reforms opened the door for increased levels of immigration. As a result, the percentage of American workers who are foreign-born is approaching the level reached at the peak of pre–World War I immigration. In 1900, 20.3% of the labor force was foreign-born; after dropping for most of the twentieth century, the percentage began to rise again in the 1980s and had reached 15.6% of the labor force by 2007 (Newburger and Gryn 2009). Moreover, levels of immigration to the United States in the late twentieth and early twenty-first century rivaled those of earlier periods, with more than a million new *legal* permanent residents being admitted in many years (U.S. Department of Homeland Security 2010).

As levels of immigration rose, a sense developed that the most recent immigration waves were different. New immigration rules gave priority to those with educational credentials, which influenced the types of immigrants entering the country and their ability to enter the good jobs being cultivated in the new economy. As discussed later in this chapter, this dynamic can help explain why some recent immigrant groups have succeeded in ways that resident African American groups have not. However, because priority was given to immigrants with close family in the United States, many legal immigrants continue to arrive with limited education and skills (Alba and Nee 2003). This could potentially lead these immigrants to become a burden on society or bid down wages and displace more expensive American-born workers, an issue we discuss at greater length later in this chapter. Particular attention has been directed to cultural issues, as Latino migrants were (falsely, as it turns out) believed to be resistant to learning English (Portes and Rumbaut 2001). Some also feel that, in an age of easy electronic communication and cheap travel, immigrants, particularly from nearby Mexico, would remain tied to their cultures of origin and would resist "Americanization" (Alba and Nee 2003).

In this context, hostility to immigrants has reemerged, as evidenced by the construction of the barricades along the U.S.-Mexican border, growing support for aggressive government efforts to detect and deport illegal immigrants and their children, and the emergence of vigilante groups such as the Minute Men, who patrol for illegal immigrants. The concerns expressed in Exhibit 7.1 are echoed by the thesis of politician and commentator Patrick Buchanan's (2006) book *State of Emergency*. The only difference is that, instead of focusing concern on the Chinese, this book directs fear and hostility toward Mexican immigrants.

Magnitude of Racial Inequality in the New Economy

It is hard to argue that race and ethnicity are no longer major factors in determining one's fate in the workplace after considering the extent of the differences between Latino, African American, and white American incomes. One way of measuring these disparities is to examine per capita earnings, that is, the total of all earnings within a racial group divided by total group membership. Note, however, that the way these estimates are usually created

Exhibit 7.2   Mean Income of Men With Earnings: United States, 1970–2012 (Adjusted to 2012 Dollars)

Source: Statistical Abstract of the United States, U.S. Census Bureau.

considers only those who have incomes, leaving out of the analysis individuals who lack incomes (disproportionately members of racial minorities). Exhibit 7.2 reveals that average incomes for men with incomes in the four major racial groups have remained largely stagnant during the past three decades and have actually declined since 2000.[2] Exhibit 7.3 shows that averages for women with incomes have risen more rapidly and have not declined since 2000 (although women continue to trail men by significant margins). These exhibits also show the continued existence of income gaps between whites, Asian Americans, African Americans, and Latinos. For men, whites and Asian Americans outearn African Americans and Latinos by a significant margin, and that margin has not narrowed appreciably over the past decade. The gaps among women wage earners are considerably smaller and have not changed significantly in the past ten years. Asian American women have the highest incomes, followed by white women. African American women's incomes are only slightly lower than white women's, while Latinas earn substantially less, on average, than women in any of the other three groups.[3]

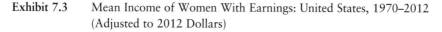

Exhibit 7.3   Mean Income of Women With Earnings: United States, 1970–2012 (Adjusted to 2012 Dollars)

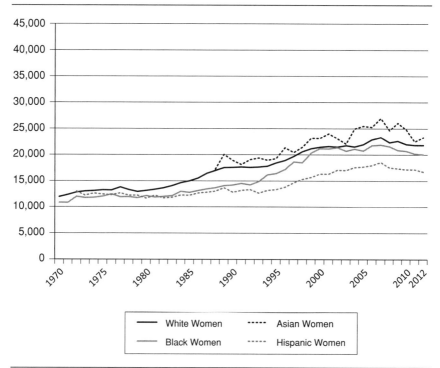

Source: Statistical Abstract of the United States, U.S. Census Bureau.

The large gaps in men's incomes are only part of the story. Another important question is whether the jobs obtained by African Americans and Latinos are sufficient to bring families to a reasonable standard of living. Answering this requires shifting analysis from individuals to families and considering all the sources of income a family possesses. Family structures vary across social groups, with significant consequences for their earnings. For instance, African American families are far more likely than are white families to be single-parent families relying on a single income. Latino and Asian American families, on the other hand, are much more similar in structure to white families than they are to African American families. Having two adult wage earners in the household may help to compensate partially for the limited returns received from low-wage jobs. As Exhibit 7.4 shows, African Americans and Latino Americans are more than twice as likely as white Americans to be living below the poverty line. This reveals that race and ethnicity are closely tied to the ability to find the types of jobs that enable families to achieve reasonable standards of living. For one in four African American or Latino families, these opportunities are very limited.

Exhibit 7.4   Percentage of People Living Below the Poverty Line: United States, 2012

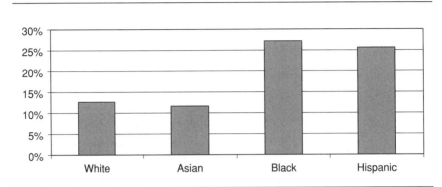

Source: U.S. Census Bureau.

The existence of a significant income gap between whites and African Americans or Latinos has fueled speculation that a racially and ethnically distinctive "underclass" has emerged in the United States. This argument was first made about African Americans, whose higher rates of poverty and bad employment prospects are an old and (as the earlier data indicate) continuing story. Scholars have speculated that a similar phenomenon is developing among Latinos. These scholars argue that, unlike earlier European immigrants, Latinos are not rapidly assimilating into the American economy and moving their way up the economic ladder. Instead, a process of "segmented assimilation" is occurring, in which Latinos become part of the American economy but in roles much like those of lower-class African Americans; that is, in poorly paid, unstable, secondary labor market jobs. Not everyone agrees with this view. Some contend that Latinos *are* gradually making their way up the ladder, although their progress is slowed by the shrinkage of factory employment (the traditional route for upward mobility among immigrants) (Alba and Nee 2003). Still others argue that Latinos are following a path of "working-class assimilation"; that is, they are moving up the economic ladder but not as fast as they would if they were not members of an identifiable minority group (Waldinger, Lim, and Cort 2007). Though not fully agreeing on the pace of assimilation, all these studies conclude that being Latino has a significant negative effect on the ability to find good, secure, well-paying jobs.

Thus, we are left with a puzzle. How is it possible—in a society where the legal constraints limit discrimination on the basis of race and ethnicity, where evidence indicates that some cultural attitudes have changed, where the belief is that equal opportunity exists, and where examples of successful minorities abound—that African Americans and Latinos lag so far behind whites and people of Asian descent? In the sections that follow, we argue that the reasons for racial and ethnic inequalities in the workplace are tied to three overarching sources of inequality and that each of these sources of inequality involves persistent problems from the old economy and emerging problems linked to the new one. One source is the ability of parents to prepare their children for the world of work, a process that requires intergenerational transmission of resources. Another source involves aspects of social structure, such as the ways work opportunities, race, and geography intertwine. Finally, interpersonal dynamics play a role as well, as members of different ethnic groups face different prospects of being perceived and treated equitably in the workplace. As discussed later, these separate explanations—resources, opportunity, and discrimination—work together in a cumulative manner to fashion racial and ethnic disadvantages in the new economy. And while race and ethnicity create barriers for some members of society, they can create advantages for others by facilitating the formation of social connections that help members of some ethnic groups adapt to the new opportunity structures.

Intergenerational Transmission of Resources

For most workers in today's economy, a successful career requires strategic investments of time, energy, and financial resources. Here we consider four types of resources passed through intergenerational relations. These resources constitute capital (or assets) that can be used to enhance future career prospects (Bourdieu 1986). One type of capital is economic, that is, income and property that can be devoted to education or entrepreneurial endeavors. But prospects for success also can be elevated through the development of marketable skills (human capital), network ties (social capital), and the ability to interact comfortably with others who have resources (cultural capital). As we discuss next, race maps onto access to all of these assets.

Race, Ethnicity, and Economic Capital

In comparison with whites, African Americans and Latinos have less **economic capital**, fewer financial resources essential to pursuing a college education or the start-up funds needed for entrepreneurial endeavors. In addition to income differentials, racial minorities are disadvantaged in respect to wealth—the sum total of all possessions. Wealth is difficult to measure because it is not formally tracked in the way that income is assessed, but Exhibit 7.5 shows some of the extent of the differences. In 2011, only one in two African Americans or Latino American households had interest-earning bank accounts or owned a home. Fewer than one in ten owned stocks, and only about one in four participated in 401(k) retirement accounts. Taken together, these statistics indicate that most African Americans and Latino Americans are essentially propertyless, possessing virtually no economic resources to pass on to the next generation, either in the form of inheritance or in the form of enhanced resources in the home. Note also that the absence of retirement accounts inverts the relationships between parents and children, as the children of African Americans and Latinos are far more likely to funnel resources *to* their parents in later life, which in turn saps the financial resources that they might send to their own children. The problem has only grown worse in the aftermath of the Great Recession, as African Americans and Latinos lost their homes through foreclosure at almost twice the rate as white homeowners (Bocian, Li, and Ernst 2010). And as the stock market has returned to record highs, most African American and Latino households saw no positive gains in wealth, as they were not positioned to benefit from owning stocks or retirement portfolios. In contrast, those who were able to retain control of their wealth that existed before the Great Recession have seen those assets grow as the economy recovered.

Exhibit 7.5   Percentage of Households Owning Select Assets by Race: United States, 2011

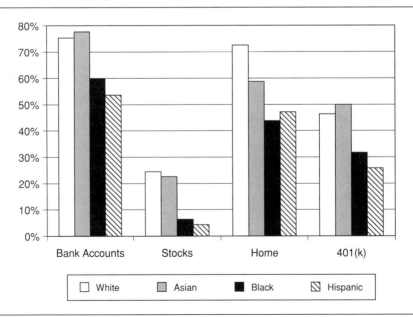

Source: U.S. Census Bureau.

Wealth deprivation is especially important to consider in the contemporary economic situation because it plays a significant role in decreasing the likelihood that disadvantaged children will successfully apply to competitive college programs. Opportunities to take advanced placement exams or to engage in extracurricular activities (necessary for entry into elite college programs) are in many cases absent from the rural and urban schools where African American and Latino students are concentrated. Movement to desirable school districts requires the financial wherewithal to afford down payments and hefty mortgages, often beyond the reach of disadvantaged parents (Kozol 2006). In other words, the possession of a home can be directly linked to access to high-quality education. Consider, for example, that in Hillsborough Hills, California, in 2012 (where the population is 66% white and the median household income is $250,000) parents *donate* $2,300 per pupil *in addition to* the regular funds that this affluent school district budgets for education. Twenty miles away, in East Palo Alto (where the population is 29% white and the median household income is $48,700 per year), the school's foundation receives donations that equate to $100 per student. Here we see how race intersects with place, resulting in chasms that block prospects for mobility and advantages that secure success (Reich 2013).

How can the economic capital differences among racial and ethnic groups be reduced? One solution is to rework the distribution of resources so that members of the lower classes (who are disproportionately members of minority groups) have a more equitable share of the collective pool of income. This could involve, for instance, revising the minimum wage standard to enable those in low-wage jobs to earn enough to get by and to invest in their children's lives. Improved incomes would, in turn, help African Americans and Latinos begin to accumulate wealth (through savings, home ownership, and even investment), though efforts also would need to be made to overcome problems such as obstacles to home ownership (e.g., discriminatory lending practices and continued housing segregation) (Shapiro 2004). Finding ways to loosen the connection between property ownership and access to high-quality education also would be important. This would require rethinking how community resources are directed, for instance, reversing the current system so that greater proportions of social resources are directed to schools in disadvantaged (minority) neighborhoods.

Race, Ethnicity, and Human Capital

At the beginning of the movie *The Graduate*, Mr. Robinson offers Benjamin Braddock a piece of advice about how to make his fortune— "Plastics . . . enough said." The message was straightforward; all Ben needed to do was develop the skills and apply himself to that industry, and his future would be made. Such advice fits well within human capital theory, a perspective that focuses on the value of the skills different employees apply to their jobs. **Human capital** comprises capabilities vested in individuals, such as technical skills, education, and experience. Those individuals who have the most human capital generally are the most valued employees, earn the highest wages, and have the strongest prospects for upward mobility. Conversely, those who lack skills, or who possess skills that do not fit current opportunity structures, experience economic hardship.

One approach to documenting differences in human capital is to study achievements in formal schooling. In 2010 the percentage of African Americans (84%) who had earned high school degrees was only modestly lower than whites (87%) and Asians (88%), a dramatic change from the past, when African Americans were far less likely to complete high school than other groups. Latinos, on the other hand, continued to lag far behind (62%), a dynamic that largely reflects the recent arrival of poorly educated immigrants from Mexico and other parts of Latin America (Waldinger 2001). But even if high school graduation rates among the various ethnic groups were at complete parity, African Americans and Latinos are far more likely to attend schools that provide inferior learning opportunities compared with those offered in the suburban schools whites and Asians are more likely to attend.

More revealing are differences in the likelihood of completing postsecondary education; these trends are illustrated in Exhibit 7.6. While college completion rates have increased for all groups during the latter part of the twentieth century, Asian Americans have the highest college completion rates, with whites second. African Americans and Latinos are significantly less likely to have a college degree, which puts members of these groups at a distinct disadvantage in the competition for the higher-skill and higher-paying positions in the new economy.

Identification of racial differences in educational attainment helps resolve one of the major questions concerning race and work: why are so many Asian Americans (many of whom are recent immigrants) succeeding when large numbers of African Americans and Latinos are not? One explanation can be found in Asian Americans' possession of the type of human capital valued in today's economy: the skills and credentials obtained through a college education. They are what some sociologists call "human capital immigrants" (such as computer programmers and doctors from India), who typically adapt to the United States quickly and get jobs fairly similar to those obtained by nonimmigrants (although there is evidence that Asian Americans with degrees from outside the United States do less well than those with degrees from American universities and that "silicon ceilings"

Exhibit 7.6   Percentage Graduating From College (Age Twenty-Five Years and Older) by Race: United States, 1970–2013

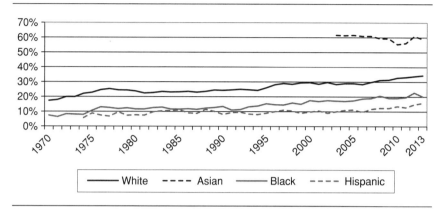

Source: U.S. Census Bureau.

exist in high-tech firms for Indians). Latinos are much more likely to be "labor migrants," who arrive with limited education and, consequently, make slower economic progress and get trapped in low-wage jobs (Alba and Nee 2003; Varma 2006; Zeng and Xie 2004).

The strong effect of human capital differences on economic inequality points to the need to improve opportunities—especially for members of disadvantaged minority groups—for education and training. But this alone is not a solution to the problem of inequality because many jobs in today's economy are designed to be performed by low-skill workers. Even if one could wave a wand and make all members of society hold PhDs, there would still be hamburgers to flip, shelves to stock, and cash registers to operate. This indicates the need for initiatives to improve the returns on work and supports for the disproportionate shares of minority workers channeled into the low end of the new economy.

Race, Ethnicity, and Social Capital

Human capital is about "what you know," and as just discussed, it can account for some of the variation in job attainment and earnings. **Social capital** is wealth that can be created through "who you know," such as kinship and friendship relationships, as these types of social ties can open doors. Even more distant relationships, or loose ties, can make a profound difference by simply increasing awareness that opportunities exist (Granovetter 1973, 1995).[4] Social capital does not operate instead of human capital; it operates in concert with it, with social ties opening opportunities to exercise and develop skills in the context of employment. For example, a Mexican construction worker may find a first job in the United States via kinship ties and then learn skills as an *ayudante* (helper/ apprentice). When he progresses to *albañil* (craftsman), he may *brincando* (job jump) to other employers, and these jumps may be independent of existing social ties (Hagan, Lowe, and Quingla 2011). The social capital made it possible for the immigrant to move from nonworker to novice worker to skilled worker, and the human capital gained over time makes it possible for him to achieve upward mobility that operates independently of kinship ties.

People tend to form social ties within racially **homogamous networks**— sets of social relations with others who are similar in race and economic position. White men are especially advantaged by their integration in networks with other white men, such that they become aware of not only better opportunities but also a wider volume of opportunities in comparison to women and members of disadvantaged minority groups (McDonald, Nan, and Ao 2009). In contrast, those at the lower end of the class structure are less likely to have much contact with people who can help them move up occupational ladders (Fernandez and Fernandez-Mateo 2006). Moreover, among the poorest groups in the new economy (where African Americans and Latinos are overrepresented), social networks often get used, out of necessity, primarily for day-to-day survival and can even create demands (especially on women, who are most frequently called on to help in times of need) that challenge personal capacities to maintain stable employment (Dominguez and Watkins 2003).

The existence of social capital plays an important role in explaining career mobility patterns. For instance, when Nicaraguan professionals migrated to Florida in the 1980s, they experienced difficulty finding good jobs, despite their high levels of education. In contrast, relatively poor and uneducated groups such as the Vietnamese who settled in Louisiana during the same period tended to do better, despite possessing weak English skills. The key difference was the strength and extent of the Vietnamese family networks that helped new members learn of job opportunities and placed them in positions in locally owned businesses (Portes and Rumbaut 2001). Other studies reveal similar effects for other ethnic groups that have had a longer history in the United States. For example, one classic study compared the employment experiences of young men growing up in three ethnic neighborhoods in Brooklyn, all of whom had high risk for entering criminal careers. When young Italian American men got into trouble, male relatives helped them get into the industrial work that they themselves performed. By contrast, Latino youths tended to work various kinds of neighborhood jobs with friends and relatives (especially those involving automobiles), which led them into more organized illegal work (in "chop shops") or into auto mechanics jobs (Sullivan 1989).

Access to networks and social capital is also an important factor in explaining the differences between African Americans and recent Latino immigrants. Both groups suffer a poverty of social capital but in different ways. One problem for inner-city African American young people is that their teachers and family members have few social ties with employers, and, as a consequence, they have fewer doors opened for them (Moss and Tilly 2001; Royster 2003). They also have far fewer contacts with jobholders and, as a result, have limited information about opportunities or mentorship on how to develop a successful career (W. Wilson 1997). Of note, Latino immigrants in inner-city locations appear to be finding jobs, despite the shortage of available opportunities, partly because of their social ties to other Latinos who hold jobs (Mouw 2002). These networks are so effective that some workplaces have developed internal norms of referring and hiring only Latino workers. Given language barriers, these tightly knit work groups can make it difficult for employers to hire members of other ethnic groups (Waldinger and Lichter 2003). Even though inner-city Latinos are more likely to be employed than are African Americans, their network ties tend to link them to relatively low-wage jobs (Fernandez and Fernandez-Mateo 2006; Waldinger 2001; Waldinger and Der-Martirosian 2001).

Differences in social capital also make enormous differences in chances for upward mobility within organizations. One's ability to move up the ladder depends not just on merit but also on mentoring and sponsorship received from senior employees who provide resources, opportunities, and protection when the going gets rough. Members of racial and ethnic minorities are at a disadvantage in getting this kind of help partly because of their scarce representation in positions of power, which creates a dearth of the kinds of social ties available to well-connected white protégés. When members of minority groups *do* have access to strong, resource-rich networks, they are much more successful in gaining access to high-level jobs and senior positions (Zweigenhaft and Domhoff 2003). In addition, because racial similarities guide the formation of social ties, these ties not only influence access to jobs, they also influence perceptions of competence. Consider, for example, that managers who are racially similar will tend to have greater agreement on the merits of the same supervisee's performance. And managers tend to view employees who are racially similar to themselves as performing better. The implications are that if a white employee is being supervised by a white manager, that employee will tend to be viewed more favorably than a comparable minority employee. And the bias will be compounded if the employee's white manager is in the same social network with other white managers who have supervised this same employee (Castilla 2011). As we discuss later, despite the many problems of affirmative action programs, understanding these types of dynamics offers some of the best justifications for the continued application of these policies, as they not only open doors for underrepresented members to enter into positions that have been exclusionary, they also enhance prospects for organizations to function with greater fairness.

Race, Ethnicity, and Cultural Capital

The best jobs in the new economy require not only technical skills but also the ability to work effectively with people. This requires knowing when and how to discuss issues and how to comport oneself appropriately, especially when interacting with others who can open up opportunities. The focus on **cultural capital**—habitual orientations and dispositions that can be used for gain—shows that it is not simply the ability to work but also the ability to "fit in" that influences success (Bourdieu 1986). Acquiring cultural capital requires more than simply earning a college degree; it necessitates the ability to harmonize interaction, create friendships, know the right conversational skills, operate within taken-for-granted behavioral norms, and master other intangibles that are not part of formal job descriptions.

Culture operates like a tool kit, enabling individuals to navigate the worlds in which they live (Swidler 1986). But depending on the social world, the tools in that kit will vary. Members of racial and ethnic minority groups are more likely to come from families at the bottom of the economic ladder, so many have not been initiated into middle-class culture by their families or the schools they attended. Consider, for instance, what it is like to be like Mike, the young African American adult introduced in Chapter 1, who grew up in an inner-city neighborhood where illegal drug use is prevalent. In this world, the code of the street is to gain and maintain "respect," and success in the neighborhood requires toughness and the ability to exert masculine dominance. Although these cultural skills facilitate survival in the neighborhood, they prove counterproductive to presenting oneself in ways that would be appropriate to work in downtown offices. When these young men venture into this world, they feel awkward and inadequate, aware that they do not fit in and that their language and attire is too "street." They also find it difficult to take orders or tolerate indignities, especially those they perceive as coming from women supervisors (Anderson 1999). Nor is this simply a matter of their own attitudes; employers also look for the "right" cultural capital in prospective employees. Unconventional (from the middle-class perspective) forms of dress or appearance (e.g., braids, dreadlocks, beaded hair), nonstandard English, and other characteristics of inner-city African American life are often looked down on by employers, who see these as markers of unreliability and an inability to fit in (Moss and Tilly 2001).

Cultural capital is not learned in the same way one might learn computer programming. It comes from years of socialization that form a **habitus**—the habitual ways of interacting with and understanding one's world (Bourdieu 1984). This requires more than memorizing whether forks go on the left or the right. It requires the development of a natural ease in the situations that matter and the ability to belong with those who count. And it involves developing perspectives about what to expect for oneself and what to expect from others. One study of successful African Americans found that they stressed the need to learn to fit into the social world of more affluent whites. These African Americans argued that their experiences in private schools had taught them to be confident and comfortable in a social environment very different from the one into which they were born (Zweigenhaft and Domhoff 2003).

Classic studies of lower-class young men indicate that they often lack a clear sense of what types of jobs are available, may have unrealistic aspirations, and often develop a perspective of self-blame when things do not work out as they had hoped (Liebow 1967; MacLeod 1995). And even when disadvantaged youth believe that they can succeed, they are not well positioned to do so. For example, a study of young African American men living in Chicago found that they held fairly conventional (if often unrealistic) goals in a community where it was unlikely that they would find good work. They wanted "good jobs" that brought respect; they talked about city jobs, starting small businesses, and, notably, getting blue-collar jobs in factories, even though few such jobs remained in the communities in which they lived. However, when asked what they *expected* to be doing in a few years' time, they had no clear sense of the future or of how their aspirations would pan out. They possessed only a sketchy knowledge of efforts that might benefit them in obtaining work in the contemporary economy. In sum, they thought they could succeed but lacked the cultural capital to know how (Young 1999, 2003).

The importance of cultural capital in an economy where most work involves social interaction should not be underestimated. But how does one teach culture? Part of the problem is the extent of economic segregation, which has increased since 1970. As long as the social networks of those from poor backgrounds are restricted to others in similar situations, and as long as community environments promote different cultural codes and values, this will remain an enduring problem.

Geographic Distribution of Race and Work Opportunity

Understanding the interaction of race and work requires considering residential patterns, the geographic distribution of work, and the prospect that individuals can find good jobs that match the skills they possess. Although proximity does not guarantee that one will get a job, the chances of finding a good job will be better if jobs are located near one's home and community and if one resides next to other people who have jobs. The **spatial mismatch hypothesis**—that is, the idea that people often have trouble getting jobs if they are located where employment is scarce—has been shown by many studies to help explain why minority workers (who are often spatially concentrated) have limited access to good employment (Fernandez and Su 2004). One of the most striking examples of how geography has affected the economic experiences of an ethnic group can be found in the case of Native Americans. The reservation system, established in the nineteenth century, virtually ensured that indigenous communities, established in remote rural areas, would be at the margins of the economy. The lack of work opportunity is one of the primary causes for this ethnic group's escalated risk for suicide, alcoholism, and out-of-wedlock births.

William Julius Wilson (1987, 1997) demonstrated comparable effects on the experiences of African Americans in the Northeast and Midwest. In the middle of the twentieth century, when the industrial economies of cities like Detroit, Cleveland, and Chicago were booming, African American men found work in factories, and their families created stable communities. However, from the 1970s to the 1990s, those factory jobs disappeared, followed by the middle class, which left many neighborhoods in central cities populated by relatively low-income African American populations (Bartlett and Steele 1992; Bensman and Lynch 1987; Bluestone and Harrison 1982). The same types of economic and demographic shifts also occurred across much of rural America (Duncan 1999). In many of these places, a "hyper-ghettoization" of concentrated poverty resulted in increased crime, drug use, and out-of-wedlock births, which in turn undermined the prospects of these communities nurturing new workers or attracting new employers (Sampson, Raudenbush, and Earls 1997; Sampson, Morenoff, and Gannon-Rowley 2002). The effects of industrial decline on African Americans do seem to have varied across the country. Waldinger (1996) for example, found that manufacturing was not so important to African American employment in New York City, so its decline there did not have the same racial consequences as it did in cities like Chicago. But different racial groups appear to be queued for disadvantage, with African Americans commonly positioned to be the most at risk. Consider, for example, that Latinos in Chicago were also highly concentrated in manufacturing but did not suffer the same consequences as African Americans when industry there declined (Parks 2011). It is important to recognize that deindustrialization had an especially profound effect on African American men who came of age as job opportunities were being dismantled, as this group experienced declining career options not only in comparison to previous birth cohorts but also in comparison to white men who had similar levels of educational attainment (Wagmiller and Lee 2014).

For those who are remarkably disadvantaged, career death spirals follow an all too typical pattern. Maturing in a community that has few opportunities and a lack of work-oriented role models can lead to unstable work patterns and inclinations to work and escape in the underground economy of drugs and crime. Such was the case of Mike, the young African American man presented in Chapter 1. Conviction for these offenses, even if it leads only to short-term incarceration, undermines prospects of securing future meaningful work (Apel and Sweeten 2010). In the context of hypersurveillance, even if African Americans are not disproportionately more likely to engage in crime, they are more at risk of being identified as criminals and punished more harshly for that behavior (Goffman 2014). And while incarceration has a negative impact on career prospects, following release from prison, African American men's wages are lower and their wage trajectories progress at a slower rate in comparison to white men who had similar criminal records and similar preincarceration experiences or in comparison to similar men who had not been incarcerated at all (Lyons and Pettit 2011). In other words, the careers of some African American men suffer because they have a greater likelihood of becoming stigmatized and also have that stigma intensified.

Part of the challenge for the new economy is shifting work opportunities to the communities that are currently work-poor and facilitating the movement of families to locations where jobs are more plentiful (Newman 2006). The Gautreaux Program in Chicago illustrates what can happen when people are moved to employment-rich communities. It was designed to move some residents of public housing in the city of Chicago into private-sector housing and thereby reduce the impact of concentrated poverty on the lives of the disadvantaged (W. Wilson 1997). Half of the participants were randomly selected to move into suburban housing, and the other half were moved into housing within the city of Chicago. Those who had moved to the suburbs were significantly more likely to become employed. There were various reasons for this, including the transplants' sense that the neighborhood was safer (so leaving their kids alone was less of a problem) and that *not* working was socially unacceptable. But perhaps the most powerful reason for the change in work outcomes was that the suburbs offered more opportunity to work and that the African American transplants had little trouble finding jobs for which they were qualified (something that could not be said for those who remained in the city). Other studies have shown that moving to suburban locations does not, by itself, always improve the employment prospects of African Americans (Fernandez and Su 2004). But the Gautreaux experience provides strong evidence that it *can*.

If many African Americans are disadvantaged by living in declining inner-city neighborhoods where employment opportunities are scarce, what about immigrants who also are likely to settle in urban areas? Here, the nature of ethnic communities produces complex, perhaps contradictory effects. In some cases, ethnic communities provide opportunities for migrants to find work in businesses owned by (or at least dominated by) others from the same ethnic group. This can provide immigrants with better jobs than they would have found outside the ethnic economy (Wilson and Portes 1980). For example, Cubans who migrated to the Miami area established a significant number of businesses, most of which were small, but that employed many of the Cuban Americans who settled there. Those Cuban Americans who worked in the Cuban "enclave" were not all trapped in low-paying jobs. The ethnic enclave provided significant opportunities for many to learn new skills, including business skills, and open their own businesses, serving as an avenue to economic success for at least some immigrants.

In other cases, working for or with coethnics has been a real disadvantage in the longer term, trapping the immigrant in a subculture and limiting opportunities to move into the economic mainstream (Alba and Nee 2003; Waldinger and Der-Martirosian 2001). For example, Asian immigrants like Rain (the Chinese restaurant worker introduced in Chapter 1) benefit from their ethnic enclave, at least at first, because it provides them with employment and other benefits when their language and cultural skills were still poor. However, the kinds of jobs they find in the ethnic economy typically provide low wages. If they remain within the ethnic enclave, they become trapped in low-wage undesirable employment, unless they are among the few who successfully establish businesses (such as Rain's employer, who not only owns a restaurant but also owns a house that he rents to Rain and his coworkers). Fortunately, Asian immigrants have been largely successful, over time, in moving out into the larger economy as they become more acculturated. Their children, in turn, are even more likely to enjoy upward mobility and improved wages as a result (Nee, Sanders, and Sernau 1994).

People work in jobs but live in communities. In present-day America, racial segregation and economic segregation operate together to create concentrations of poverty that are also concentrations on the basis of minority membership. These communities are far removed from the opportunity structures that exist for Middle America (Quillian 2012). The movement of jobs out of areas where ethnic minorities are concentrated can have a profound impact on current and future generations of minority workers. As William J. Wilson (1997) found, when work disappears, it sets the stage for a wide variety of social problems to emerge. The solution, from a work opportunity perspective, is to redistribute work throughout the various communities and to consider not just the racial characteristics of workers but also the patterns of racial and ethnic concentration in neighborhoods and cities.

Racial Prejudice and Discrimination

The creation of a truly inclusive society requires that there be opportunities to work, that individuals have the resources to develop the skills to gain employment, and that once they are employed they are treated in a fair and equitable manner. Here, we consider the extent to which members of racial and ethnic minorities continue to experience employment discrimination. As shown by the shootings in places like Ferguson, Missouri, and North Charleston, South Carolina, and by the reactions to them, the United States is far from a "postracial" society with respect to racial attitudes and actions based on those attitudes.

Officially, employment discrimination is illegal in the United States. Laws passed in the civil rights era stipulate that employers may not discriminate against potential or current employees on the basis of their race (or gender), and that has resulted in a genuine decline in overt forms of racial exclusion (e.g., the deliberate exclusion of African Americans from apprenticeship programs or professional training programs). But research evidence indicates that race has not been entirely eliminated from employers' decisions about whom to hire and promote. In fact, employers are surprisingly willing to admit to generalizing about members of racial groups and to express a preference for (or reluctance to hire) members of different racial groups as employees. Though not all feel this way, many employers still have strongly negative—and often hostile—opinions of African American employees, particularly African American men, many of whom employers regard as unreliable and difficult employees. The harshest appraisals are directed at African Americans from the inner city—that is, those who live in "bad" neighborhoods, attended urban public schools, who speak "black English," and dress distinctively. Employers associate inner-city residents with a variety of negative behaviors (e.g., drug use, crime, poor education) and express reluctance to hire people from those neighborhoods. Employers respond more negatively to job applicants with inner-city addresses or with African American–sounding names, like Jamal or Lakisha (Bertrand and Mullainathan 2004; Fernandez and Su 2004).

The strength and persistence of employers' reluctance to hire African Americans is well-documented in research by Devah Pager (2003). Her research involved an experimental design in which matched pairs of job applicants (chosen to be similar in most respects other than their race or ethnicity) applied for entry-level jobs, and reactions to their applications were then tracked to determine whether race or ethnicity affected the outcome. As in previous research of this type, Pager found that whites received more positive outcomes than African Americans, with Latinos somewhere in the middle. Not only were African Americans less likely to get called back after an initial application, but they also were channeled into lower-status positions, while whites were more likely to be directed toward better positions than the ones for which they had applied (Pager, Western, and Bonikowski 2009). Remarkably, Pager found that employers were more likely to react positively to white applicants with a felony conviction on their record than they were to comparable African American or Latino applicants who did not have a criminal record.

Discrimination also plays a role in shaping experiences after workers have been hired. Analysis of verified racial discrimination cases in Ohio found that the most common complaint in such cases concerned dismissal. The records contained numerous cases of African American workers who complained, successfully, that they had been dismissed unfairly. These workers reported various forms of discriminatory treatment at work, including receiving less help on the job, being assigned different tasks than coworkers, and being subjected to harsher penalties than white workers for various workplace infractions. Unfairly dismissed African American workers also often complained that, prior to their dismissal, they had been subject to various forms of harassment by both their managers and coworkers (Mong and Roscigno 2010).

Negative views of African American employees seem to focus particularly on African American men. However, a somewhat different (but also negative) perception of African American women has consequences for their chances of finding good jobs. Employers do not think of African American women as lazy or "difficult" in the way that employers tend to stereotype African American men (Browne and Kennelly 1999; Kennelly 1999).

Actually, employers are more likely to perceive African American women positively, in some respects, emphasizing their role as breadwinners for their families and their role as parents. Unfortunately, this is combined with a tendency to stereotype African American women as single mothers and to project onto them problems that employers imagine go along with this status. For example, employers express concerns about tardiness and frequent absences from work in connection with African American women, believing that single parenthood will create complex work-family conflicts that cannot be resolved. Though many African American women are *not* single mothers, and though married women *and* men experience problems associated with work-family conflicts, employers continue to perceive African American women as single mothers and to have concerns about their value as employees as a result.

For many entry-level jobs in particular, employers place a great deal of emphasis on applicants' "soft skills," including communication and people skills as well as qualities such as "attitude" and "personality" (Moss and Tilly 2001). Employers generally have a negative view of African Americans' soft skills, believing that they are less reliable and more likely to "have an attitude" and experience difficulties interacting with members of other racial groups. As a result, employers often are reluctant to hire African Americans for jobs that demand interaction with clients or customers. In some cases, employers try to exclude African Americans altogether; in others, employers try to "match" the characteristics of the employee to the racial characteristics of the workplace or clientele (e.g., by choosing to hire African Americans for settings in which they work with or serve other African Americans). The result is different, and diminished, employment opportunities.

Recent increases in Latino immigration (both legal and illegal) have led to questions about whether employers prefer Latino employees to African Americans. There has been some suspicion that employers are choosing to hire Latinos for jobs once held by African Americans, such that Latinos are benefiting economically at the expense of African Americans. But the research evidence suggests that the reality is more complex. Employers tend to perceive Latino workers as hardworking and deferential (Waldinger and Lichter 2003). Given the prevalence of negative views of African Americans as workers, it would not be surprising to find that employers prefer Latinos for jobs where skill demands are low and the main requirements are hard work and subservience. That these preferences exist, however, does not mean that Latino workers are displacing African American workers, as some suspect. To begin with, employers' preferences vary according to the type of position they are trying to fill (Waldinger and Lichter 2003). Consider, for example, the hiring practices of dairy farmers in Wisconsin, who have access to a large population of migrant Hispanic labor that is willing to work long hours. These farmers express a clear preference for these workers for milking and pushing jobs (pushers move the cows to milking stations). But this does not mean that Latinos are taking the jobs away from others, as these same farmers report that they have little success in keeping any workers (white or black) for the low pay and intense demands of these jobs. This illustrates a context in which race is not used against African Americans but used in favor of Latinos. At the same time, race is used against Latinos, in that they are generally not considered for more favorable positions on these farms (Harrison and Lloyd 2013). The willingness of some immigrants to accept low wages reduces the pressure on employers to pay more (which would make these jobs more attractive to other ethnic groups). The impression that low-wage immigrants "push out" African Americans (who then become unemployed) is an oversimplification of a complex set of race-related dynamics.

Eliminating stereotypical views of racial and ethnic groups is not something that the passage of a law or the implementation of a sensitivity program alone can achieve. However, developing and enforcing effective policies for combating the discrimination that results from prejudice *does* increase opportunity for the disadvantaged (Stainback, Robinson, and Tomaskovic-Devey 2005). And the belief that people cannot do something tends to weaken when they demonstrate that they can.

Racialized Jobs

Another factor that perpetuates inequalities in the new economy is the continued existence of **racialized jobs,** or those jobs typecast to be held by members of specific racial or ethnic groups. One familiar example of this phenomenon can be seen in personal service jobs, such as those held by maids who perform work within other people's households. There is a long tradition in the United States of expecting African American and Latina women to perform domestic labor for others. Racial attitudes have changed, but race still affects maids' work experiences. African American and Latina maids are much more likely than are whites to be asked by employers to perform personal services, to engage in stigmatizing tasks (changing bedclothes, washing underwear, scrubbing on one's hands and knees), and to experience a variety of intentional or unintentional slights at work (Wrigley 1999).

Racialized jobs and work roles also can be seen in higher-level occupations. The case of the growing African American middle class is illustrative. In the past, the African American middle class tended to be confined to restricted niches. African American professionals, business owners, and the like existed, but they were largely concentrated in African American neighborhoods, providing services to African American customers and clients. In the past few decades, middle-class African Americans have been finding their way into predominately white organizations, especially in the public sector. In fact, some have argued that public-sector employment has been more important to the economic fortunes of African Americans than manufacturing (which was important largely in midwestern cities such as Chicago and Detroit). In this view, the expansion of public-sector employment, particularly in the 1960s and 1970s, provided paths to upward mobility for many African Americans. However, the concentration of middle-class African Americans in public-sector jobs has made them vulnerable. Recent cuts in the public sector have undermined previous gains, and African American men in particular have lost access to some of the well-paid government jobs previously available to them (Parks 2011).

The contemporary African American middle class also suffers from other kinds of "ghettoization" at work, and studies have shown that African American managers and professionals are funneled into smaller, peripheral firms; have less authority; earn less even when in positions of authority; and are more likely to supervise African Americans than whites (Elliott and Smith 2001; Smith 1997; Vallas 2003b). Evidently, being an African American professional or manager is not exactly the same experience as being a white one. Findings such as these indicate that many African Americans who enter the corporate world encounter a contradictory reality (Collins 1996). On the one hand, a desire to integrate workplaces, combined with affirmative action programs, makes minorities highly desired, and companies often actively seek these types of employees. However, even though the obstacles to entering the corporate world may have been reduced, what happens afterward is different. Many African Americans find that, once they have been hired, their progress up the corporate ladder is slow. It seems to take longer to get promoted, and they suspect that they have to meet a higher standard than do their white counterparts with similar kinds of education and experience (G. Wilson 1997). They also find themselves "steered" toward dead-end jobs in areas such as community relations and diversity offices, which offer attractive starting pay and a chance to "give back" to the community, but provide few avenues for career growth (Collins 1997).

Racialized jobs operate on the assumption that there are specific positions that minority group members are especially well suited to fit. On the whole, racial preferences tend to operate in favor of whites, directing them into positions of leadership. This is especially evident within collegiate athletics. Consider this example. In 2014, 57% of NCAA Division 1 basketball players were African American, but African American head coaches of these teams constituted a mere 19%. While this is more than the share of African Americans in the overall U.S. population, it still is underrepresentation, given the huge numbers of African American players who had received the kinds of training needed to become a head coach. When we look further into the role played by race in coaching assignments, two other racial disadvantages become clear. First, African American coaches were much more likely to gain jobs at historically black colleges and universities and were much less likely to get jobs coaching powerhouse teams. Furthermore, they were more likely to get jobs with teams that had poorer win-loss records. In this type of situation, these minority coaches were placed in positions where they were unlikely to be wildly successful, as well as placed on "glass cliffs" and set up to fail. This in turn set up situations that make it understandable why teams with continued losing streaks tend to replace African American coaches with white coaches, who were then positioned to be saviors (Cook and Glass 2013).

Race, Ethnicity, and Work: Social Policy

The persistence of racial and ethnic inequality at work, and the tensions and conflicts surrounding its resolution, raise a host of policy issues. Earlier, we examined the dominant theories regarding why some racial and ethnic groups lag behind and why others are advancing in the new economy. For each theory, we highlighted some general implications for policy reform. Here we consider two specific policy debates: the continued use of affirmative action programs and changes in the United States' approach to both legal and illegal immigration.

Affirmative Action

Affirmative action is the most visible effort in the past forty years to confront racial (and gender) inequality in the workplace. In 1968, the federal government began requiring firms with significant government contracts ($50,000 or more) and at least fifty employees to produce annual affirmative action reports and to demonstrate a commitment to hiring minority workers (including women). This became the basis of the programs we now know as affirmative action, which have been subsequently adopted by many companies, as well as by colleges and universities in their selection and recruitment of students (Stainback, Robinson, and Tomaskovic-Devey 2005).

How does affirmative action work? In most cases, the policy simply requires that employers make a "good faith effort" to recruit and retain employees from underrepresented groups—specifically minorities and women. This means that employers must advertise vacancies in ways visible to minority candidates, explain why they did not hire minority candidates if qualified candidates applied for the positions, and produce regular affirmative action reports documenting their efforts.

Opponents of affirmative action label it as a quota system and conclude that it leads to the hiring of unqualified individuals. They also express concerns that affirmative action leads to reverse discrimination, whereby minority candidates are favored over whites in hiring and promotion decisions. Individuals not favored by the program commonly conclude that difficulties experienced in securing work result from opportunities being unfairly directed to minorities and women. Even some minority group members express concern that they are stigmatized by assumptions that they have been hired only because of their skin color. National opinion polls, such as the General Social Survey, reveal that most whites do not favor affirmative action and that the African American community is divided on the issue.

On the other hand, proponents argue that affirmative action does not operate on the basis of quotas because specific positions are not set aside for minority candidates. Proponents also argue that affirmative action does not undermine the appointment of qualified individuals. To be hired under affirmative action programs, all candidates must meet base level qualifications. Once those criteria are met, race and gender are considered for two reasons. First, it is in the interests of society to distribute opportunities more equally, and this system (despite its flaws) is needed to combat discrimination and other factors that limit opportunity. Second, creating a diverse workforce or student body enhances organizational functioning in a multicultural society. National survey data indicate that although Americans generally oppose policies called "affirmative action," they are actually sympathetic to efforts to seek out and retain minority employees (Bowen and Bok 1998; Reskin 1998).

The courts have upheld the constitutionality of affirmative action. But they have put constraints on how it is practiced by ruling that seniority rules take precedence over affirmative action (*Firefighters v. Stotts* 1984), by shifting the burden of proof in claims of discrimination to the person making the complaint (which makes it much more difficult to prove) (*Ward's Cove Packing Co. v. Antonio* 1989), and by making it easier for employees to challenge race-based hiring practices (*Martin v. Wilks* 1989). The Supreme Court decision regarding the University of Michigan's admissions policies further restricted affirmative action (*Gratz v. Bollinger* 2003). While the Court ruled that race *could* be considered as part of a holistic approach to admissions decisions, it prohibited the university from continuing to use a quantitative rating system in which applicants were awarded points simply for minority status. An even more recent decision (*Schuette v. Coalition to Defend Affirmative Action* 2014) upheld the constitutionality of Michigan's state law banning the use of affirmative action in university admissions decisions.

One of the most important questions today concerns the effectiveness of affirmative action programs—are they opening doors that would otherwise be closed? Strong evidence indicates that affirmative action policies have helped African American and women workers, especially those from the middle class, by pressuring major employers to alter their hiring practices (Reskin 1998). The most visible effects of affirmative action have been in the public sector, where minority employment has increased significantly, partly because of the greater effectiveness of enforcement. However, the effects have been less noticeable in recent years, as the political desire to enforce them has eroded (Stainback, Robinson, and Tomaskovic-Devey 2005). The key to expanding the impact of diversity enhancement programs (such as affirmative action) is building into organizations mechanisms for account-ability, such that agents such as hiring managers understand not only that diversity achievement is a goal, but it is a goal they are partially responsible in helping the organization achieve (Kalev, Dobbin, and Kelly 2006).

There are limits to the success of affirmative action. One concern is that the programs primarily help African Americans, Latinos, and women who possess college degrees because they force employers to consider them for higher-skilled jobs. In contrast, affirmative action has been of limited help to people at the bottom of the class structure, those who lack the qualifications for desirable employment. Additionally, although affirmative action opens some doors into workplaces, it does not combat the glass ceilings, "racial-ized jobs," and dead ends that minority and female employees often encoun-ter after they enter large organizations and attempt to move up the ladder (Collins 1997).

Immigration Policy

A second policy issue that has dominated the recent headlines concerns what to do about immigration. Rising numbers of immigrants have led to concern about their economic impact and to calls for a return to a more restrictive approach. Much of the concern focuses on illegal immigration, but many Americans seem worried, especially in a period of stagnating wages and rising insecurity, that immigration *in general* has gotten out of hand.

A primary source of hostility to immigration is the belief that immigrants compete with American citizens for jobs. Economists and others have argued long and hard about the economic effects of immigration. Some conclude that the effects are largely negative, at least for American workers. They argue that an increase in immigration tends to result in lower wages because immigrants are willing to work "for less" and are vulnerable to unscrupulous employers. In addition, the growth in the supply of workers reduces the pressure on employers to raise wages to attract employees. Others argue that the situation is more complex. Areas with high rates of immigration (including *illegal* immigration) are not atypical in their wage structures (Broder 2006; Lowenstein 2006). Also, the argument that poorly educated immigrants compete with American workers is weakened by the fact that most American workers have an education at the high school level or beyond and so face only a limited threat of competition from such immigrants.

Analyses of local labor markets indicate that the effects of immigration on wages in particular areas tend to be slight (Sassen 1995). Some have argued that the real effect is at the national level; they contend that if immigration had not occurred, the wages earned by low-skill workers in particular would have been significantly higher (Borjas et al. 1997). However, these studies are inconclusive, and some economists conclude that the safest assessment is that immigration has had only a modest negative impact on the wage growth of low-skill individuals in the United States (and a somewhat positive effect on others' wages) (Card 2001; Saiz 2003). Other critics suggest that the problem with immigration is that it results in higher unemployment. Immigration increases the labor supply, creating more competition for jobs, and may encourage employers to replace Americans with less expensive immigrant labor. However, the outcomes on the careers of American workers may operate in a different manner. Evidence suggests that immigrants tend to increase the motivation of native workers to pursue the types of entry-level jobs that have greater career growth potential. In other words, a young worker might choose to become a carpenter if that job paid good wages. But if the job paid lower wages because of increased competition from foreign-born workers, that same young person would be more likely to go on to college, which would positively impact her or his long-term career outcomes (Pais 2013). In addition, the availability of low-cost immigrant workers also may cause employers to expand employment (since they can afford additional workers) so hiring immigrants may not displace anyone at all (Porter 2006). Thus, an influx of low-skilled immigrants does not always necessarily result in harm to low-skilled American workers.

The issue of highly skilled immigrants has excited controversy as well. Under current immigration law, employers are allowed to sponsor a number of immigrants from overseas on the grounds that they possess scarce skills that the employer requires and has difficulty obtaining in the U.S. labor market. The H-1B program allows employers to bring in skilled employees for temporary employment (though the employer also can choose to sponsor their application for permanent residency in the United States); the L-1 program allows international companies to "import" skilled employees who work for one of their overseas offices. As a result of such programs, the number of foreign-born workers with expertise in science, technology, engineering, and mathematics in the United States has increased significantly in recent decades (Lowell 2010). Defenders of these programs argue that they help the American economy by bringing in talented people from overseas and by enabling employers to fill vacancies that would have otherwise gone unfilled. However, critics argue that the programs are being abused. One such criticism holds that the employees being brought in are not, in fact, highly skilled and that they are not paid the appropriate wages for the positions they occupy (since the employer holds the visa, the employee is vulnerable to such treatment). In this view, these programs undercut American workers' wages and create unnecessary unemployment and underemployment among native-born technically skilled employees. In addition, some of the heavier users of these visas are companies that critics claim are major outsourcers of high-skill work—foreign workers are being brought to the United States to receive training and experience, then return overseas where they perform jobs that used to be or could be done in the United States (Hira 2010; Lowell 2010).

If the effects of legal immigration are complex, what about *illegal* immigration? The United States has been experiencing a high level of illegal immigration, primarily (but not exclusively) from Mexico and other Latin American countries. While it is difficult to get an accurate count of the number of illegal immigrants in the United States, government estimates are that their numbers were as high as 12.2 million in 2007, although they dropped off slightly to 11.7 million in 2012 (Passel, Cohn, and Gonzalez-Barrera 2013). Over half of this population is concentrated in five states: California, Florida, Texas, Illinois, and Arizona (Hoefer, Rytina, and Baker 2011). The growth of immigration from Latin America has been fueled by a variety of causes. The Bracero program introduced many Mexican families and communities to the American labor market as temporary guest workers, but when the program ended in 1964, the immigration continued in different forms. Changes in immigration law in the 1960s made it easier for those in the United States to sponsor relatives as immigrants. And changes in the economy of Mexico (particularly in agriculture, where traditional small farmers confronted more efficient, better-capitalized farms producing for global markets) pushed more Mexicans to leave their communities or to send family members away in search of income (Alba and Nee 2003). Illegal immigration has grown, in part, because changes in U.S. immigration policy have gradually made it more difficult for relatively unskilled Latin American migrants to enter the United States legally. The attraction of better-paying employment in the United States has been sufficiently powerful to overcome the dangers of entering the United States illegally and risking detection and deportation. Most recently, there have been growing numbers of immigrants from Central America, some of whom are children, who enter the United States through Mexico, fleeing drug- and gang-related violence and poverty in their home countries (Robles 2014).

The passage of the 1986 Immigration Reform and Control Act attempted to restrict the flow of illegal immigrants through a combination of increased border patrols and stricter sanctions on employers, who were made subject to penalties for hiring undocumented workers. During the administration of George W. Bush, it was rare for employers to be fined for employing undocumented workers, and only of late has the Obama administration changed tactics by shifting the focus from punishing the undocumented workers to the punishment of their employers (Preston 2011). This change in response may prove more effective because evidence is scarce that increased apprehension of illegal immigrants has discouraged these individuals from making an initial attempt or from trying again (Cornelius 2005; Massey 2006). Moreover, focusing on interdiction at the border ignores the fact that many undocumented workers enter the country legally, on short-term visas, and simply stay on once their visas have expired. Building walls between Mexico and the United States does little to affect this aspect of the problem.

In 2010, Arizona passed legislation that attempted to go beyond interdiction at the border, and a number of other states have begun discussing similar initiatives. Arizona's law focused on improving law enforcement officials' ability to detect undocumented immigrants by giving police officers broad powers to detain people suspected of being in the country illegally and by making it a criminal offense not to carry immigration documents. The law has been challenged in the courts and has excited considerable controversy, as it likely will expand the use of racial profiling. Nevertheless, laws such as this one reflect growing public concern about illegal immigration (Archibold 2010).

As Exhibit 7.7 shows, illegal immigrants compose sizable proportions of the labor force in jobs that require low-skill work, especially in farming, cleaning, construction, and food preparation, where from 5% to 25% of workers are illegal immigrants. Clearly, if the use of undocumented labor ceased tomorrow, the U.S. economy would be crippled as a result.

Exhibit 7.7   Illegal Immigrants as Percentage of Workers in Select Industries: United States, 2009

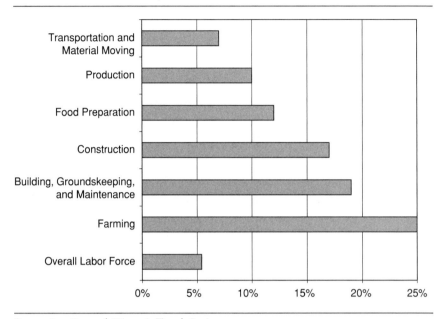

Source: Pew Research Hispanic Trends Project.

Illegal immigration is believed to allow large numbers of undocumented aliens to enter the United States, drain public resources, take away jobs from legal residents of the United States, and exert a downward pressure on wages and working conditions (Buchanan 2006). Others object to these assumptions, noting that high levels of immigration (legal or illegal) are often linked to economic prosperity. For example, undocumented workers enable the production of less expensive consumer goods, partly because they accept terms of employment deemed unacceptable by legal residents. It also bears noting that illegal immigrants often pay taxes but do not use the public services to which they are entitled (either out of fear or because they lack required documents). When illegal immigration drops, furthermore, American workers do not rush to fill the jobs that theoretically become available. On the contrary, employers often wind up pressuring politicians to loosen immigration laws so that they can obtain needed labor. And immigration proponents argue that immigrants, legal or illegal, benefit the American economy because they are hardworking, motivated, and enterprising (Broder 2006; Lowenstein 2006).

It is difficult to assess the extent to which illegal immigration depresses wages because evidence is contradictory on this point. It is possible that employers do not raise wages because the supply of cheap illegal migrants exists. Alternatively, it is possible that these are simply low-wage jobs that would go unfilled if migrants stopped coming. Some support for the first argument can be found in the reality that it would not be all that economically difficult to raise wages in sectors where illegal immigrants work. For example, wages represent a tiny percentage of the cost of the fruits and vegetables that Americans consume. Raising wages significantly in that sector would result in a small (2% or 3%) increase in the cost of produce; thus, the argument that employers *can't* raise wages rings somewhat hollow (Broder 2006).

What should be done about illegal immigration? Most of the discussion has focused on stricter border enforcement, an approach that has, thus far, proven to be ineffective. Arresting and deporting large numbers of illegal immigrants also has been discussed, but the evidence suggests that many deportees simply return. Moreover, many illegal immigrants have children who were born in the United States, creating a moral dilemma for those seeking to deport the parents. Such children receive citizenship under the provision of the Fourteenth Amendment, but some conservative legislators have called for a change in this rule because they accuse undocumented workers of deliberately having children (so-called anchor babies) to discourage deportation. The alternative is to focus on employers by strictly enforcing sanctions against those who hire illegal immigrants. This would have the effect of reducing demand for illegal immigrants (Cornelius 2005). However, employers and their advocates typically object to such policies, arguing that they unfairly burden them and that it is difficult to determine the legal status of prospective employees.[5] Additionally, as we discussed previously in this book, policy needs to respond not only to "pull factors" (what is attracting these workers to the work in the United States), but also the "push factors" (labor problems in the developing world and how poor job prospects at home compel workers in these societies to seek work elsewhere). A domestic work policy, especially as it relates to the issue of illegal immigration, would have to be coupled with an international work policy that ensures opportunity for workers irrespective of their nationalities (Kochan 2005).

Conclusion

Race, ethnicity, and work are commonly thought of as issues of the past, especially by those who are not directly or indirectly discriminated against. In this chapter, we show that the opportunities to work, and to succeed at work, remain strongly tied to issues of race and ethnicity, both because old problems persist and because new ones have emerged. They influence opportunities to obtain resources, to develop the skills needed to get good jobs, to tap into social networks that open doors, and to fit into work environments dominated by white and male power holders. Race and ethnicity also influence the opportunity to find jobs, which are often far removed from ethnic communities.

To shape a work policy for the new economy, one that is truly inclusive of all groups, race and ethnicity need to be included as important consider-ations. Part of the solution will necessarily involve creating greater equality of opportunity and directing more resources (e.g., finances, skills, and social connections) to disadvantaged minority groups. This will require increased allocation of funds to underprivileged families and communities. The persis-tence of racial and ethnic preferences in hiring and the continued application of racial and ethnic stereotypes point to the need for further development of multicultural sensitivities. This will be challenging to accomplish as long as geographies divide the population on the basis of both race and class. And efforts need to be made to promote the creation of good jobs in places where quality employment has largely disappeared. But perhaps some of the most effective initiatives to reduce racial inequalities will involve creating a situa-tion in which those at the bottom of the economy can be adequately rewarded in this affluent society. This can be done by increasing the resources that come from jobs (e.g., by raising the minimum wage to a living wage) and by providing collective resources, irrespective of racial identity, class, and geographic location. This would help disadvantaged people of *all* racial and ethnic backgrounds and would do much to promote racial equality as well.

There has been remarkable progress in advancing racial inclusion at work, but old interracial tensions remain and new ones are emerging. Far from having eliminated the problem, the new economy continues to fragment opportunity along racial and ethnic lines. There are few indications that recent economic transformations signal that racial convergence is within sight.

Notes

1. The U.S. Census treats *Hispanic* as a broad ethnic category that includes many different groups (Mexican Americans, Cuban Americans, Puerto Ricans, and so on). Some have objected to this term, both because it is artificial (clustering together groups who think of themselves as different) and because it includes groups who do not speak Spanish (for example, many Guatemalans or Peruvians speak native languages rather than Spanish). The term *Latino* has been suggested as an

alternative, yet there is no consensus about which term is preferable. We have used *Latino* primarily to emphasize the issue of ethnic diversities. However, in the tables, we have used the term *Hispanic*, as it is used in the government sources from which the data originate.

2. Because costs of living change over time, we converted these income figures to "constant dollars"—the values of these earnings are adjusted for the effects of inflation.

3. It should be added that these data consider only people who have incomes. Because African Americans are much less likely to be employed than either whites or Latinos, these data probably understate the gap in income between the average African American and the average member of other groups in American society.

4. Imagine how much better off Benjamin Braddock would have been if Mr. Robinson had owned a plastics company!

5. For example, the U.S. Chamber of Commerce opposed provisions in the recent Arizona immigration law that made businesses responsible for enforcing immigration policies and imposed sanctions on those not in compliance. See http://topics.law.cornell.edu/supct/cert/09-115 for a summary of their arguments.

Chapter Eight

Reshaping the Contours of the New Economy

There is little evidence that the new economy is moving in a direction that will ensure everyone will have opportunities to engage in meaningful work, to earn a comfortable income, or possess resources needed to construct satisfactory lives outside of work. On the contrary, employer practices and institutional arrangements continue to sustain—and have sometimes even deepened—the chasms that separate workers from opportunity.

In this final chapter, we consider ways to reshape the new economy so that opportunities and resources are more equitably distributed. To do this, we first revisit the issue of opportunity divides to highlight the major concerns facing workers and discuss what would need to change to address those concerns. We then turn our attention to the process of social change and strategies to make workers' interests a priority in the ongoing development of the new economy and some obstacles that will be encountered along the way. Our hope is that strategic action, built through individual and collective efforts, can bring about needed changes. Finally, we conclude this book with a brief reflection on the prospects for liberated work in the new economy, work that would match the potential contributions—and needs—of a diverse workforce.

Opportunity Chasms

Class Chasms

One of the major problems in the new economy is that so many workers find it difficult or impossible to find satisfying and secure jobs that pay.

There are both old and new aspects to this problem. Although workers across the class spectrum face problems of strained schedules, insecure jobs, and uncertain futures, these concerns are felt most strongly by those working in the numerous "McJobs" that emerged as a result of efforts to deskill work in the old economy. Today, legions of workers labor in jobs that offer low pay, few benefits, and few opportunities for growth. These workers can expect scant rewards and slim prospects that diligent efforts will result in upward mobility. And because women and minorities tend to be funneled into these low-end jobs, this class divide contributes to gender and racial inequalities. There also have been efforts to chip away at the security and leisure time available to those in the middle class. Insecurity extends to nearly all segments of the workforce, and most workers contend with strong prospects that their (or their spouse's) employer will close shop, lay them off, or restructure their jobs away. Careers commonly require working long hours and affect abilities to form rewarding family lives. Access to more favorable jobs increasingly depends on (but is not guaranteed by) access to education, and that, in turn, depends on whether one comes from a family with the resources to underwrite the costs of staying in school into early adulthood. The lives of workers occupying good jobs remain very different from the lives of those laboring in bad jobs, but a feature of the new economy is that many "good" jobs have acquired features once associated with less desirable employment. At the same time, the transition to the new economy witnessed the richest members of society becoming even wealthier and further separating their lives from the rest of society. In contemporary America, the significant gaps are not just between the middle class and the poor but also between the affluent and everyone else. It is hard not to conclude that the good fortunes of those at the top of the class structure have come from the bad fortunes of those at the bottom and the increasingly fragile middle.

What can be done? One of the most pressing concerns is to address the economic problems faced by low-wage workers and to reshape the terms under which their jobs operate. There needs to be a national dialogue, and action, to rebalance the equation of a fair day's effort and a fair day's pay, including issues of compensation, scheduling, and security. But beyond those issues, resources and institutional arrangements will need to be restructured in ways that enable workers to move from dead-end, low-skill positions into jobs that offer greater rewards. This will require, among other things, designing and supporting educational opportunities that fit the structure of the new economy. And because the returns to work are so lopsidedly allocated, the lion's share of the financial burden of paying for these changes must be borne by the affluent.

Issues of job insecurity, unmanageable schedules, limited (and sometimes nonexistent) vacations, summary dismissal, and a variety of other concerns cut across class lines. Creating entitlements to reasonable treatment and reinforced safety nets will help all workers, not just those who labor in bad jobs. Launching initiatives to address these concerns will require abandoning cultural mind-sets that divide groups of workers from one another. As long as low-wage workers see themselves as pitted against those with education, or the middle class sees itself as being pitted against those receiving welfare, the effort to mobilize support for collective resources will be hampered. As was the case in bringing about the Fair Labor Standards Act and Social Security legislation in the wake of the Great Depression, catalyzing change almost necessarily will require recruiting the fragile middle class into the struggle.

Gender Chasms

In the old economy, social policies, organizational cultures, job designs, and personal expectations were shaped by the assumption that men would be breadwinners and women would be homemakers. Within this gender regime, women's efforts in the home were defined as something other than real work, and care work was not given its economic due. In the new economy, women are nearly as likely as men to work outside of the home and to aspire to meaningful careers. And it is not simply women's desires that influenced their increased integration into the paid labor force—most families need two earners to make ends meet. Inequalities between men and women persist in no small degree because of the ideas and structures that place most of the burden of care work on women.

Gendered work standards, modeled on what men used to bring to the workplace, are now structured into job designs and employers' definitions of who are "ideal workers." Workers have been socialized to accept a career mystique, an unsustainable set of expectations promoting an intense commitment to work. These structures and beliefs chafe against the resources available to the new workforce, one composed increasingly of dual-earner and single-parent families. How are workers responding? Most commonly by laboring long hours, shifting the timing and sequencing of life events (such as marriage and childbirth), doing without, and shouldering the burden of increased stress. Their ability to manage also often is predicated on their ability to employ low-wage workers to care for children or aging parents. Recognizing these facts highlights the need to dismantle a gender regime that continues to assign men and women to different jobs inside and outside the home. But beyond countering the forces of socialization and interpersonal discrimination, structural changes will have to occur as well. Compensation will need to be recalibrated so that care work receives equitable returns as a recognized form of labor. And career and job templates that assume workers have the capacity to work like men with full-time, stay-at-home spouses will need to be reconfigured.

Workers and employers in the new economy need to redefine how much work employees should be expected to perform and to redesign jobs to be reasonably compatible with what workers can provide across their careers. Efforts to develop a "one-size-fits-all" approach to work and family strains are unlikely to succeed, as the potential contributions of most workers vary over the life course. A more fruitful direction for change involves creating new templates for flexible careers (Moen and Sweet 2004). These can include opportunities to scale back work hours or to take time-outs from the labor force. And individuals and couples will need to have the resources to effectively plan careers so that they can land on their feet when jobs are lost.

The issues surrounding gender and work are commonly cast as "women's problems," but the reality is that these are family problems that affect men, women, children, aging parents, and their communities. Accelerating the pace and extending the range of reform will require bringing men into the movement to humanize work by persuading them of the benefits to be reaped from reconfigured gender roles and resources. This is actually an easy argument to make. Which stressed worker would not want to see the establishment of reasonable work schedules, expanded vacations, and opportunities to secure time-outs from his job? If more men are convinced that they lose out with gendered divisions of labor—particularly in their access to time to spend with their children—the clamor for change will increase, and coalitions for change will strengthen. Mobilizing this support requires recasting workplace reform as more than a question of how to increase gender equality.

Racial and Ethnic Chasms

Though civil rights–era legislation imposed legal barriers against discrimination, racial and ethnic ties continue to influence access to jobs. Today, race and ethnicity play a role in determining where one lives, the resources families have to pass from one generation to the next, and the attitudes gatekeepers hold about individuals from different backgrounds. Like the gender chasm, the race chasm is maintained through social structures that differentially allocate resources and opportunities, as well as cultural orientations that shape expectations.

If the new economy is to become truly race-blind, it will need to address—but also go beyond—sources of interpersonal discrimination, such as the widespread use of stereotypes that label potential employees as suspect. The disadvantages minority group members face stem from being raised in families that lack the economic resources to afford college tuition, the social connections to facilitate entry into good jobs, and the cultural capital that provides the soft skills needed for success in the new economy. But family disadvantages and interpersonal discrimination are not the only source of racial inequity. It also results from community-level resource deficits. The forces that concentrate members of underprivileged racial and ethnic minority groups into disadvantaged neighborhoods deprive members of these groups of quality education, information about work and careers, and the types of social ties that link potential works to jobs.

Racial tensions continue to divide the U.S. workforce, with controversies over immigration, affirmative action programs, and welfare reform all exhibiting strong racial overtones. The dialogue about whether illegal immigrants are "taking jobs from American workers" or "doing jobs that no one else will perform" distracts from the larger question of how to regulate low-wage work. A crucial step in reorienting this debate will be to shift the focus away from blaming the victims of globalization and economic restructuring and toward analyzing the conditions of work—at home and abroad. Only of late has there been renewed consideration of the exploitative conditions under which most low-wage work occurs or of the role of employers who provide jobs to undocumented workers. Building racial coalitions will be a great challenge because prejudice and discrimination are etched so deeply into the culture and structure of American society. Still, these barriers can be dismantled by groups that share common interests, and as this happens, prospects for opening opportunities for underrepresented minority groups will be enhanced.

International Chasms

The new economy's global reach is profoundly affecting work opportunities around the world. It is impossible to ignore the remarkable transformations occurring in China, India, and many other developing nations. Longer life expectancies, as well as access to medical care, educational opportunities, and consumer goods, reflect a variety of positive outcomes of globalization. But at the same time, globalization has contributed to a number of new problems in the developing world, including pollution, overpopulation of cities, and the creation of hazardous work environments. Inequalities persist, both within and across developing nations.

The emergence of an affluent, educated business and professional class in countries such as China or Brazil has occurred in tandem with both old and new forms of low-income work in factories, in informal economies, and in fractured cityscapes. Some societies are advancing, but other places in the global economy, especially in sub-Saharan Africa, have been largely left behind. The flow of work opportunities into the developing world and the movement of employment away from its traditional locations in the United States and Europe have contributed to American workers' feelings of insecurity and fueled international antagonisms.

The solutions to these problems are unlikely to come from the free market. As Karl Marx observed (an observation reiterated by Thomas Piketty [2014]), the forces that make capitalism so productive are intertwined with the drive to exploit labor around the globe:

> The need of a constantly expanding market for its products chases the bourgeoisie over the whole surface of the globe. It must nestle everywhere, settle everywhere, establish connections everywhere. . . . All old-established industries have been destroyed or are daily being destroyed. They are dislodged by new industries, whose introduction becomes a life and death question for all civilized nations, by industries that no longer work up indigenous raw material, but raw material drawn from the remotest zones; industries whose products are consumed, not only at home, but in every quarter of the globe. In place of the old wants, satisfied by the production of the country, we find new wants, requiring for their satisfaction the products of distant lands and climes. (Marx and Engels 1972 [1848])

The current system enables largely unfettered mobility of capital and creates incentives for employers to move jobs to locations where labor and the environment can be most easily exploited. Developing societies will not necessarily benefit from this movement, because the same mechanisms that enable capital to move also make it possible to shift the profits to other locations. Noted analysts such as Thomas Friedman (2005) optimistically assert that globalization will "flatten" the divides between developed and developing countries. Though this may be true in cultural terms, in economic terms the divides between developed and many developing countries are expanding. This is not to say that life will not continue to improve in most developing nations, but it will not be nearly as good as it could be if reasonable checks and controls, designed to ensure more equitable returns from work, were placed on free-market capitalism. This needs to be done not only for ethical reasons but also because it is in the interests of workers in the United States to do so.

Agents of Change

Throughout this book, we posed questions concerning the contours of the new economy and the origins of the divides that separate workers from opportunity. In this final section, we consider two remaining important issues: identifying the types of changes that are feasible and the forces that can make these transformations happen. Our argument is that refashioning the new economy will require the concerted efforts of multiple agents, ranging from individual consumers to activist groups, unions, employers, government, and international organizations. However, not every agent will carry the same level of force, and when their efforts are misapplied (or misrepresented), they can actually impede change rather than accelerate it.

Individuals

Efforts to reshape the workings of the new economy, and to remedy its problems, often encourage a "do-it-yourself" approach. But can the cumulative efforts of disconnected individuals lead to the types of changes needed to refashion substantially the contours of work and opportunity? Consider, for example, the advice manual *The Better World Handbook: From Good Intentions to Everyday Actions* (Jones et al. 2002). This book (like a number of others) suggests that the path to reform leads through self-reflection and conscious efforts to "do the right thing." Toward that end, consumers are advised to limit their trade with companies that are less than environmentally sensitive or labor friendly, as well as to treat coworkers and subordinates with the dignity that they deserve. Investors are encouraged to buy stocks in companies that have a positive track record on issues of public concern. And, like innumerable other self-help books, it offers advice on the best ways to "balance" work and family.

Though intuitively appealing, these do-it-yourself solutions are unlikely to create truly meaningful change unless they are coupled with organized collective action and government engagement. One problem with the focus on the isolated consumer is that individuals face the Herculean challenge of identifying those brands and companies that are "responsible." To do so requires not only understanding the actions of distributors but also the various companies linked to them in vast global supply chains. And companies can have mixed histories—for example, they may be strong on environmental concerns but much weaker on labor concerns. Socially responsible consumers also experience considerable difficulty determining which products to buy because the information they receive is often confusing and misleading (Nestle 2003; Seidman 2007). And even if consumers did have access to the relevant information, options to purchase responsibly do not always exist. This is a classic example of the exit/voice dilemma: individual consumers may possibly influence policy through exit (by avoiding choices they reject) but lack voice; that is, they cannot *create* options that correspond to their preferences. Of equal concern is the observation that consumers are reluctant to purchase fair trade products that cost much more than standard goods. In practice, people tend to place higher premiums on issues of style and price than on ethical business practices (Iwanow, McEachern, and Jeffrey 2005; Pelsmacker, Driesen, and Rayp 2005).

The expectation that individuals will provide solutions for collective problems has a long history in American culture. For conservatives, individualism reflects an American virtue, and they reference Tocqueville (1969 [1836]) in their observations of the ways their country's successes hinged on Americans' embrace of autonomy and volunteerism. They tout the merits of an "ownership society" that allocates as many resources as possible to individuals. Thus, rather than invest in a national health care system or Social Security, the individualistic approach is to offer health "savings accounts" and personally managed retirement portfolios. Nor is it only conservatives who place individualistic perspectives at the forefront of social policy; so do many liberals. This can be witnessed, for example, in neoliberal efforts to end "welfare as a way of life" and to introduce strict limits on support through the Personal Responsibility and Work Opportunity Reconciliation Act. In all of these cases, reforms were presented as empowerment but actually had the consequence of shifting the responsibility for managing risk to individuals. As Jared Bernstein (2006) argues, these programs rest on an underlying philosophy that says "you're on your own" and that individuals have no right to expect support or protection from hardship (see also Hacker 2006).

Numerous cultural critics have argued that individualism results in a diminished capacity to empathize and understand how one's fortunes (or misfortunes) are connected to larger social processes (Bellah et al. 1985; Mills 1959; Putnam 2000; Riesman, Glazer, and Reuel 2001 [1961]). Even when sympathy exists, notice how individual volunteers are assigned the task of ameliorating hardship, supplanting bolder initiatives to challenge oppressive structural arrangements. For example, consider two of the most prominent volunteer and semivolunteer groups in America today: Habitat for Humanity and Teach for America. As of 2013, Habitat for Humanity International, with a nearly all-volunteer membership, has built or repaired approximately 750,000 homes in America and abroad since its inception. Teach for America had approximately 10,000 dedicated young teachers working in impoverished school districts in 2013. Without disparaging these accomplishments, it is important to place them in context. In 2013, in the United States alone, *43 million* people lived in poverty and *one in ten* children did not graduate from high school. And that is just in the United States. As well-intentioned as volunteers are, they commonly do little (if anything) to eliminate structural barriers or establish a more equitable distribution of social resources, and these types of efforts tend to make (at best) small dents in the problems at hand.

In sum, individualistic solutions are hampered by three fundamental problems. First, people may not have the inclination or the capacity to behave in a manner that will transform the new economy. Second, individualistic efforts generally leave untouched the underlying forces that shape the contours of work and opportunity. Third, as a cultural framework, individualism reinforces the shift of risks to individuals, rather than building on the strength of collectivities. This does not mean that individuals cannot make a difference by trying to be socially conscious or that these efforts cannot create good outcomes. But these efforts *alone* will not be sufficient to address the root sources of the problems or make a significant impact on the operations of the new economy.

Activist, Advocacy, and Interest Groups

What about activist groups? These groups comprise individuals who band together to exert pressure on governments, employers, and consumers. Their goals are to use collective action, primarily directed at the local level, to influence employment and trade practices, not only at home in America but also abroad in developing countries. Consider the successes of activist groups, such as United Students Against Sweatshops and United Students for Fair Trade, illustrated in Exhibit 8.1, which have influenced their own educational institutions to sever contracts with producers with histories of labor abuse (Crawford 2003; Glover 2003). Among their accomplishments is increased public awareness of exploitative labor practices within the production of well-known consumer items, such as those endorsed by P. Diddy, Kathie Lee Gifford, and Michael Jordan. By putting pressure on institutions from within, and by mobilizing public opinion, these groups engage in a "name-and-shame" strategy to persuade employers to change their business practices (Seidman 2007). And activist groups devoted to specific segments of the workforce, such as women's advocacy groups like the National Organization for Women (NOW), can make substantial differences in not only increasing the visibility of disadvantage but also advancing policies that address these types of concerns (Akchurin and Lee 2013).

Some grassroots organizations have attempted to pressure local governments and employers to implement reasonable terms of employment. For example, activist groups such as Jobs with Justice operate almost entirely through local volunteers, organizing social awareness campaigns and proposing legislation at the local level to control employment practices (O'Brien and Gupta 2005). As a result of their efforts, more than one hundred cities

Exhibit 8.1   Student Protesters Outside a Gap Store in Manhattan

and jurisdictions had implemented living-wage ordinances by 2003 (Freeman 2005).[1] We witnessed these effects firsthand, as a small group of students at Ithaca College (where one of the authors teaches) staged a series of press releases, articles in the student newspaper, and small demonstrations, demanding that the college pay all of its workers a living wage. The students used the college's image (or brand) for leverage, as the college presented itself as being a socially conscious organization devoted to sustainability. The students revealed to the wider community that the college was not fully living up to its ideals, as the institution subcontracted its food services to the subcontractor Sodexo, which did not pay its employees a living wage. In response to the pressure exerted by the students, the college renegotiated the terms of its agreement with Sodexo, which in 2011 instituted new wage rates at the Ithaca College campus.

Although these types of successes provide reason for hope, it is important to assess them relative to the magnitude of the problems. Even the most successful grassroots initiatives tend to have limited reach in sparking change in employment practices in the new economy. In part, they are hampered by limited resources and fluctuating memberships. When they do effect change, gains can be fleeting, as companies remain free to move facilities to "employer-friendly" locations (Armbruster-Sandoval 2005). Another problem is related to the strategy of focusing change at the local level, which can sometimes be trumped by more macro-level initiatives. For example, companies can influence the creation of legislation at the state level to restrict the right of local communities to set their own labor standards. And focusing on the local level tends to produce changes confined to small groups of workers in particular locations. Careful study of living-wage initiatives, for example, reveals that comparatively few low-wage workers have been affected (most studies estimate the number to be less than 100,000, a small fraction of today's workforce) (Freeman 2005).

Arguably, the biggest success of activist groups has not been in local reforms but in increasing public awareness of labor and environmental abuses. In response, companies have become more conscious of their public image, which in turn has influenced some major employers to reform labor and trade practices. For example, once the widespread use of child labor gained public recognition, companies such as Nike, Reebok, and Adidas agreed to monitor their suppliers' employment practices. Coffee distributors such as Starbucks have signed agreements with "preferred suppliers," who have promised to pay better wages, not to employ child labor, and to have their operations monitored (Schrage 2004). Still, critics, such as the Organic Consumers Association, claim that Starbucks makes only limited use of "fair trade" coffee beans and that the company's commitment to economic justice is superficial. As we discuss later, employers have developed a variety of strategies to maintain the impression of being socially responsible, while often avoiding being truly responsible (Seidman 2007).

The impact of grassroots organizations necessarily depends on recruitment, alliances with other organizations, and the ability to identify and target institutions that can effect change. Perhaps these concerns are most effectively illustrated by considering the contributions and limited success of the Occupy Wall Street movement. In October 2011, a series of protests were staged in New York, demonstrations intended to make visible the link between corporate greed, the global recession, and the problems facing Middle America. This culminated with a month-long encampment at Zuccotti Park that ended after a series of confrontations with the police led to the park being cleared. On the one hand, the Occupy movement was very successful at bringing an issue to the public consciousness, introducing new phrases to our lexicon (such as the "99 percenter") and making the issue of inequality (for a time) a part of the national dialogue. On the other hand, it is important to recognize that beyond these achievements, the movement did not create any identifiable change to the legal or political structures that guide wealth accumulation. This exemplifies the inherent constraints within which activist groups operate. Because these groups tend to rely on economically deprived and relatively unorganized volunteers, they operate from a distinctly disadvantaged position. Even if these groups have justice and public sentiment on their side, they engage in conflict in an uphill battle against big money. Sometimes all it takes to counter a grassroots organization such as this is time for the group members to lose energy and the capacity to carry on.

One other type of interest group that is often underrecognized in public discourse but can be critically important in catalyzing or paralyzing change is private foundations. While foundations often start as the product of an individual's inclination to direct money toward particular types of objectives, they operate as entities unto themselves, with boards of directors, program officers, and other staff. On the one hand, they can finance efforts to block the types of changes outlined in this chapter. On the other hand, a number of foundations are directly charged with advancing issues relating to social justice and have a genuine stake in trying to support efforts to develop and encourage ways of working that serve the interests of both employers and workers. The Sloan Foundation is a notable example of this type of work, having invested over $130 million in research projects intended to identify and resolve the tensions between work and family role performance. Had the Sloan Foundation not invested these resources, there would be far less recognition of the types of tensions facing working families and far less clarity about what needs to be done (Christensen 2013).

In sum, activist, advocacy, and interest groups are not going to solve the problems on their own. Their resources and reach are limited, and they are likely to compete against one another. What will determine their impact is the extent to which individual groups are positioned to harness resources and effectively use resources, such that the balance favors those intent on advancing the interests of workers and their families over those who would rather see promising initiatives vetoed.

Unions and Organized Labor

The American union movement has been in decline for much of the past fifty years, and efforts to reverse this trend have proven largely unsuccessful. As we noted in Chapter 2, unions face a variety of problems in the new economy, including the decline of manufacturing employment, a legal framework that makes organizing difficult, capital mobility, and the proliferation of smaller workplaces. The problems facing organized labor are compounded by public relations concerns. Many American workers have ambivalent feelings toward unions, which are commonly perceived as the reason why jobs move overseas, as protecting deadbeat employees, as corrupt, and as undermining the principle that individual workers (rather than classes of workers) should be compensated according to their efforts (Lichtenstein 2002). Only one in five Americans (20%) thinks that unions are "excellent" or "very good" for the country, about one in three (36%) believes that unions block economic progress, and two in three (69%) think unions have enough or too much power.[2]

Though unions have diminished power in the new economy, it is important to recognize that they still hold considerable sway. Unions play a vital role in influencing job contracts for those who are members or who work in unionized workplaces. Today, even though smaller proportions of the labor force are organized, they remain a substantial political force, particularly within the Democratic Party (Dark 2001). Approximately one in ten workers is a union member, and many more Americans belong to a family in which at least one person is a union member.

There are some indications that unions could make a comeback in the United States. Although it is true that surveys find evidence that many Americans have ambivalent feelings about unions and their role in society, they also reveal that nonunion workers are increasingly likely to say that they would definitely or probably vote to join a union (and now outnumber those who say they would not) (Freeman 2007). New patterns of labor migration also have brought to the United States new groups of workers. Some of these recent immigrants are difficult to organize: some are hostile to unions, others may have been frightened by labor repression at home, some are undocumented and fear deportation, and still others are "sojourners" who intend to return to their home countries. However, as was true in the nineteenth and twentieth centuries, many immigrants (particularly those from Latin America) bring with them receptive attitudes to unionization and, in some cases, experience with organizing (Gordon 2005; Milkman 2006; Waldinger and Der-Martirosian 2000).

Several recent examples of successful organizing campaigns give proponents hope that the resurgence of union activity has already begun. In some cases, conventional unions have succeeded in organizing previously unorganized groups of workers. The Justice for Janitors campaign has made remarkable progress in organizing and winning better conditions for building maintenance workers (Milkman and Voss 2004). Similarly, the Hotel and Restaurant Workers Union succeeded in negotiating labor contracts with most of the full-service hotels in San Francisco (Wells 2000). Unions are even attracting the interest of professional workers, such as graduate students, who successfully gained union representation at several major universities (Lafer 2003). Surprisingly, some of the most successful organizing campaigns have been conducted by some of the oldest (and allegedly most "conservative") unions, those once affiliated with the American Federation of Labor (AFL). Ruth Milkman (2006) argues that this is because they are concentrated in growing sectors of the economy, in industries unaffected by capital mobility (such as hotels), and because their approaches are better suited to a volatile economy.[3]

Although conventional unions have had some successes, organizing low-wage workers, especially immigrants, sometimes requires another approach. One strategy that has shown promise is the creation of worker centers. These are community-based organizations, typically representing immigrants, that attempt to help low-wage workers in a variety of ways. They provide services such as legal help and education, they advocate, and they help to organize workers (Fine 2006). Some have succeeded in improving wages, stimulating organization, and making legislative gains for workers, even in places like suburban Long Island, where low-wage workers are often undocumented and isolated from one another in small workplaces (Gordon 2005).

One challenge confronting unions is adjusting their expectations to match the needs and interests of workers in the new economy. For example, in a system where jobs are constantly in flux, and where manufacturing only constitutes a small portion of the job market, the approach of using seniority systems to protect workers makes less sense than it did in the old economy. New methods for protecting workers are needed, some of which may be learned from earlier efforts. For example, rather than employers controlling who gets jobs, unions could collectively manage the placement of employees as opportunities expand and contract. This method of managing insecurity was commonly used in the craft union halls of the early twentieth century and its time may have come again (Lichtenstein 2002). Others suggest that the future of unions depends on their regaining their militancy and energy. Only in this way, they argue, can unions overcome the negative image they have acquired and persuade workers that they are not bureaucratic, corrupt, and irrelevant (Lopez 2003). Dan Clawson (2003), for example, calls for a new "upsurge" of union activity, which would require unions to organize new workplaces and industries and, most importantly, change the political and cultural climate in which unions exist. He argues that something like this happened in the 1930s, when the last big flurry of new organizing activity took place. He believes this can happen again, if unions are creative and respond to new problems and opportunities.[4] It is also important to make it easier for workers to unionize, to decrease antiunion sentiments, and to more effectively establish the vital role that unions can play in setting equitable terms of employment (Kalleberg 2013).

A resurgent union movement will have to confront globalization and develop a means of collaborating and organizing workers on an international level. The expansion of international corporations and the development of global supply chains has weakened unions by making it easier for employers to move production to low-wage, nonunion locations. As Russia, China, and India entered the global capitalist economy in the early 1990s, the global labor force grew enormously, shifting bargaining power to employers (Luce 2014). Unions have long recognized the need to organize globally. Even in the late nineteenth century, labor "internationals" existed, and many twentieth-century unions belonged to a variety of international union federations. More recently, an attempt to consolidate these international organizations led to the formation in 2006 of the International Trade Union Confederation (ITUC), which claims more than three hundred affiliates in a wide range of countries. However, most international labor organizations, including the ITUC, do not engage in organizing efforts but rather serve as clearinghouses for information, protest various forms of injustice against workers around the world, and pressure national and international organizations (such as the World Bank) on behalf of workers. Today, there are other opportunities for cross-national cooperation, such as an American union working together with a sister union at a branch plant overseas. Alternately, workers in one country could be organized to act in sympathy with workers in the same industry overseas. This happened in 1998, when American workers refused to unload ships affected by an Australian dock strike. There have also been efforts to foster labor cooperation along supply chains, including a 2010 campaign by American labor groups to pressure Walmart to get its subcontractors to drop criminal charges against protesting workers employed by one of its subcontractors in Bangladesh (Luce 2014).

Unions will be better positioned to promote change when they integrate themselves with other activist groups, such as the antisweatshop campaigns and living-wage efforts mentioned earlier. In the past, unions and new social movements have not been receptive to one another. During the Vietnam War era, unions were often perceived (sometimes accurately) as opposed to the student movement. Nevertheless, when unions work in concert with other grassroots organizations, an approach that has been called *social movement unionism*, the results are often superior to when they operate alone (Gordon 2005; Milkman 2006). Successful living-wage campaigns illustrate this well; so do the much-discussed demonstrations in Seattle in 2001, in which labor groups cooperated with church groups, environmentalists, and others to protest the meetings of the World Trade Organization and its policies regarding global trade (Clawson 2003). And the remarkably successful organizing drives in Las Vegas hotels and casinos also owe much to a conscious strategy of working together with other community organizations (Fantasia and Voss 2004).

In short, labor organization could, again, become a powerful force for workplace reform. However, there is no guarantee that this will happen. Obstacles to union organization remain powerful and the gains discussed here are fragile. The New York University (NYU) graduate students' union, which organized in 2002 and made substantial gains in wages, benefits, and rights to overtime, was essentially shattered in 2005 (Arenson 2005; Epstein 2005). A much talked about effort to establish a union at one of the big-box retailers, Target, recently failed, illustrating the continued effectiveness of employer efforts to keep unions out (Greenhouse 2011b). Similarly, mass worker walkouts and protests were staged in 2014 to help galvanize support for fast-food workers' efforts to unionize, but they did not succeed. Government action also can have a negative effect on unions' chances. There has been increased discussion of passing right-to-work laws in numerous states. These laws prohibit making union membership or the payment of union dues a condition for employment, and the passage of these types of laws will hamper both membership and the resources available to unions (Maher 2011). As we saw in Chapter 2, several major states have passed legislation that would, if not overturned, significantly limit public-sector unions. Worker centers, too, often find their gains to be temporary or unenforceable and struggle both to forge links with nonimmigrant groups and to grow beyond a few hundred members (Gordon 2005). So, although it may be premature to announce the death of American unions, unions are unlikely to become suddenly powerful enough to reshape American workplaces by themselves. Their efforts can have an important incremental effect, however, when they occur in concert with those of other change agents.

Even a resurgent union movement may not improve the situation of all American workers. A strength and core contribution of the organized labor movement has been to enhance work conditions for union members. It has had a lesser impact on individuals who are not in unionized organizations, and the union movement has historically benefited men more than women. For example, while unions have the potential to address social concerns, such as negotiating work arrangements to enhance men's engagement in care work, to date unions have not exercised a strong voice in movements to create "family friendly" workplaces (Haas and Hwang 2013). This suggests that while unions can play an important role in enhancing work quality, their focus may not be on solving problems of particular importance to significant groups in the contemporary workplace, and the benefits of unionization are likely to be enjoyed only by some workers.

Employers

The tensions between work and family life, and the growing awareness of the problems of global trade, are creating pressures to implement more socially responsible designs for workplace operations. But are these pressures sufficient to motivate employers to advance meaningful change from within? What is the likelihood that "internal" actions by the leading agents in the new economy will foster new approaches to work that serve the interests of workers and the communities in which they live?

One strategy to make employers take ownership of change relies on demonstrating how responsive policies can actually benefit companies. Work-family scholars call this the *dual agenda* and posit that what is good for working families, or the wider society, does not necessarily come at a cost to employers. Some family responsive policies, such as flexible work arrangements (when applied in specific types of settings to specific types of workers) can actually work in the employer's interests (Pavalko and Henderson 2006). Fulfilling the dual agenda requires demonstrating the potential for positive "returns on investment" that can be measured by increased productivity, greater profits, better employee retention, consumer loyalty, or other indicators of success. This **business case** for reform shows employers how their companies can benefit from altering production practices and taken-for-granted ways of working (Kossek and Fried 2006).

In many industries, a business case can be made to enhance labor standards through increased wages, benefits, or the creation of flexible work arrangements. For instance, recognition as a "best employer" in publications such as *Working Mother* magazine can help a company market itself to consumers and attract the most desirable employees. Similarly, a business case can be made to respond to brand tarnishing that results from naming-and-shaming pressures brought to bear by activist groups. A marketing business case can be made for developing products that fill the emerging niche for fair trade products. And opening opportunities for bridge jobs or flexible employment can provide a means to retain the talents, experience, and knowledge of an aging workforce (DeLong 2004). Researchers at the Massachusetts Institute of Technology (MIT) have worked with employers to design collaborative experiments to test how dismantling and replacing entrenched ways of organizing work affect the bottom line (Bailyn et al. 2006). Other researchers, in collaboration with employers, are documenting the extent to which companies are implementing worker-responsive practices and then publicizing findings from which companies can "benchmark" their own performance relative to that of the wider corporate community (Harrington and James 2006). Expanding the control workers have in managing their schedules has helped limit the extent of employee turnover and ease work-family conflict at companies such as Best Buy (Kelly, Moen, and Tranby 2011; Moen, Kelly, and Hill 2011).

Although these approaches show some promise, the employers in these studies tend to be those that want to retain and focus the energies of skilled workers. It is much harder, and sometimes impossible, to identify a business case to improve the conditions of work for those engaged in low-end jobs at home or abroad. If one traces the history of work from industrialization forward, it becomes apparent that the business case is often strongest for *dismantling*, rather than implementing, worker-responsive practices (such as providing high wages, secure jobs, health insurance, retirement benefits, and safe working environments—all of which have been eroded in the new economy). This is not to say that a dual agenda cannot sometimes be satisfied, especially for flexible work arrangements for highly skilled workers. But it is important to recognize the limitations of this approach because it is unlikely to close many of the major opportunity chasms, such as those that channel the lowest strata of the workforce into poorly paid, low-skill work. For those workers, the business case (established by history and numerous current cases) is to degrade work and opportunity.

Beyond the business case strategy, others suggest that employers may move the new economy forward as they embrace an ethos of **corporate citizenship** or **corporate social responsibility (CSR)**. In this case, the internal force is an open commitment, by corporate leadership, to understand their roles as stewards of the new economy (Blowfield 2005). CSR requires managers not to direct their actions simply to expand profit within the narrow confines of the law but also to follow normative standards of professional conduct that go beyond what is obligatory or customary (Carter 2004). Perhaps most familiar to American consumers is Ben & Jerry's ice cream, a company that maintains that community-mindedness is a core component of the brand.[5] Beyond this company, the adoption of corporate social responsibility codes has been demonstrated to have a positive impact in the textile, leather tanning, and shoe industries in South Asia and in the wine industry in South Africa (Luken and Stares 2005; Nelson, Martin, and Ewert 2005; Winstanley, Clark, and Leeson 2002). And individual socially responsive leaders can make a difference in the lives of their workers. For example, because of the challenges of being a single parent following his wife's death, CEO Lewis Platt created sweeping changes at Hewlett-Packard, including the introduction of expansive flextime, flexplace, and family leave policies (Abelson 1999).

Will grassroots pressures and CSR lead to a more humane new economy? Gay Seidman (2007) offers a skeptical appraisal, basing her conclusions on the ways companies reformed (or failed to reform) their labor practices in South Africa, India, and Guatemala. She found that, even when the need for change was the focus of considerable public attention, corporate leaders largely failed to demonstrate a commitment to social responsibility. For example, even as the South African system of apartheid was exposed to widespread condemnation, American-based multinational corporations avoided challenging the South African government on human rights violations. Their primary goal was to keep operating within an oppressive regime. And when corporations did respond, they were slow and tempered and acted in ways that generally respected the political system enforcing differential treatment of white and black South Africans. Even when companies signed pacts that required fair labor treatment, they were lax in enforcement, swayed evaluations to oversell their successes, and underreported the incidence and the implications of their failures.

Seidman concluded that companies are not strongly motivated on their own volition to "do the right thing." Nor does pressure directly applied by consumers or activist organizations necessarily create a market-driven response that will lead corporations to "come to their senses" and act in responsible ways. A case in point is the much-publicized Rugmark program in India, a voluntary program in which manufacturers vow to not employ children in the manufacture of carpets. In return, participating employers receive a Rugmark tag that is sewn to the back of the carpet. This is then used as a marketing tool, giving consumers comfort in believing that the rug they are purchasing is made in accordance with fair labor practices. The Rugmark approach relies on a voluntary program that employers sign on to, which in turn is used to ratchet up the value of their product (and puts pressure on other employers to behave in a similar socially responsible fashion). Although Rugmark was initially lauded as an innovative market-based approach to stamping out child labor, subsequent analysis of its effects revealed serious flaws. One problem is lax oversight because the program is not supervised by the Indian government or international agents but by a small number of inspectors employed by the Rugmark program. Inspections are rare, so that even when a rug is certified, it is uncertain that children were not involved. Rugmark also spawned competing marks, such as Care and Fair, that assure consumers that a portion of the proceeds from their purchase will be returned to benefit children and others in the carpet district. This latter approach leaves intact the practice of employing children in grueling, hazardous work and leaves consumers with the false impression that their purchase is child labor–free. Another concern is that the voluntary approach to enforcing fair labor practices can foster a two-tiered distribution system, in which some products produced by the same manufacturer can be exported to societies (or stores) that care about fair labor practices, whereas others can be exported to societies that do not. Finally, as Seidman (2007) notes, fair trade labels may matter for luxury or visible product lines such as rugs, but they cannot be effectively applied to other products (such as ball bearings) that are hidden from the consumer.

An interesting, and potentially important, variation on the theme of corporate responsibility is the emergence of groups of activists and socially responsible businesses attempting to pioneer a new approach to economic activity. These groups, some of which are for-profit organizations, some of which are not, are developing alternatives to conventional ways of doing business, including implementing environmentally friendly, sustainable practices; creating jobs in poor urban communities abandoned by conventional businesses (e.g., the "green" businesses developed by the Evergreen Cooperatives in Cleveland); and experimenting with reward structures that limit income inequality (such as cooperative ownership or limits on the pay gap between CEOs and ordinary workers). The successes of some of these enterprises may inspire others to start new ones or may inspire other organizations to "rethink business as usual." On the other hand, pursuing these strategies requires major changes in conventional approaches to business activity, and other groups in society may find reasons to oppose them (for example, it is easy to present sustainability as expensive and hostile to job creation, especially in bad economic times) (Alperovitz 2011).

Another wrinkle in the CSR movement concerns the question of what is meant by "social responsibility." Consider, for example, the case of the family owned craft store chain Hobby Lobby. In some respects, Hobby Lobby represents the ideal CSR employer, structuring work in accordance with the Christian ideals of its owners (including closing the store on Sundays and paying its workers a living wage). On the other hand, Hobby Lobby protested the Affordable Care Act, arguing that the company should not be expected to provide birth control to its employees through the government-mandated health care program (the U.S. Supreme Court ultimately sided with Hobby Lobby). Thus Hobby Lobby's definition of social responsibility led it to successfully deny resources to its employees that most other employers remain obligated to provide.

Is corporate leadership likely to guide companies to be "good citizens" in the new economy? Or are corporations more likely to continue to engage in "a race to the bottom" and seek ways to maximize profit at the expense of workers and the communities in which they live? As we illustrate throughout this book, if corporate action is left unchecked, considerable evidence indicates that the latter path is more likely. It is important to remember that capitalism itself discourages social responsibility because there are clear financial motivations to employ the populations that can be most easily exploited and to move to locations where environmental protections are weakest. The case of Walmart, the world's largest employer and retailer, amply demonstrates this proposition. In the wake of widespread condemnation of its employment and trade practices, Walmart has directed far greater attention to its strategies for managing public opinion than it has to reforming its labor practices, and its profits and power continue to increase (Goldberg 2007). However, these outcomes are not inevitable, nor are organizations completely immune to social pressures or emergent industry standards. In fact, research that focuses on the ways organizations respond to normative pressures reveals that sometimes companies shift their practices because they see others doing likewise (DiMaggio and Powell 1983; Kelly 2003). From an institutional perspective, one might think of individual companies as being like the homeowner who mows his lawn because he sees his neighbors doing likewise. The more practices (such as flexible work arrangements) are viewed as "taken-for-granted" ways of doing work, the more new companies will incorporate these practices into their talent management strategies.

Government

Political conservatives commonly caution against the interference of "big government" and the impediments regulation creates for the functioning of the economy. This perspective on government's role in the regulation of the new economy has a number of problems. First, government is *always* involved in economic activity. As economic historian Karl Polanyi (1944) argued, the market itself could not exist unless the government had been there to help create it and continued to provide the political, legal, and military framework within which it operates. Second, government has a long history of making trade possible and shielding workers from abusive work conditions. Most of the protections workers have today are the result of government intervention; these include child labor laws, unemployment insurance, environmental regulations, social security, minimum wage standards, rights to overtime pay, workplace safety oversight, the right to unionize, prohibitions against discrimination, and the right to family medical leave (see the appendix for a regulatory time line). Those who espouse laissez-faire capitalism often overlook these necessary "intrusions" into the economy, and we suspect very few Americans would want to see the regulation of work return to the standards of the early twentieth century.

In the preceding chapters, we argued that the U.S. government generally has been reluctant to interfere in the contests between workers and their employers regarding pay, schedules, security, and other conditions of work. And the U.S. government's efforts pale in comparison with the more active role that governments have played in Western Europe. We also observed that, during the twentieth century, the U.S. government went from being virtually absent from the regulation of work to being much more involved. The directions government actions will take in the future, and its speed of response, are not foregone conclusions. As in the old economy, competing interest groups will sway legislation, and the process will be political, not inevitable. Ultimately, government action will hinge on the ability of individuals, activist groups, unions, and others to influence its operations.

What role should the American government play in the new economy? The types of action we advocate will require reenvisioning the regulation of work, in much the same way as happened during the New Deal. This reenvisioning should consider specific workplace regulations, as well as the collective responsibility to provide for the basic needs of citizens, irrespective of their attachment to the labor force. We suggest three types of policy initiatives. First, there must be a revisiting of the issue of what constitutes reasonable conditions for work and a revision of the standards enacted under the Fair Labor Standards Act (and other legislation) to consider both the nature of jobs and the composition of the labor force in the new economy. Second, there needs to be a national discussion of the means by which affluence and opportunities can be more equitably distributed. Third, though much attention has been focused on the U.S. government's role in promoting the interests of employers and protecting jobs at home, there needs to be a forceful discussion of its role in regulating the terms under which global supply chains operate and the role of the United States in fostering *positive* development abroad.

A Fair Labor Standards Act for the New Economy

When the Fair Labor Standards Act was enacted in 1938, it offered Americans, for the first time, the right to overtime pay and a minimum wage. Since its passage, its provisions have received modest updates and some new worker protections have been instituted. However, current regulations largely fail to address the needs of many workers in the new economy. Today, employers can expect workers to labor for below poverty-level wages; employers are at liberty to impose long, short, or unpredictable schedules that interfere with employees' family responsibilities; and they are not obligated to provide information sufficient to enable employees to plan lives and careers. Redefining what constitutes the minimum standards of fair treatment is long overdue.

In 2015, the federal minimum wage remained at a scant $7.25 per hour and had a real value lower than it was thirty years earlier. Teenagers are commonly considered to be the typical minimum wage workers, but the reality is that nearly one in two (44%) minimum wage workers is older than age twenty-five, and one in three (36%) works full time (Bureau of Labor Statistics 2014). And because the minimum wage is not indexed to any objective standard, or automatically adjusted to correspond with inflation, its level will continue to be subject to the vagaries of political will. If occupying low-wage jobs were simply a temporary condition, such as holding a summer job in high school, the problem would not be as severe as it actually is. In the new economy, low-wage jobs are usually not stepping-stones on the path to upward mobility, and most low-wage workers are adults. Not only do these jobs trap these workers, they also appear to trap their children. Nearly half (41%) of the children born into low-wage families in the 1960s occupied low-wage jobs when they became adults in the 1990s, a rate of intergenerational mobility far lower than in most other advanced economies (Osterman and Shulman 2011).

One fix involves addressing the issue of low-wage work head-on, to make a one-time adjustment that simultaneously changes the minimum wage to more closely approximate that of a living wage and to tie this standard to future inflation adjustments. The most frequent objection to this proposition is that it will strip away jobs, making it too expensive to employ workers. Proponents argue that the workers who receive raises will spend more money, resulting in increased demand and the creation of additional jobs. Comparative data offer support for the proponents of minimum wages hikes, as employment rates of adults in the United States compare unfavorably to nations that have higher minimum wage standards (Osterman and Shulman 2011). And, while economists disagree as to the effects of raising the minimum wage, it is worth noting that the Economic Policy Institute's statement on increasing the minimum wage to $10.10 per hour was endorsed by more than six hundred economists, including four Nobel laureates (Economic Policy Institute 2014). In the spring of 2015, Los Angeles became the latest American city (following Seattle and San Francisco) to raise the minimum wage to $15 an hour, and Chicago and New York were considering following suit (Kasperkevic 2015). These local experiments may provide testing grounds for a national increase in the minimum wage.

During the Great Depression, the problem of unemployment was exacerbated because those who had jobs were expected to work long hours, which in turn deprived others of the opportunity to work. The Fair Labor Standards Act responded by implementing overtime provisions that penalized employers for working their employees beyond forty hours per week.

By mandating time-and-a-half compensation for overtime, the act stimulated a reduction in work hours, as well as dispersed work opportunity. But because full-time employees are typically the only ones who receive benefits, and because the costs of benefits like health care have increased substantially, the penalty for overworking employees has decreased in the new economy. And because of changing opportunity structures, many more employees in the new economy are exempt from overtime provisions, as they labor in salaried positions and within organizational cultures that treat long hours as desirable and normal.

Today, the forty-hour workweek plus time-and-a-half pay for overtime is a taken-for-granted arrangement, but one that needs to change. Although the current threshold may have been a reasonable expectation for a husband/breadwinner–wife/homemaker arrangement, today many dual-earner couples work a combined eighty to one hundred hours per week (and sometimes more), leaving them frazzled and exhausted. One approach to fixing this problem can be found in France, a country that reduced the threshold for overtime eligibility to thirty-five hours per week. The result of this legislation has been to increase work opportunity and to decrease the level of stress shouldered by working families. One study of the impact of the French law found that nearly two in three workers responded that it had made it easier for them to combine work life with their family life (Fagnani and Letablier 2004). If shortening the workweek turns out not to be an option for the United States, an alternative would be increasing the penalty for overworking employees—perhaps from time-and-a-half to double-time compensation.

A Fair Labor Standards Act for the New Economy needs to address the issue of overwork in other ways as well. For example, to bring the country more in line with the treatment of workers in Europe, Americans would need the opportunity to take four to five weeks of paid vacation a year. Current labor standards need to go far beyond the twelve weeks of unpaid leave provided by the Family and Medical Leave Act, and, at a minimum, the current standard needs to be modified to mandate paid leaves of absence (which in turn will make family leave available to all workers). The variety of family leave and family supports enacted in Europe in the past thirty years provide valuable lessons to inform efforts to reshape American family leave policy.

Finally, a Fair Labor Standards Act for the New Economy needs to address the issue of job insecurities. In part, adjustments of family leave and overtime provisions may help to reduce insecurity by discouraging underemployment and forced "voluntary" exits from the labor force. Again, lessons from Europe may help to craft this legislation, as well as anticipate its impact on worker performance. In France, for example, complex *licencie-ment* laws regulate the conditions under which employees can be fired. To terminate a worker, companies commonly have to demonstrate that the employee could not be retained, show that the company cannot afford to keep the job in existence, or prove that the employee is incompetent. These laws substantially shift the onus of responsibility back to employers to legitimate why a good worker is being let go. However, this solution is not without problems. For example, in France when employees underperform, rather than firing them outright (as is commonly done in America), employers sometimes pay them to disappear graciously and even go so far as to keep problematic employees on the books but not assign them important work (Smith 2006). Though this type of legislation could have the result of keeping greater numbers of "deadbeat" employees on the payroll, French workers are actually more productive (as measured by productivity per hour worked) than American employees are (Krugman 2005). Whether American culture could embrace such commitments remains to be seen, but the key to winning the debate will be a concerted effort to shift the discussion from employer rights to worker rights and from "you're on your own" to "we're in this together" (Bernstein 2006).

It is important to recognize that simply putting new regulations on the books is not an entirely sufficient response. The reality is that many existing regulations are not enforced (access to a private space to accommodate breastfeeding being an especially notable example, but wage and safety standards are frequently ignored as well). And existing penalties are not sufficient to serve as effective deterrents. What is needed is for government to place worker interests at the forefront of enforcement efforts and to direct resources accordingly (Bernhardt 2012; Osterman and Shulman 2011).

Decreasing Inequities in Affluence and Opportunity

Some would argue that the U.S. government should not be in the business of equalizing opportunity, but the fact is that it has been active in this capacity for some time. Were it not for government intervention, rural America would not have paved roads or be electrified, those living downstream or downwind would drink and breathe far stronger toxins, and the public airwaves would not exist. The passage of the Civil Rights Act, Equal Pay Act, and Americans With Disabilities Act, as well as landmark court decisions such as *Brown v. Board of Education*, all demonstrate commitments to equalize opportunities. And government is the source of a number of entitlements—resources that all individuals have access to, regardless of their attachment to the labor force. One such entitlement is public education, which is available to all citizens through the twelfth grade. Social Security, often presented as an "insurance" to which individuals "contribute," is also an entitlement, in that it provides incomes to older citizens and the disabled through the tax revenues generated by the current generation of workers.

At the domestic level, the primary impediment to the provision of collective supports is not scarcity of available resources but, rather, the *distribution* of those resources. In 2012, the most affluent fifth of the population received more than *half* of the nation's collective income. In contrast, the poorest fifth of the population received only a 3% share. Most other developed nations have implemented systems to offer broad access to quality health care, child care, and educational opportunities. Why can Americans, who live in one of the world's most prosperous economies, not have the same resources?

Health Care. In the past, many Americans lacked access to health care, because their jobs did not provide it, because they could not afford to purchase it privately, and because they were not eligible for government-supported programs that aided the elderly (Medicare) and the poor (Medicaid). Efforts to make health insurance more broadly available were unsuccessful until, in 2010, President Obama signed into law the Affordable Care Act (otherwise known as Obamacare), legislation that introduced incentives and penalties with the goal of expanding access to health insurance and, if eligible, receive subsidies to purchase insurance or be enrolled in Medicare or Medicaid. With this law, among other new protections, insurance companies are prohibited from excluding individuals because of preexisting conditions or from capping payments. However, as we write, a concerted effort is underway to challenge this law through both legislation and through court appeals. While the Affordable Care Act represents a remarkable advance, time will tell if the new approach is given a sufficient chance to work, how effective it will be in distributing health care opportunity, and whether unintended outcomes result. Early appraisals point toward optimistic conclusions.

Child Care. Access to quality child care is uneven, expensive, and often inadequate (Children's Defense Fund 2005; Heymann 2000). Today, low-income workers commonly lack access to good child care arrangements, and the middle class feels the financial pinch as well. One possibility is to follow the model offered by Finland and France, which have publicly funded high-quality day care facilities to help working parents remain in their jobs (Pfau-Effinger 2004). Instituting such changes in America will require demonstrating that child care centers can offer care that is as good (or better) than that which is received in the home. Establishing these centers will require directing public resources to constructing buildings, hiring trained personnel, and compensating them at the professional-level wages that care work deserves.

Ironically, as the need to care for disadvantaged children has increased, welfare reform efforts in the United States have undermined the prospects that poor single mothers can nurture their children (Crouter and Booth 2004). If the poor are expected to work, then jobs should pay wages sufficient to support families, and workers should have access to the resources to ensure that children have reasonable care and supervision. Lacking those resources, or the opportunity or ability to work, they should have sufficient public support to enable a reasonable standard of living.

Education. International comparisons of educational attainment are commonly used to make an argument that American public schools are not equipping students with the skills for work in the global economy. The reality is more complex. Those students who are fortunate enough to attend the better schools score as well—and usually higher—than students in nearly all other countries. However, students in disadvantaged school districts perform at low levels. Remedying class and racial divides will involve increasing resources to underfunded schools and combating racial and economic segregation. Beyond this obvious concern, there needs to be a national discussion about how to make a quality college education accessible to all members of society, especially to those students who lack financial resources (Duncan and Murnane 2011; Kozol 2006). The United States also trails behind countries such as Germany and Japan in providing noncollege training linked to desirable forms of employment. The American public education system could be made to benefit a wider range of young people if it abandoned a one-size-fits-all approach to education that imposes lifelong economic penalties on those students who cannot or do not wish to complete a college degree (Rosenbaum, Cepa, and Rosenbaum 2013).

The United States has among the highest rates of working poverty, meaning that even after individuals combine their wages and any assistance they might receive, they remain poor nonetheless. One reason for this is that the wages and work hours that many low-wage workers receive are not sufficient to bring them above the poverty line. However, an added component is that government assistance provided to low-wage workers is more modest in the United States than the types of assistance offered elsewhere. One study revealed that if the United States offered the types of welfare state benefits that are typically available in advanced economies, its working poverty rate would be cut in half. If the United States offered welfare state programs comparable to those that exist in very generous states, such as Denmark or France, the rate would be cut by 75% (Brady, Fullerton, and Cross 2010). There is a choice to be made. One path is to maintain the status quo: low-wage work, unpredictable work hours, and meager assistance. The alternate path is to adjust all of these factors, boosting wage rates, increasing access to work, and providing assistance that raises all families out of poverty. This is possible.

Some suggest that Europe's slow economic recovery has much to do with workers' receiving too many protections that impose unsustainable costs and lead to unforeseen consequences (as evidenced by rising debts and high youth unemployment). In contrast, the argument continues, the U.S. economy appears to be thriving (as evidenced by stock market surges). Critics of this argument point to the fact that most of the benefits of economic recovery in the United States went to the most affluent; they contend, as well, that the slow European recovery has less to do with workers' protections and more to do with the fact that European governments did little to stimulate their economies (Krugman 2015). In the wake of the Great Recession, and the opportunities presented by an economic recovery, both Americans and Europeans confront an opportunity to rethink the reasonableness of existing arrangements. Under current conditions, American workers navigate careers in contexts of insecurity and inflexibility, whereas Europeans currently have difficulty initiating careers but with far greater protections. The appropriate role for government in stimulating employment and providing for the economic needs of workers has yet to be defined. On the basis of both objective and comparative standards, if other countries have gone too far in providing supports and protections for workers, the United States has certainly not gone far enough.

International Organizations and International Controls

The latter part of the twentieth century witnessed the creation of international trade agreements covering multiple countries. The most famous example is the North American Free Trade Agreement (NAFTA), but there are others around the world, including the creation of the European Union (EU), which goes well beyond a simple trade agreement. These arrangements are fueled by the belief that free trade promotes economic growth and that allowing unlimited capital mobility and tariff-free exchanges will boost all the economies involved, create employment, and generate profits. Because of this motivation, most attempts to assess the impact of these arrangements have focused on job creation. Critics argue that agreements like NAFTA encourage employers to shift employment to low-wage areas, but advocates respond that low-end jobs leave the United States, and new managerial and professional jobs are created as the result of business growth (Bair and Gereffi 2003). Sorting out precisely what the economic impact of NAFTA has been has proven to be tremendously difficult.

NAFTA was accompanied by multinational side agreements on labor and environmental issues, which were intended to provide protections for workers and for the environment in all of the countries signing the agreement.

Advocates for organized labor and for environmental causes complain that these have proven largely ineffective (Tseming 2004). Indeed, the fear is considerable that free trade will lead to a global race to the bottom, with countries reducing standards to stay competitive. But it could have been, and could still be, otherwise. If the best labor practices from each country became the standard in all of the participating nations, and if the enforcement mechanisms built into agreements like NAFTA are used effectively, this would improve the working conditions of workers throughout the region. There is much discussion of this within the European Union, and in some ways, this may be happening—for example, in the efforts to standardize the maximum number of hours of work. The European Union also has used its influence to require improved labor standards in nonmember countries with which it makes bilateral agreements. In other words, international economic agreements *can* become mechanisms for raising labor standards on a global scale.

Conversely, an opposite strategy of withdrawing trade can be used to bring countries with poor labor and environmental records into line. Should the United States "interfere" with the domestic policies of other countries in such a manner? The answer is that it has openly (as well as covertly) done so for some time. Currently, the U.S. government prohibits American businesses from trading with Myanmar (Burma), North Korea, and Iran over human rights issues. And although the exploitation of workers abroad appears external to U.S. interests, it is one of the chief factors that stimulates the migration of jobs from the United States to developing countries. Here is a nexus where activist groups and unions can play a crucial role in influencing discussion of the conduct of international trade relations.

Human rights abuses at work come in a variety of forms, but one of the most devastating is child labor. UNICEF estimates that 246 million children work in the global economy and that approximately half are employed in hazardous environments. In Benares, India, as many as 200,000 children work in virtual bondage for manufacturers producing saris and carpets (Davis 2006). In Bangladesh, two-thirds of children aged twelve to sixteen labor on average eight to ten hours per day (Delap 2001). Throughout the developing world, children are employed in a wide variety of endeavors in the apparel, shoe, fishing, rug, and construction industries. They are also major contributors to informal economies, working as (among other occupations) prostitutes, servants, and firewood collectors.

Some lessons can be learned from considering why child labor declined in Europe and America but persists in the developing world.[6] In the mid-nineteenth century, children composed as much as 60% of the workforces in the factories that emerged in the wake of the Industrial Revolution

(Gratton and Moen 2004). In the United States, children contributed one-quarter to one-third of the typical household's income in the early twentieth century, which was more than the average contribution of wives (Cunningham 2000). Looking back at the decline of child labor in America reveals two forces at play. One force was cultural: children were redefined as needing protection (Aries 1965; Zelizer 1994). But equally and perhaps even more important were the changing rewards received from work, which made it possible for families to remove their children from the labor force and still maintain a reasonable quality of life (Cunningham 2000; Edmonds 2005). In developing nations, where per capita earnings are in the hundreds of dollars per year, a child's income can be critical to family survival. If standards of living rise in the developing world, we would anticipate child labor declines similar to those that occurred in the early twentieth century in the United States. Reaching this goal almost certainly will require developing more effective means of regulating global supply chains.

One would hope that international agencies, such as the United Nations, would be well positioned to regulate global work, but this does not appear to be the case. Consider, for example, the United Nations' response to the problem of child labor in the new economy. In 1989, the United Nations ratified the following resolution:

> Children have the right to be protected from economic exploitation and from performing any work that is likely to be hazardous or to interfere with the child's education, or to be harmful to the child's health or physical, mental, spiritual, moral or social development. Additionally, states must (a) Provide for a minimum age or minimum ages for admission to employment; (b) Provide for appropriate regulation of the hours and conditions of employment; (c) Provide for appropriate penalties or other sanctions to ensure the effective enforcement of the present article. (United Nations 1989)

Although the United Nations condemns child labor, enforcement of this resolution has been hamstrung by vague standards on who is (or is not) a child, as well as how many hours and what conditions are "appropriate." Even in countries like India that have laws prohibiting the use of child labor, lax oversight of employers is common. As one analyst noted, it is ironic that India forbids child labor in the carpet weaving industry, yet the Indian government itself runs a training program for carpet weavers and recruits children as young as age six. And though the world community condemns child labor, global investment practices (discussed shortly) continue to provide millions of dollars of funds to support the expansion of the carpet industry, with no barriers to prevent the use of child labor (Arat 2002).

The ability and the will of international organizations to go beyond symbolic gestures on the problem of labor abuse are questionable. The International Labor Organization (ILO) is the United Nations' branch concerned with labor questions. In principle, the ILO could become a force for improving the conditions of labor on a global scale and for using the United Nations' enforcement authority to combat labor abuses in particular parts of the world. However, the ILO has largely defined itself as a clearinghouse for information, a center for research, and a forum for discussion of the problems of the workplace, but not as an enforcement agency.

Today, there appears to be a greater emphasis on opening trade than on regulating and controlling the terms under which it occurs. Consider, for example, the ways in which the World Bank and International Monetary Fund (IMF) approach the issue of fostering the development of the global economy. Although these are separate organizations formed for different reasons, by the end of the twentieth century they shared three common concerns:

1. Crisis management: to provide economic resources to help countries avert financial crises.
2. Transition: to foster countries' efforts to restructure to market-oriented economies.
3. Development: to help the poorest countries obtain resources to integrate themselves into global markets.

Their approach to resolving these problems has been to provide loans to countries in need but under conditions that require political reforms in support of market-based economies. By providing loans to countries in need, the World Bank and International Monetary Fund invest in high-risk economies, putting money where it is lacking. But the structural adjustment programs that accompany these loans typically require reduced government supports for workers, privatization, diminished regulation, and a series of other measures that at best require no improvement in the conditions of labor and at worst lead to deterioration. These programs also provide little protection against loans being squandered through political waste and outright corruption. One of the IMF's and World Bank's goals is to foster economic development, but there is no clear evidence that they have been successful and some evidence that their lending practices may have even undermined economic development. Such is the case of lending to sub-Saharan Africa. Lacking the resources to pay these loans, already poor countries can become trapped in debt-borrowing spirals that now impoverish them, rather than help them develop (Babb 2005; Woods 2006).

The United States is in no position to tell other societies that they cannot use child labor or to dictate wages and environmental practices. But it can dictate that, unless specific expectations are met, U.S. investors will be prohibited from engaging in trade with those societies. The first step is to initiate a national discussion of what these standards should be and to foster a public awareness that it is in the interests of U.S. workers to have such standards enforced. As an alternative to (or in addition to) the name-and-shame strategy that activist groups might launch, the U.S. government and unions can support workers' movements at home and abroad (Seidman 2007).

The United States also could play a greater role in stimulating positive development. Despite being the major recipient of wealth generated in the global economy, the U.S. government lags far behind most countries in the share of its wealth it redistributes to developing countries. Of equal concern is the expectation that agencies such as the IMF and World Bank increasingly perform the needed development work. In 2010, the United States allotted less than 1% of its budget to foreign aid (only 18 cents per $100 of the country's GDP). The largest share of aid given was directed to military and political efforts, and far smaller proportions were directed to true development efforts in impoverished regions of the world such as Africa and Southeast Asia. It also bears noting that the amount of aid being given, as a percentage of the United States' GDP, has declined steadily from the years following World War II to the present (Tarnoff and Lawson 2011).

Conclusion

In this book, we argued that the new economy has many new characteristics but that it also has integrated old practices into the design of jobs and the allocation of resources. Some of the problems evident today are new, but many reflect unresolved problems that emerged in the old economy, failed approaches to those problems, and lagging responses to emerging concerns. Today, America faces challenges analogous to those it confronted at the turn of the twentieth century. Old means of working are being discarded, as new technologies and organizational practices are introduced. Previously dominant sectors of the economy are in decline, as new jobs and industries are emerging. And the workforce is changing, as are communities of workers. Along with the challenges these changes present, there remain persistent concerns—of inequalities, overwork, underemployment, and insecurity.

If left unchanged, the contours of work in the new economy will be all too familiar. The future of work will be characterized by divided opportunities, with workers segregated on the basis of class, gender, race, and nationality. Some workers, particularly women and members of minority groups, will have careers dislodged or never make it onto career tracks at all. Large portions of the workforce will labor in alienating, low-skill, low-wage jobs. Some will have careers disrupted when they have children; others will keep their careers intact by foregoing having children altogether. Large numbers of workers will experience stress from having too much work, whereas many others will be work-poor and labor in jobs with unpredictable schedules (if they can find work at all). And most workers will labor under conditions of uncertainty and have inadequate resources to plan careers and to weather job loss.

Economies should work for people, not the other way around. The shape of the new economy is not immutable, nor is its future inevitable. One of the lessons learned by looking at work in historical perspective is that people have been able to effect positive change—even when faced with formidable resistance. Throughout this book, we present ideas for change and illustrations of how these changes have been introduced in other countries. A wide variety of existing examples show how societies and organizations have reduced overwork, fostered employment, expanded flexibilities, increased securities, and equalized opportunities.

Essential to resolving all of the issues presented in this book is recognizing that the problem is not a scarcity of wealth or resources. Rather, the problem is the ways in which resources are allocated in a tremendously productive economy. There is no reason to accept the premise that good jobs and a good life will inevitably be beyond the reach of the hardworking men and women who make it all possible.

Notes

1. Such ordinances commit communities to do business only with employers who pay wages above minimum wage levels and that enable a family to live at a level above the federally defined poverty line.

2. Authors' analysis of the General Social Survey.

3. For example, Milkman notes that the AFL tries to get all (or most) of the employers in an area to agree to labor standards so that a single employer's threat to move or close down is less effective.

4. In 1995, when John Sweeney became leader of the AFL-CIO, he promised to rebuild the union movement by prioritizing organizing activities. The new regime did have some successes, most notably the Justice for Janitors campaign. However, the AFL-CIO's efforts in this regard may have stalled. Careful analysis of contemporary unions shows that only a few of the AFL-CIO's affiliates have made organizing new groups of workers a priority (Bronfenbrenner and Hickley 2003). In 2005,

the AFL-CIO suffered a major split. A number of unions, including some of its largest and most vigorous members (SEIU, AFSCME) left to form their own federation (Change to Win) dedicated to more aggressive organizing (Moberg 2005). However, the secession has not made the breakaway unions more effective organizers than they were previously, and several of them have subsequently left Change to Win (Aleks 2015).

5. However, Ben & Jerry's has been purchased by an international conglomerate. There has been an effort to preserve the company's socially conscious image, but it remains to be seen whether this can be sustained over the long haul.

6. One notable contradiction in the United States is the continued acceptance of child labor on farms, where they are engaged in work that is dangerous, backbreaking, and largely tedious. Because farm workers are largely excluded from the protections of the Fair Labor Standards Act, children at age twelve (and in some instances even younger) can legally be employed for wages lower than the conventional minimum wage and with no limit on the number of hours the child may be compelled to work each day. Limited regulation of farm work and lax enforcement of the laws that do exist result in exposure to dangerous equipment and chemical contamination (Tucker 2000).

Appendix

Legislative and Regulatory Time Line of Worker Rights and Protections in the United States

Primarily adapted from the Bureau of Labor Statistics with information from other relevant sources included. (See http://www.bls.gov/opub/cwc/charts/cm20030124ar06c2.pdf.)

1884

Federal Labor Bureau, the predecessor of the Bureau of Labor Statistics, is established by the Hopkins Act.

1891

Kansas establishes the first state prevailing wage law.

1903

Department of Commerce and Labor is established by an act of Congress.

1912

Massachusetts adopts first minimum wage law for women and minors.

1913

U.S. Department of Labor is established by an act of Congress. It includes the Bureau of Labor Statistics, the Bureau of Immigration and Naturalization, and the Children's Bureau.

1914

Clayton Act limits the use of injunctions in labor disputes and provides that picketing and other union activities should not be considered unlawful.

1916

First federal child labor law is signed but later struck down by the U.S. Supreme Court.

1920

Women's Bureau is established as a federal agency to represent the needs of wage-earning women in the public policy process.

1926

Railway Labor Act requires railroad employers to not discriminate against employees for joining a union and provides for the rights of workers to collectively bargain.

1931

Davis-Bacon Act provides for the payment of prevailing wage rates to laborers and mechanics employed by contractors and subcontractors on public construction.

1932

Norris-LaGuardia Act outlaws "yellow dog" contracts that required workers to sign away their rights to join unions as a precondition for employment.

1933

Wagner-Peyser Act creates the U.S. Employment Service in the Department of Labor.

1935

Federal Social Security Act provides a nationwide system of social insurance to protect wage earners and their families in old age, in the event of illness and disability, and in the event of economic hardship. Many key social programs of the twentieth century developed from this act, including Social Security, unemployment insurance, and Aid to Families with Dependent Children (AFDC). The National Labor Relation (Wagner) Act establishes the first national policy of protecting the rights of workers to organize and elect their representatives for collective bargaining purposes.

1936

Public Contracts (Walsh-Healy) Act sets labor standards on government contracts requiring the manufacture or purchase of materials.

1938

Fair Labor Standards Act sets minimum wage, maximum hours, and time pay, as well as equal pay and child labor standards.

1947

Labor-Management Relations (Taft-Hartley) Act reiterates policies protecting rights of workers to organize and elect union representatives. This act also places checks on union tactics, including secondary strikes and organizing procedures and as such is commonly viewed by labor activists as a step backward in the labor movement.

1949

An amendment to the Fair Labor Standards Act directly prohibits child labor for the first time.
Courts decide that benefits are subject to collective bargaining.

1958

Welfare and Pension Disclosure Act requires administration of health insurance, pension, and supplementary unemployment compensation plans to file plan descriptions and annual financial reports with the Secretary of Labor.

1959

Labor-Management Reporting (Landrum-Griffin) Act prohibits improper activities by labor and management, such as secondary boycotts; provides certain protection for the rights of union members; and requires filing of certain financial reports by unions and employers.

1962

Manpower Development and Training Act requires the federal government to determine manpower requirements and resources and to "deal with the problems of unemployment resulting from automation and technological changes and other types of unemployment."

1963

Equal Pay Act prohibits wage differentials based on sex for workers covered by the Fair Labor Standards Act.

1964

Title VII of the Civil Rights Act establishes the U.S. Equal Employment Opportunity Commission to enforce federal statutes prohibiting employment discrimination.

1965

Medicare is established under Social Security. The McNamara-O'Hara Service Contract Act provides wage standards for employees performing work on federal service contracts.

1967

Age Discrimination in Employment Act makes it illegal to discharge, refuse to hire, or otherwise discriminate against persons ages forty to sixty-five.

1969

Federal Coal Mine Health and Safety Act protects the health and safety of the nation's coal miners.

1970

Occupational Safety and Health Act (OSHA) places certain duties on employers and employees to assure safe and healthful working conditions.

1974

Employer Retirement Income Security Act (ERISA) imposes standards on employer-provided benefit plans. The act is designed to protect the security of pension promises made by private-sector firms.

1978

Pregnancy Discrimination Act requires employee benefit programs to treat pregnancy in the same way as illnesses.

1982

Job Training Partnership Act (JTPA) prepares youths and adults facing serious barriers to employment by providing job training and other services that would result in increased earnings, increased education and occupational skills, and decreased welfare dependency.

1985

Consolidated Omnibus Budget Reconciliation Act (COBRA) requires employers that provide health care benefits to continue such benefits to formerly covered individuals for a period of time after employer coverage ends.

1989

Worker Adjustment and Retraining Notification Act (WARN) provides protection to workers, their families, and their communities by requiring employers to provide notification sixty calendar days in advance of plant closings and mass layoffs.

1990

Americans With Disabilities Act (ADA) establishes a clear and comprehensive prohibition of discrimination on the basis of disability.

1993

Family and Medical Leave Act (FMLA) mandates employers to provide many types of workers up to twelve weeks of unpaid time off for worker and family medical purposes.

1996

The Personal Responsibility and Work Opportunity Reconciliation Act introduces work expectations for the receipt of welfare, replacing the earlier program of Aid to Families With Dependent Children (AFDC) with Temporary Assistance for Needy Families (TANF). Especially important changes are a maximum five years' cumulative support and the introduction of expectations that welfare recipients work (or prepare to work).

1998

The Workforce Investment Act (WIA) focuses on the needs of companies and how to make industries more productive by providing services that increase the number of jobs and the placement of individuals into those jobs.

1999

Ticket to Work and Work Incentives Act (TWWIA) provides health care and employment preparation and placement services to individuals with disabilities.

2009

Lilly Ledbetter Act amends the Civil Rights Act of 1964 to specify that the 180-day statute of limitations for filing an equal-pay lawsuit regarding pay discrimination resets with each new discriminatory paycheck.

2010

Fair Labor Standards Act is amended to require employers to provide reasonable break time and a private, nonbathroom place for nursing mothers to express breast milk during the workday, for one year after the child's birth.

The Patient Protection and Affordable Care Act includes a provision that penalizes employers (who have more than fifty employees) if they do not provide health coverage to their full-time workers.

References

Abelson, Reed. 1999. "A Push from the Top Shatters a Glass Ceiling." *New York Times*, August 22, A1.

AFL-CIO. 2014. "Ceo-to-Worker Pay Ratios around the World." http://www.aflcio .org/Corporate-Watch/Paywatch-Archive/CEO-Pay-and-You/CEO-to-Worker -Pay-Gap-in-the-United-States/Pay-Gaps-in-the-World.

Akchurin, Maria and Cheol-Sung Lee. 2013. "Pathways to Empowerment: Repertoires of Women's Activism and Gender Earnings Equality." *American Sociological Review* 78(4):679–701.

Alba, Richard and Victor Nee. 2003. *Remaking the American Mainstream: Assimilation and Contemporary Immigration*. Cambridge, MA: Harvard University Press.

Aleks, Rachel. 2015. "Estimating the Effect of 'Change to Win' on Union Organizing." *ILR Review* 68(3):584–605.

Alperovitz, Gar. 2011. "The New-Economy Movement." *The Nation*, June 13, pp. 20–24.

Altonji, Joseph and Jennifer Oldham. 2003. "Vacation Laws and Annual Work Hours." *Federal Reserve Bank of Chicago Economic Perspectives* (3rd Quarter):19–29.

Altucher, Kristine and Lindy B. Williams. 2003. "Family Clocks: Timing Parenthood." Pp. 49–59 in *It's About Time: Career Strains, Strategies, and Successes*, edited by P. Moen. Ithaca, NY: Cornell University Press.

Amott, Teresa and Julie Matthaei. 1996. *Race, Gender and Work: A Multicultural Economic History of Women in the United States*. Boston: South End Press.

Anderson, Elijah. 1999. *Code of the Street: Decency, Violence and the Moral Life of the Inner City*. New York: W. W. Norton.

Annie E. Casey Foundation. 2015. "Kids Count: 2015 Data Book: State Trends in Child Well-Being." http://www.aecf.org/m/resourcedoc/aecf-2015kidscountdata book-2015.pdf.

Apel, Robert and Gary Sweeten. 2010. "The Impact of Incarceration on Employment During the Transition to Adulthood." *Social Problems* 57(3):448–79.

Appelbaum, Eileen. 2011. "Macroeconomic Policy, Labour Market Institutions and Employment Outcomes." *Work, Employment & Society* 25(4):596–610.

Appelbaum, Eileen and Rosemary Batt. 1992. *The New American Workplace: Transforming Work Systems in the United States*. Ithaca, NY: ILR Press.

Aquilino, William. 2005. "Impact of Family Structure on Parental Attitudes toward the Economic Support of Adult Children over the Transition to Adulthood." *Journal of Family Issues* 26:143–67.

Arat, Zehra F. 2002. "Analyzing Child Labor as a Human Rights Issue: Its Causes, Aggravating Policies, and Alternative Proposals." *Human Rights Quarterly* 24(1):177.

Archibold, Randall. 2010. "Arizona Enacts Stringent Law on Immigration." *New York Times*, April 23. http://www.nytimes.com/2010/04/24/us/politics/24immig.html.

Arenson, Karen. 2005. "N.Y.U. Moves to Disband Graduate Students Union." *New York Times*, June 17, B2.

Aries, Phillipe. 1965. *Centuries of Childhood: A Social History of Family Life*. New York: Vintage.

Armbruster-Sandoval, Ralph. 2005. "Workers of the World Unite? The Contemporary Anti-Sweatshop Movement and the Struggle for Social Justice in the Americas." *Work and Occupations* 32:464–85.

Arnett, Jeffrey. 2004. *Emerging Adulthood: The Winding Road from the Late Teens through the Twenties*. New York: Oxford University Press.

Arnett, Jeffrey. 2007. "Afterword: Aging Out of Care: Toward Realizing the Possibilities of Emerging Adulthood." *New Directions for Youth Development* 113:151–62.

Arthur, Michael and Denise Rousseau, eds. 1996. *The Boundaryless Career: A New Employment Principle for a New Organizational Era*. New York: Oxford University Press.

Arthur, Michelle and Alison Cook. 2004. "Taking Stock of Work-Family Initiatives: How Announcements of 'Family-Friendly' Human Resource Decisions Affect Shareholder Value." *Industrial & Labor Relations Review* 57(4):599–613.

Arum, Richard and Josip Roksa. 2011. *Academically Adrift: Limited Learning on College Campuses*. Chicago: University of Chicago Press.

Aspray, William. 2010. "IT Offshoring and American Labor." *American Behavioral Scientist* 53(7):962–82.

Autor, David, Lawrence Katz, and Melissa Kearney. 2006. "The Polarization of the US Labor Market." *American Economic Association Papers and Proceedings* 96(2): 189–94.

Babb, Sarah. 2005. "The Social Consequences of Structural Adjustment: Recent Evidence and Current Debates." *Annual Review of Sociology* 31:199–222.

Bailyn, Lotte, Ann Bookman, Mona Harrington, and Thomas Kochan. 2006. "Work-Family Interventions and Experiments: Workplaces, Communities, and Society." Pp. 651–64 in *The Work and Family Handbook: Multidisciplinary Perspectives, Methods, and Approaches*, edited by M. Pitt-Catsouphes, E. E. Kossek, and S. Sweet. Mahwah, NJ: Lawrence Erlbaum.

Bailyn, Lotte, Robin Collins, and Yang Song. 2007. "Self-Scheduling for Hospital Nurses: An Attempt and Its Difficulties." *Journal of Nursing Management* 15(1):72–77.

Bair, Jennifer and Gary Gereffi. 2003. "Upgrading, Uneven Development, and Jobs in the North American Apparel Industry." *Global Networks* 3(1):143–69.

Bandura, Albert. 1982. "Self-Efficacy Mechanism in Human Agency." *American Psychologist* 37:122–47.

Barnett, Rosalind C. and Karen C. Gareis. 2000a. "Reduced-Hours Employment." *Work and Occupations* 27(2):168–87.

Barnett, Rosalind Chait and Karen C. Gareis. 2000b. "Reduced-Hours Employment: The Relationship between Difficulty of Trade-Offs and Quality of Life." *Work and Occupations* 27(2):168–87.

Barrett, Rowena. 2004. "Working at Webboyz: An Analysis of Control Over Software Development Labour Process." *Sociology* 38(4):777–94.

Bartlett, Donald and James Steele. 1992. *America: What Went Wrong?* Kansas City, MO: Andrews and McMeel.

Batt, Rosemary, Virginia Doellgast, Hyunji Kwon, Mudit Nopany, Priti Nopany, and Anil da Costa. 2005. *The Indian Call Centre Industry: National Benchmarking Report Strategy, HR Practices, and Performance.* Ithaca, NY: Cornell University.

Beck, Ulrich. 2000. *The Brave New World of Work.* Cambridge, UK: Polity Press.

Becker, Gary S. 1981. "Division of Labor in Households and Families." Pp. 30–53 in *A Treatise on the Family*, edited by G. S. Becker. Cambridge, MA: Harvard University Press.

Becker, Penny Edgell and Phyllis Moen. 1999. "Scaling Back: Dual-Earner Couples' Work-Family Strategies." *Journal of Marriage and the Family* 61(4):995–1007.

Beers, Thomas. 2000. "Flexible Schedules and Shift Work: Replacing the '9 to 5' Workday?" *Monthly Labor Review* 123(6):33–40.

Belanger, Jacques and Paul Edwards. 2013. "The Nature of Front-Line Service Work: Distinctive Features and Continuity in the Employment Relationship." *Work, Employment & Society* 25(4):596–610.

Bell, Daniel. 1973. *The Coming of Post-Industrial Society.* New York: Basic Books.

Bellah, Robert, Richard Madsen, William Sullivan, Ann Swidler, and Steven Tipton. 1985. *Habits of the Heart: Individualism and Commitment in American Life.* New York: Harper and Row.

Bennhold, Katrin. 2008. "Sarkozy Wins Battle to Loosen 35-Hour Workweek." *New York Times*, July 24. http://www.nytimes.com/2008/07/24/world/europe/24iht -france.4.14765628.html.

Bensman, David and Roberta Lynch. 1987. *Rusted Dreams: Hard Times in a Steel Community.* Berkeley: University of California Press.

Bergman, Helena and Barbara Hobson. 2002. "Compulsory Fatherhood: The Coding of Fatherhood in the Swedish Welfare State." Pp. 92–124 in *Making Men into Fathers: Men, Masculinities and the Social Politics of Fatherhood*, edited by B. Hobson. Cambridge, UK: Cambridge University Press.

Bernhardt, Annette. 2012. "The Role of Labor Market Regulation in Rebuilding Economic Opportunity in the United States." *Work & Occupations* 39(4):354–75.

Bernhardt, Annette, Martina Morris, Mark Handcock, and Marc Scott. 2001. *Divergent Paths: Economic Mobility in the New American Labor Market*. New York: Russell Sage Foundation.

Bernhardt, Annette, Heather Boushey, Laura Dresser, and Chris Tilly. 2008. *The Gloves-Off Economy: Workplace Standards at the Bottom of America's Labor Market*. Champaign, IL: Labor and Employment Relations Association.

Bernstein, Jared. 2006. *All Together Now: Common Sense for a Fair Economy*. San Francisco: Berrett-Koehler.

Bertrand, Marianne and Sendhil Mullainathan. 2004. "Are Emily and Greg More Employable Than Lakisha and Jamal? A Field Experiment on Labor Market Discrimination." *The American Economic Review* 94:991–1013.

Bianchi, Suzanne M., Liana C. Sayer, Melissa A. Milkie, and John P. Robinson. 2012. "Housework: Who Did, Does or Will Do It, and How Much Does It Matter?" *Social Forces* 91(1):55–63.

Bidwell, Matthew and Forrest Briscoe. 2009. "Who Contracts? Determinants of the Decision to Work as an Independent Contractor among Information Technology Workers." *Academy of Management Journal* 52(6):1148–68.

Blair-Loy, Mary. 2003. *Competing Devotions: Career and Family among Women Executives*. Cambridge, MA: Harvard University Press.

Blau, Francine and Lawrence Khan. 2006. "The U.S. Gender Pay Gap in the 1990s: Slowing Convergence." *Industrial Relations Section Working Paper* 508. http://www.nber.org/papers/w10853.pdf.

Blinder, Alan S. 2006. "Offshoring: The Next Industrial Revolution?" *Foreign Affairs* 85(2):113–28.

Blowfield, Michael. 2005. "Corporate Social Responsibility: Reinventing the Meaning of Development?" *International Affairs* 81(3):515–24.

Bluestone, Barry and Bennett Harrison. 1982. *The Deindustrialization of America: Plant Closings, Community Abandonment and the Dismantling of Basic Industry*. New York: Basic Books.

Bocian, Debbie Gruenstein, Wei Li and Keith Ernst. 2010. "Foreclosures by Race and Ethnicity: The Demographics of a Crisis." Washington, DC: Center for Responsible Lending.

Bookman, Ann. 2004. *Starting in Our Own Backyards: How Working Families Can Build Community and Survive the New Economy*. New York: Routledge.

Boris, Eileen and Carolyn Lewis. 2006. "Caregiving and Wage-Earning: A Historical Perspective on Work and Family." Pp. 73–98 in *The Work and Family Handbook: Multidisciplinary Perspectives, Methods and Approaches*, edited by M. Pitt-Catsouphes, E. E. Kossek, and S. Sweet. Boston: Lawrence Erlbaum.

Borjas, George, Richard Freeman, Lawrence Katz, John DiNardo, and John Abowd. 1997. "How Much Do Immigration and Free Trade Affect Labor Market Outcomes?" *Brookings Papers on Economic Activity* 1997(1):1–90.

Bourdieu, Pierre. 1984. *Distinction: A Social Critique of the Judgment of Taste*. Cambridge, MA: Harvard University Press.

Bourdieu, Pierre. 1986. "The Forms of Capital." Pp. 487–510 in *Handbook of Theory and Research for the Sociology of Education*, edited by J. Richardson. New York: Greenwood Press.

Bowen, William and Dereck Bok. 1998. *The Shape of a River: Long-Term Consequences of Considering Race in College and University Admissions.* Princeton, NJ: Princeton University Press.

Boydston, Jeanne. 1990. *Home and Work: Housework, Wages, and the Ideology of Labor in the Early Republic.* New York: Oxford University Press.

Bradsher, Keith. 2002. "A High-Tech Fix for One Corner of India." *New York Times*, December 27.

Brady, David, Andrew S. Fullerton, and Jennifer Moren Cross. 2010. "More Than Just Nickels and Dimes: A Cross-National Analysis of Working Poverty in Affluent Democracies." *Social Problems* 57(4):559–85.

Brand, Jennie E. and Xie Yu. 2010. "Who Benefits Most from College? Evidence for Negative Selection in Heterogeneous Economic Returns to Higher Education." *American Sociological Review* 75(2):273–302.

Braverman, Harry. 1974. *Labor and Monopoly Capital.* New York: Monthly Review Press.

Broder, John. 2006. "Immigrants and the Economics of Hard Work." *New York Times,* April 2, WK 3.

Brody, Hugh. 2002. *Maps and Dreams.* New York: Pantheon.

Bronfenbrenner, Kate. 2009. "No Holds Barred: The Intensification of Employer Opposition to Organizing." Washington, DC: Economic Policy Institute.

Bronfenbrenner, Kate and Robert Hickley. 2003. "Changing to Organize: A National Assessment of Union Strategies." Pp. 17–61 in *Rebuilding Labor: Organizers and Organizing in the New Labor Movement*, edited by R. Milkman and K. Voss. Ithaca, NY: ILR Press.

Brooks, Clem and Jeff Manza. 2013. "A Broken Public? Americans' Responses to the Great Recession." *American Sociological Review* 78(5):727–48.

Brooks, David. 2005. "The Education Gap." *New York Times*, September 25. http://query .nytimes.com/gst/fullpage.html?res=9B03E1DA1430F936A1575AC0A9639C8B63.

Brooks, Michael. 2001. "Law Enforcement Physical Fitness Standards and Title VII." *FBI Law Enforcement Bulletin* 70(5):26–32.

Browne, Irene and Ivy Kennelly. 1999. "Stereotypes and Realities: Images of Black Women in the Labor Market." Pp. 302–26 in *Latinas and African American Women at Work: Race, Gender and Economic Inequality*, edited by I. Brown. New York: Russell Sage Foundation.

Buchanan, Patrrick. 2006. *State of Emergency: The Third World Invasion of America.* New York: Thomas Dunne Books.

Budig, Michelle. 2006. "Intersections on the Road to Self-Employment: Gender, Family and Occupational Class." *Social Forces* 84:2223–39.

Budig, Michelle J. and Melissa J. Hodges. 2010. "Differences in Disadvantage: Variation in the Motherhood Penalty across White Women's Earnings Distribution." *American Sociological Review* 75(5):705–28.

Burawoy, Michael. 1979. *Manufacturing Consent: Changes in the Labor Process under Monopoly Capitalism*. Chicago: University of Chicago Press.

Bureau of Labor Statistics. 2012. "Number of Jobs Held and Job Duration for Baby Boomers, 1978–2010." *TED: The Economics Daily*. Washington, DC: U.S. Bureau of Labor Statistics.

Bureau of Labor Statistics. 2014. *Characteristics of Minimum Wage Workers, 2013*. Washingon, DC: U.S. Bureau of Labor Statistics. http://www.bls.gov/cps/min wage2013.pdf.

Buss, Terry F. and F. Stevens Redburn. 1987. "Plant Closings: Impacts and Responses." *Economic Development Quarterly* 1(2):170–77.

Bygren, Magnus and Michael Gähler. 2012. "Family Formation and Men's and Women's Attainment of Workplace Authority." *Social Forces* 90(3):795–816.

Callahan, Raymond. 1962. *Education and the Cult of Efficiency*. Chicago: University of Chicago Press.

Cappelli, Peter. 1997. *The New Deal at Work*. Cambridge, MA: Harvard Business School Press.

Cappelli, Peter. 1999. "Career Jobs Are Dead." *California Management Review* 42:168–79.

Cappelli, Peter. 2008. *Talent on Demand: Managing Talent in an Age of Uncertainty*. Cambridge, MA: Harvard Business School Press.

Carbone, June and Naomi Cahn. 2014. *Marriage Markets: How Inequality Is Remaking the American Family*. Oxford, UK: Oxford University Press.

Card, David. 2001. "Immigrant Inflows, Native Outflows, and the Local Labor Market Impacts of Higher Immigration." *Labor Economics* 19:22–64.

Carr, Deborah. 1996. "Two Paths to Self Employment? Women's and Men's Self Employment in the United States, 1980." *Work and Occupations* 23:26–53.

Carter, Craig R. 2004. "Purchasing and Social Responsibility: A Replication and Extension." *Journal of Supply Chain Management: A Global Review of Purchasing & Supply* 40(4):4–16.

Castells, Manuel. 2000. *The Rise of the Network Society*. Oxford, UK: Blackwell.

Castilla, Emilio J. 2011. "Bringing Managers Back In: Managerial Influences on Workplace Inequality." *American Sociological Review* 76(5):667–94.

Catalyst. 2014. "Women CEOs of the Fortune 1000." http://www.catalyst.org/knowl edge/women-ceos-fortune-1000.

Cech, Erin A. 2013a. "The Self-Expressive Edge of Occupational Sex Segregation." *American Journal of Sociology* 119(3):747–89.

Cech, Erin A. 2013b. "Ideological Wage Inequalities? The Technical/Social Dualism and the Gender Wage Gap in Engineering." *Social Forces* 91(4):1147–82.

Ceci, Stephen and Wendy Williams. 2010. *The Mathematics of Sex: How Biology and Society Conspire to Limit Talented Women and Girls*. New York: Oxford University Press.

Ceci, Stephen, Wendy Williams, and Susan Barnett. 2009. "Women's Underrepresentation in Science: Sociocultural and Biological Considerations." *Psychological Bulletin* 135(2):218–61.

Cha, K., R. Weagly and L. Reynolds. 2005. "Parental Borrowing for Dependent Children's Higher Education." *Journal of Family and Economic Issues* 26(3):299–321.

Cha, Youngjoo. 2010. "Reinforcing Separate Spheres: The Effect of Spousal Overwork on Men's and Women's Employment in Dual-Earner Households." *American Sociological Review* 75(2):303–29.

Chakravartty, Paula. 2001. "Flexible Citizens and the Internet: The Global Politics of Local High-Tech Development in India." *Emergences: Journal for the Study of Media & Composite Cultures* 11(1):69–88.

Chandler, Alfred. 1990. *Scale and Scope: The Dynamics of Industrial Capitalism.* Cambridge, MA: Belknap Press.

Chase-Dunn, Christopher, Yukio Kawano, and Benjamin D. Brewer. 2000. "Trade Globalization since 1795: Waves of Integration in the World-System." *American Sociological Review* 65(1):77–95.

Children's Defense Fund. 2005. *State of America's Children 2005.* Washington, DC: Children's Defense Fund.

Christensen, Kathleen. 2013. "Launching the Workplace Flexibility Movement: Work Family Research and a Program of Social Change." *Community, Work & Family* 16(3):261–84.

Chronicle of Higher Education. 2010. *Almanac of Higher Education.* http://chronicle .com/section/Almanac-of-Higher-Education/463/.

Clawson, Dan. 2003. *The Next Upsurge: Labor and the New Social Movements.* Ithaca, NY: ILR Press.

Clawson, Dan and Naomi Gerstel. 2014. *Unequal Time: Gender, Class and Family in Employment Schedules.* New York: Russell Sage Foundation.

Cohen, Barney. 2003. "Urban Growth in Developing Countries: A Review of Current Trends and a Caution Regarding Existing Forecasts." *World Development* 32:23–51.

Cohen, Lizabeth. 1991. *Making a New Deal: Industrial Workers in Chicago, 1919–1939.* New York: Cambridge University Press.

Collins, Sharon M. 1996. *Black Corporate Executives: The Making and Breaking of a Black Middle Class.* Philadelphia: Temple University Press.

Collins, Sharon M. 1997. "Black Mobility in White Corporations: Up the Corporate Ladder but out on a Limb." *Social Problems* 44(1):55–67.

Committee on Maximizing the Potential of Women in Academic Science and Engineering, National Academy of Sciences, National Academy of Engineering, and Institute of Medicine. 2006. *Beyond Bias and Barriers: Fulfilling the Potential of Women in Academic Science and Engineering.* Washington, DC: National Academies Press.

Cook, Alison and Christy Glass. 2013. "Glass Cliffs and Organizational Saviors: Barriers to Minority Leadership in Work Organizations?" *Social Problems* 60(2):168–87.

Coontz, Stephanie. 1997. *The Way We Really Are: Coming to Terms with America's Changing Families.* New York: Basic Books.

Coontz, Stephanie. 2000. *The Way We Never Were: American Families and the Nostalgia Trap*. New York: Basic Books.

Cooper, Michael and Mary Williams Walsh. 2011. "Public Pensions, Once Off Limits, Face Budget Cuts." *New York Times*. April 25. http://www.nytimes.com/2011/04/26/us/26pensions.html?_r=2&hp.

Cornelius, Wayne. 2005. "Controlling 'Unwanted' Immigration: Lessons from the United States, 1993–2004." *Journal of Ethnic and Migration Studies* 31:775–94.

Correll, Shelley. 2001. "Gender and the Career Choice Process: The Role of Biased Self-Assessments." *American Journal of Sociology* 106(4):1691–730.

Correll, Shelley. 2004. "Constraints into Preferences: Gender, Status, and Emerging Career Aspirations." *American Sociological Review* 69(1):93–113.

Correll, Shelley. 2007. "Getting a Job: Is There a Motherhood Penalty?" *American Journal of Sociology* 112(5):1297–338.

Costa, Dora. 2000. "Hours of Work and the Fair Labor Standards Act: A Study of Retail and Wholesale Trade, 1938–1950." *Industrial and Labor Relations Review* 53:648–64.

Cottle, Thomas J. 2001. *Hardest Times: The Trauma of Long Term Unemployment*. Westport, CT: Praeger.

Cowie, Jefferson. 2001. *Capital Moves: RCA's 70-Year Quest for Cheap Labor*. New York: New Press.

Crawford, Elizabeth. 2003. "Good to the Last Drop." *Chronicle of Higher Education* 49:A8.

Creamer, Elizabeth and Associates. 2001. *Working Equal: Academic Couples as Collaborators*. New York: RoutledgeFalmer.

Crittenden, Ann. 2001. *The Price of Motherhood*. New York: Henry Holt.

Crouter, Ann and Alan Booth. 2004. *Work-Family Challenges for Low-Income Parents and Their Children*. Mahwah, NJ: Lawrence Erlbaum.

Crowley, Martha. 2010. "Neo-Taylorism at Work: Occupational Change in the Post-Fordist Era." *Social Problems* 57(3):421–47.

Cunningham, Hugh. 2000. "The Decline of Child Labour: Labour Markets and Family Economies in Europe and North America since 1830." *Economic History Review* 53:409–28.

Curry, James. 1993. "The Flexibility Fetish." *Capital and Class* 50:99–126.

Dark, Taylor. 2001. *The Unions and the Democrats: An Enduring Alliance* (2nd ed.). Ithaca, NY: Cornell University Press.

Darrah, Charles. 2006. "Ethnography and Working Families." Pp. 367–86 in *The Work and Family Handbook: Multidisciplinary Perspectives, Methods and Approaches*, edited by M. Pitt-Catsouphes, E. E. Kossek, and S. Sweet. Mahwah, NJ: Lawrence Erlbaum.

Davis, Julie. 2014. "U.S. Acts to Curb Firms' Move Overseas to Avoid Taxes." *New York Times*, September 22. http://www.nytimes.com/2014/09/23/business/treasury-creates-new-hurdles-to-inversion-moves.html?_r=0.

Davis, Mike. 2006. *Planet of Slums*. London: Verso Books.

de Graaf, John, David Wann, and Thomas Naylor. 2001. *Affluenza: The All Consuming Epidemic*. San Francisco: Berrett-Koehler.

Delap, Emily. 2001. "Economic and Cultural Forces in the Child Labour Debate: Evidence from Urban Bangladesh." *Journal of Development Studies* 37(4):1.

Dellinger, Kirsten and Christine Williams. 2002. "The Locker Room and the Dorm Room: Workplace Norms and the Boundaries of Sexual Harassment in Magazine Editing." *Social Problems* 49:242–57.

DeLong, David. 2004. *Lost Knowledge: Confronting the Threat of an Aging Workforce.* New York: Oxford University Press.

DeSilver, Drew. 2014. "American Unions' Membership Declines as Public Support Fluctuates." Pew Research Center Fact Tank. http://www.pewresearch.org/fact-tank/2014/02/20/for-american-unions-membership-trails-far-behind-public-support/.

Deyo, Frederic. 1989. *Beneath the Miracle: Labor Subordination in the New Asian Industrialisation.* Berkeley: University of California Press.

DiMaggio, Paul and Walter Powell. 1983. "The Iron Cage Revisited: Institutional Isomorphism and Collective Rationality in Organizational Fields." *American Sociological Review* 48(2):147–60.

Dominguez, Silvia and Celeste Watkins. 2003. "Creating Networks for Survival and Mobility: Social Capital among African-American and Latin-American Low-Income Mothers." *Social Problems* 50(1):11–35.

Duncan, Cynthia. 1999. *Worlds Apart: Why Poverty Persists in Rural America.* New Haven, CT: Yale University Press.

Duncan, Greg J. and Richard J. Murnane. 2011. *Whither Opportunity: Rising Inequality, Schools and Children's Life Chances.* New York: Russell Sage Foundation.

Durkheim, Emile. 1964 [1895]. *The Division of Labor in Society.* New York: Free Press.

Dwyer, Rachel E. 2013. "The Care Economy: Gender, Economic Restructuring, and Job Polarization in the U.S. Labor Market." *American Sociological Review* 78(3):390–416.

Eccles, J. and N. Zarrett. 2006. "The Passage to Adulthood: Challenges of Late Adolescence." *New Directions for Youth Development* 111:13–28.

Economic Policy Institute. 2014. "Over 600 Economists Sign Letter in Support of $10.10 Minimum Wage: Economist Statement on the Federal Minimum Wage." Economic Policy Institute.

Economist. 2014. "What's Next: Future Global Trends Affecting Your Organization. Evolution of Work and the Worker." New York: The Economist Intelligence Unit.

Economy, Elizabeth. 2005. *The River Runs Black: The Environmental Challenge to China's Future.* Ithaca, NY: Cornell University Press.

Edmonds, Eric V. 2005. "Does Child Labor Decline with Improving Economic Status?" Pp. 77–99 in *Journal of Human Resources*, Vol. 40: University of Wisconsin Press.

Edwards, Richard. 1979. *Contested Terrain: The Transformation of the Workforce in the Twentieth Century.* New York: Basic Books.

Ehrenreich, Barbara. 2001. *Nickel and Dimed: On (Not) Getting by in America.* New York: Metropolitan.

Eisenbrey, Ross and Ross Bernstein. 2003. "Eliminating the Right to Overtime Pay: Department of Labor Proposal Means Lower Pay, Longer Hours for Millions of Workers." Washington, DC: Economic Policy Institute.

Elder, Glen. 1998. "The Life Course and Human Development." Pp. 939–91 in *Handbook of Child Psychology, Vol. 1: Theoretical Models of Human Development*, edited by R. Lerner. New York: Wiley.

Elder, Glen. 1999. *Children of the Great Depression: Social Change in Life Experience*. Boulder, CO: Westview Press.

Elger, Tony and Chris Smith. 1994. *Global Japanization: The Transnational Transformation of the Labour Process*. London: Routledge.

Elliott, James and Ryan Smith. 2001. "Ethnic Matching of Supervisors to Subordinate Work Groups: Findings on 'Bottom-up' Ascription and Social Closure." *Social Problems* 48:258–76.

Elliott, James and Ryan Smith. 2004. "Race, Gender and Workplace Power." *American Sociological Review* 69:365–86.

Emirbayer, Mustafa and Ann Mische. 1998. "What Is Agency?" *American Journal of Sociology* 103(4):692–1023.

Engels, Friederich. 1936 [1845]. *The Condition of the Working-Class in England in 1844*. New York: Allen & Unwin.

England, Paula, Michelle Budig, and Nancy Folbre. 2002. "Wages of Virtue: The Relative Pay of Care Work." *Social Problems* 49(4):455–73.

Epstein, David. 2005. "Fired up at NYU." *Inside Higher Ed*, July 13. http://inside highered.com/news/2005/07/13/nyu.

Erickson, Rebecca and Wendy Grove. 2007. "Why Emotions Matter: Age, Agitation and Burnout among Registered Nurses." *Online Journal of Issues in Nursing* 12(1):1–13.

European Foundation for the Improvement of Living and Working Conditions. 2011. "Changes Over Time – First Findings from the Fifth European Working Conditions Survey." http://www.eurofound.europa.eu/sites/default/files/ef_publi-cation/field_ef_document/ef1074en_0.pdf.

Ewing, Jack. 2013. "Swiss Voters Decisively Reject a Measure to Put Limits on Executive Pay." *New York Times*, November 24. http://www.nytimes .com/2013/11/25/business/swiss-reject-measure-to-curb-executive-pay.html?mab Reward=relbias:r,{%221%22:%22RI:11%22}&_r=0&adxnnl=1&module=Sear ch&adxnnlx=1410977192-3qqpR36ExvQg2aK1ZDGVkg.

Fagnani, Jeanne and Marie-Therese Letablier. 2004. "Work and Family Life Balance: The Impact of the 35 Hour Laws in France." *Work, Employment and Society* 18(3):551–72.

Fantasia, Rick and Kim Voss. 2004. *Hard Work: Remaking the American Labor Movement*. Berkeley: University of California Press.

Farnesworth-Riche, Martha. 2006. "Demographic Implications for Work-Family Research." Pp. 125–40 in *The Work and Family Handbook: Multidisciplinary Perspectives and Methods*, edited by M. Pitt-Catsouphes, E. E. Kossek, and S. Sweet. Mahwah, NJ: Lawrence Erlbaum.

Fernandez, Roberto and Celina Su. 2004. "Space in the Study of Labor Markets." *Annual Review of Sociology* 30:545–69.

Fernandez, Roberto and Isabel Fernandez-Mateo. 2006. "Networks, Race and Hiring." *American Sociological Review* 71:42–71.

Fine, Janice. 2006. *Worker Centers: Organizing Communities at the Edge of the Dream.* Ithaca, NY: Cornell University Press.

Firefighters v. Stotts, 467 U.S. 561 (1984).

Fletcher, Joyce. 2001. *Disappearing Acts: Gender, Power, and Relational Practice at Work.* Cambridge, MA: MIT Press.

Florida, Richard. 2002. *The Rise of the Creative Class: And How It's Transforming Work, Leisure, Community, and Everyday Life.* New York: Basic Books.

Freeman, Richard. 2005. "Fighting for Other Folks' Wages: The Logic and Illogic of Living Wage Campaigns." *Industrial Relations* 44:14–31.

Freeman, Richard. 2007. "Do Workers Still Want Unions? More Than Ever." Washington, DC: Economic Policy Institute.

Freud, Sigmund. 1961 [1929]. *Civilization and Its Discontents.* New York: W. W. Norton.

Freund, Peter and George Martin. 2000. "Driving South: The Globalization of Auto Consumption and Its Social Organization of Space." *Capitalism, Nature, Socialism* 11(4):51–71.

Friedan, Betty. 1963. *The Feminine Mystique.* New York: W. W. Norton.

Friedman, Thomas. 2005. *The World Is Flat: A Brief History of the Twenty-First Century.* New York: Farrar, Straus and Giroux.

Fröbel, Folker, Jürgen Heinrichs, and Otto Kreye. 1982. *The New International Division of Labour: Structural Unemployment in Industrialised Countries and Industrialisation in Developing Countries* New York: Cambridge University Press.

Fuchs-Epstein, Cynthia. 2007. "Great Divides: The Cultural, Cognitive, and Social Bases of the Global Subordination of Women." *American Sociological Review* 72(1):1–22.

Gabriel, Yiannis, David E. Gray, and Harshita Goregaokar. 2013. "Job Loss and Its Aftermath among Managers and Professionals: Wounded, Fragmented and Flexible." *Work, Employment & Society* 27(1):56–72.

Galtry, Judith. 2000. "Extending the "Bright Line": Feminism, Breastfeeding, and the Workplace in the United States." *Gender & Society* 14(2):295–317.

Galtry, Judith. 2002. "Child Health: An Underplayed Variable in Parental Leave Policy Debates?" *Community, Work and Family* 5(3):257–78.

Garey, Anita Ilta. 1999. *Weaving Work and Motherhood.* Philadelphia: Temple University Press.

Garfinkel, Harold. 1967. *Studies in Ethnomethodology.* Englewood Cliffs, CA: Prentice Hall.

Gereffi, Gary. 1994. "Capitalism, Development and Global Commodity Chains." Pp. 211–31 in *Capitalism and Development*, edited by G. Gereffi. London: Routledge.

Gerson, Kathleen. 2009. *The Unfinished Revolution: How a New Generation Is Reshaping Family, Work, and Gender in America.* New York: Oxford University Press.

Gerstel, Naomi and Natalia Sarkisian. 2006. "Sociological Perspectives on Families and Work: The Import of Gender, Class, and Race." Pp. 73–98 in *The Work and Family Handbook: Multidisciplinary Perspectives, Methods and Approaches*, edited by M. Pitt-Catsouphes, E. E. Kossek, and S. Sweet. Boston: Lawrence Erlbaum.

Gilbert, Dennis. 2003. *The American Class Structure in an Age of Growing Inequality.* New York: Wadsworth.

Gitelson, Idy and Dana McDermott. 2006. "Parents and Their Young Adult Children: Transitions to Adulthood." *Child Welfare* 85(5):853–66.

Glauber, Rebecca. 2008. "Race and Gender in Families and Work: The Fatherhood Wage Premium." *Gender and Society* 22(1):110–22.

Glover, Katherine. 2003. "No Sweat in Minneapolis." *Dollars and Sense* 249:8–9.

Glyn, Andrew. 2005. "The Imbalance of the Global Economy." *New Left Review* 34:5–37.

Glynn, Sarah Jane. 2012. "The New Breadwinners: 2010 Update; Rates of Women Supporting Their Families Economically Increased Since 2007." Center for American Progress Issue Brief, April 16. http://www.americanprogress.org/issues/2012/04/epd_breadwinners.html.

Goffman, Alice. 2014. *On the Run: Fugitive Life in an American City.* Chicago: University of Chicago Press.

Goldberg, Jeffrey. 2007. "Selling Wal-Mart: Annals of Spin." *The New Yorker*, April 2, pp. 32–40.

Golden, Lonnie. 2001. "Flexible Work Schedules: What Are We Trading Off to Get Them?" *Monthly Labor Review* 124(3):50–67.

Golden, Lonnie. 2005. "Overemployment in the US: Which Workers Face Downward Constrained Hours." Pp 209–34 in *Decent Working Time: New Trends, New Issues*, edited by Y. Boulin, J. Lallement, J. Messenger, and F. Michon. New York: International Labor Organization.

Goldin, Claudia. 2014. "A Grand Gender Convergence: Its Last Chapter." *American Economic Review* 104(4):1091–1119.

Goldscheider, Frances, Calvin Goldscheider, Patricia St. Clair, and James Hodges. 1999. "Changes in Returning Home in the United States, 1925–1985." *Social Forces* 78(2):695–728.

Gordon, Jennifer. 2005. *Suburban Sweatshops: The Fight for Immigrant Rights.* Cambridge, MA: Harvard University Press.

Gornick, Janet and Marcia Meyers. 2003. *Families That Work: Policies for Reconciling Parenthood and Employment.* New York: Russell Sage Foundation.

Gould, William. 2007. "Independent Adjudication, Political Process, and the State of Labor-Management Relations: The Role of the National Labor Relations Board." *Indiana Law Journal* 82(2):460–97.

Granovetter, Mark. 1973. "The Strength of Weak Ties." *American Journal of Sociology* 78:1360–80.

Granovetter, Mark. 1995. *Getting a Job.* Chicago: University of Chicago Press.

Gratton, Brian and Jon Moen. 2004. "Immigration, Culture, and Child Labor in the United States, 1880–1920." *Journal of Interdisciplinary History* 34(3):355–91.

Gratz v. Bollinger, 539 U.S. 244 (2003).

Green, Francis. 2006. *Demanding Work: The Paradox of Job Quality in the Affluent Economy*. Princeton, NJ: Princeton University Press.

Green, James. 2006. *Death in the Haymarket*. New York: Pantheon.

Greenhouse, Steven. 2011a. "A Watershed Moment for Public-Sector Unions." *New York Times*, February 18. http://www.nytimes.com/2011/02/19/us/19union.html?_r=1.

Greenhouse, Steven. 2011b. "Losing Vote at a Target in New York, Union Vows to Try Again." *New York Times*, June 18. http://www.nytimes.com/2011/06/19/business/19target.html.

Greenhouse, Steven. 2014. "Bangladesh Inspections Find Gaps in Safety." *New York Times*, March 11 http://www.nytimes.com/2014/03/12/business/safety-flaws-found-in-new-inspections-of-factories-in-bangladesh.html?_r=0.

Gregory, Paul. 2012. "Outsourcer-in-Chief: Obama of General Motors." *Forbes*, August 12. http://www.forbes.com/sites/paulroderickgregory/2012/08/12/outsourcer-in-chief-obama-of-general-motors/.

Grunberg, Leon, Richard Anderson-Connolly, and Edward S. Greenberg. 2000. "Surviving Layoffs: The Effects on Organizational Commitment and Job Performance." *Work and Occupations* 27(1):7–31.

Grusky, David and Maria Charles, eds. 2004. *Occupational Ghettos*. Stanford, CA: Stanford University Press.

Gusfield, Joseph. 1963. *Symbolic Crusade: Status Politics and the Urban Temperance Movement*. Chicago: University of Illinois.

Haas, Linda and Tine Rostgaard. 2011. "Fathers' Rights to Paid Parental Leave in the Nordic Countries: Consequences for the Gendered Division of Leave." *Community, Work & Family* 14(2):179–97.

Haas, Linda and C. Philip Hwang. 2013. "Trade Union Support for Fathers' Use of Work–Family Benefits – Lessons from Sweden." *Community, Work & Family* 16(1):46–67.

Hacker, Jacob. 2006. *The Great Risk Shift: The Assault on American Jobs, Families, Health Care and Retirement and How You Can Fight Back*. New York: Oxford University Press.

Hagan, Jacqueline, Nichola Lowe, and Christian Quingla. 2011. "Skills on the Move: Rethinking the Relationship between Human Capital and Immigrant Economic Mobility." *Work & Occupations* 38(2):149–78.

Hakim, Catherine. 2001. *Work-Lifestyle Choices in the Twenty-First Century*. New York: Oxford University Press.

Haley-Lock, Anna, Danielle Berman, and Jeffrey M. Timberlake. 2013. "Employment Opportunity for Workers without a College Degree across the Public, Nonprofit, and for-Profit Sectors." *Work & Occupations* 40(3):281–311.

Harden, Jeni. 2001. "Mother Russia at Work: Gender Divisions in the Medical Profession." *European Journal of Women's Studies* 8:181–99.

Hareven, Tamara. 1982. *Family Time and Industrial Time: The Relationship between the Family and Work in a New England Industrial Community*. New York: Cambridge University Press.

Hareven, Tamara and Randolph Langenbach. 1978. *Amoskeag*. New York: Pantheon Books.

Harrington, Brad and Jaquelyn James. 2006. "The Standards of Excellence in Work-Life Integration: From Changing Policies to Changing Organizations." Pp. 665–84 in *The Work and Family Handbook: Multidisciplinary Perspectives, Methods, and Approaches*, edited by M. Pitt-Catsouphes, E. E. Kossek and S. Sweet. Mahwah, NJ: Lawrence Erlbaum.

Harrington, Brad, Fred Van Deusen, and Iyar Mazar. 2012. "The New Dad: Right at Home." Boston: Boston College Center for Work & Family. http://www.bc.edu/content/dam/files/centers/cwf/pdf/The%20New%20Dad%20Right%20at%20Home%20BCCWF%202012.pdf.

Harris, Jeanne and Iris Junglas. 2013. "Decoding the Contradictory Culture of Silicon Valley." Accenture Institute for High Peformance. http://www.register.accenture.com/SiteCollectionDocuments/PDF/Accenture-Decoding-Contradictory-Culture-Silicon-Valley.pdf.

Harrison, Jill Lindsey and Sarah E. Lloyd. 2013. "New Jobs, New Workers, and New Inequalities: Explaining Employers' Roles in Occupational Segregation by Nativity and Race." *Social Problems* 60(3):281–301.

Harvey, Adia. 2005. "Becoming Entrepreneurs: Intersections of Race, Class and Gender at the Black Beauty Salon." *Gender and Society* 19(3):789–808.

Hatton, Erin. 2011. *The Temporary Economy: From Kelly Girls to Permatemps in Postwar America*. Philadelphia: Temple University Press.

Hays, Sharon. 2003. *Flat Broke with Children: Women in the Age of Welfare Reform*. New York: Oxford University Press.

Head, Simon. 2003. *The New Ruthless Economy: Work and Power in the Digital Age*. New York: Oxford University Press.

Head, Simon. 2004. "Inside the Leviathan." *New York Review of Books*, pp. 80–89.

Head, Simon. 2014. "Worse Than Wal-Mart: Amazon's Sick Brutality and Secret History of Ruthlessly Intimidating Workers." *Salon*, February 23. http://www.salon.com/2014/02/23/worse_than_wal_mart_amazons_sick_brutality_and_secret_history_of_ruthlessly_intimidating_workers/.

Heckscher, Charles. 1988. *The New Unionism: Employee Involvement in the Changing Corporation*. New York: Basic Books.

Hegewisch, Ariane and Janet Gornick. 2011. "The Impact of Work-Family Policies on Women's Employment: A Review of Research from OECD Countries." *Community, Work & Family* 14(2):119–37.

Henson, Kevin. 1996. *Just a Temp*. Philadelphia: Temple University Press.

Henson, Kevin and Jackie Krasas Rogers. 2001. "Why Marcia You've Changed! Male Temporary Clerical Workers Doing Masculinity in a Feminized Occupation." *Gender and Society* 15:218–38.

Herrnstein, Richard and Charles Murray. 1994. *The Bell Curve: Intelligence and Class Structure in American Life*. New York: The Free Press.

Hessler, Peter. 2003. "Underwater." *The New Yorker*, July 7, pp. 28.

Heymann, Jody. 2000. *The Widening Gap: Why America's Working Families Are in Jeopardy and What Can Be Done About It*. New York: Perseus.

Hilbrecht, Margo and Donna S. Lero. 2014. "Self-Employment and Family Life: Constructing Work–Life Balance When You're 'Always On.'" *Community, Work & Family* 17(1):20–42.

Hira, Ron. 2010. "U.S. Policy and the Stem Workforce System." *American Behavioral Scientist* 53(7):949–61.

Hochschild, Arlie Russell. 1983. *The Managed Heart: Commericalization of Human Feeling*. Berkeley: University of California Press.

Hochschild, Arlie Russell. 1989. *The Second Shift*. New York: Avon Books.

Hochschild, Arlie Russell. 1997. *The Time Bind: When Work Becomes Home and Home Becomes Work*. New York: Metropolitan Books.

Hoefer, Michael, Nancy Rytina, and Ryan Baker. 2011. *Estimates of the Unauthorized Immigrant Population Residing in the United States: January 2010*. http://www.dhs.gov/xlibrary/assets/statistics/publications/ois_ill_pe_2010.pdf.

Holzer, Harry, Julia Lane, David Rosenblum, and Fredrik Andersson. 2011. *Where Are All the Good Jobs Going? What National and Local Job Quality and Dynamics Mean for U.S. Workers*. New York: Russell Sage Foundation.

Honey, Michael. 1999. *Black Workers Remember: An Oral History of Segregation, Unionism and the Freedom Struggle*. Berkeley: University of California Press.

Hostetler, Andrew, Stephen Sweet, and Phyllis Moen. 2007. "Gendered Career Paths: A Life Course Perspective on the Return to School." *Sex Roles* 56:85–103.

Hutchens, Robert and Karen Grace-Martin. 2006. "Employer Willingness to Permit Phased Retirement: Why Are Some More Willing Than Others." *Industrial and Labor Relations Review* 59(4):525–46.

Iwanow, H., M. G. McEachern, and A. Jeffrey. 2005. "The Influence of Ethical Trading Policies on Consumer Apparel Purchase Decisions." *International Journal of Retail and Distribution Management* (33):371–87.

Jacobs, Jerry A. and Kathleen Gerson. 2004. *The Time Divide: Work, Family, and Gender Inequality*. Cambridge, MA: Harvard University Press.

Jacoby, Sanford. 1985. *Employing Bureaucracy*. New York: Columbia University Press.

Jacoby, Sanford. 1991. *Masters to Managers*. New York: Columbia University Press.

Jacoby, Sanford. 1999. "Are Career Jobs Headed for Extinction?" *California Management Review* 42:123–45.

Jacoby, Sanford. 2001. "Risk and the Labor Market: Societal Past as Economic Prologue." Pp. 31–60 in *Sourcebook of Labor Markets: Evolving Structures and Processes*, edited by I. Berg and A. Kalleberg. New York: Kluwer.

Jones, Ellis, Ross Haenfler, Brett Johnson, and Brian Klocke. 2002. *The Better World Handbook: From Good Intentions to Everyday Actions*. Gabriola Island, Canada: New Society.

Jones, Marc T. 2005. "The Transnational Corporation, Corporate Social Responsibility and the 'Outsourcing' Debate." *Journal of American Academy of Business, Cambridge* 6(2):91–97.

Kahlenberg, Richard. 2004. *America's Untapped Resource: Low-Income Students in Higher Education*. New York: Century Foundation Press.

Kahn, Joseph. 2003. "Ruse in Toyland: Chinese Workers' Hidden Woe." *New York Times*, December 7, A2.

Kalev, Alexandra. 2014. "How You Downsize Is Who You Downsize: Biased Formalization, Accountability, and Managerial Diversity." *American Sociological Review* 79(1):109–35.

Kalev, Alexandra, Frank Dobbin, and Erin Kelly. 2006. "Best Practices or Best Guesses? Assessing the Efficacy of Corporate Affirmative Action and Diversity Policies." *American Sociological Review* 71(3):589–617.

Kalleberg, Arne L. 2007. *The Mismatched Worker*. New York: W. W. Norton.

Kalleberg, Arne L. 2009. "Precarious Work, Insecure Workers: Employment Relations in Transition." *American Sociological Review* 74(1):1–22.

Kalleberg, Arne L. 2013. *Good Jobs, Bad Jobs: The Rise of Polarized and Precarious Employment Systems in the United States, 1970s to 2000s*. New York: Russell Sage Foundation.

Kalleberg, Arne, Barbara Reskin, and Ken Hudson. 2000. "Bad Jobs in America: Standard and Nonstandard Employment Relations and Job Quality in the United States." *American Sociological Review* 65(2):256–78.

Kan, Man Yee. 2007. "Work Orientation and Wives' Employment Careers: An Evaluation of Hakim's Preference Theory." *Work and Occupations* 34(4):430–62.

Kanter, Rosabeth Moss. 1977. *Men and Women of the Corporation*. New York: Basic Books.

Karlin, Carolyn Aman, Paula England, and Mary Richardson. 2002. "Why Do 'Women's Jobs' Have Low Pay for Their Educational Level?" *Gender Issues* 20(4):0–22.

Kasperkevic, Jana. 2015. "LA Becomes Largest US City to Increase Minimum Wage to $15 an Hour." *The Guardian*, May 19. http://www.theguardian.com/us-news/2015/may/19/la-minimum-wage-rise-vote.

Katz, Michael. 1996. *In the Shadow of the Poorhouse*. New York: Basic Books.

Kelly, Erin. 2003. "The Strange History of Employer-Sponsored Child Care: Interested Actors, Uncertainty, and the Transformation of Law in Organizational Fields." *American Journal of Sociology* 109(3):606–49.

Kelly, Erin, Ellen Ernst Kossek, Leslie Hammer, Mary Durham, Jeremy Bray, Kelly Chermack, Laurne Murphy and Dan Kaskubar. 2008. "Getting There from Here: Research on the Effects of Work-Family Initiatives on Work-Family Conflict and Business Outcomes." Pp. 305–49 in *The Academy of Management Annals (Volume 2)*, edited by J. Walsh and A. Brief. New York: Academy of Management.

Kelly, Erin, Phyllis Moen, and Eric Tranby. 2011. "Changing Workplaces to Reduce Work-Family Conflict: Schedule Control in a White-Collar Organization." *American Sociological Review* 76(2):265–90.

Kelly, Erin, Phyllis Moen, J. Michael Oakes, Wen Fan, Cassandra Okechukwu, Kelly D. Davis, Leslie B. Hammer, Ellen Ernst Kossek, Rosalind Berkowitz King, Ginger C. Hanson, Frank Mierzwa, and Lynne M. Casper. 2014. "Changing Work and Work-Family Conflict: Evidence from the Work, Family, and Health Network." *American Sociological Review* 79(3):485–516.

Kenessey, Zoltan. 1987. "Primary, Secondary, Tertiary and Quarternary Sectors of the Economy." *The Review of Income and Wealth* 33:359–86.

Kennelly, Ivy. 1999. "'That Single Mother Element.' How White Employers Typify Black Women." *Gender and Society* 13:168–92.

Kennelly, Ivy. 2002. "'I Would Never Be a Secretary': Reinforcing Gender in Segregated and Integrated Occupations." *Gender and Society* 16:603–24.

Kennelly, Ivy. 2006. "Secretarial Work, Nurturing, and the Ethic of Service." *NWSA Journal* 18:170–92.

Khadria, Binod. 2001. "Shifting Paradigms of Globalization: The Twenty-First Century Transition Towards Generics in Skilled Migration from India." Pp. 45–71 in *International Migration*, Vol. 39: Blackwell.

Killewald, Alexandra. 2013. "A Reconsideration of the Fatherhood Premium: Marriage, Coresidence, Biology, and Fathers' Wages." *American Sociological Review* 78(1):96–116.

Kim, Chigon and Mark Gottdiener. 2004. "Urban Problems in Global Perspective." Pp. 172–92 in *Handbook of Social Problems: A Comparative International Perspective*, edited by G. Ritzer. Thousand Oaks, CA: Sage.

Kim, Young-Mi. 2013. "Diverging Top and Bottom: Labour Flexibilization and Changes in Career Mobility in the USA." *Work, Employment & Society* 27(5):860–79.

Kimmel, Michael. 2006. "A War against Boys?" *Dissent* 53:65–70.

Kleiner, Sibyl and Eliza K. Pavalko. 2014. "Double Time: Is Health Affected by a Spouse's Time at Work?" *Social Forces* 92(3):983–1007.

Kochan, Thomas. 2005. *Restoring the American Dream: A Working Families' Agenda for America*. Cambridge, MA: MIT Press.

Kocieniewski, David. 2011. "G.E. Strategies Let It Avoid Taxes Altogether." *New York Times*, March 25. http://www.nytimes.com/2011/03/25/business/economy/25tax.html?_r=0.

Koeber, Charles. 2002. "Corporate Restructuring, Downsizing and the Middle Class: The Process and Meaning of Worker Displacement in the 'New Economy.'" *Qualitative Sociology* 25:217–46.

Kossek, Ellen Ernst and Alyssa Fried. 2006. "The Business Case: Managerial Perspectives on Work and Family." Pp. 611–26 in *The Work and Family Handbook: Multidisciplinary Perspectives, Methods, and Approaches*, edited by M. Pitt-Catsouphes, E. E. Kossek, and S. Sweet. Boston: Lawrence Erlbaum.

Kossek, Ellen Ernst, Suzan Lewis, and Leslie Hammer. 2010. "Work-Life Initiatives and Organizational Change: Overcoming Mixed Messages to Move from the Margins to the Mainstream." *Human Relations* 63(1):3–19.

Kossek, Ellen Ernst and Brenda Lautsch. 2012. "Work-Family Boundary Management Styles in Organizations: A Cross Level Model." *Organizational Psychology Review* 2(2):152–71.

Kozol, Jonathan. 2006. *The Shame of the Nation*. New York: Three Rivers Press.

Kraft, Philip. 1984. *Programmers and Managers: The Routinization of Computer Programming*. Secaucus, NJ: Springer Verlag.

Kreiner, Glen, Elaine Hollensbe, and Mathew Sheep. 2009. "Balancing Borders and Bridges: Negotiating the Work-Home Interface Via Boundary Work Tactics." *Academy of Management Journal* 52(4):704–30.

Kremer, Monique. 2006a. "Consumers in Charge of Care: The Dutch Personal Budget and Its Impact on the Market, Professionals, and the Family." *European Societies* 8:385–401.

Kremer, Monique. 2006b. "The Politics of Ideals of Care: Danish and Flemish Child Care Policy Compared." *Social Politics* 13:261–85.

Krugman, Paul. 2005. "French Family Values." *New York Times*, July 29, C1.

Krugman, Paul. 2015. "The Austerity Delusion." *The Guardian*, April 29. http://www.theguardian.com/business/ng-interactive/2015/apr/29/the-austerity-delusion.

Ku, Manwai C. 2011. "When Does Gender Matter? Gender Differences in Specialty Choice among Physicians." *Work & Occupations* 38(2):221–62.

Kurlansky, Mark. 1998. *Cod: A Biography of the Fish That Changed the World*. New York: Penguin.

Lafer, Gordon. 2003. "Graduate Student Unions: Organizing in a Changed Academic Economy." *Labor Studies Journal* 28(2):25–43.

Lambert, Susan J. 2009. *Making a Difference for Hourly Employees*, edited by A. Crouter and A. Booth. Washington, DC: Urban Institute Press.

Lambert, Susan J., Anna Haley-Lock, and Julia R. Henly. 2012. "Schedule Flexibility in Hourly Jobs: Unanticipated Consequences and Promising Directions." *Community, Work & Family* 15(3):293–315.

Lasch, Christopher. 1995. *Haven in a Heartless World: The Family Besieged*. New York: W. W. Norton.

Lash, Scott and John Urry. 1987. *The End of Organized Capitalism*. Madison: University of Wisconsin Press.

Ledbetter v. Goodyear Tire & Rubber Co., 550 U.S. 618 (2007).

Lee, Ching Kwan. 1998. *Gender and the South China Miracle*. Berkeley: University of California Press.

Lee, Ching Kwan. 2007. *Against the Law: Labor Protests in China's Rustbelt and Sunbelt*. Berkeley: University of California Press.

Leidner, Robin. 1993. *Fast Food, Fast Talk: Service Work and the Routinization of Everyday Life*. Los Angeles: University of California Press.

Levy, Frank. 1998. *The New Dollars and Dreams*. New York: Russell Sage.

Lichtenstein, Nelson. 2002. *State of the Union: A Century of American Labor*. Princeton, NJ: Princeton University Press.

Liebow, Eliot. 1967. *Tally's Corner*. Boston: Little, Brown.

Lipset, Seymour. 1996. *American Exceptionalism: A Double-Edged Sword*. New York: W. W. Norton.

Liptak, Adam. 2011. "Jutices Rule for Wal-Mart in Class-Action Bias Case." *New York Times*, June 20. http://www.nytimes.com/2011/06/21/business/21bizcourt.html.

Liu, Yujia and David B. Grusky. 2013. "The Payoff to Skill in the Third Industrial Revolution." *American Sociological Review* 118(5):1330–74.

Lopez, Steven. 2003. "Overcoming Legacies of Business Unionism: Why Grassroots Organizing Activities Succeed." Pp. 114–32 in *Rebuilding Labor: Organizers and*

Organizing in the New Labor Movement, edited by R. Milkman and K. Voss. Ithaca, NY: ILR Press.

Lopez, Steven. 2006. "Culture Change Management in Long-Term Care: A Shop Floor View." *Politics and Society* 34(1):55–80.

Lowell, Lindsay. 2010. "A Long View of America's Immigration Policy and the Supply of Foreign-Born Stem Workers in the United States." *American Behavioral Scientist* 53(7):1029–44.

Lowenstein, Roger. 2006. "Do Illegal Immigrants Take Jobs?" *New York Times Magazine*, July 9, 34–43, 69–71.

Luce, Stephanie. 2014. *Labor Movements: Global Perspectives*. Cambridge, UK: Polity Press.

Luken, Ralph and Rodney Stares. 2005. "Small Business Responsibility in Developing Countries: A Threat or an Opportunity?" *Business Strategy & the Environment* 14(1):38–53.

Lyness, Karen S., Janet C. Gornick, Pamela Stone, and Angela R. Grotto. 2012. "It's All About Control: Worker Control over Schedule and Hours in Cross-National Context." *American Sociological Review* 77(6):1023–49.

Lyons, Christopher J. and Becky Pettit. 2011. "Compounded Disadvantage: Race, Incarceration, and Wage Growth." *Social Problems* 58(2):257–80.

Machlowitz, M. M. 1980. *Workaholics: Living with Them, Working with Them.* Reading, MA: Addison-Wesley.

MacLeod, Jay. 1995. *Ain't No Makin' It*. Boulder, CO: Westview Press.

MacMillan, Ross, ed. 2005. *The Structure of the Life Course: Standardized? Individualized? Differentiated?* Vol. 9. New York: Elsevier.

Maher, Kris. 2011. "Unions Fend Off Right to Work Bill in New Hampshire." *Wall Street Journal*, June 24. http://online.wsj.com/article/SB1000142405270230423 1204576404092860800676.html.

Mandel, Hadas and Moshe Semyonov. 2004. "Family Policies, Wage Structures, and Gender Gaps: Sources of Earnings Inequality in 20 Countries." *American Sociological Review* 70:949–67.

Mandel, Hadas. 2011. "Rethinking the Paradox: Tradeoffs in Work-Family Policy and Patterns of Gender Inequality." *Community, Work & Family* 14(2):159–77.

Mandel, Hadas and Moshe Semyonov. 2006. "A Welfare State Paradox: State Interventions and Women's Employment Opportunities in 22 Countries." *American Journal of Sociology* 111(4):1910–49.

Marglin, Steven. 1982. "What Do Bosses Do?" Pp. 285–98 in *Classes, Power and Conflict: Classical and Contemporary Debates*, edited by A. Giddens and D. Held. Berkeley: University of California Press.

Marks, Alexandra. 2004. "United's Pension Woes: Sign of a Bigger Issue." *Christian Science Monitor*, October 4, 1–2.

Martin v. Wilks, 490 U.S. 755 (1989).

Marx, Karl. 1964 [1844]. "Economic and Philosophic Manuscripts." Pp. 61–219 in *Karl Marx: Economic and Philosophic Manuscripts*, edited by T. Bottomore. New York: McGraw Hill.

Marx, Karl and Friedrich Engels. 1972 [1848]. "Manifesto of the Communist Party." Pp. 331–62 in *The Marx-Engels Reader*, edited by R. C. Tucker. New York: W. W. Norton.

Masser, Barbara and Dominic Abrams. 2004. "Reinforcing the Glass Ceiling: The Consequences of Hostile Sexism for Female Managerial Candidates." *Sex Roles* 51:609–15.

Massey, Douglas. 2006. "The Wall That Keeps Illegal Workers In." *New York Times*, April 4. 8–12.

Mattingly, Doreen. 1999. "Making Maids." Pp. 61–78 in *Gender, Migration & Domestic Service*, edited by D. Mattingly and J. Momsen. New York: Routledge.

Mattsson, Lars-Gunnar. 2003. "Reorganization of Distribution in Globalization of Markets: The Dynamic Context of Supply Chain Management." *Supply Chain Management* 8(5):416–26.

McCann, Deirdre. 2005. "Working Time Laws: A Global Perspective: Findings from the Ilo's Conditions of Work and Employment Database." Geneva, Switzerland: International Labor Office.

McDonald, Steve, Lin Nan, and Dan Ao. 2009. "Networks of Opportunity: Gender, Race, and Job Leads." *Social Problems* 56(3):385–402.

McElhinney, Stephen. 2005. "Exposing the Interests: Decoding the Promise of the Global Knowledge Society." *New Media & Society* 7(6):748–69.

McLaughlin, Heather, Christopher Uggen, and Amy Blackstone. 2012. "Sexual Harassment, Workplace Authority, and the Paradox of Power." *American Sociological Review* 77(4):625–47.

McPhee, John. 2005. "Out in the Sort; Annals of Transport." *New Yorker* 81(9):161–67.

Meiksins, Peter. 1998. "The Time Bind." *Monthly Review* 49:1–13.

Meiksins, Peter and Peter Whalley. 2002. *Putting Work in Its Place: A Quiet Revolution*. Ithaca, NY: ILR Press.

Meiksins, Peter and Peter Whalley. 2004. "Labor and Leisure: Should Europe Work More, or America Less?" *International Herald Tribune*, August 11, 1–4.

Meixell, Brady and Ross Eisenbrey. 2014. "An Epidemic of Wage Theft Is Costing Workers Hundreds of Millions of Dollars a Year." Economic Policy Institute Issue Brief: Economic Policy Institute Issue Brief. http://www.epi.org/publication/epidemic-wage-theft-costing-workers-hundreds.

Meyerson, Harold. 2011. "Editorial: The US: Where Europe Comes to Slum." *Los Angeles Times*, May 15. http://readersupportednews.org/opinion2/279-82/5943-the-us-where-europe-comes-to-slum.

Milanovic, Branko. 2005. *Worlds Apart: Measuring International and Global Inequality*. Princeton, NJ: Princeton University Press.

Milberg, William. 2004. "The Changing Structure of Trade Linked to Global Production Systems: What Are the Policy Implications?" *International Labour Review* 143(1/2):45–90.

Milkman, Ruth. 2006. *L.A. Story: Immigrant Workers and the Future of the U.S. Labor Movement*. Berkeley: University of California Press.

Milkman, Ruth and Kim Voss. 2004. *Rebuilding Labor: Organizers and Organizing in the New Labor Movement*. Ithaca, NY: ILR Press.

Mills, C. Wright. 1959. *The Sociological Imagination*. New York: Oxford University Press.

Mills, C. Wright. 2002 [1951]. *White Collar: The American Middle Classes*. London: Oxford University Press.

Mir, Ali, Biju Mathew, and Raza Mir. 2000. "The Codes of Migration: Contours of the Global Software Labor Market." *Cultural Dynamics* 12(1):5.

Mischel, Lawrence, Jared Bernstein, and Sylvia Allegretto. 2005. *The State of Working America 2004/2005*. Ithaca, NY: Economic Policy Institute.

Mischel, Lawrence, Jared Bernstein, and Heidi Shierholz. 2009. *The State of Working America 2008/2009*. Ithaca, NY: Economic Policy Institute.

Misra, Joya, Michelle Budig, and Irene Boeckman. 2011. "Work-Family Policy and the Effects of Children on Women's Employment, Hours, and Earnings." *Community, Work & Family* 14(2):139–57.

MIT. 1999. "A Study on the Status of Women Faculty in Science at MIT." Boston: Massachusetts Institute of Technology. http://web.mit.edu/fnl/women/women.html.

Moberg, David. 2005. "Look Who's Walking." *The Nation*, July 26. http://www.thenation.com/article/look-whos-walking.

Moen, Phyllis. 2001a. "Constructing a Life Course." *Marriage and Family Review* 30:97–109.

Moen, Phyllis. 2001b. "The Gendered Life Course." Pp. 179–96 in *Handbook of Aging and the Social Sciences*, edited by L. George and R. H. Binstock. San Diego, CA: Academic Press.

Moen, Phyllis. 2007. "Not So Big Jobs and Retirements: What Workers (and Retirees) Really Want." *Generations* 31(1):31–36.

Moen, Phyllis and Stephen Sweet. 2003. "Time Clocks: Couples' Work Hour Strategies." Pp. 17–34 in *It's About Time: Career Strains, Strategies, and Successes*, edited by P. Moen. Ithaca, NY: Cornell University Press.

Moen, Phyllis, Ronit Waismel-Manor, and Stephen Sweet. 2003. "Success." Pp. 17–34 in *It's About Time: Couples and Careers*, edited by P. Moen. Ithaca, NY: Cornell University Press.

Moen, Phyllis and Stephen Sweet. 2004. "From 'Work-Family' to 'Flexible Careers': A Life Course Reframing." *Community, Work and Family* 7(2):209–26.

Moen, Phyllis and Patricia V. Roehling. 2005. *The Career Mystique*. Boulder, CO: Rowman & Littlefield.

Moen, Phyllis and Donna Spencer. 2006. "Converging Divergences in Age, Gender, Health, and Well-Being: Strategic Selection in the Third Age." Pp. 127–44 in *Handbook of Aging and the Social Sciences*, edited by R. Binstock and L. George. New York: Elsevier Academic Press.

Moen, Phyllis, Erin Kelly, and Rachelle Hill. 2011. "Does Enhancing Work-Time Control and Flexibility Reduce Turnover? A Naturally Occurring Experiment." *Social Problems* 58(1):69–98.

Moen, Phyllis, Erin Kelly, Eric Tranby, and Quinlei Huang. 2011. "Changing Work, Changing Health: Can Real Work-Time Flexibility Promote Health Behaviors and Well-Being?" *Journal of Health and Social Behavior* 52(4):404–29.

Moen, Phyllis, Jack Lam, Samantha Ammons, and Erin L. Kelly. 2013. "Time Work by Overworked Professionals: Strategies in Response to the Stress of Higher Status." *Work & Occupations* 40(2):79–114.

Mohanty, Chandra Talpade. 2003. *Feminism without Borders: Decolonizing Theory, Practicing Solidarity*. Durham, NC: Duke University Press.

Moller, Stephanie and Beth Rubin. 2008. "The Contours of Stratification in Service-Oriented Economies." *Social science research* 37(4):1039–60.

Mong, Sherry and Vincent Roscigno. 2010. "African American Men and the Experience of Employment Discrimination." *Qualitative Sociology* 33(1):1–21.

Montgomery, David. 1979. *Workers' Control in America: Studies in the History of Work, Technology, and Labor Struggles*. Cambridge, UK: Cambridge University Press.

Morgan, Kimberly. 2005. "The 'Production' of Child Care: How Labor Markets Shape Social Policy and Vice Versa." *Social Politics* 12:243–63.

Morgan, Kimberly and Kathrin Zippel. 2003. "Paid to Care: The Origins and Effects of Care Leave Policies in Western Europe." *Social Politics* 10:49–85.

Moss, Philip and Chris Tilly. 2001. *Stories Employers Tell: Race, Skill and Hiring in America*. New York: Russell Sage Foundation.

Mouw, Ted. 2002. "Are Black Workers Missing the Connection? The Effect of Spatial Distance and Employee Referrals on Interfirm Racial Segregation." *Demography* 39:507–28.

Mouw, Ted and Arne Kalleberg. 2010. "Occupations and the Structure of Wage Inequality in the United States, 1980s to 2000s." *American Sociological Review* 75(3):402–31.

Muller v. Oregon, 208 U.S. 412 (1908).

Munsch, Christin L., Cecilia L. Ridgeway, and Joan C. Williams. 2014. "Pluralistic Ignorance and the Flexibility Bias: Understanding and Mitigating Flextime and Flexplace Bias at Work." *Work and Occupations* 41(1):40–62.

Murray, Charles. 1995. *Losing Ground: American Social Policy, 1950–1980*. New York: Basic Books.

Myrdal, Gunnar. 1995 [1954]. *An American Dilemma: The Negro Problem and Modern Democracy*. New York: Transaction Press.

Nakano Glenn, Eveyln. 2002. *Unequal Freedom: How Race and Gender Shaped American Citizenship and Labor*. Cambridge, MA: Harvard University Press.

National Center for Education Statistics. 2013. "Percentage of 18- to 24-Year-Olds Enrolled in Degree-Granting Institutions, by Level of Institution and Sex and Race/Ethnicity of Student: 1967 Through 2012." http://nces.ed.gov/programs/digest/d13/tables/dt13_302.60.asp.

National Institute of Population and Social Security Research. 2012. "Population Projections for Japan (January 2012): 2011 to 2060." http://www.ipss.go.jp/site-ad/index_english/esuikei/gh2401e.asp.

Nau, Michael. 2013. "Economic Elites, Investments, and Income Inequality." *Social Forces* 92(2):437–61.

Neal, Margaret and Leslie Hammer. 2006. *Working Couples Caring for Children and Aging Parents: Effects on Work and Well-Being*. Mahwah, NJ: Lawrence Erlbaum.

Nee, Victor, Jimy Sanders, and Scott Sernau. 1994. "Job Transitions in an Immigrant Metropolis: Ethnic Boundaries and the Mixed Economy." *American Sociological Review* 59:849–72.

Nelson, Daniel. 1980. *Frederick W. Taylor and the Rise of Scientific Management.* Madison: University of Wisconsin Press.

Nelson, Valerie, Adrienne Martin, and Joachim Ewert. 2005. "What Difference Can They Make? Assessing the Social Impact of Corporate Codes of Practice." *Development in Practice* 15(3/4):539–45.

Nestle, Marion. 2003. *Food Politics.* Los Angeles: University of California Press.

Newburger, Eric and Thomas Gryn. 2009. *The Foreign-Born Labor Force in the United States: 2007.* Congress, ACS-10. http://www.census.gov/prod/2009pubs/acs-10.pdf.

Newman, Kathleen. 2006. *Chutes and Ladders.* New York: Russell Sage Foundation.

Ngai, Pun. 2005. *Made in China: Factory Workers in a Global Workplace.* Durham, NC: Duke University Press.

Noble, David. 1979. *America by Design: Science, Technology, and the Rise of Corporate Capitalism.* New York: Alfred Knopf.

Nowicki, Carol. 2003. "Family and Medical Leave Act." Sloan Work and Family Encyclopedia. http://wfnetwork.bc.edu.

O'Brien, Helena and Sarita Gupta. 2005. "Local Power Can Change Wal-Mart: The Acorn and Jobs with Justice Organizing Strategy." *Social Policy* 36:16–20.

O'Leary, Christopher and Stephen Wandner. 1997. "Summing Up: Achievements, Problems and Prospects." Pp. 669–722 in *Unemployment Insurance in the United States: Analysis of Policy Issues*, edited by C. O'Leary and S. Wandner. New York: W. E. Upjohn Institute.

O'Reilly, Brian. 1994. "The New Deal: What Companies and Employees Owe One Another." *Fortune*, June 13, pp. 44–50.

O'Riain, Sean. 2007. "New Deal or No Deal? Knowledge Workers in the Information Economy." Pp. 63–77 in *Surviving the New Economy*, edited by J. Amman, T. Carpenter, and G. Neff. Boulder, CO: Paradigm.

Ochs, Elinor, Anthony Graesch, Angela Mittmann, Thomas Bradbury, and Rena Repetti. 2006. "Video Ethnography and Ethnoarcheaological Tracking." Pp. 387–410 in *The Work and Family Handbook: Interdisciplinary Perspectives, Methods, and Approaches*, edited by M. Pitt-Catsouphes, E. E. Kossek, and S. Sweet. Mahwah, NJ: Lawrence Erlbaum.

Offer, Shira and Barbara Schneider. 2011. "Revisiting the Gender Gap in Time-Use Patterns: Multitasking and Well-Being among Mothers and Fathers in Dual-Earner Families." *American Sociological Review* 76(6):809–33.

Osnowitz, Debra. 2010. *Freelancing Expertise: Contract Professionals in the New Economy.* Ithaca, NY: ILR Press.

Osterman, Paul. 2001. *Securing Prosperity.* Princeton, NJ: Princeton University Press.

Osterman, Paul and Beth Shulman. 2011. *Good Jobs America: Making Work Better for Everyone.* New York: Russell Sage Foundation.

Osterud, N. G. 1987. "'She Helped Me Hay It as Good as a Man': Relations among Women and Men in an Agricultural Community." Pp. 87–97 in *"To Toil the*

Livelong Day": America's Women at Work, 1780–1980, edited by C. Groneman and M. B. Norton. Ithaca, NY: Cornell University Press.

Pager, Devah. 2003. "The Mark of a Criminal Record." *American Journal of Sociology* 108(5):937-75.

Pager, Devah, Bruce Western, and Bart Bonikowski. 2009. "Discrimination in a Low-Wage Labor Market: A Field Experiment." *American Sociological Review* 74(5):777–99.

Pagnan, Colleen E., Donna S. Lero, and Shelley M. MacDermid Wadsworth. 2011. "It Doesn't Always Add Up: Examining Dual-Earner Couples' Decision to Off-Shift." *Community, Work & Family* 14(3):297–316.

Pais, Jeremy. 2013. "The Effects of U.S. Immigration on the Career Trajectories of Native Workers, 1979–2004." *American Journal of Sociology* 119(1):35–74.

Parker, Mike. 1985. *Inside the Circle: A Union Guide to QWL.* Boston: South End Press.

Parker, Mike and Jane Slaughter. 1988. *Unions and the Team Concept.* Boston: South End Press.

Parks, Virginia. 2011. "Revisiting Shibboleths of Race and Urban Economy: Black Employment in Manufacturing and the Public Sector Compared 1950–2000." *International Journal of Urban and Regional Research* 35(1):110–29.

Parthasarathy, Balaji. 2004. "India's Silicon Valley or Silicon Valley's India? Socially Embedding the Computer Software Industry in Bangalore." *International Journal of Urban and Regional Research* 28(3):664–85.

Passel, Jeffrey, D'Vera Cohn, and Ana Gonzalez-Barrera. 2013. "Population Decline of Unauthorized Immigrants Stalls, May Have Reversed." Pew Research Hispanic Trends Project. http://www.pewhispanic.org/2013/09/23/population -decline-of-unauthorized-immigrants-stalls-may-have-reversed.

Patel, Reena. 2010. *Working the Night Shift: Women in India's Call Center Industry.* Stanford, CA: Stanford University Press.

Patni, Ambika. 1999. "Silicon Valley of the East." *Harvard International Review* 21(4):8.

Paules, Greta Foff. 1991. *Dishing It Out: Power and Resistance among Waitresses in a New Jersey Restaurant.* Philadelphia: Temple University Press.

Pavalko, Eliza and Kathryn Henderson. 2006. "Combining Care Work and Paid Work: Do Workplace Policies Make a Difference?" *Research on Aging* 28:359–74.

Pelsmacker, Patrick De, Liesbeth Driesen, and Glenn Rayp. 2005. "Do Consumers Care About Ethics: Willingness to Pay for Fair Trade Coffee." *Journal of Consumer Affairs* 39:363–86.

Peng, Thomas. 2011. "The Impact of Citizenship on Labour Process: State, Capital and Labour Control in South China. *Work, Employment and Society* 25(4):726–41.

Perpitone, Julianne. 2010. "More Wives Outearning Their Husbands." *CNN Money .com*, January 19. http://money.cnn.com/2010/01/19/news/economy/married_ women_salaries.

Perrucci, Robert and Carl Wysong. 2002. *The New Class Society: Goodbye American Dream?* New York: Rowman and Littlefield.

Pettit, Becky and Jennifer Hook. 2005. "The Structure of Women's Employment in Comparative Perspective." *Social Forces* 84:779–801.

Pfau-Effinger, Birgit. 2004. *Development of Culture, Welfare States and Women's Employment in Europe.* Burlington, VT: Ashgate.

Pietrykowski, Bruce. 1999. "Beyond the Fordist/Post-Fordist Dichotomy: Working through the Second Industrial Divide." *Review of Social Economy* 57:177–98.

Piketty, Thomas. 2014. *Capital in the Twenty-First Century.* Cambridge, MA: Harvard University Press.

Piore, Michael. 1977. "The Dual Labor Market and Its Implications." Pp. 91–95 in *Problems in Political Economy*, edited by D. Gordon. Lexington, MA: D. C. Heath.

Piore, Michael and Charles Sabel. 1984. *The Second Industrial Divide: Possibilities for Prosperity.* New York: Basic Books.

Pitt-Catsouphes, Marcie, Ellen Ernst Kossek, and Stephen Sweet. 2006. "Charting New Territory: Advancing Multi-Disciplinary Perspectives, Methods, and Approaches in the Study of Work and Family." Pp. 1–16 in *The Work and Family Handbook: Multi-Disciplinary Perspectives, Methods and Approaches*, edited by M. Pitt-Catsouphes, E. E. Kossek, and S. Sweet. Mahwah, NJ.: Lawrence Erlbaum.

Pixley, Joy. 2008. "Life Course Patterns of Career-Priorizing Decisions and Occupational Attainment in Dual Earner Couples." *Work and Occupations* 35(2):127–63.

Polanyi, Karl. 1944. *The Great Transformation.* New York: Farrar and Rinehart.

Pollert, Anna. 1988. "Dismantling Flexibility." *Capital and Class* 34:42–75.

Porter, Eduardo. 2006. "Cost of Illegal Immigration May Be Less Than Meets the Eye." *New York Times*, April 16. http://www.nytimes.com/2006/04/16/business/yourmoney/16view.html.

Portes, Alejandro and Ruben Rumbaut. 2001. *Legacies: The Story of the Immigrant Second Generation.* Berkeley: University of California Press.

Poster, Winifred and Srirupa Prasad. 2005. "Work-Family Relations in Transnational Perspective: A View from High-Tech Firms in India and the United States." *Social Problems* 52(1):122–46.

Presser, Harriet B. 2000. "Nonstandard Work Schedules and Marital Instability." *Journal of Marriage and the Family* 62:93–110.

Presser, Harriet B. 2003a. "Race-Ethnic and Gender Differences in Nonstandard Work Shifts." *Work and Occupations* 30:412–39.

Presser, Harriet B. 2003b. *Working in a 24/7 Economy: Challenges for American Families.* New York: Russel Sage Foundation.

Preston, Anne. 2004. *Leaving Science: Occupational Exit from Scientific Careers.* New York: Russell Sage Foundation.

Preston, Julia. 2011. "A Crackdown on Employing Illegal Workers." *New York Times*, May 29. http://www.nytimes.com/2011/05/30/us/politics/30raid.html.

Pugh, Allison. 2009. *Longing and Belonging: Parents, Children, and Consumer Culture.* Los Angeles: University of California Press.

Putnam, Robert. 2000. *Bowling Alone: The Collapse and Revival of American Community.* New York: Simon and Schuster.

Quillian, Lincoln. 2012. "Segregation and Poverty Concentration: The Role of Three Segregations." *American Sociological Review* 77(3):354–79.

Raider, Holly and Ronald Burt. 1996. "Boundaryless Careers and Social Capital." Pp. 187–200 in *The Boundaryless Career: A New Employment Principle for a New Organizational Era,* edited by M. B. Arthur and D. M. Rousseau. New York: Oxford University Press.

Reich, Rob. 2013. "Not Very Giving." *New York Times,* September 4. http://www.nytimes.com/2013/09/05/opinion/not-very-giving.html?_r=0.

Reskin, Barbara. 1998. *The Realities of Affirmative Action in Employment.* Washington, DC: The American Sociological Association.

Reskin, Barbara, Debra McBrier, and Julie Kmec. 1999. "The Determinants and Consequences of Workplace Sex and Race Composition." *Annual Review of Sociology* 25:335–61.

Restifo, Salvatore J., Vincent J. Roscigno, and Zhenchao Qian. 2013. "Segmented Assimilation, Split Labor Markets, and Racial/Ethnic Inequality: The Case of Early-Twentieth-Century New York." *American Sociological Review* 78(5):897–924.

Richardson, Pete. 2006. "The Anthropology of the Workplace and the Family." Pp. 165–88 in *The Work and Family Handbook: Multi-Disciplinary Perspectives, Methods and Approaches,* edited by M. Pitt-Catsouphes, E. E. Kossek, and S. Sweet. Mahwah, NJ: Lawrence Erlbaum.

Richman, Amy, Janet Civian, Laurie Shannon, Jeffrey Hill, and Robert Brennan. 2008. "The Relationship of Pereived Flexibility, Supportive Work-Life Policies, and Use of Formal Flexible Arrangements and Occasional Flexibility to Employee Engagement and Expected Retention." *Community, Work & Family* 11(2):183–97.

Riesman, David, Nathan Glazer, and Denney Reuel. 2001 [1961]. *The Lonely Crowd: A Study of the Changing American Character.* New Haven, CT: Yale University Press.

Rifkin, Jeremy. 2004. *The End of Work.* New York: Jeremy P. Tarcher/Putnam Books.

Rimer, Sara. 2007. "For Girls, It's Be Yourself, and Be Perfect, Too." *New York Times,* April 1, A1.

Rinehart, James, Christopher Huxley, and David Robertson. 1997. *Just Another Car Factory? Lean Production and Its Discontents.* Ithaca, NY: ILR Press.

Rippeyoung, Phyllis L. F. and Mary C. Noonan. 2012. "Is Breastfeeding Truly Cost Free? Income Consequences of Breastfeeding for Women." *American Sociological Review* 77(2):244–67.

Ritzer, George. 2011. *The Mcdonaldization of Society.* Thousand Oaks, CA: Pine Forge Press.

Rivera, Jorge and Chang Hoon Oh. 2013. "Environmental Regulations and Multinational Corporations' Foreign Market Entry Investments." *Policy Studies Journal* 41(2):243–72.

Roberts, Bryan. 2005. "Globalization and Latin American Cities." *International Journal of Urban and Regional Research* 29:110–23.

Robles, Frances. 2014. "Fleeing Gangs, Children Head to a U.S. Border." *New York Times*, July 10, A1.

Rosenbaum, James, Kennan Cepa, and Janet Rosenbaum. 2013. "Beyond the One-Size-Fits-All College Degree." *Contexts* 12(1):48–52.

Rosenfeld, Jake and Meredith Kleykamp. 2012. "Organized Labor and Racial Wage Inequality in the United States." *American Journal of Sociology* 117(5):1460–502.

Rousseau, Denise. 2005. *I-Deals: Idiosyncratic Deals Employees Bargain for Themselves*. Armonk, NY: M. E. Sharpe.

Roy, Donald. 1955. "Efficiency and 'the Fix.'" *American Journal of Sociology* 60:255–66.

Roychowdhury, Poulami. 2014. "Brothers and Others: Organizing Masculinity, Disorganizing Workers." *Social Problems* 61(1):22–41.

Royster, Deirdre. 2003. *Race and the Invisible Hand: How White Networks Exclude Black Men from Blue Collar Jobs*. Berkeley: University of California Press.

Rubin, Beth A. and Charles Brody. 2005. "Contradictions of Commitment in the New Economy: Insecurity, Time, and Technology." *Social Science Research* 34:843–61.

Rudnyckyj, Daromir. 2004. "Technologies of Servitude: Governmentality and Indonesian Transnational Labor Migration." *Anthropological Quarterly* 77:407–34.

Rybczynski, Witold. 1991. *Waiting for the Weekend*. New York: Viking.

Sahlins, Marshall. 1972. *Stone Age Economics*. Chicago: Aldine-Atherton.

Saiz, Albert. 2003. "The Impact of Immigration on American Cities: An Introduction to the Issues." *Business Review* Q4:4–23.

Salzman, Hal, Daniel Kuehn, and Lindsay Lowell. 2013. "Guestworkers in the High-Skill US Labor Market: An Analysis of Supply, Employment and Wage Trends." Washington, DC: Economic Policy Institute. http://www.epi.org/publication/bp359-guestworkers-high-skill-labor-market-analysis.

Sampson, Robert, S. W. Raudenbush, and Felton Earls. 1997. "Neighborhoods and Violent Crime: Multilevel Study of Collective Efficacy." *Science* 277:918–24.

Sampson, Robert, Jeffrey D. Morenoff, and Thomas Gannon-Rowley. 2002. "Assessing 'Neighborhood Effects': Social Processes and New Directions in Research." *Annual Review of Sociology* 51(1):443–78.

Santorum, Rick. 2006. *It Takes a Family: Conservatism and the Common Good*. New York: Intercollegiate Studies Institute.

Sarkesian, Natalia and Naomi Gerstel. 2004. "Explaining the Gender Gap in Help to Parents: The Importance of Employment." *Journal of Marriage and Family* 66:431–51.

Sassen, Saskia. 1995. "Immigration and Local Labor Markets." Pp. 87–127 in *The Economic Sociology of Immigration: Essays on Networks, Ethnicity, and Etrepreneurship*, edited by A. Portes. New York: Russell Sage Foundation.

Sassen, Saskia and R. C. Smith. 1992. "Post-Industrial Growth and Economic Reorganization: The Impact on Immigrant Employment." Pp. 87–127 in *United States-Mexico Relations: Labour Market Interdependence*, edited by J. A. Bustamante, C. W. Reynolds, and R. A. Honojosa Ojeda. Stanford: Stanford University Press.

Saunders, Doug. 2010. *Arrival Cities: How the Largest Migration in History Is Reshaping Our World*. New York: Pantheon Books.

Saxenian, Anna Lee. 1996. "Beyond Boundaries: Open Labor Markets and Learning in Silicon Valley." Pp. 23–39 in *The Boundaryless Career: A New Employment Principle for a New Organization Age*, edited by M. B. Arthur and D. M. Rousseau. New York: Oxford University Press.

Schiebinger, Londa, Andrea Davies Henderson, and Shannon Gilmartin. 2008. *Dual-Career Academic Couples: What Universities Need to Know*. Stanford, CA: Stanford University Press.

Schlosser, Eric. 2005. *Fast Food Nation*. New York: Harper Perennial.

Schmidt, Stefanie. 2000. "Job Security Beliefs in the General Social Survey: Evidence on Long-Run Trends and Comparability with Other Surveys." Pp. 300–34 in *On the Job: Is Long-Term Employment a Thing of the Past*, edited by D. Neumark. New York: Russell Sage Foundation.

Schneider, Daniel. 2011. "Market Earnings and Household Work: New Tests of Gender Performance Theory." *Journal of Marriage and the Family* 73(4):845–60.

Schneider, Nathan. 2015. "End of the 8-Hour Day? Unpredictable Days and Digital Scheduling – Welcome to the New Fight Over the Clock." *The Nation*, May 11, 12–16.

Schoeni, Robert and Karen Ross. 2005. "Material Assistance Received from Families During the Transition to Adulthood." Pp. 396–416 in *On the Frontier of Adulthood: Theory, Research, and Public Policy*, edited by S. Richard, F. Furstenberg, and R. Rumbaut. Chicago: University of Chicago Press.

Schor, Juliet. 1998. *The Overspent American: Upscaling, Downshifting, and the New Consumer*. New York: Basic Books.

Schrage, Elliot. 2004. "Supply and the Brand." *Harvard Business Review* 82(6):20–21.

Schrank, Andrew. 2004. "Ready-to-Wear Development? Foreign Investment, Technology Transfer, and Learning by Watching in the Apparel Trade." *Social Forces* 83(1):123–56.

Schuette v. Coalition to Defend Affirmative Action, 572 U.S. (2014).

Schultz, Derek. 2006. "Myths and Realities About High Tech Work." Pp. 15–32 in *Surviving in the New Economy*, edited by J. Amman, T. Carpenter, and G. Neff. Boulder, CO: Paradigm.

Schuman, Howard, Charlotte Steeh, Lawrence Bobo, and Maria Krysan. 1998. *Racial Attitudes in America: Trends and Interpretations* (Rev. ed.). Cambridge, MA: Harvard University Press.

Schumpeter, Joseph. 1989. *Essays: On Entrepreneurs, Innovations, Business Cycles, and the Evolution of Capitalism*. New Brunswick, NJ: Transaction.

Scott, Robert. 2015. "The Manufacturing Footprint and the Importance of US Manufacturing Jobs." *EPI Briefing Paper #388*. Economic Policy Institute. http://www.epi.org/publication/the-manufacturing-footprint-and-the-importance-of-u-s-manufacturing-jobs/.

Seidman, Gay. 2007. *Beyond the Boycott: Labor Rights, Human Rights and Transnational Activism*. New York: Russell Sage Foundation.

Sennett, Richard. 1998. *The Corrosion of Character: The Personal Consequences of Work in the New Capitalism*. New York: W. W. Norton.

Shapiro, Thomas. 2004. *The Hidden Cost of Being African American: How Wealth Perpetuates Inequality*. New York: Oxford University Press.

Shephard, Roy and Jean Bonneau. 2002. "Assuring Gender Equity in Recruitment Standards for Police Officers." *Canadian Journal of Applied Physiology* 27(3):263–95.

Shih, Johanna. 2004. "Project Time in Silicon Valley." *Qualitative Sociology* 27:223–45.

Shockley, Kristen M. and Tammy D. Allen. 2012. "Motives for Flexible Work Arrangement Use." *Community, Work & Family* 15(2):217–31.

Silva, Jennifer M. 2012. "Constructing Adulthood in an Age of Uncertainty." *American Sociological Review* 77(4):505–22.

Skocpol, Theda. 1992. *Protecting Soldiers and Mothers: The Political Origins of Social Policy in the United States*. Boston: Harvard University Press.

Smith, Chris and Peter Meiksins. 1995. "System Society and Dominance Effects in Cross-National Organisational Analysis." *Work, Employment and Society* 9:241–61.

Smith, Craig. 2006. "Letter from Paris: 4 Simple Rules for Firing an Employee in France." *New York Times*, March 28, C1.

Smith, Ryan. 1997. "Race, Income and Authority at Work: A Cross-Temporal Analysis of Black and White Men, 1972–1994." *Social Problems* 44:19–37.

Smith, Ryan. 2012. "Money, Benefits and Power: A Test of the Glass Ceiling and Glass Escalator Hypotheses." *Annals of the American Academy of Political and Social Science* 39:149–72.

Smith, Vicki. 1990. *Managing in the Corporate Interest: Control and Resistance in an American Bank*. Berkeley: University of California Press.

Smith, Vicki. 2002. *Crossing the Great Divide: Worker Risk and Opportunity in the New Economy*. Ithaca, NY: Cornell University Press.

Smith, Vicki and Esther Neuwirth. 2008. *The Good Temp*. Ithaca, NY: Cornell University Press.

Stainback, Kevin, Corre Robinson, and Donald Tomaskovic-Devey. 2005. "Race and Workplace Integration: A Politically Mediated Process?" *American Behavioral Scientist* 48:1200–28.

Stone, Pamela. 2007. *Opting Out? Why Women Really Quit Careers and Head Home*. Los Angeles: University of California Press.

Stuart, Mark, Irena Grugulis, Jennifer Tomlinson, Chris Forde, and Robert MacKenzie. 2013. "Reflections on Work and Employment into the 21st Century: Between Equal Rights, Force Decides." *Work, Employment & Society* 27(3):379–95.

Sturges, Jane. 2013. "A Matter of Time: Young Professionals' Experiences of Long Work Hours." *Work, Employment & Society* 27(2):343–59.

Sullivan, Mercer. 1989. *Getting Paid: Youth, Crime and Work in the Inner City*. Ithaca, NY: Cornell University Press.

Swanberg, Jennifer, Marcie Pitt-Catsouphes, and Krista Drescher-Burke. 2005. "A Question of Justice: Disparities in Employees' Access to Flexible Schedule Arrangements." *Journal of Family Issues* 26(6):866–95.

Sweet, Stephen. 2007. "The Older Worker, Job Insecurity and the New Economy." *Generations* 31:45–49.

Sweet, Stephen. 2009. "When Is a Person Too Young or Too Old to Work: Cultural Variations in Europe." Vol. 2. *Global Issue Brief.* Boston: The Sloan Center on Aging and Work.

Sweet, Stephen and Phyllis Moen. 2004. "Intimate Academics: Coworking Couples in Two Universities." *Innovative Higher Education* 28(4):252–74.

Sweet, Stephen and Phyllis Moen. 2006. "Advancing a Career Focus on Work and Family: Insights from the Life Course Perspective." Pp. 189–208 in *The Work and Family Handbook: Multi-Disciplinary Perspectives, Methods and Approaches*, edited by M. Pitt-Catsouphes, E. E. Kossek, and S. Sweet. Mahwah, NJ: Lawrence Erlbaum.

Sweet, Stephen and Phyllis Moen. 2007. "Integrating Educational Careers in Work and Family: Women's Return to School and Family Life Quality." *Community, Work & Family* 10:233–52.

Sweet, Stephen and Phyllis Moen. 2011. "Dual Earners Preparing for Job Loss: Agency, Linked Lives and Resilience." *Work and Occupations* 20(4):1–36.

Sweet, Stephen, Raymond Swisher, and Phyllis Moen. 2005. "Selecting and Assessing the Family Friendly Community: Adaptive Strategies of Middle Class Dual-Earner Couples." *Family Relations* 54:596–606.

Sweet, Stephen, Phyllis Moen, and Peter Meiksins. 2007. "Dual Earners in Double Jeopardy: Preparing for Job Loss in the New Risk Economy." Pp. 437–61 in *Workplace Temporalities*, Vol. 17, *Research in the Sociology of Work*, edited by B. Rubin. New York: Elsevier.

Sweet, Stephen, Elyssa Besen, Marcie Pitt-Catsouphes, and Lonnie Golden. 2014. "Explaining Organizational Variation in Flexible Work Arrangements: Why the Pattern and Scale of Availability Matter." *Community, Work and Family* 17(2):115–41.

Swidler, Ann. 1986. "Culture in Action: Symbols and Strategies." *American Sociological Review* 51:273–86.

Swisher, Raymond, Stephen Sweet, and Phyllis Moen. 2004. "The Family-Friendly Community and Its Life Course Fit for Dual-Earner Couples." *Journal of Marriage and Family* 66:281–92.

Takaki, Ronald. 2008. *A Different Mirror: A History of Multicultual America.* Boston: Back Bay Books.

Tarnoff, Curt and Marian Leonardo Lawson. 2011. *Foreign Aid: An Introduction to U.S. Programs and Policy.* http://fas.org/sgp/crs/row/R40213.pdf.

Tax Policy Center. 2014a. "Historical Marginal Effective Tax Rates on Capital Income." Tax Facts. Urban Institute and Brookings Institute. http://www.tax policycenter.org/taxfacts/displayafact.cfm?Docid=323&Topic2id=70.

Tax Policy Center. 2014b. "Historical Corporate Top Tax Rate and Bracket: 1909–2013." Tax Facts. Urban Institute and Brookings Institute. http://www .taxpolicycenter.org/taxfacts/content/pdf/corporate_historical_bracket.pdf.

Taylor, Frederick Winslow. 1964 [1911]. *The Principles of Scientific Management.* New York: Harper.

Taylor, Phil and Peter Bain. 2005a. "India Calling to the Far Away Towns: The Call Centre Labour Process and Globalization." *Work, Employment & Society* 19(2):261–82.

Taylor, Phil and Peter Bain. 2005b. "Call Centre Offshoring to India: The Revenge of History?" *Labour & Industry*. 14(3):15–38.

Teitelbaum, Michael. 2014. *Falling Behind: Boom, Bust and the Global Race for Scientific Talent*. Princeton, NJ: Princeton University Press.

Thernstrom, Stephan. 1980. *Poverty and Progress*. Cambridge, MA: Harvard University Press.

Thomas, William I. and Dorothy Thomas. 1928. *The Child in America* (2nd ed.). New York: Knopf.

Thomas, William I. and Florian Znaniecki. 1958. *The Polish Peasant in Europe and America*. New York: Dover.

Thompson, E. P. 1963. *The Making of the English Working Class*. New York: Pantheon Books.

Thompson, E. P. 1967. "Time, Work-Discipline, and Industrial Capitalism." *Past and Present* 38:56–97.

Thompson, Paul. 2003. "Disconnected Capitalism: Or Why Employers Can't Keep Their Side of the Bargain." *Work, Employment & Society* 17(2):359–78.

Thurow, Lester C. 1999. "Jobless Figures Deceptive." *Boston Globe*, April 20, C4.

Tiano, Susan. 1994. *Patriarchy on the Line: Labor, Gender and Ideology in the Mexican Maquila Industry*. Philadelphia: Temple University Press.

Tilcsik, András. 2011. "Pride and Prejudice: Employment Discrimination against Openly Gay Men in the United States." *American Journal of Sociology* 117(2):586–686.

Tilly, Chris. 2011. "The Impact of the Economic Crisis on International Migration: A Review." *Work, Employment & Society* 25(4):675–92.

Tocqueville, Alexis de. 1969 [1836]. *Democracy in America*. New York: Doubleday.

Tracy, James F. 1999. "Whistle While You Work: The Disney Company and the Global Division of Labor." *Journal of Communication Inquiry* 23(4):374.

Trattner, Walter. 1999. *From Poor Law to Welfare State*. New York: Free Press.

Trefalt, Spela. 2010. "Interpersonal Aspects of Justice in Workplace Flexibility." in *Work and Family Encyclopedia*. Sloan Work and Family Research Network. http://wfnetwork.bc.edu/encyclopedia_entry.php?id=16766&area=All.

Tseming, Yang. 2004. "The Effectiveness of the NAFTA Environmental Side Agreement's Citizen Submission Process: A Case Study of the Metales y Derivados Matter." Rochester, NY: Social Science Research Network.

Tucker, Lee. 2000. *Fingers to the Bone: United States Failure to Protect Child Farmworkers*. Washington, DC: Human Rights Watch.

Tulin, Roger. 1984. *A Machinist's Semi-Automated Life*. San Pedro, CA: Singlejack Books.

Uchitelle, Louis. 2006. *The Disposable American: Layoffs and Their Consequences*. New York: Knopf.

Uchitelle, Louis. 2011. "From Two Breadwinners to One." *The Nation*, May 4, 17–20.

Uggen, Christopher and Amy Blackstone. 2004. "Sexual Harassment as a Gendered Expression of Power." *American Sociological Review* 69(1):64–92.

Ulrich, Laurel. 1982. *Good Wives: Image and Reality in the Lives of Women in Northern New England 1650–1750*. New York: Oxford University Press.

United Nations Statistics Division. 2011. "Demographic and Social Indicators: Statistics and Indicators on Women and Men." http://unstats.un.org/unsd/demo graphic/products/indwm/tab4e.htm.

U.S. Department of Homeland Security. 2010. "Yearbook of Immigration Statistics 2009." Washington, DC: U.S Department of Homeland Security, Office of Immigration Statistics. http://www.dhs.gov/xlibrary/assets/statistics/year book/2009/ois_yb_2009.pdf.

Vallas, Steven. 2003a. "The Adventures of Managerial Hegemony: Teamwork, Ideology, and Worker Resistance." *Social Problems* 50:204–25.

Vallas, Steven 2003b. "Rediscovering the Color Line within Work Organizations: The 'Knitting or Racial Groups' Revisited." *Work and Occupations* 30:379–400.

Vallas, Steven and John Beck. 1996. "The Transformation of Work Revisited: The Limits of Flexibility in American Manufacturing." *Social Problems* 43:339–61.

Varma, Roli. 2006. *Harbiners of Global Change: India's Techno-Immigrants in the United States*. Lanham, MA: Lexington Books.

Vaughan, Diane. 2006. "Air Traffic Control Today: Politics, Labor History, and Cultural Reproduction." *Critical Solidarity, Newsletter of the Labor and Labor Movements Section of the American Sociological Association* 6(2):1–3.

Veblen, Thorstein. 1994 [1899]. *The Theory of the Leisure Class*. New York: Penguin Classics.

Volscho, Thomas W. and Nathan J. Kelly. 2012. "The Rise of the Super-Rich: Power Resources, Taxes, Financial Markets, and the Dynamics of the Top 1 Percent, 1949 to 2008." *American Sociological Review* 77(5):679–99.

Voydanoff, Patricia. 2007. *Work, Family, and Community: Exploring Interconnections*. Mahwah, NJ: Lawrence Erlbaum.

Wagar, Terry H. 2001. "Consequences of Work Force Reduction." *Journal of Labor Research* 22(4):851–62.

Wagmiller, Robert L. Jr. and Kristen Schultz Lee. 2014. "Are Contemporary Patterns of Black Male Joblessness Unique? Cohort Replacement, Intracohort Change, and the Diverging Structures of Black and White Men's Employment." *Social Problems* 61(2):305–27.

Waldinger, Roger. 1996. *Still the Promised City: African-Americans and the New Immigrants in Postindustrial New York*. Cambridge, MA: Harvard University Press.

Waldinger, Roger. 2001. "Up from Poverty? 'Race,' Immigration and the Fate of Low-Skilled Workers." Pp. 80–116 in *Strangers at the Gates: New Immigrants in Urban America*, edited by R. Waldinger. Berkeley: University of California Press.

Waldinger, Roger and Claudia Der-Martirosian. 2000. "Immigrant Workers and American Labor: Challenge or Disaster?" Pp. 49–80 in *Organizing Immigrants: The Challenge for Unions in Contemporary California*, edited by R. Milkman. Ithaca, NY: Cornell University Press.

Waldinger, Roger and Claudia Der-Martirosian. 2001. "The Immigrant Niche: Pervasive, Persistent, Diverse." Pp. 228–71 in *Strangers at the Gates: New Immigrants in Urban America*, edited by R. Waldinger. Berkeley: University of California Press.

Waldinger, Roger and Michael Lichter. 2003. *How the Other Half Works: Immigration and the Social Organization of Labor*. Berkeley: University of California Press.

Waldinger, Roger, Nelson Lim, and David Cort. 2007. "Bad Jobs, Good Jobs, No Jobs? The Employment Experience of the Mexican-American Second Generation." *Journal of Ethnic and Migration Studies* 33:1–35.

Wallerstein, Immanuel. 1979. *The Capitalist World Economy*. Cambridge, UK: Cambridge University Press.

Wallerstein, Immanuel. 1983. *Historical Capitalism*. London: Verso.

Wandner, Stephen and Andrew Stettner. 2000. "Why Are Many Jobless Workers Not Applying for Benefits?" *Monthly Labor Review* 123:21–32.

Ward's Cove Packing Co. v. Antonio, 490 U.S. 642 (1989).

Warren, Elizabeth and Amelia Warren Tyagi. 2003. *The Two-Income Trap: Why Middle-Class Mothers and Fathers Are Going Broke*. New York: Basic Books.

Weber, Max. 1998 [1905]. *The Protestant Ethic and the Spirit of Capitalism*. Los Angeles: Roxbury.

Weller, Christian and Edward Wolff. 2005. *Retirement Income: The Crucial Role of Social Security*. Washington, DC: Economic Policy Institute.

Wells, Miriam. 2000. "Immigration and Unionization in the San Francisco Hotel Industry." Pp. 109–29 in *Organizing Immigrants: The Challenge for Unions in Contemporary California*, edited by R. Milkman. Ithaca, NY: Cornell University Press.

West, Candace and Don Zimmerman. 1987. "Doing Gender." *Gender and Society* 1(2):125–51.

Western, Bruce and Jake Rosenfeld. 2011. "Unions, Norms, and the Rise in U.S. Wage Inequality." *American Sociological Review* 76(4):513–37.

Westman, Mina, Dalia Etzion, and Shoshi Horovitz. 2004. "The Toll of Unemployment Does Not Stop with the Unemployed." *Human Relations* 57(7):823–44.

Whaples, Robert. 2010. "Hours of Work in U.S. History." Economic History Association. https://eh.net/encyclopedia/hours-of-work-in-u-s-history.

Wharton, Amy. 1999. "The Psychosocial Consequences of Emotional Labor." *Annals of the American Academy of Political and Social Sciences* 56(1):158–76.

Whyte, William H. 1956. *The Organization Man*. New York: Simon and Schuster.

Williams, Christine. 1991. *Gender Differences at Work: Women and Men in Non-traditional Occupations*. Los Angeles: University of California Press.

Williams, Christine, Patti Giuffre, and Kirsten Dellinger. 1999. "Sexuality in the Workplace: Organizational Control, Sexual Harassment, and the Pursuit of Pleasure." *Annual Review of Sociology* 25:73–93.

Williams, Damian. 2009. "Grounding the Regime of Precarious Employment: Homeless Day Laborers' Negatiation of the Job Queue." *Work and Occupations* 36(2):209–46.

Williams, Joan. 2000. *Unbending Gender: Why Family and Work Conflict and What to Do About It*. New York: Oxford University Press.

Wilson, George. 1997. "Pathways to Power: Racial Differences in the Determinants of Job Authority." *Social Problems* 44:38–54.

Wilson, Kenneth and Alejandro Portes. 1980. "Immigrant Enclaves: An Analysis of the Labor Market Experiences of Cubans in Miami." *American Journal of Sociology* 86:295–319.

Wilson, W. J. 1987. *The Truly Disadvantaged: The Inner City, the Underclass, and Public Policy*. Chicago: University of Chicago Press.

Wilson, W. J. 1997. *When Work Disappears: The World of the New Urban Poor*. New York: Alfred A. Knopf.

Winslow-Bowe, Sarah. 2006. "The Persistence of Wives' Income Advantage." *Journal of Marriage and Family* 68(4):824–42.

Winstanley, D., J. Clark, and H. Leeson. 2002. "Approaches to Child Labour in the Supply Chain." *Business Ethics: A European Review* 11(3):210–23.

Wolkinson, Benjamin and Russell Ormiston. 2006. "The Arbitration of Work-Family Conflicts." Pp. 685–704 in *The Handbook of Work and Family: Multidisciplinary Perspectives, Methods and Approaches*, edited by M. Pitt-Catsouphes, E. E. Kossek, and S. Sweet. Mahwah, NJ: Lawrence Erlbaum.

Wood, Ellen Meiksins. 2003. *Empire of Capital*. London: Verso Books.

Woods, Ngaire. 2006. *The Globalizers: The IMF, the World Bank, and Their Borrowers*. Ithaca, NY: Cornell University Press.

Wright, Eric Olin. 1985. *Classes*. London: Verso Books.

Wrigley, Julia. 1999. "Is Racial Oppression Intrinsic to Domestic Work? The Experiences of Children's Caregivers in Contemporary America." Pp. 97–123 in *The Cultural Territories of Race: Black and White Boundaries*, edited by M. Lamont. Chicago: University of Chicago Press.

Yakura, Elaine. 2001. "Billables: The Valorization of Time in Consulting." *American Behavioral Scientist* 44:1076–95.

Yang, Tiantian and Howard E. Aldrich. 2014. "Who's the Boss? Explaining Gender Inequality in Entrepreneurial Teams." *American Sociological Review* 79(2):303–27.

York, Richard, Eugene Rosa, and Thomas Dietz. 2003. "Footprints on the Earth: The Environmental Consequences of Modernity." *American Sociological Review* 68:279–300.

Young, Alford. 1999. "Navigating Race: Getting Ahead in the Lives of 'Rags to Riches' Young Black Men." Pp. 30–62 in *The Cultural Territories of Race: Black and White Boundaries*, edited by M. Lamont. Chicago: University of Chicago Press.

Young, Alford. 2003. *The Minds of Marginalized Black Men: Making Sense of Mobility, Opportunity and Future Life Chances*. Princeton, NJ: Princeton University Press.

Young, Cristobal. 2012. "Losing a Job: The Nonpecuniary Cost of Unemployment in the United States." *Social Forces* 91(2):609–34.

Youngjoo, Cha and Kim A. Weeden. 2014. "Overwork and the Slow Convergence in the Gender Gap in Wages." *American Sociological Review* 79(3):457–84.

Zelizer, Viviana. 1994. *Pricing the Priceless Child: The Changing Social Value of Children*. Princeton, NJ: Princeton University Press.

Zeng, Zhen and Yu Xie. 2004. "Asian-Americans' Earnings Disadvantage Reexamined: The Role and Place of Education." *American Journal of Sociology* 109:1075–108.

Zweigenhaft, Richard and William Domhoff. 2003. *Blacks in the White Elite: Will the Progress Continue?* Lanham, MD: Rowman and Littlefield.

Index

Note: Exhibits and notes are indicated with e or n after the page number.